Natural History General And Particular, 6

George Louis Leclerc Buffon

CONTENTS.

DIRECTIONS to the BINDER.

NATURAL HISTORY.

THE ELEPHANT*.

IF the human species be excepted, the Elephant is the moſt reſpectable animal in the world. In ſize he ſurpaſſes all other terreſtrial creatures ; and, by his intelligence, he makes as

near

* The Elephant has a long cartilaginous trunk, formed of multitudes of rings, pliant in all directions, and terminated with a ſmall moveable hook. The noſtrils are at the end of the trunk, which is uſed, like a hand, to convey any thing into the mouth. This animal has no cutting teeth, but four large flat grinders in each jaw, and in the upper, two vaſt tuſks, pointing forwards, and bending a little upwards; the largeſt of them imported into Britain are ſeven feet long, and weigh 152 pounds each. The eyes are ſmall, and the ears long, broad and pendulous. The back is much arched. The legs are thick, and very clumſy and ſhapeleſs. The feet are undivided; but their margins are terminated by five round hoofs. The tail is like that of a hog. The colour of the ſkin is duſky, with a few ſcattered hairs on it ; *Pennant's Synopſ.*

In Greek, Ελεφας; in Latin, *Elephantus, Barrus*; in Spaniſh, *Elephante*; in German, *Helphant*; in the Eaſt, *Elfil. Phil,* or *Fil,* is a Chaldean word which ſignifies *ivory,* and Munſter uſes it to denote the *Elephant.* In the Eaſt Indies the elephant

near an approach to man as matter can approach fpirit *. Of all animated beings, the elephant, the dog, the beaver, and the ape, have the moft admirable inftinct. But this inftinct, which is only a refult of all the animal powers, both internal and external, manifefts itfelf by very different effects in each of thefe fpecies. Naturally, and when left at full liberty, the dog is as cruel and bloody as the wolf; but amidft all this ferocity of difpofition, there is one flexible point which we have cherifhed. Hence the natural difpofitions of the dog differ not from thofe of other rapacious animals, but by this point of fenfibility, which renders him fufceptible of affection and attachment. It is from nature that he de-

---

was formerly called *Barre*; and it is probable that *Barrus* was derived from this word, and afterwards applied by the Latins to the elephant; *Gefner. cap. de Elephanto.* At Congo, it is called *Manzao* or *Manzo*; *Drake, p.* 104.

Elephas; *Plinii, lib.* viii. *cap.* 1. *Raii Synopf. Quad. p.* 131. *Klein. Quad. p.* 36. *Ludolph. Æthiop. p.* 54. *Boullaye-le-Gouz. p.* 250. *Dellon's Voyage, p.* 71. *Leo Afric. p.* 336. *Kolben's Cape vol.* ii. *p.* 98. *Bofman's Hift. of Guiney, p.* 230. *Linfchottan. Iter. p.* 55. *Du Halde's China, vol.* ii. *p.* 224. *Addanfon's Voyage, p.* 138. *Moor's Travels, p.* 31. *Borri's Account of Cochin China, p.* 795. *Barbot's Guiney, p.* 141. 206. *Seba, tom.* i. *p.* 175. *tab.* 3. *Edwards, p.* 221.

L'Elephant; *Briffon. Quad. p.* 28.

Elephas maximus; *Linn. Syft. Nat. p.* 48.

* Valet fenfu et reliqua fagacitate ingenii excellit elephas; *Arift. Hift. Anim. lib.* ix. *cap.* 46.—Elephanti funt natura mites et manfueti, ut ad rationale animal proxime accedant; *Strabo.* —Vidi elephantos quofdam qui prudentiores mihi videbantur quam quibufdam in locis homines; *Vartomannus, apud Gefner. cap. de Elephanto.*

rives

rives this germ of fentiment, which man has cultivated and expanded by living long and conftantly in fociety with this animal. The dog alone was worthy of this diftinguifhed regard; for, being more fufceptible of foreign impreffions than any other quadruped, all his relative powers have been brought to perfection by his commerce with man. His fenfibility, his docility, his courage, his talents, and even his manners, are modified and formed by the example and qualities of his mafter. We ought not, therefore, to afcribe to him all the powers he appears to poffefs. His moft brilliant qualities are borrowed from us. He has acquired more than other animals, becaufe he is more capable of making acquifitions. Inftead of having a repugnance to man, he has a natural bias in favour of the human race. This gentle fentiment, which is always alive, is made evident by the defire of pleafing, and has produced docility, fidelity, perpetual fubmiffion, and, at the fame time, that degree of attention which is neceffary for acting accordingly, and for giving ready obedience to all the commands he receives.

The ape, on the contrary, is as untractable as he is extravagant. His nature, in every point, is equally ftubborn. He has no relative fenfibilities, no gratitude, no recollection of good treatment, or of benefits received. Averfe to the fociety of man, and to every kind of reftraint, he has a violent propenfity to do every thing that

is hurtful or difpleafing. But thefe real faults
are compenfated by apparent perfections. In his
external figure, he refembles man : He has arms,
hands, and fingers. The ufe of thefe parts alone
renders him fuperior in addrefs to other animals ; and the relations they give him to us, in
fimilarity of movements and conformity of
actions, pleafe and deceive us, and lead us to afcribe to internal qualities, what depends folely
on the ftructure of his members.

The beaver, whofe individual qualities feem
far inferior to thofe of the dog and ape, has, notwithftanding, received from Nature a gift almoft
equivalent to that of fpeech. He makes himfelf fo well underftood to his own fpecies, that
they unite in fociety, act in concert, undertake
and execute large and long continued works ;
and this focial attachment, as well as the refult
of their mutual intelligence, are more entitled
to our admiration than the addrefs of the ape, or
the fidelity of the dog.

Hence the genius of the dog (if I may be
permitted to profane this term) is borrowed ;
the ape has only the appearance of it ; and the
talents of the beaver extend no farther than to
what regards himfelf and his affociates. But
the elephant is fuperior to all the three ; for in
him all their moft exalted qualities are united.
In the ape, the hand is the principal organ of
addrefs. The trunk of the elephant affords him
the fame means of addrefs as the ape. It ferves

inftead

inftead of an arm and a hand; and by it heis enabled to raife and lay hold of fmall as well as of large objects, to carry them to his mouth, to place them on his back, to embrace them faft, or to throw them at a diftance. He has, at the fame time, the docility of the dog, and, like that animal, he is fufceptible of gratitude, capable of attachment, is eafily accuftomed to man, fubmits lefs by force than good treatment, ferves him with zeal, fidelity, knowledge, &c. In fine, the elephant, like the beaver, loves the fociety of his equals, and can make himfelf to be under-ftood by them. They are often obferved to af-femble together, to difperfe, and act in con-cert; and if they receive no mutual edification, if they carry on no common operation, it muft, perhaps, be afcribed to the want of room and of tranquillity; for men have been very anciently multiplied in all the countries inhabited by the elephant; he is, therefore, perpetually difturbed, and is no where a peaceable poffeffor of fuf-ficient fpace to eftablifh a fecure abode. We have feen, that all thefe advantages are necef-fary to unfold the talents of the beaver, and that, in every place frequented by men, he lofes his induftry, and receives no edification from affo-ciating. Every being has its relative value in Nature. To form a juft eftimation of the ele-phant, he muft be allowed to poffefs the fagacity of the beaver, the addrefs of the ape, the fentiment of the dog, together with the peculiar advan-

tages

tages of ſtrength, largeneſs, and long duration of life. Neither ſhould we overlook his arms, or tuſks, which enable him to transfix and conquer the lion. We ſhould alſo conſider that the earth ſhakes under his feet; that with his hand he tears up trees *; that by a puſh of his body, he makes a breach in a wall; that, though tremendous in ſtrength, he is rendered ſtill more invincible by his enormous maſs, and by the thickneſs of his ſkin; that he can carry on his back an armed tower filled with many warriors; that he works machines, and carries burdens which ſix horſes are unable to move; that to this pro-

---

* Veteres proboſcidem elephanti manum appellaverunt.—Eadem aliquoties nummum e terra tollentem vidi, et aliquando detrahentem arboris ramum, quem viri viginti-quatuor fune trahentes ad humum flectere non potueramus; cum ſolus elephas tribus vicibus motum detrahebat; *Vartomannus, apud Geſner. cap. de Elephanto.*—Silveſtres elephanti ſagos, oleaſtros, et palmas dentibus ſubvertunt radicitus; *Oppian.*—Promuſcis elephanti naris eſt qua cibum, tam ſiccum quam humidum, ille capiat, orique perinde ac *manu* admoveat. Arbores etiam eadem complectendo evellit; denique ea non alio utitur modo niſi ut manu; *Ariſtot. de Partib. Animal. lib.* ii. *cap.* 16.—Habet præterea talem tantamque narem elephantus, ut ea manus vice utatur..... Suo etiam rectori erigit atque offert, arbores quoque eadem proſternit, et quoties immerſus per aquam ingreditur, ea ipſa edita in ſublimi reflat atque reſpirat; *Ariſt. Hiſt. Anim. lib.* ii. *cap.* 1.—The ſtrength of the elephant is ſo amazing that it can only be known from experience. I have ſeen an elephant carry on his tuſks two cannons, fixed together with cables, each weighing three thouſand pounds, which he firſt raiſed from the ground, and then carried them to the diſtance of five hundred paces. I have alſo ſeen an elephant draw ſhips and gallies upon land, in order to ſet them afloat; *Voyages de Fr. Pyrard, tom.* ii. *p.* 356.

digious

digious strength he adds courage, prudence, coolness, and punctual obedience; that he preserves moderation even in his most violent passions; that he is constant and impetuous in love *; that, when in anger, he mistakes not his friends; that he never attacks any but those who offend him; that he remembers favours as long as injuries; that, having no appetite for flesh, he feeds on vegetables alone, and is born an enemy to no living creature; and, in fine, that he is universally beloved, because all animals respect, and none have any reason to fear him.

Men likewise, in all ages, have had a kind of veneration for this first and grandest of terrestrial creatures. The ancients regarded him as a miracle of Nature; and, indeed, he is her highest effort. But they have greatly exaggerated his faculties. They have, without hesitation, ascribed to him intellectual powers and moral virtues. Pliny, Ælian, Solinus, Plutarch, and other authors of a more modern date, have given to these animals rational manners, a natural and innate religion †, a kind of daily adoration of

the

---

* Nec adulteria novere, nec ulla propter fœminas inter se prælia, cæteris animalibus pernicialia, non quia desit illis amoris vis, &c.: *Plin. lib.* viii. *cap.* 5.—Mas quam impleverit coitu, eam amplius non tangit; *Aristot. Hist. Anim. lib.* ix. *cap.* 49.

† Hominum indigenarum linguam elephanti intelligunt; *Ælian. lib.* iv. *cap.* 24. , ... Luna nova nitescente, audio elephantos naturali quadam et ineffabili intelligentia e silva, ubi pascuntur, ramos recens decerptos auferre, eosque deinde in

the fun and moon, the ufe of ablution before
worfhip, a fpirit of divination, piety towards heaven and their fellow-creatures, whom they affift at the approach of death, and after their
deceafe, bedew them with tears, cover them with
earth, &c. The Indians, prejudiced with the
notion of the metempfycofis or tranfmigration of
fouls, are ftill perfuaded, that a body fo majeftic
as that of the elephant muft be animated with
the foul of a great man or a king. In Siam *,

Laos,

fublime tollere, ut fufpicere, et leviter ramos movere, tanquam fupplicium quoddam Deæ protendentes, ut ipfis pro-
pria et benevola effe vellit; *Ælian. lib.* iv. *cap.* 10.—Elephas
eft animal proximum humanis fenfibus. . . . . Quippe intel-
lectus illis fermonis patrii et imperiorum obedientia, officio-
rumque, quæ didicere, memoria, amoris et gloriæ voluptas:
Imo vero, quæ etiam in homine rara, probitas, prudentia,
æquitas, religio quoque fiderum, folifque ac lunæ veneratio.
Autores funt, nitefcente luna nova, greges eorum defcendere;
ibique fe purificantes folenniter aqua circumfpergi, atque, ita
folutato fidere, in filvas reverti. . . . . Vifique funt feffi
ægritudine, herbas fupini in cœlum jacentes, veluti tellure
precibus allegata. *Plin. Hift. Nat. lib.* viii. *cap.* 1.—Se abluunt
et purificant, dein adorant folem et lunam.——Cadavera fui
generis fepeliunt.—Lamentant, ramos et pulverem injiciunt
fupra cadaver.——Sagittas extrahunt tanquam Chirurgi periti;
Plin. Ælian. Solin. Tzetzes, &c.

* M. Conftance conducted the ambaffador to fee the white
elephant which is fo efteemed in India, and has given rife to
fo many wars. He is very fmall, and fo old, that he is all
wrinkled. Several mandarins are appointed to take care of
him, and his victuals are ferved up to him in large golden
veffels. His apartment is magnificent, and the infide of it is
handfomely gilded; *Premier Voyage du P. Tachard, p.* 239. In
a country-houfe belonging to the king, fituated upon the
river about a league from Siam, I faw a fmall white ele-

phant,

Laos, Pegu *, &c. the white elephants are regarded as the living *manes* of the Indian Emperors. Each of thefe animals has a palace, a number of domeftics, golden veffels filled with the choiceft food, magnificent garments, and they are abfolved from all labour and fervitude. The emperor is the only perfonage before whom they bow the knee, and their falute is returned by the Monarch. By all thefe attentions,

phant, which was deftined to be fucceffor to the one in the palace, which is faid to be three hundred years old. This little elephant is fomewhat larger than an ox, and is attended by many mandarins; and, out of refpect to him, his mother and aunt are kept along with him; *Idem, p.* 273.

* When the King of Pegu walks abroad, four white elephants, adorned with precious ftones and ornaments of gold, march before him; *Recueil des Voyages de la Compagnie des Indes de Hollande, tom.* iii. *p.* 43. . . . When the King of Pegu gives audience, the four white elephants are prefented to him, who do him reverence by raifing their trunks, opening their mouths, making three diftinct cries, and then kneeling. When raifed, they are led back to their ftables, and there each of them are fed in large golden veffels. They are twice a day wafhed with water taken from a filver veffel. . . . During the time of their being dreffed in this manner, they are under a canopy fupported by eight domeftics, in order to defend them from the heat of the fun. In going to the veffels which contain their food and water, they are preceded by three trumpets, and march with great majefty, regulatiug their fteps by mufic, &c.; *Idem, tom.* iii. *p.* 40.—White elephants are held to be facred by the natives of Pegu: Having learned that the King of Siam had two, they fent ambaffadors offering any price that fhould be demanded for them. But the king of Siam would not fell them. His Majefty of Pegu, incenfed at this refufal, came with his army, and not only carried off the elephants by force, but rendered the whole country tributary to him; *Idem, tom.* ii. *p.* 223.

honours,

honours, and marks of refpect, they are flatter-
ed, but not corrupted. This circumftance alone
fhould be fufficient to convince the Indians, that
thefe animals are not endowed with human
fouls.

After removing the fabulous credulities of
antiquity, and the puerile fictions of fuperftition, which ftill exift, the elephant, even to phi-
lofophers, poffeffes enough to make him be regarded as a being of the firft diftinction. He
deferves to be known, and to be ftudied. We
fhall, therefore, endeavour to write his hiftory
with impartiality. We fhall firft confider him
in a ftate of nature, when he is perfectly free
and independent, and afterwards in a ftate of
fervitude, when the will of his mafter is partly
the motive of his actions.

In a wild ftate, elephants are neither fangui-
nary nor ferocious. Their difpofitions are gentle, and they make not a wrong ufe of their arms
or their ftrength; for they never exert them
but in defending themfelves, or in protecting
their companions. Their manners are focial;
for they are feldom feen wandering alone. They
generally march in troops, the oldeft keeping
foremoft*, and the next in age bringing up the
rear. The young and the feeble are placed in
the middle. The mothers carry their young

* Elephanti gregat imfemper ingrediuntur; ducit agmen
maximus natu, cogit ætate proximus. Amnes tranfituri mi-
nimos præmittunt, ne majorum inceffu atterente alveum,
crefcat gurgitis alitudo; *Plin. Hift. Nat. lib.* viii. *cap.* 5.

firmly

firmly embraced in their trunks. They obferve not this order, except in perilous marches, when they want to pafture on cultivated fields. In the deferts and forefts, they travel with lefs precaution, but without feparating fo far as to exceed the poffibility of receiving affiftance from one another. Some of them, however, occafionally wander, or lag behind the troop; and it is thefe alone whom the hunters dare attack; for a little army is neceffary to affail a whole troop *; and they are never vanquifhed but at the expence of feveral lives. It is even dangerous to do them the fmalleft injury†; for they run ftraight upon the offender,

* I ftill tremble when I think of the danger to which we expofed ourfelves in purfuing a wild elephant; for, though there were only ten or a dozen of us, the one half of which were not well armed, if we could have come up with him, we fhould have been foolifh enough to make the attack. We thought we might kill him by two or three fhot. But I afterwards faw that this bufinefs requires two or three hundred men; *Voyage de Guinée, par Guillaume Bofman, p.* 436.

† Solent elephanti magno numero confertim incedere, et fi quemdam obvium habuerint, vel devitant, vel illi cedunt; at fi quemdam injuria afficere velit, probofcide fublatum in terram dejicet, pedibus deculcans donec mortuum reliquerit; *Leonis Africani Defcript. Africæ, p.* 744.—The Negroes unanimoufly relate, that the elephants, when they meet any perfon in the woods, do him no harm, unlefs they are attacked; but that, when fhot at, and not mortally wounded, they become extremely furious; *Voyage de Guinée, par Bofman, p.* 245.—The wild elephant is provoked to purfue a man, and is then caught in a pit-fall; *Journal du Voyage de Siam, par l'Abbée de Choify, p.* 242.—Thofe who hurt

or

der, and though the weight of their bodies be great, their steps are so long, that they easily overtake the most agile man. They then transfix him with their tusks, or, laying hold of him with their trunk, throw him against a stone, and put an end to his existence by trampling him under their feet. But it is when provoked only that they kill men in this manner, and never injure those who do not disturb them. But as they are extremely suspicious and sensible of injuries, it is proper to avoid them; and the travellers who frequent the countries inhabited by elephants, kindle fires during the night, and beat drums to prevent their approach. When they have been once attacked by men, or have fallen into a snare, they are said never to forget it, but take every opportunity of revenge. As their sense of smelling is, perhaps, more perfect than that of any other animal, the smell of a man strikes them at a great distance, and they can easily follow him by the scent. The ancients relate, that the elephants tear the grass off the ground upon which the hunters had passed, and that they hand it about to each other for the purpose of receiving information concerning the passage and march of the enemy.

or insult an elephant, should be much on their guard; for these animals do not easily forget injuries, until they accomplish their revenge; *Recueil des Voyages de la Compagnie des Indes de Hollande, tom.* i. *p.* 413.

Thefe

Thefe animals love the banks of rivers *, deep valleys, and fhady moift places. They cannot difpenfe with water, which they trouble before they drink. They often fill their trunk with water, either to carry it to their mouth, or folely for refrefhing their nofe, and amufing themfelves by throwing it back into the river, or befprinkling it around. They cannot fupport cold, and likewife fuffer by extreme heat. To avoid the ardour of the fun's rays, they retire into the moft fhady receffes of the forefts. They frequently take to the water: The enormous fize of their bodies rather aids than retards their fwimming; for they fink not proportionably fo deep as other animals; and the length of their trunk, which they hold up in the air, and through which they refpire, removes from them all apprehenfions of being drowned.

Roots, herbs, leaves, and tender wood, are their common food. They likewife eat grains and fruits. But they difdain flefh and fifh †. When one of them difcovers a plentiful pafture, he calls to the others, and invites them to eat with him ‡. As they require a vaft quantity of

---

* Elephanti naturæ proprium eft rofcida loca et mollia amare et aquam defiderare, ubi verfari maxime ftudet; ita ut animal paluftre nominari poffit; *Ælian. lib.* iv. *cap.* 24.

† The moft favage of thefe animals eat no flefh, but live folely upon leaves, branches, and twigs of trees, which they break off with their trunk, and even browfe pretty ftrong wood; *Voyage de Fr. Pyrard, tom.* ii. *p.* 367.

‡ Cum eis cætera pabula defecerint, radices effodiunt, quibus pafcuntur;

of forage, they often change their place of pafturing; and, when they come upon cultivated. fields, they do incredible damage. Their bodies being of an enormous weight, they deftroy ten times more with their feet than they ufe for food, which generally amounts to one hundred and fifty pounds of grafs a day; and, as they always go in troops, they lay a whole country wafte in a fingle hour. For this reafon, the Indians and Negroes ufe every artifice to prevent the approach of thefe animals, or to fright them away. They make great noifes, and kindle large fires round· their cultivated fields. But, notwithftanding thefe precautions, the elephants fometimes pay them a vifit, drive off the domeftic cattle, put the men to flight, and, not unfrequently, overturn their limber habitations. It is difficult to fcare them; and they are not fufceptible of fear. Nothing can furprife them, or ftop their progrefs, but artificial fires *, or crackers, which the natives throw at them, and

pafcuntur; e quibus primus qui aliquam prædam repererit, regreditur ut'et fuos gregales advocet, et in prædæ communionem deducat; *Ælian. lib. ix. cap.* 56.

* When the elephant is enraged, nothing ftops his career but artificial fires. When fighting, the fame means are employed to difengage them from the combat; *Relat. par Thevenot, tom.* iii. *p.* 133.——The Portuguefe know no other mode of defending themfelves againft the elephant, but by throwing fquibs or torches in his eyes; *Voyage de Feynes, p.* 89.——In the Mogul empire, elephants are made to combat with each other. They fight fo obftinately, that they can only be feparated by throwing artificial fires between them; *Voyage de Bernier, tom.* ii *p.* 64.

the

the fudden and repeated noife fometimes induces
them to turn back. It is not eafy to make them
feparate from each other; for they generally act
in concert, whether they attack, march, or fly.

When the females come in feafon, this attachment to fociety yields to a ftronger paffion. The
troop feparates into pairs, which love had pre-
vioufly formed. They unite from choice, fteal
off in queft of retirement, and their march feems
to be preceded by love, and followed by modefty; for all their pleafures are accompanied
with the profoundeft myftery. They have never
been detected in their amours. They anxioufly
avoid the prefence or infpection of their neighbours; and know, perhaps, better than the human race, how to enjoy pleafure in fecret, and to
be entirely occupied with a fingle object. They
fearch for the deepeft folitudes of the woods,
that they may give full vent, without difturbance or referve, to all the impulfes of Nature *,
which are lively and durable, in proportion to
the long interval of abftinence. The female goes
with young two years †: When impregnated,
the male abftains; and his feafon of love returns

---

* Elephanti folitudines petunt coituri, et præcipue fecus flumi-
na; *Arift. Hift. Anim. lib.* v. *cap.* 1.——Pudore nunquam nifi in
abdito coeunt; *Plin. lib.* viii. *cap.* 5.

† Mas coitum triennio interpofito repetit. Quam gravidam
reddidit, eandem præterea tangere nunquam patitur. Uterum
biennio gerit; *Arift. Hift. Anim. lib.* v. *cap.* 14.—Elephantus
biennio geftatur, propter exuperantiam magnitudinis; *Idem, de
Generat. Anim. lib.* iv. *cap.* 10.

but

but once in three years. The females produce only one young *; which, at the moment of birth, has teeth †, and is as large as a wild boar. There is no appearance, however, of the horns or tusks. Soon after, they begin to shoot; and, at the age of six months, they are several inches long ‡. The animal is then larger than an ox, and the tusks continue to grow and enlarge till the most advanced age, provided the creature enjoys health and liberty; for it is not to be imagined what changes may be introduced into the temperament and habits of the elephant by slavery and unnatural food. They are easily tamed, instructed, and rendered submissive; and, as they are stronger and more intelligent than any other animal, their service is more ready, more extensive, and more useful. But the disgust arising from their situation is probably never eradicated: For, though they feel, from time to time, the most lively impressions of love, they neither intermix nor produce in a domestic state. Their constrained passion degenerates into fury. Being unable to gratify themselves without witnesses, they fret, lose patience, and, at last, their indignation becomes so violent, that the strongest

---

* Quæ maxima inter animalia sunt, ea singulos pariunt, ut elephas, camelus, equus; *Arist. de Generat. Anim. lib.* iv. *cap.* 4.

† Statim cum natus est elephantus dentes habet, quanquam grandes illos (dentes) non illico conspicuos obtinet; *Arist. Hist. Anim. lib.* ii. *cap.* 5.

‡ Thomas Lopes, apud Gesnerum, cap. de Elephanto.

chains,

chains, and fetters of every kind, are neceſſary to repreſs their movements, and to allay their rage. Hence they differ from all other domeſtic animals, who are managed by men as if they had no will of their own. They are not of the number of thoſe born ſlaves, which we propagate, mutilate, or multiply, purely to anſwer our own purpoſes. Here the individual alone is a ſlave. The ſpecies remain independent, and uniformly refuſe to augment the ſtores of their tyrants. This circumſtance ſhows the elephant to be endowed with ſentiments ſuperior to the nature of common brutes. To feel the moſt ardent paſſion, and, at the ſame time, to deny the gratification of it, to experience all the fury of love, and not to tranſgreſs the laws of modeſty, are, perhaps, the higheſt efforts of human virtue; and yet, in theſe majeſtic animals, they are only common and uniform exertions. The indignation they feel, becauſe they cannot be gratified in ſecret, becomes ſtronger than the paſſion of love, ſuſpends and deſtroys the effects of it, and, at the ſame time, excites that fury, which, during theſe paroxyſms, renders them more dangerous than any wild animal.

We are inclined, were it poſſible, to doubt of this fact; but all naturaliſts, hiſtorians, and travellers, concur in aſſuring us, that the elephants never produce in a domeſtic ſtate *. The Prin-

ces

* It is remarkable, that the male never covers the female, though ſhe indicates the ſtrongeſt mark of deſire, in ſituations

ces of India keep great numbers of elephants;
and, after many fruitless attempts to multiply
them like other domestic animals, they found it
neceſſary to ſeparate the males from the females,
in order to diminiſh the frequency of thoſe in-
effectual ardours, which are always accompanied
with fury. Hence there are no domeſtic elephants which have not formerly been wild;
and the manner of taking, taming, and rendering them ſubmiſſive *, merits particular attention.

where they may be expoſed to the obſervation of men ; *Voyage de
Fr. Peyrard, p.* 357.——The elephants never couple but in
ſecret, and produce only one at a birth; *Coſmographie du Levant,
par Thevot, p.* 70.

* I went to ſee the grand hunting of the elephants, which
was performed in the following manner: The King ſent a
great number of women into the woods; and, when the re-
port was brought that they had diſcovered a troop of elephants, he diſpatched thirty or forty thouſand men, who
made a large circle round the place. They poſted themſelves
in fours at the diſtance of twenty or twenty-five feet from
each other, and at every ſtation they kindled a fire, which
was raiſed about three feet above the ſurface of the earth.
There was another circle compoſed of elephants trained to
war, diſtant from one another about a hundred or a hundred
and fifty paces; and, in ſuch places as the wild elephants
might moſt eaſily eſcape, the war elephants were poſted
cloſer. There were cannons in ſeveral places, which are diſ-
charged when the wild elephants attempt to force a paſſage ;
for they are terrified at fire. This circle is daily diminiſhed,
and at laſt becomes ſo ſmall, that the fires are not above five
or ſix paces diſtant. As the elephants hear a great noiſe all
round them, they dare not fly, though it is not uncommon
for ſome of them to make their eſcape; for I was told that
ten of them got off in one day. When the hunters want to
ſeize them, they are made to enter a place ſurrounded with
ſtakes,

tion. In the midst of the forest, and in the neighbourhood of places frequented by the elephants, a spot is chosen, and surrounded with strong pallisades. The largest trees of the wood serve as the principal stakes, to which are fixed cross bars that support the other stakes. A large opening is left, through which the elephant may enter; and over this door there is a trap, or rather it receives a strong bar, which is shut after the animal passes. To draw him into this enclosure, the hunters go in quest of him: They carry along with them into the forest a tamed female in season; and, when they imagine themselves to be near enough to be heard, her governor makes her utter the cry of love. The wild male instantly replies, and hastens to join her. She is then made to march towards the enclosure, repeating the cry from time to time. She arrives first; and the male, following her by the scent, enters by the same port. As soon as he perceives the hunters, and sees himself surround-

---

stakes, where there are also some trees, between which a man can easily pass. There is another circle of war elephants and soldiers, into which some men enter mounted on elephants, who are extremely dexterous in throwing ropes round the hind legs of these animals. When fixed in this mannner, the wild elephant is put between two tame elephants, and a third one is appointed to push him behind in such a manner, as obliges him to go forward; and, when he grows mischievous, the others give him blows with their trunks. He is then led off into captivity; and the others are seized in the same manner. I saw ten of them taken. The King was present, and gave every necessary order; *Relation de la l' Ambassade de M. Chevalier de Chaumont à la Cour du Roi de Siam, p.* 91.

ed,

ed, his ardour vanifhes, and is changed into fury. Ropes and fetters are thrown round his legs and trunk. Two or three tamed elephants, conducted by men expert in that bufinefs, are brought to him, and they endeavour to fix him to one of thefe animals. In fine, by addrefs, by force, by torture, and by careffes, he is tamed in a few days. I will not enter into a more particular detail, but content myfelf with quoting from thofe travellers who have been eye-witneffes of the hunting of elephants*, which

* At a quarter of a league from Luovo, there is a kind of large amphitheatre, of a rectangular figure, furrounded with high terrafs walls, upon which the fpectators are placed. Within thefe walls, there is a pallifade of ftrong pofts fixed in the ground, behind which the hunters retire when purfued by the enraged elephants. A large opening is left on the fide next the fields, and oppofite to it, next the city, there is a fmaller one, which leads to a narrow alley, through which an elephant can pafs with difficulty, and this alley terminates in a large fhade where the operation of taming is finifhed.

When the day deftined for the chafe arrives, the hunters enter the woods, mounted on female elephants trained to this exercife. The men cover themfelves with leaves of trees, to prevent their being obferved by the wild elephants When they have advanced into the forefts, and think that fome elephants may be in the neighbourhood, they make the females utter certain cries, fitted to allure the males, who inftantly reply by frightful roarings. Then the hunters, when they perceive the elephants at a proper diftance, return, and lead the females gently back toward the amphitheatre above defcribed. The wild elephants never fail to follow. The male, which we faw tamed, entered the inclofure fpontaneoufly along with the females, and the paffage was immediately fhut. The females continued their march acrofs the amphitheatre,

and

which differs in different countries, and according to the strength and dexterity of the people who

and filed off one by one into the narrow alley at the other end. The wild elephant, who had followed them all along, stopt at the entrance of this defile. Every method was tried to make him enter. The females, who were now beyond the alley, were made to cry. Some Siamese irritated him, by clapping their hands, and crying *pat, pat*. Others teaze him with long poles armed with sharp points; and, when pursued, they slip through between the posts, and conceal themselves behind the pallisade, which the elephant cannot surmount. Lastly, after having pursued several hunters in vain, he singles out one, whom he sets upon with extreme fury. This man runs into the narrow alley, and the elephant follows him. But, he no sooner enters but he perceives himself to be in a snare; for the man escapes, and two portcullises, one before and another behind, are instantly let fall; so that, being unable either to advance or retreat, the animal makes the most astonishing efforts, and raises the most hideous cries. The hunters endeavour to sooth him by throwing pails of water on his body, by rubbing him with leaves, by pouring oil upon his ears, and by bringing to him tamed elephants, both male and female, who caress him with their trunks. They fix ropes, however, round his body, and hind legs, to enable them to drag him out, and they continue to throw water on his trunk and body, in order to refresh him. In fine, a tamed elephant, accustomed to instruct noviciates, is made to approach him. The former is mounted by a servant, who makes the animal advance and retire, to show the wild elephant that he has nothing to fear, and that he may go out. The port is then opened, and he follows his neighbour to the end of the alley. When there, two elephants are tied, one to each side of him, another marches before, leads him in the way they want him to go, while a third pushes him behind with its head, till they arrive at a kind of shade, where he is tied to a large post, which turns round like the capstan of a ship. There he is left till next day, to allow his rage to subside. But, while he frets around this post, a Bramin, one of those Indian priests who are ex-

tremely

who make war againſt them; for, inſtead of
making, like the king of Siam, walls, terraſſes,
pallifades,

tremely numerous in Siam, dreſſed in white, approaches the animal, mounted on an elephant, turns gently round him, and
bedews him with a confecrated water, which the prieſt carries
in a golden veſſel. They believe that, by this ceremony, the
elephant loſes his natural ferocity, and is rendered fit for the
King's ſervice. Next day, he walks along with his enſlaved
neighbours; and, at the end of fifteen days, he is completely
tamed; *Premier Voyage du P. Tachard, p.* 298.

They had no ſooner alighted from their horſes, and mounted
the elephants which were prepared for them, than the King appeared, accompanied with a great number of mandarins, riding
on elephants of war. They all proceeded about a league into
the wood, when they arrived at the place where the wild elephants were encloſed. This was a ſquare park, of three or four
hundred geometrical paces, the ſides of which were fenced with
large ſtakes; in which, however, conſiderable openings were left
at certain diſtances. It contained fourteen large elephants. As
ſoon as the royal train arrived, a circle was formed, conſiſting
of a hundred war elephants, which were placed round the park
to prevent the wild ones from forcing through the pallifades.
We were ſtationed behind this fence, near the King A dozen
of the ſtrongeſt tame elephants were puſhed into the park, each
of them being mounted by two men, furniſhed with large ropes
and nooſes, the ends of which were fixed to the elephants they
rode. They firſt ran againſt the elephant they wiſhed to ſeize,
who, ſeeing himſelf purſued, endeavoured to force the barrier
and make his eſcape. But the whole was blockaded by the
war elephants, who puſhed him back; and, in his courſe, the
hunters, mounted on the tame elephants, threw their nooſes
ſo dexterouſly upon the ſpots where it behoved the animal to
place his feet, that the whole were ſeized in the ſpace of an hour.
Each elephant was then bound with ropes, and two tame ones
placed on each ſide of him, by means of which he is tamed in
fifteen days; *Idem, p.* 340.

A few days after, we had the pleaſure of being preſent at the
hunting of elephants. The Siameſe are very dexterous at this
ſpecies

pallifades, parks, and vaft enclofures, the poor
Negroes content themfelves with the moft fimple
artifices.

fpecies of hunting, which they have feveral modes of performing. The eafieft, and not the leaft entertaining, is executed by
means of female elephants. When a female is in feafon, fhe is
conducted to the foreft of Luovo. Her guide rides on her back,
and covers himfelf with leaves, to prevent his being perceived
by the wild elephants. The cries of the tame female, which fhe
never fails to fet up upon a certain fignal given by the guide,
collect all the elephants within the reach of hearing, who foon
follow her. The guide, taking advantage of their mutual cries,
returns flowly towards Luovo with all his train, and enters an
enclofure made of large ftakes, about a quarter of a league from
the city, and pretty near the foreft. A great troop of elephants
were, in this manner, brought together; but one of them only
was large, and it was very difficult to feize and to tame him.—
The guide who conducted the female, went out of the enclofure
by a narrrow paffage in the form of an alley, and about the
length of an elephant. Each end of this alley was provided
with a portcullis, which was eafily raifed or let down. All the
young elephants followed the female at different times. But a
paffage fo narrow alarmed the large one, who always drew
back. The female was made to return feveral times; he uniformly followed her to the port; but, as if he forefaw his lofs of
liberty, he would never pafs. Several Siamefe, who were in
the park, then advanced and endeavoured to force him, by goad-
ing him with fharp pointed poles. The elephant, being enraged
by this treatment, purfued them with fuch fury and quicknefs,
that not one of them would have efcaped, had they not
nimbly retired behind the ftakes of the pallifade, againft which
the ferocious creature broke its large tufks three or four times.
In the heat of the purfuit, one of thofe who attacked him moft
brifkly, and who was moft keenly purfued, run into the alley,
which the elephant entered in order to kill him. But the animal no fooner fell into the fnare, than the Siamefe efcaped by
a fmall paffage, and the two portcullifes were inftantly let down.
The elephant ftruggled much; but he found himfelf obliged to

remain

artifices. They dig *, in the places where the elephants are suppofed to pafs, ditches fo deep, that after falling into them, there is no poffibility of getting out,

　　　　　　　　　　　　　　　　The

remain in his prifon. To appeafe him they threw pailfulls of water on his body. Ropes, however, were put round his legs and neck. After being fatigued for fome time, he was brought out by means of two tame elephants who drew him forward with ropes, while other two pufhed him behind, till he was fixed to a large poft, round which he could only turn. In an hour after, he became fo tractable, that a Siamefe mounted on his back; and next day he was let loofe, and conducted to the ftables along with the others; *Second Voyage du P. Tachard, p.* 352.

* Though thefe animals be large and favage, great numbers of them are taken in Æthiopia by the following ftratagem: In the thickeft parts of the foreft, where the elephants retire during the night, an enclofure is made of ftakes, interlaced with large branches, in which a fmall opening is left, which has a door lying flat on the ground. When the elephant enters, the hunters, from the top of a tree, draw up the door by means of a rope. They then defcend and flay the animal with arrows. But if, by accident, they mifs their aim, and the creature efcapes from the enclofure, he kills every man he meets; *L'Afrique de Marmol, tom.* i. *p.* 58.—There are different modes of hunting elephants. In fome places, caltrops are fpread on the ground, by means of which the animals fall into ditches, from whence, after being properly entangled, they are eafily drawn out. In others, a tame female is led into a narrow defile, and allures the male to approach by her cries. When he arrives, the hunters fhut him up by barriers, which they have in readinefs for the purpofe; and though he finds the female on her back, he copulates with her, contrary to the practice of other quadrupeds. After this, he endeavours to retire. But, while he goes about in queft of an outlet, the hunters, who are upon a wall, or fome elevated fituation, throw ropes and chains of different dimenfions, by which they fo entangle his trunk and the reft of his body, that they can approach him without danger; and, after

The elephant, when tamed, becomes the moſt gentle and moſt obedient of all domeſtic animals. He is ſo fond of his keeper, that he careſſes him, and anticipates his commands, by foreſeeing

ter taking ſome neceſſary precautions, they carry him off, accompanied with two tame elephants, to ſhew him a proper example, or to chaſtiſe him, if he rebels.——There are many other methods of hunting elephants; for every country has its own mode; *Relation d'un Voyage par Thevenot, tom.* iii. *p.* 131.—— The inhabitants of Ceylon dig pretty deep ditches, which they cover with thin planks and ſtraw. During the night, the elephants having no ſuſpicion of the deceit, come upon the planks, and fall into the ditch, from which they are unable to eſcape, but would infallibly periſh by hunger, if victuals were not brought to him by ſlaves, to whom they gradually become accuſtomed, and at laſt are rendered ſo tame, that they are brought to Goa, and other adjacent countries, to gain their own livelihood and that of their maſters; *Divers Memoires touchant les Indes Orientales, premier diſcours, tom.* ii. *p.* 257. *Recueil des Voyages de la Compagnie des Indes, Amſt.* 1711.——As the Europeans give a high price for elephants teeth, the love of gain arms the Negroes perpetually againſt theſe animals. For this ſpecies of hunting they ſometimes aſſemble in great bodies, with their arrows and darts. But the moſt common and moſt ſucceſsful method is that of digging ditches in the woods, becauſe they are never deceived in diſtinguiſhing the track of the elephants.——There are two methods of taking theſe animals, either by digging ditches and covering them with the branches of trees, into which the creatures inadvertently fall, or by hunting them, which is performed in the following manner. In the iſland of Ceylon, where the elephants are very numerous, the hunters keep female elephants, which they call *alias*. As ſoon as they learn that there are wild elephants in any place, they repair thither, accompanied with two of theſe alias, which, whenever a male is diſcovered, they let looſe. The females come up on each ſide of him, and, keeping him in the middle, ſqueeze him ſo hard that he cannot eſcape; *Voyage d'Orient. du P. Philippe de la tres-ſainte Trinité, p.* 361.

every

every thing that will pleafe him. He foon learns to comprehend figns, and even to underftand the expreffion of founds. He diftinguifhes the tones of command, of anger, or of approbation, and regulates his actions accordingly. He never miftakes the voice of his mafter. He receives his orders with attention, executes them with prudence and eagernefs, but without any degree of precipitation; for his movements are always meafured, and his character feems to partake of the gravity of his mafs. He eafily learns to bend his knees for the accommodation of thofe who mount him. His friends he careffes with his trunk, falutes with it fuch people as are pointed out to him, ufes it for raifing burdens, and affifts in loading himfelf. He allows himfelf to be clothed, and feems to have a pleafure in being covered with gilded harnefs and brilliant houfings. He is employed in drawing chariots*,

ploughs,

* I was an eye-witnefs to the following facts. At Goa, thére are always fome elephants employed in the building of fhips. I one day went to the fide of the river, near which a large fhip was building in the city of Goa, where there is a large area filled with beams for that purpofe. Some men tie the ends of the heavieft beams with a rope, which is handed to an elephant, who carries it to his mouth, and after twifting it round his trunk, draws it, without any conductor, to the place where the fhip is building, though it had only once been pointed out to him. He fometimes drew beams fo large, that more than twenty men would have been unable to move. But what furprifed me ftill more, when other beams obftructed the road, he elevated the ends of his own beams, that they might run eafily over thofe which lay in his way. Could the moft enlightened man

do

ploughs, waggons, &c. He draws equally, and never turns reſtive, provided he is not inſulted with improper chaſtiſement, and the people who labour with him have the air of being pleaſed with the manner in which he employs his ſtrength. The man who conducts the animal generally rides on his neck, and uſes an iron rod *, hooked at the end, or a bodkin, with which he pricks the head or ſides of the ears, in order to puſh the creature forward, or to make him turn. But words are generally ſufficient †, eſpecially if the animal has had time to acquire a complete acquaintance with his conductor, and to put entire confidence in him. The attachment of the elephant becomes ſometimes ſo ſtrong, and his affection ſo warm and durable, that he has been known to die of ſorrow, when,

do more ? *Voyage d'Orient. du P. Philippe de la tres-ſainte Trinité, p. 367.*

* The conductor rides on the elephant's neck, and uſes no bridle, reins, or any kind of ſtimulus, but only a large iron rod, ſharp and hooked at the end, with which he ſpurs on the animal, and likewiſe directs the way, by pricking his ears, muzzle, and other places that have moſt ſenſibility. This rod, which would kill any other animal, is hardly ſufficient to make an impreſſion on the ſkin of the elephant, or to keep him in ſubjection when irritated; *Voyage de Pietro della Valle, tom. iv. p. 247.*— Two ſervants, the one mounted on the neck, and the other on the crupper, manage the elephant, by means of a large iron hook; *Premier Voyage du P. Tachard, p. 273.*

† Non fræno aut habenis aut aliis vinculis regitur bellua, ſed inſidentis voci obſequitur; *Vartoman. apud Geſner. cap. de Elephanto.*

in

in a paroxyfm of rage, he had killed his guide*.

Though the elephant produces but a fingle young one in two or three years, the fpecies is very numerous. The prolific powers of animals are proportioned to the fhortnefs of their lives. In elephants the duration of life compenfates their fterility; and, if it be true that they live two centuries, and can propagate till they are one hundred and twenty years old, each couple may produce forty in this period. Befides, as they have nothing to fear from other animals, and are taken with much difficulty and hazard by men, the fpecies is eafily fupported, and is generally diffufed over all the fouthern regions of Africa and Afia. Elephants abound in Ceylon †,

---

* Quidam iracundia permotus cum cefforem fuum occidiffet, tam valde defideravit, ut, pœnitudine et mœrore confectus, obierit; *Arrianus in Indicis.*

† In Ceylon there are many elephants, whofe teeth bring much riches to the inhabitants; *Voyage de Fr. Peyrard, tom.* ii. *p.* 151.——There are vaft numbers of elephants in India, moft of which are brought from the ifland of Ceylon; *Voyage de la Boullaye-le-Goux, p.* 250.—— At Deli, as well as other parts of India, there are different kinds of elephants; but thofe brought from Ceylon are preferred to all the reft; *Relation d'un Voyage, par Thevenot, tom.* iii. *p.* 131.——In the ifland of Ceylon there are many elephants, and they are more generous and noble than thofe of other countries; *Voyage d'Orient. du P. Philippe, p.* 361. Recueil *des Voyages qui ont fervi à l'Etabliffement de la Compagnie des Indes de Holland. Les Voyages de Tavernier, tom.* iii. *p.* 237.

in

in the Mogul empire*, in Bengal †, in Siam ‡, in Pegu ‖, and in all the other territories of India. They are, perhaps, still more numerous in all the southern regions of Africa, except certain cantons which they have abandoned, because they are totally occupied by men. Elephants are faithful to their country, and never change their climate; for though they can live in temperate regions, yet they appear not to have ever attempted to establish themselves, or even to travel into these climates. They were formerly unknown in Europe. Homer, though he mentions ivory §, seems not to have been acquainted with the animal by which that substance is produced. Alexander the Great was the first European who ever mounted an ele-

---

* Voyage de Fr. Bernier au Mogul, tom ii. p. 64.——— Voyage de de Feynes à la Chine, p. 88.——Relation d'un Voyage, par Thevenot, tom. iii. p. 131.——Voyage d'Edward Terei, aux Indes Orientales, p. 15.

† The country of Bengal abounds in elephants; and it is from thence they are conveyed to the other parts of India; *Voyage de Fr. Peyrard, tom.* i. *p.* 353.

‡ M. de Constance informed me, that the King of Siam had twenty thousand elephants in his dominions, without reckoning those that are wild, and live in the woods and mountains, of which fifty, sixty, and even eighty, are sometimes taken at a single hunting match; *Premier Voyage du P. Tachard, p.* 288.

‖ Recueil des Voyages de la Compagnie des Indes.—Voyage de Vander Hagen, tom. iii. p. 40. &c.

§ Herodotus is the most ancient author who mentions ivory to have been a matter derived from elephants teeth; *Vid. Plin. Hist. Nat. lib.* viii. *cap.* 3.

phant.

phant*. Thofe which he took from Porus, he caufed to be brought to Greece; and they were, perhaps, the fame which Pyrrhus †, feveral years after, employed againft the Romans in the Tarentine war, and with which Curius came triumphant into Rome. Annibal afterwards tranfported elephants from Africa, made them pafs the Alps, and conducted them almoft to the gates of Rome.

The Indians, from a period beyond the records of hiftory, have employed elephants in war ‡. Among thefe undifciplined nations, the elephants formed their beft troop ; and, as long as fteel weapons alone were employed, they generally decided the fate of battles. We learn from hiftory, however, that the Greeks and Romans were foon accuftomed to thefe monfters of war. They opened their ranks to let them pafs, and directed all their weapons, not againft the animals, but their conductors, who ufed all their efforts to turn and appeafe thofe which had

---

* Elephantes ex Europæis primus Alexander habuit, cum fubegiffet Porum ; *Paufanias, in Atticis.*

† Manius Curius Dentatus, victo Pyrrho, primum in triumpho elephantum duxit ; *Seneca de Brevitate Vitæ, cap.* 13.

‡ From time immemorial, the Kings of Ceylon, of Pegu, and of Aracan, have ufed elephants in wars. Naked fabres were tied to their trunks, and on their backs were fixed fmall wooden caftles, which contained five or fix men armed with javelins, and other weapons. They contribute greatly to diforder the enemy; but they are eafily terrified by the fight of fire; *Recueil des Voyages de la Compagnie des Indes, tom.* vii.—*Voyage de Schonten, p.* 32.

feparated

feparated from the reft of the troop. Now that fire has become the element of war, and the chief inftrument of death, elephants, which are terrified both at the noife and flame *, would be more dangerous than ufeful in our combats. The Indian Kings ftill arm elephants in their wars; but this practice is defigned more for fhow than utility. One advantage, however, is derived from them. Like every other military order, they ferve the purpofe of enflaving their equals, and are, accordingly, ufed in taming the wild elephants. The moft powerful monarchs of India have not now above two hundred war elephants †. They keep many others for the purpofes of labour, and for tranfporting their women in large cages covered with foliage. It is a very fafe mode of riding; for the elephant never ftumbles: But to be accuftomed to his brifk and fwinging movements, requires time and practice. The neck is the beft feat; for there

---

* The elephants are afraid of fire; and, therefore, fince the ufe of fire-arms, thefe animals are of no value in war. Some of thofe brought from Ceylon are not fo daftardly; but it is only after being daily accuftomed to the firing of guns, and to having crackers thrown among their feet; *Voyage de Fr. Bernier, tom.* ii. *p.* 65.

† Few people in India have elephants. Even their nobles have not many; and the great Mogul keeps not above five hundred for his houfhold, and for tranfporting his baggage and women, in wattled cages or bafkets. I have been affured, that he has not above two hundred war elephants, part of which are employed in carrying fmall pieces of artillery; *Relation d'un Voyage, par Thevenot, tom.* iii. *p.* 132.

the

the fuccuffions are not fo hard as on the fhoulders, back, or crupper. But for the purpofes of war or of hunting, each elephant is always mounted by feveral men *. The conductor rides aftraddle on their neck, and the hunters or combatants fit on the other parts of the body.

In thofe happy regions where cannon, and other murdering engines, are imperfectly known, they ftill fight with elephants †. At Cochin, and other parts of Malabar ‡, horfes are not ufed, and all the warriors who fight not on foot are mounted on elephants. The practice is nearly the fame in Tonquin §, Siam ||, and

* Of all animals, the elephant is the moft ferviceable in war; for he can eafily carry four men armed with muſkets bows, or fpears; *Recueil des Voyages de la Compagnie des Indes de Hollande; Second Voyage de Vander Hagen, tom.* ii. *p.* 53.

† When the elephants are led to war, they ferve two purpofes; for they either carry fmall wooden towers, from the top of which fome foldiers fight, or they have fwords fixed to their trunks with iron chains, and in this manner they are let loofe againft the enemy, whom they affail with courage, and would unqueftionably cut to pieces, if they were not repelled by fpears, which throw out fire; for, as elephants are terrified at fire, this artifice is employed to put them to flight; *Voyage d'Orient. par le P. Philippe, p.* 367.

‡ In Cochin, as well as in other parts of Malabar, no horfes are ufed in war. Thofe who fight not on foot, are mounted on elephants, of which there are great numbers in the mountains; and thefe mountain elephants are the largeft in India; *Relation d'un Voyage, par Thevenot, tom.* iii. *p.* 261.

§ In the kingdom of Tonquin, the women of rank generally ride upon elephants, fo very tall and maffy, that they can carry without any danger, a tower with fix men in it, befide the conductor on their neck; *Il Genio Vagante del Conte Aurelio degli Anzi, tom.* i. *p.* 282.

|| See Le Journal du Voyage de l'Abbé de Choify, p. 242.

Pegu,

Pegu, where the King and great Lords always
ride upon elephants. At festivals, they are preceded and followed by a numerous train of these
animals, pompously adorned with pieces of
shining metal, and covered with rich stuffs. Their
tufks are ornamented with rings of gold and
filver *; their ears and cheeks are painted;
they are crowned with garlands; and a number of little bells are fixed to different parts of
their body. They feem to delight in rich at-
tire; for they are cheerful and careffing in proportion to the number of their ornaments. But
it is only in the fouthern parts of India where
the elephants have acquired this degree of po-
lifh. In Africa, it is with difficulty that they
can be tamed †. The Afiatics, who have been

* We have feen elephants whofe teeth were extremely large
and beautiful. In fome, they are more than four feet long,
and garnifhed with rings of gold, filver, and copper; *Premier
Voyage du P. Tachard, p.* 273.—The grandeur of the princes
confifts in the number of elephants they are able to keep,
which is the chief fource of their expence. The Great Mogul
has feveral thoufands of them. The King of Madura, the
Lords of Narzinga and of Bifnager, and the Kings of Naires
and of Manful, have feveral hundreds, which they diftinguifh
into three claffes. The largeft are deftined for the fervice of
the Prince. Their harnefs is extremely rich. They are covered with cloth embroidered with gold, and ftudded with
pearls. Their teeth are adorned with fine gold and filver,
and fometimes with diamonds. Thofe of a middle fize are
employed in war; and the leaft are ufed for common labour; *Voyage du P. Vincent Marie de Ste Catherine de Sienne,
chap.* xi.

† The inhabitants of Congo have not the art of taming elephants, which are very mifchievous, take crocodiles with their
trunks, and throw them to a great diftance; *Il Genio Vag.
del Conte Aurelio, tom.* ii. *p.* 473.

very

very anciently civilized, made the education of the elephant a kind of art, and have inſtructed and modified him according to their own manners But, of all the African nations, the Carthaginians alone formerly trained the elephants to war; becauſe, at the ſplendid period of their republic, they were perhaps the moſt civilized people of the Eaſt. There are now no wild elephants in all that part of Africa on this ſide of Mount Atlas. There are even few beyond theſe mountains, till we arrive at the river Senegal. But they are numerous in Senegal*, in Guiney † in Congo ‡, on the Teeth coaſt §, in the countries

* The elephants, of which I daily ſaw great numbers along the banks of the river Senegal, no longer aſtoniſh me. On the fifth day of November, I walked into the woods oppoſite to the village of Dagana, where I found a number of their freſh tracks, which I followed near two leagues, and at laſt diſcovered five of theſe animals; three of them lay wallowing, like hogs, in their own ſoil, and the fourth was ſtanding with its cub, eating the branches of an acacia tree, which they had broken off. By comparing the animal with the height of the tree, I perceived that its crupper was at leaſt eleven or twelve feet high, and its tuſks near three feet long. Though my preſence did not diſturb them, I thought it proper to retire. In purſuing my route, I met with the impreſſions of their feet, which meaſured near a foot and a half in diameter. Their dung, which reſembled that of a horſe, formed balls ſeven or eight inches in diameter; *Voyage au Senegal, par M. Adanſon, p.* 75. See alſo *Voyage de la Maire, p.* 97.

† Voyage de Guinée, par Boſman, p. 243.

‡ In the province of Pamba, which belongs to the kingdom of Congo, there are many elephants, on account of the number of rivers and foreſts with which that country abounds; *Drake's Voyages.* See likewiſe, in the Dutch collection of Eaſt India Voyages, *Le Voyage de Vander Broeck, tom.* ii. *p.* 319. and *Il Genio Vagante del Conte Aurelio, tom.* ii. *p.* 473.

§ The firſt country where elephants are frequent is that part

countries of Anta*, Acra, Benin, and all the other fouthern territories of Africa †, as far as thofe which are terminated by the Cape of Good Hope; except fome well inhabited provinces, fuch as Fida ‡, Ardra, &c. We even find

of the coaft called by the Flemifh *Tand-kuft*, or *Teeth-coaft*, on account of the number of elephants teeth, of which the natives make a lucrative traffic. Towards the gold coaft, and in the countries of Awiné, Jaumoré, Eguira, Abocroé, Ancober, and Axim, many elephants are daily flain; and, the more any country is defert and uninhabited, it is proportionally more frequented by elephants and other favage animals; *Voyage de Guinée, par Guil. Bofman, p. 244.*

* The country of Anta likewife abounds in elephants; for many of them are not only killed on the main land, but they daily come down to the fea-coaft, and under our forts, from which our people defcry them, and make great ravages upon them. From Anta to Acra, very few are found, but in the places mentioned above, becaufe the countries between Anta and Acra have been a long time tolerably peopled, except that of Fetu, which, for five or fix years, has been almoft deferted, and the elephants, for that reafon, have taken it into their poffeffion. On the coaft of Acra, vaft numbers are annually flain; becaufe in thefe diftricts there is much defert and uninhabited land. . . . In the country of Benin, as well as on the Rio de Calbari, Camerones, and other adjacent rivers and countries, thefe animals are fo numerous, that it is difficult to conceive how the natives can or dare live in them; *Idem, p. 246.*

† Below the Bay of St. Helen's, the country is divided into two portions by the Elephant river, which has received its name from the elephants, who love running waters, and are found in great numbers upon their banks; *Defcription du Cap de Bonne Efperance, par Kolbe, tom. i. p. 114. et tom. iii. p. 12.*

‡ There are no elephants in Ardra, nor in Fida, though, in my time, one was killed there. But the Negroes affirm, that fuch an event had not happened for fixty years before. I, therefore, imagine that this animal had wandered thither from fome other country: *Voyage de Guinée, par Bofman, p. 245.*

them

them in Abyssinia *, in Æthiopia †, in Nigritia ‡, upon the eastern coasts, and in all the interior parts of Africa. They likewise exist in the large islands of India and Africa, as Madagascar §, Java ||, and as far as the Philippine islands **.

After comparing the testimonies of travellers and historians, it appears that elephants are more

* See Voyage Historique d'Abyssinie du P. Lobo, tom. i. p. 57. where troops of elephants are said to be found in Abyssinia.

† The Æthiopians have elephants in their country; but they are smaller than those of India; and, though their teeth are hollow, and of less value, they constitute a considerable article of trade; *Voyage de Paul Lucas, tom. iii. p. 186.*—There are many elephants in Æthiopia, and in the country of Prester John, beyond the island of Mosambique, where the Caffres or Negroes kill a great number for the sake of their teeth; *Recueil des Voyages de la Compagnie des Indes de Hollande, tom. i. p. 413.* See also *L'Afrique de Marmol, tom. i. p. 58.*

‡ Elephas magna copia in silvis Nigritarum regionis invenitur. Solent magno numero confertim incedere, &c.; *Leonis Afric. Descript. Africæ, tom. ii. p. 774. et 745.*

§ In the island of Madagascar, elephants are supposed to be more numerous than in any other country. Madagascar, and an adjacent island, called *Cuzibet*, furnish such vast quantities of ivory, that, in the opinion of merchants, the rest of the world does not produce an equal number of elephants teeth; *Descript. de l' Inde Orient. par Marc Paul, p. 114.*

|| The animals found in the island of Java, are, 1. elephants, which are tamed and hired out for labour; *Recueil des Voyages de la Compagnie des Indes de Hollande, tom. i. p. 411.*—At Tuban, the King's elephants are each placed under a particular shade supported by four pillars; and, in the middle of the area, which is likewise covered, there is a large stake, to which the elephant is fixed by a chain; *Idem, tom. i. p. 526.*

** Mandanar is the only Philippine island which produces elephants; and, as the natives do not tame these animals, as in Siam and Cambaya, they are prodigiously numerous; *Voyage autour du Monde, par Gemelli Careri, tom. v. p. 209.*

nume-

numerous and common in Africa than in Afia.
They are alfo lefs fufpicious, and retire not to
fuch diftant folitudes. They feem to know the
unfkilfulnefs and debility of the men who inhabit this part of the world; for they daily approach the villages, without difcovering any apprehenfions *. They treat the Negroes with
that natural and fupercilious indifference which
they entertain for all animals. They regard not
man as a powerful or formidable being, but
as a crafty creature, who knows only how to
lay fnares in their way, but who dares not attack
them face to face, and is ignorant of the art of
reducing them to flavery. It is by this art alone,
which has been long known in the Eaftern nations, that the number of thefe animals has been
diminifhed. The wild elephants, which thefe
people render domeftic, become by captivity fo
many voluntary eunuchs, in whom the fources
of generation are daily dried up. But, in
Africa, where the elephants are all free, the
fpecies is fupported, and might even increafe,
though more of them were deftroyed; becaufe
every individual is conftantly labouring to repair the wafte. I perceive no other caufe to
which this difference of number can be afcribed;
for it appears, from every confideration, that the

---

* The elephants often pafs the night in the villages, and are
fo little afraid of frequented places, that, inftead of turning
when they perceive the houfes of the Negroes, they march
ftraight forward, and overturn them like nut fhells; *Voyage de
la Maire, p.* 98.

C 3   fouth

south of India and the East of Africa, are the
countries most congenial to the nature of the
elephant. He is there much larger and stronger
than in Guiney, or any other western region
of Africa. He dreads excessive heat, and never
inhabits the burning sands of the desert. Neither is the species so numerous in the country of
the Negroes, as along the rivers; and they are
never found in the mountainous parts of Africa.
But, in India, the strongest and most coura-
geous of the species, and which have the largest
tusks, are called *Mountain Elephants :* They inhabit the elevated parts of the country, where,
the air being more temperate, the waters less
impure, and the food more wholesome, they acquire all the perfections of which their nature
is capable.

In general, the elephants of Asia exceed, in
size, strength, &c. those of Africa ; and those
of Ceylon, in particular, are superior to all those
of Asia, not only in magnitude, but in courage
and intelligence. These qualities they perhaps
derive from a more perfect education. However this may be, all travellers have celebrated
the elephants of this island *, where the surface
of

<hr />

* The elephants of Ceylon are preferred to all others, because they have most courage. . . . The Indians say, that all
the other elephants respect those of Ceylon; *Relation d'un Voyage
par Thevenot,* p. 261.—The elephants of Ceylon are the boldest
of the species; *Voyage de Bernier, tom.* ii. *p.* 65.—The best and
most intelligent elephants come from the island of Ceylon; *Recueil*

of the earth is variegated with mountains, which are more elevated in proportion as they advance toward the centre of the ifland, and where the heat, though great, is not fo exceffive as in Senegal, Guiney, and the other weftern parts of Africa. The ancients, who knew nothing of this quarter of the world, except the territories fituated between Mount Atlas and the Mediterranean, had remarked, that the Lybian elephants were much fmaller than thofe of India *. There are now no elephants in that part of Africa; which proves what was alledged under the article *Lion* †, that men are at prefent more numerous there than they were in the days of the Carthaginians. The elephants have retired in proportion to the difturbance they have met with from the human fpecies. But, in travelling through the climates of Africa, they have not changed their nature; for the elephants of Senegal, Guiney, &c. are ftill much fmaller than thofe of India.

The ftrength of thefe animals is proportioned to their magnitude. The Indian elephants carry

cueil des *Voyages, tom.* i. *p.* 413.; *tom.* ii. *p.* 256.; *tom.* iv. *p.* 363. —In Ceylon the elephants are numerous, and more generous, and noble than any others. . . . All other elephants revere thofe of Ceylon, &c.; *Voyage d'Orient. du P. Philippe, p.* 130. *et* 367.

*'Indicum (elephantum) Afri pavent, nec contueri audent; nam et major Indicis magnitudo eft; *Plin. Hift. Nat. lib.* viii. *cap.* 9.

† See above, vol. v. p. 66.

with

with eafe three or four thoufand weight *: The fmaller, or thofe of Africa, can eafily raife with their trunk a weight of two hundred pounds, and place it on their own fhoulders †. They draw up into their trunks large quantities of water, which they fquirt into the air, or all around, to the diftance of feveral fathoms. They can carry a weight of above a thoufand pounds on their tufks. They ufe their trunks for breaking branches, and their tufks for tearing up trees. The greatnefs of their ftrength may be ftill farther conceived from the quicknefs of their movements, compared with the magnitude of their bodies. At their ordinary ftep, they cut as much ground as a horfe at a gentle trot; and they run as faft as a horfe can gallop: But, in a ftate of liberty, they never run, unlefs when enraged or terrified. Domeftic elephants are generally walked, and they perform eafily, and without fatigue, a journey of fifteen or twenty leagues in a day; and, when pufhed, they can travel thirty or forty leagues a day‡. Their tread is heard at a great diftance, and they may be eafily followed by the tracks of their feet,

* Relation d'un Voyage par Thevenot, p. 261.

† The elephant raifes with his trunk a weight of two hundred pounds, and places it on his own fhoulders. . . . . He draws up into his trunk one hundred and fifty pounds of water, which he fquirts to a confiderable height in the air; *L'Afrique de Marmol, tom.* i. *p.* 58.

‡ When an elephant is pufhed, he can perform, in one day, as much as a man generally does in fix; *L'Afrique de Marmol, tom.* i. *p.* 58.

w hich

which, in soft ground, measure fifteen or eighteen inches in diameter.

A domestic elephant performs more work than perhaps six horses *; but he requires from his master much care, and a great deal of good victuals, which cost about four francs, or a hundred pence a-day †. He is generally fed with rice, raw or boiled, and mixed with water. To keep him in full vigour, he is said to require daily a hundred pounds of rice, besides fresh herbage to cool him; for he is subject to be over-heated, and must be led to the water twice or thrice a-day for the benefit of bathing. He easily learns to bathe himself. He takes the water up in his trunk, carries it to his mouth, drinks part of it, and, by elevating his trunk, allows the remainder to run over every part of his body. To

---

* The price of elephants is very high. They are sometimes sold from a thousand pagodas of gold to fifteen thousand roupees, that is, from nine or ten thousand livres to thirty thousand; *Notes de M. de Buffy.*—At Ceylon, an elephant is worth, at least, eight thousand *pardaons*; and, when very large, he brings twelve, and even fifteen thousand pardaons; *Hist. de l'Isle de Ceylon, par Ribeyro, p.* 144.

† The food of an elephant costs about half a pistole each day; *Relation d'un Voyage par Thevenot, p.* 261. ——Tamed elephants are very delicate in their feeding. They require rice well boiled, and seasoned with butter and sugar, which is given to them in large balls. They devour daily a hundred pounds of rice, besides leaves of trees, particularly those of the Indian fig, called *bananas* or *plantane*, which are given them by way of refreshment; *Voyage de Pyrard, tom.* ii. *p.* 367. See also, *Voyages de la Boullaye-le-Goux, p.* 250.;—and *Recueil des Voyages de la Compagnie des Indes de Hollande, tom.* i. *p.* 473.

give an idea of the labour he performs, it is sufficient to remark, that all the tuns, facks, and bales, tranfported from one place to another in India, are carried by elephants; that they carry burdens on their bodies, their necks, their tufks, and even in their mouths, by giving them the end of a rope, which they hold faft with their teeth; that, uniting fagacity to ftrength, they never break or injure any thing committed to their charge; that from the margins of the waters, they put thefe bundles into boats without wetting them, laying them down gently, and arranging them where they ought to be placed; that when difpofed in the places where their mafters direct, they try with their trunk whether the goods are properly ftowed; and, if a tun or cafk rolls, they go, of their own accord, in queft of ftones to prop and render it firm.

When the elephant is properly managed, though in captivity, he lives a long time; and, it is probable, that, in a ftate of liberty, his life is ftill longer. Some authors affirm, that he lives four or five hundred years* others two or three hundred †, and others a hundred and twenty,

* Onefimus, according to Strabo, *lib*. 15. fays, that elephants live five hundred years.—Philoftratus, *Vit. Apoll. lib*. xvi. relates, that the elephant Ajax, which fought for Porus againft Alexander the Great, lived four hundred years after that battle,———Juba, King of Mauritania, afferts, that an elephant was taken in Mount Atlas, which was known to have been in a battle four hundred years before.

† Elephantum alii annos ducentos vivere aiunt, alii trecentos;

twenty, a hundred and thirty, and a hundred and forty *. I believe that a medium between the two extremes is the truth; and that, if captive elephants live a hundred and twenty, or a hundred and thirty years, those which are free, and enjoy all the conveniencies and rights of Nature, ought to exist at least two hundred. Besides, if they go two years with young, and require thirty before they obtain their full growth, we may, with still more certainty, conclude, that their life extends beyond the period we have affixed. But captivity abridges their existence less than the injuries arising from change of climate. Whatever care is bestowed on him, the elephant lives not long in temperate, and still shorter in cold countries. That which the King of Portugal sent to Louis XIV.

centos; *Arist. Hist. Anim. lib.* viii. *cap.* 9.—Elephas ut longissimum annos circiter ducentos vivit; *Arrian. in Indicis.* - I saw a white elephant, which was destined to be the successor of that in the palace, and was said to be near three hundred years old; *Premier Voyage de Siam du P. Tachard, p.* 273.

* The elephants grow during one half of their existence, and generally live a hundred and fifty years; *Drake's Voyage, p.* 104.—The female elephants go two years with young, and live a hundred and fifty years; *Recueil des Voyages de la Compagnie des Indes de Hollande, tom.* vii. *p.* 31.——Notwithstanding all the inquiries I have made, I could never learn exactly how long the elephant lives. The keepers of these animals can give no other information, than that such an elephant was in the possession of their father, grandfather, and great-grandfather; and, by computing the length of time which these people lived, it is sometimes found to amount to a hundred and twenty, or a hundred and thirty years; *Voyage de Tavernier, tom.* iii. *p.* 242.

in 1668*, and which was then only four years old, died in the month of January 1681, at the age of feventeen, and lived at Verfailles only thirteen years, though he was fed plentifully, and managed with the greateft attention. He had daily eighty pounds of bread, twelve pints of wine, and two pails of pottage, mixed with four or five pounds of bread; and every fecond day, in place of pottage, he had two pails of boiled rice, without reckoning what was given him by vifitors. He had, befides, a fheaf of corn every day for his amufement; for, after eating the ears, he made a kind of whip of the ftraw, with which he drove away the flies. He delighted in breaking the ftraw into fmall morfels, which he did very dexteroufly with his trunk; and, as he was daily led out to walk, he pulled and eat the grafs. The elephant which was lately at Naples, though the heat is greater there than in France, lived but a few years. Thofe which were fent to Peterfburgh, though well fheltered, clothed, and warmed with ftoves, all died fucceffively. Hence we may conclude, that this animal is incapable of fubfifting, and far lefs can he multiply, in any part of Europe. But I am aftonifhed that the Portuguefe, who firft knew the value and utility of elephants in the Eaft Indies, did not tranfport them to the warm climate of Brazil, where, by leaving them at liberty, they would

* Mem. pour fervir à l'Hiftoire des Animaux, part. iii. p. 101 et 127.

probably

probably have multiplied. The elephants are generally afh-coloured, or blackifh. White elephants, as formerly remarked, are extremely rare *; and authors are quoted who have feen white and red elephants in different parts of India, where they are highly valued †. Befides, thef

* Some perfons who lived long in Pondicherry, feem to doubt the exiftence of white and red elephants; for they affirm, that in this part of India, at leaft, the elephants are all black. It is true, they remark, that, when thefe animals are long neglected to be wafhed, the duft which adheres to their oily and naked fkin gives them the appearance of a dirty gray colour; but when wafhed with water, they become as black as formerly. I believe that black is the natural colour of elephants, and none of any other colour are to be found in thofe parts of India which thefe people have had an opportunity of feeing. But, at the fame time, it feems not to admit of a doubt, that in Ceylon, Siam, Pegu, Cambaya, &c. fome white and red elephants are accidentally to be met with. For ocular witneffes of this fact, we might quote le Chevalier Chaumont, l'Abbé de Choify, le P. Tachard, Vander Hagen, Jooft Schuten, Thevenot, Ogilvy, and other travellers of lefs note. Hortenfels, who has collected, in his *Elephantographia*, a great number of facts from different voyages, affures us, that the white elephant has not only a white fkin, but that the hair of its tail is alfo white. To thefe teftimonies, we might add the authority of the ancients. Ælian, lib. iii. cap 46. mentions a fmall white elephant in India, and feems to infinuate that the mother was black. This variety in the colour of elephants, though rare, is certain, and very ancient. It has, perhaps, proceeded from their domeftic condition, to which the Indians have been long accuftomed to reduce thefe animals.

† In the proceffion of the King of Pegu, two red elephants are led before, harneffed with filk and gold ftuffs, which are followed by four white elephants, harneffed in a fimilar manner, with the addition of precious ftones, and the tufks covered

with

thefe varieties are fo uncommon, that, inftead of confidering them as diftinct races, they ought to be regarded as qualities purely individual and accidental; for, if it were otherwife, we fhould know the countries of white, red, and black elephants, in the fame manner as we know the climates of white, red, and black men. ‘In India,’ fays P. Vincent Marie, ‘ there are three ‘ kinds of elephants: The white, which are the ‘ largeft, the moft gentle, and peaceable, are ‘ adored as gods by feveral nations: The red, ‘ fuch as thofe of Ceylon, though the fmalleft in ‘ fize, are the moft valorous, the ftrongeft, and ‘ the beft for the purpofes of war; the other ‘ elephants, whether from natural inclination, or ‘ from recognifing fomething fuperior, pay great ‘ refpect to thofe of Ceylon: The black is the ‘ third kind, and they are the moft common, and ‘ in moft eftimation *.’ This is the only author who feems to hint, that Ceylon is the peculiar climate of red elephants; for other travellers make no mention of fuch a fact. He likewife afferts, that the Ceylon elephants are the fmalleft. Thevenot fays the fame thing in his voyage, p. 260. But other writers relate the reverfe. In fine, P. Vincent is the only author who fays,

with rubies; *Voyage de la Compagnie des Indes de Hollande,* *tem.* iii. *p.* 60.

* *Voyage du P. Fr. Vincent Marie de St. Catherine de Sienne,* *chap.* 9. tranflated from the Italian by M. le Marquis de Montmirail.

that

that the white elephants are the largeſt. P.
Tachard, on the contrary, aſſures us, that the
King of Siam's white elephant was diminutive,
though very old. After comparing the teſtimonies of travellers with regard to the magnitude
of elephants in different climates, it appears,
that the ſmalleſt are thoſe of the weſt and north
of Africa, and that the ancients, who knew only
the northern part of Africa, were right in
their general aſſertion, that the Indian elephants
were much larger than thoſe of Africa. But, in
the eaſtern regions of this quarter of the world,
of which the ancients were ignorant, the elephants are as large, and perhaps larger, than
thoſe of India. In this laſt region, it appears,
that the elephants of Siam, Pegu, &c. are larger
than thoſe of Ceylon; which, however, from
the unanimous teſtimony of travellers, have
more courage and intelligence.

Having thus marked the principal facts with
regard to the ſpecies, let us next examine, in
detail, the properties of the individual, his ſenſes,
movements, ſize, ſtrength, addreſs, ſagacity, &c.
In proportion to the magnitude of his body,
the eyes of the elephant are very ſmall; but
they are lively and brilliant: What diſtin-
guiſhes them from the eyes of all other animals,
is a pathetic expreſſion of ſentiment, and an
almoſt rational management of all their actions[*].
He turns them ſlowly and with mildneſs towards

[*] Elephantographia Chriſtophori Petri ab Hartenfels.

I

his

his mafter. When he fpeaks, the animal regards him with an eye of friendfhip and attention, and his penetrating afpect is confpicuous when he wants to anticipate the inclination of his governour. He feems to reflect, to deliberate, to think, and never determines till he has feveral times examined, without paffion or precipitation, the figns which he ought to obey. The dog, whofe eyes are very expreffive, is too prompt and vivacious to allow us to diftinguifh with eafe the fucceffive fhades of his fenfations. But, as the elephant is naturally grave and moderate, we read in his eyes, whofe movements are flow, the order and fucceffion of his internal affections *.

His ear is very good ; and the external organ of hearing, like that of fmelling, is more remarkable in the elephant than in any other animal. His ears are very large, and much longer, even in proportion to his body, than thofe of the afs. They lie flat on the head, like the human ears. They are commonly pendulous ; but he can raife and move them with fuch facility, that he ufes them to defend his eyes from duft and flies †. He delights in the found of

* The eyes of the elephant are, proportionally, exceedingly fmall; but they are very active and lively, and they uniformly move in fuch a manner, as gives him the air of thought and reflection ; *Voyage au Indes Orientales du P. Fr. Vincent Marie de St. Catherine de Sienne, p.* 376.

† The elephant has very large ears. . . He perpetually moves them with much gravity, and they defend his eyes from all kinds of infects; *Id. Ibid.* . . . . See alfo *Les Memoires pour fervir à l'Hiftoire des Animaux, part* iii. *p.* 107.

mufical

mufical inftruments, and moves in cadence to the trumpet and tabor. His fenfe of fmelling is exquifite, and he is paffionately fond of perfumes of every kind, and efpecially of odoriferous flowers, which he gathers one by one, makes nofegays of them, and, after gratifying his nofe, conveys them to his mouth. The flowers of the orange conftitute one of his moft delicious morfels. With his trunk he robs an orange tree of all its verdure, eating the fruit, the flowers, the leaves, and even the fmall branches*. In the meadows, he felects the moft odoriferous plants; and, in the woods, he prefers the cocoa, the banana, the palm, and the fage trees; and, as thefe trees are foft and tender, he eats not only the leaves and fruit, but even the branches, the trunk, and the roots; for, when they are unable to pull up the trees with their trunk, they always fucceed by ufing their tufks.

With regard to the fenfe of touching, it is chiefly confined to the trunk; but, in this member, it is as delicate and diftinct as in the human hand. The trunk is compofed of membranes, nerves, and mufcles; it is both an organ of feeling and of motion. The animal can not only move and bend it, but he can contract, lengthen, and turn it on all fides. The extremity of the trunk terminates in a portube-

---

* Voyage de Guinée, par Bofman, p. 243.

rance * which ftretches out on the upper fide in the form of a finger, by means of which the elephant performs all that we do with our fingers. He lifts from the ground the fmalleft piece of money; he felects the herbs and flowers, and picks them up one by one; he unties the knots of ropes, opens and fhuts gates, by turning the keys, or pufhing back the bolts. He learns to trace regular characters with an inftrument as fmall as a quil †. It cannot be denied that the elephant's hand has feveral advantages over ours. It is equally flexible, and as dexterous in touching or laying hold of objects. Thefe operations are performed by means of the appendix or finger, fituated on the fuperior part of the border, that furrounds the extremity of the trunk, in the middle of which there is a concavity in the form of a cup, and in the bottom of the cup are the apertures of the two common canals of fmelling and of refpiration. The elephant, therefore, has his nofe in his hand, and is enabled to combine the power of his lungs with the action of his fingers, and to attract

* Mem. pour fervir a l'Hiftoire des Animaux, part. iii. p. 108. & 140.

† Mutianus ter Conful auctor eft, aliquem ex his et litterarum ductus Græcarum didiciffe, folitumque præfcribere ejus linguæ verbis: Ipfe ego hæc fcripfi, &c.; *Plin. Hift. Nat. lib.* viii. *cap.* 3.——Ego vero ipfe elephantum in tabula litteras Latinas promufcide atque ordine fcribentem vidi: Verumtamen docentis manus fubjiciebatur ad litterarum ductum et figuram eum inftituens; dejectis autem et intentis oculis erat cum fcriberet; doctos et litterarum gnaros animantium oculos effe dixiffes; *Ælian. de Nat. Anim. lib.* ii. *cap.* 11.

fluids

fluids by a ftrong fuction, or to raife heavy bodies by applying to them the edge of his trunk,
and making a vacuum within by a vigorous in-
fpiration.

Hence delicacy of feeling, acutenefs of fmelling, facility of movement, and the power of fuction, are united at the extremity of the elephant's
nofe. Of all the inftruments which Nature has fo
liberally beftowed on her moft favourite productions, the trunk of the elephant is perhaps the
moft complete and the moft admirable. It is not
only an organic inftrument, but a triple fenfe,
whofe united functions are at once the caufe, and
produce the effects of that fagacity and thofe remarkable talents which diftinguifh the elephant,
and exalt him above all other quadrupeds. He
is not fo fubject, as other animals, to errors of
vifion; becaufe he quickly rectifies them by the
fenfe of touching; and, by ufing his trunk, as
a long arm, for the purpofe of touching remote
objects, he acquires, like man, clear ideas of
diftances. But the other animals, except the
monkeys and fome others who have a kind of
arms and hands, cannot acquire ideas of diftance
but by traverfing fpace with their bodies. Of
all the fenfes, that of touching has the greateft
relation to intelligence. The delicacy of touching, the flexibility of the trunk, the power of
fuction, the fenfe of fmelling, and the length
of the arm, give the ideas of the fubftance of
bodies, of their external form, of their weight,

of

of their falutary or noxious qualities, and of their diftance. Thus, by the fame members, and by one fimultaneous act, the elephant feels, perceives, and judges of feveral things at one time. Now a multiplied fenfation is equivalent, in fome meafure, to reflection: Though this animal, therefore, is, like all others, deprived of the faculty of reflecting, as his fenfations are combined in the fame organ, contemporary, and not feparated from each other, it is not furprifing that he fhould have ideas of his own, and readily acquire thofe we wifh to communicate to him. The memory of the elephant fhould be more perfect than that of any other animal; for memory depends greatly on the circumftances of actions. No folitary fenfation, however lively, can leave any diftinct or durable impreffion; but feveral combined and contemporary fenfations make deep and lafting impreffions; fo that, if the elephant cannot recollect an idea by touch alone, the adjacent and acceffory fenfations of fmelling, and the power of fuction, which have acted at the fame time, aid him in recalling the remembrance of it. In man, the beft mode of rendering the memory faithful, is to employ fucceffively all our fenfes in examining an object; and it is owing to the neglect of habituating ourfelves to the combined ufe of our fenfes, that we forget moft things we ought to remember.

But,

But, though the elephant has more memory and intelligence than any other animal, his brain is proportionally fmaller than that of moft quadrupeds *. I mention this fact as a proof that the brain is not the feat of fenfation, the *fenforium commune*, which, on the contrary, refides in the nerves of the fenfes, and in the membranes of the head. Thus the nerves diftributed upon the trunk of the elephant, are fo numerous as to be equivalent to all thofe beftowed on the reft of the body. It is, therefore, by virtue of this fingular combination of fenfes and faculties in the trunk, that the elephant excels all other animals in fagacity, notwithftanding the enormity of his mafs, and the difproportion of his form; for the elephant is, at the fame time, a miracle of intelligence and a monfter of matter. The thicknefs and inflexibility of his body; the fhortnefs and ftiffnefs of his neck; the fmallnefs and deformity of his head; the exceffive largenefs of his ears and nofe; the minutenefs of his eyes, mouth, genitals, and tail; his ftraight, clumfy, and almoft inflexible limbs; the fhortnefs and fmallnefs of his feet †, which are hardly apparent; the thick-

---

* Mem. pour fervir à l'Hift. des Animaux, part. iii. p. 135.

† The feet of every animal except the elephant are proportionally larger than thofe of man.——The feet were fo fmall as to be hardly perceptible; becaufe the toes are covered with the fkin of the legs, which hangs down on all fides as far as the ground, and appears like the trunk of a tree cut acrofs; *Mem. pour fervir à l'Hift. des Animaux, p. 102.*

nefs

nefs and callofity of his fkin: All thefe deformities are the more confpicuous and difagreeable to the eye, becaufe they are modelled on a large fcale, and moft of them peculiar to the elephant alone; for in no animal are the head, the feet, the nofe, the ears, and the tufks, fituated like thofe of the elephant.

From this ftrange conformation, the animal is fubjected to feveral inconveniencies. He moves his head with difficulty, and cannot turn himfelf, in order to go back, without making a circuit. The hunters who attack him behind, or on the flanks, avoid the effects of his vengeance by circular movements; and they have time to renew their blows while he is turning himfelf againft them. His legs, the rigidity of which is not fo great as that of his neck and body, bend but flowly, and with difficulty. They are ftrongly articulated to the thighs. His knee is like that of man *, and his foot is equally low; but the latter has no extent, fpring, or force, and the former is hard and rigid. As long, however, as the elephant is young and in health, he bends his knees to lie down, and allows himfelf to be mounted, or charged with a load. But, when old or fick, this movement becomes fo laborious,

* His knee is fituated, like that of man, in the middle between the belly and the foot; fo that the elephant's leg is fimilar to a man's, both with regard to the pofition of the knee and the fmallnefs of the foot, the extent of which, from the heel to the toes, is very fmall; *Mem. pour fervir à l'Hift. des Animaux, part.* iii. *p.* 102.

that

that he choofes rather to fleep on his feet; and, if forced to lie down*, machines are neceffary to raife him. His tufks, which, with age, become enormoufly heavy, and not being placed, like the horns of other animals, in a vertical pofition, form two long levers, which, by their almoft horizontal direction, fatigue the head prodigioufly, and make it hang down; fo that the animal is fometimes obliged to make holes in the wall of his lodge to fupport them, and relieve him of their weight †. He has the difadvantage of having the organ of fmelling very diftant from that of tafting, and the inconvenience of not being able to feize any thing on the ground with his mouth, becaufe his neck is too ftiff and too fhort to allow his head to reach the earth. He is, therefore, obliged to lay hold of his food, and even of his drink, with his nofe, and then to convey it, not only to the entrance of his mouth, but as far as the throat; and, when the trunk is filled with water, he thrufts the end of

---

* We learned from the people who had the charge of the elephant at Verfailles, formerly mentioned, that, the firft eight years he lived, he lay down and' rofe with great facility; and that, during the laft five years, he did not lie down to fleep, but leaned againft the wall of his apartment; fo that, if he had happened to lie down when fick, it would have been neceffary to pierce the floor above, in order to raife him with engines; *Mem. pour fervir à l'Hift. des Animaux, p.* 104.

† We faw where the elephant had employed his tufks in making holes in a ftone-pillar, which projected from the wall of his lodge, and thefe holes fupported him when fleeping, his tufks being put into them: *Id. p.* 102.

it

it to the very root of the tongue*, feemingly with the intention of pufhing back the epiglottis to prevent the water which rufhes out with impetuofity, from entering into the larynx; for he forces out the water by the fame air which he employed to fuck it up, and it rufhes out of the trunk with noife, and precipitantly enters the gullet. The tongue, the mouth, and the lips, are of no ufe to him, as in other animals, to fuck or lap his drink.

From this defcription, the fingular confequence refults, that the young elephant muft fuck with its nofe, and afterwards convey the milk to its gullet. We are told, however, by the ancients, that he fucks with his mouth, and not with his trunk †. But there is reafon to believe that they never were witneffes of the fact, and that they reafoned folely from the analogy of other animals. If the young elephant ever acquired the habit of fucking with his mouth, why fhould he lofe it during the reft of his life? Why does he never employ the mouth to fuck in water? Why does he uniformly employ a double action, when a fingle one would anfwer the purpofe? Why does he never feize any object with his mouth, ex-

---

* Mem. pour fervir à l'Hift. des Animaux, part. iii. p. 109.

† Pullus editus ore fugit, non promufcide, et ftatim cum natus eft cernit et ambulat; *Arift. Hift. Anim. lib.* vi. *cap.* 27.—Anniculo quidem vitulo æqualem pullum edit elephantus, qui ftatim, ut natus eft, ore fugit; *Ælian. de Nat. Anim. lib.* vi. *cap.* 3.

cept

eept what is thrown into it when open * ? It is, therefore, extremely probable, that the young elephant fucks with his trunk only. This prefumption is not only proved by the following facts, but is founded on a ftronger analogy than that which gave rife to the opinion of the ancients. We formerly remarked, that, in general, animals, at the moment of birth, can perceive the prefence of the aliment they want by no other fenfe but that of fmelling. The ear can have no effect; neither can the eye; for moft animals are blind when they begin to fuck. The fenfe of touching can only convey a vague and indifcriminate notion of all the parts of the mother's body, or, rather, it can indicate nothing relative to appetite. But the fenfe of fmelling is alone fufficient for this purpofe: It is not only a fpecies of tafte, but a fore-tafte, which precedes, accompanies, and determines the other kind. The elephant, therefore, like all other animals, perceives by this fore-tafte, the prefence of his aliment; and, as the feat of fmelling is united with the power of fuction, at the extremity of the trunk, he applies it to the teat, fucks the milk, and conveys it to the mouth to fatisfy his appetite. Befides, the two paps, as in woman, are fituated on the breafts, and the teats being very fmall in proportion to the fize of the young

* Voyez les Memoires pour fervir à l'Hift. des Animaux, part. iii. p. 109. et 110.

one's

one's mouth, whofe neck alfo has little flexibility, the mother muft have lain on her back or fide to enable her young to lay hold of the teat with its mouth ; and, even in this fituation, it would have been difficult to extract the milk, on account of the enormous difproportion between the largenefs of the mouth and the fmallnefs of the teat. But the margin of the trunk, which the animal contracts at pleafure, is eafily accommodated to the teat, and enables the young elephant to fuck the mother either when fhe ftands or lies on her fide. Thus every circumftance concurs in invalidating the notion of the ancients on this fubject ; for none of them, nor even any of the moderns, alledge that they ever faw the elephant fucking ; and I have no hefitation in predicting, that, whenever fuch an obfervation is made, it will appear, that he fucks not with his mouth, but with his nofe. I likewife imagine that the ancients are deceived, when they tell us, that the elephants copulate like other quadrupeds, the female only lowering her crupper *, for the more eafy reception of the male. The fituation of the part feems to render this mode of junction impoffible. The female elephant has not, like other quadrupeds, the orifice of the vagina adjacent to the anus ; for it is fituated nearly in the middle of the belly, about two and a half, or

---

* Subfidit fœmina, clunibufque fubmiffis, et infiftit pedibus ac innititur ; mas fuperveniens comprimit, atque ita munere venereo fungitur ; *Arift. Hift. Anim. lib.* v. *cap.* 2.

three

three feet diftant from the anus*. On the other hand, the male organ is by no means proportioned to the magnitude of his body, nor to fo long an interval, which, in the fituation fuppofed, would preclude the practicability of his approach. Naturalifts as well as travellers agree in affirming, that the male organ of the elephant exceeds not, either in length or diameter †, that of a horfe. It is therefore impoffible that he fhould attain his end in the ordinary pofition of quadrupeds. The female muft neceffarily lie on her back. De Feynes ‡ and Tavernier ‖ pofitively affert, and the fituation of the parts confirms their evidence, that thefe animals cannot intermix in any other manner §. They require, therefore,

* Mem pour fervir à l'Hift. des Animaux, part. iii. p. 132.

† Elephantus genitale equo fimile habet, fed parvum nec pro corporis magnitudine. Teftes idem non foris confpicuos fed intus circa renes conditos habet; *Arift. Hift. Anim. lib.* ii. *cap.* 1. *L'Afrique d'Ogilby, p.* 13. *et* 14.

‡ When thefe animals couple, the female lies on her back; and, after the operation, the male raifes the female with his trunk; *Voyage par Terre à la Chine du S. de Feynes, p.* 90.

‖ Though the elephants have no intercourfe in a domeftic ftate, yet they frequently come in feafon. It is remarkable that the female, on thefe occafions, collects all kinds of herbs and leaves, of which fhe makes a bed elevated four or five feet above the ground, and, contrary to the nature of all other quadrupeds, lies down on her back, and folicits the male by her cries; *Voyage de Tavernier, tom.* iii. *p.* 240.

§ This article was written before I faw M. de Buffy's Notes concerning the elephant; and his evidence fully confirms the fact, which the fituation of the parts had fuggefted. ' The ele' phants,' fays M. de Buffy, ' copulate in a fingular manner.

' The

therefore, more time and conveniency for this operation than other quadrupeds; and it is, perhaps, for this reason, that they never copulate but when they enjoy full liberty, and have every neceffary article at their command. The female muft not only confent, but folicit the male by a pofition which fhe never affumes, unlefs when fhe thinks herfelf in perfect retirement *. May we not, therefore, conclude, that modefty is a phyfical virtue which exifts in the brute creation? It is, at leaft, like foftnefs, moderation, and temperance, a general and beautiful attribute of the female fex.

Thus the elephant neither fucks, generates, eats, nor drinks like other animals. The found of his voice is likewife extremely fingular. If we believe the ancients, the elephant utters two kinds of cries, one by the trunk, which, from its finuofities and inflexions, is rough and long, like the found of a trumpet; and another by the mouth, which is interrupted by fhort paufes and harfh fighs †. This fact, which was advanced

by

‘ The female lies down on her back. The male refts on his fore ‘ legs, bends down thofe behind, and touches not the female ‘ any farther than is neceffary to effect his purpofe.’

* Pudore nunquam nifi inabdito coeunt; *Plin. Hift. Nat. lib.* viii. *cap.* 5.—The elephants couple very rarely; and, when they do, it is with fuch fecrecy, and in places fo folitary, that they have never been obferved by any perfon. When in a domeftic ftate, they never produce; *Voyage aux Indes Orientales du P. Vincent Marie de Sainte Catherine de Sienne, chap.* xi. *p.* 396.

† Elephantus citra nares ore ipfo vocem edit fpirabundam,

quem-

by Ariftotle, and afterwards repeated by naturalifts and travellers, is probably falfe, or, at leaft,
not exactly related. M. de Buffy denies that the
elephant utters any cry through the trunk. However, as a man, by fhutting his mouth clofe, can
make a found through his nofe, the elephant
whofe nofe is fo large, may produce founds in
the fame manner. But, however this may be,
the cry of the elephant is heard at the diftance
of more than a league, and yet it excites not
terror like the roaring of the lion or tiger.

The elephant is ftill more fingular in the
ftructure of his feet, and the texture of his fkin,
which laft is not, like other quadrupeds, covered
with hair, but totally bare, as if it were fhaven.
There are only a few briftles in the fiffures of
the fkin, and thefe briftles are thinly fcattered
over the body, but very numerous on the cilia
and back of the head *, in the auditory paffages,
and the infides of the thighs and legs. In the
epidermis, or fcarf fkin, there are two kinds of
wrinkles, the one raifed and the other depreffed,
which give it the appearance of being cut into
fiffures, refembling pretty nearly the bark of an
old oak tree. In man, and the other animals,

quemadmodum cum homo fimul et fpiritum reddit et loquitur,
at per nares fimile tubarum raucitati fonat ; *Arift. Hift. Anim.
lib.* iv. *cap.* 9.—Citra nares ore ipfo fternutamento fimilem edit
fonum ; per nares autem tubarum raucitati ; *Plin. Hift. Nat.
lib.* viii.

* Memoires pour fervir à l'Hiftoire des Animaux, part. iii.
p. 113.

the

the epidermis adheres throughout to the ſkin;
but, in the elephant, it is only attached by ſome
points of inſertion, like two pieces of cloth
ſtitched together. This epidermis is naturally
dry, and very ſubject to grow thick. It often
acquires the thickneſs of three or four lines, by
the ſucceſſive drying of different layers which
are produced one above another. It is this thick-
ening of the ſcarf ſkin which gives riſe to the
elephantiaſis or *dry leproſy*, to which man, whoſe
ſkin is naked like that of the elephant, is ſometimes ſubject. This diſeaſe is very common to
the elephant; and the Indians, to prevent it,
rub him frequently with oil, and bathe him with
water, with a view to preſerve the ſkin clean and
flexible. The ſkin, where it is not callous, is
extremely ſenſible. In the fiſſures, and other
places where it is neither dry nor hardened, the
elephant feels the ſtinging of flies in ſuch a lively
manner, that he not only employs his natural movements, but even the reſources of his intelligence, to get rid of them. He ſtrikes them
with his tail, his ears, and his trunk. He contracts his ſkin, and cruſhes them between its
wrinkles. He drives them off with branches
of trees, or handfuls of long ſtraw. When all
theſe artifices are unſucceſsful, he collects duſt
with his trunk, and covers all the ſenſible parts
of his ſkin with it. He has been obſerved pul-
veriſing himſelf in this manner ſeveral times in a
day; and always at the moſt proper ſeaſon, namely,

after

after bathing *. The use of water is as necessary to these animals as air. When free, they never quit the banks of rivers, and often go into the water till it reaches their belly, and in this situation they daily spend several hours. In India, where the elephants are treated in the manner that best corresponds with their nature and temperament, they are carefully bathed, and allowed time and every possible conveniency for bathing themselves †. Their skin is cleaned by

* I was informed that the elephant at Versailles always rolled in the dust after bathing, which he did as often as he was allowed; and it was observed that he threw dust upon all the places which had been missed when he rolled himself, and that he drove of the flies with handfuls of straw, or by throwing dust with his trunk on the places where he felt himself stung, there being nothing which the flies avoid so much as falling dust; *Mem. pour servir a l'Hist. des Animaux, part.* iii. *p.* 117.

† About eight or nine o'clock before noon, we went to the river to see the elephants belonging to the King and the nobles bathed. The animal goes into the water till it reaches his belly, and, lying down on one side, fills his trunk several times, and throws the water upon the parts which are uncovered. The master then rubs off, with a kind of pumice-stone, all the dirt that has been collected on the creature's skin. Some authors tell us, that, when the elephant lies down, he is unable to raise himself. But this assertion is not founded in truth; for the master, after rubbing on one side, desires the animal to turn to the other, which he does very quickly; and after both sides are well curried, he comes out of the river, and stands some time on the bank till he dries. The master then brings a pot of red or yellow paint, and draws lines on the elephant's face, round the eyes, and upon the breast and rump. He is next rubbed over with oil, to strengthen his nerves; *Voyage de Tavernier, tom.* iii. *p.* 264.

rubbing

rubbing it with a pumice-ftone; and then they are anointed with perfumed oils, and painted with various colours.

The ftructure of the elephant's feet and legs ftill differs from that of moft other animals. The fore legs appear to be longer than the hind legs, and yet the former are fomewhat fhorter *. The hind legs are not bended in two places like thofe of the horfe and ox, in whom the thigh-bone is almoft totally concealed in the buttock, the knee is fituated near the belly, and the bones of the foot are fo high and fo long, that they appear to conftitute a great part of the leg. But the foot of the elephant is very fhort, and refts on the ground. His knee, like that of man, is placed near the middle of the leg. The fhort foot of the elephant is divided into five toes, which are fo covered with the fkin as not to be vifible. We only fee a kind of nails, the number of which varies, though that of the toes remains always the fame. There are uniformly five toes on each foot, and commonly five nails †; but fome-times there are only four ‡, or even three nails; and,

* Mem. pour fervir à l'Hift. des Anim. part. iii. p. 102.

† The royal academy of fciences recommended to me to examine whether all the elephants had nails on their feet. I never faw a fingle elephant which had not five on each foot at the extremities of the five large toes. But the toes are fo fhort, that they hardly project from the foot; *Premier Voyage du P. Tachard, p. 273.*

‡ All thofe who have written concerning the elephant, affign five nails to each foot; but, in our fubject, there were only

and, in this cafe, they correfpond not exactly with the extremities of the toes. Befides, this variety, which has only been remarked in young elephants brought to Europe, feems to be purely accidental, and probably depends on the manner the animal has been treated during the firft years of its growth. The fole of the foot is covered with a kind of leather as hard as horn, and projects outward all around. The nails confift of the fame fubftance.

The ears of the elephant are very long, moveable at pleafure, and ferve the animal as a fan. The tail is not longer than the ears, being generally from two and a half to three feet in length. It is thin, pointed, and garnifhed at the extremity with a tuft of thick hairs, or rather threads of a black, gloffy, folid, horny fubftance. This hair or horn is as thick and ftrong as iron-wire, and a man cannot break it by pulling with his hands, though it be flexible and elaftic. In fine, this tuft of hair is greatly efteemed as an ornament by the Negro women, who are probably attached to it by fome fuperftition *. An elephant's tail

only three. The fmall Indian elephant formerly mentioned had four nails both on the fore and hind feet. But there are uniformly five toes on each foot; *Mem. pour fervir à l'Hift. des Animaux, part. iii. p. 103.*

* Merolla remarks, that many of the Pagans in thefe countries, and particularly the Saggas, have a devout regard for the elephant's tail. When any of their chiefs die, they preferve, in honour of him, one of thefe tails, to which they pay a kind of religious worfhip, founded on the notion of its

tail is fometimes fold for two or three flaves;
and the Negroes often hazard their lives in en-
deavouring to cut it off from the live animal.
Befide this tuft, the tail is covered, or rather
ftrewed, through its whole extent, with briftles
as large and as hard as thofe of the wild boar.
Thefe briftles are alfo found on the convex part
of the trunk and the eye-brows, where they
fometimes exceed a foot in length. Briftles or
hairs on the eye-lids are peculiar to man, the
monkey, and the elephant.

Climate, food, and fituation, have a great influence on the growth and fize of the elephant.
In general, thofe that are taken young, and reduced to captivity, never acquire their natural dimenfions. The largeft elephants of India and the
eaftern parts of Africa are fourteen feet high;
the fmalleft, which are found in Senegal, and
other weftern regions of Africa, exceed not ten or
eleven feet; and thofe which are brought to Europe
when young, never arrive at this height. The
Verfailles elephant, which came from Congo*, at
the age of feven years, was not above feven and
a half feet high. During the thirteen years that
he lived, he acquired only one foot; fo that, at
the age of four, when he was tranfported, he was

power. They often go a hunting folely with a view to obtain a tail of this kind. But it muft be cut off with a fingle
blow from the live animal, without which, fuperftition allows
it no virtue; *Hift. Gen. des Voyages, par l'Abbé Prevoft. tom. v.
p. 79.*

* Mem. pour fervir à l'Hift. des Animaux, part. iii. p. 101.

only

only fix and a half feet in height; and, as the
rate of growth always diminifhes as animals advance in years, it cannot be fuppofed, that, if he
had lived thirty years, the common period when
the growth of elephants is completed, he would
have acquired more than eight feet in height.
Hence the domeftic ftate reduces the growth
of the elephant one third, not only in height, but
in all other dimenfions. The length of his body,
from the eye to the origin of the tail, is nearly
equal to his height at the withers. An Indian
elephant, therefore, of fourteen feet high, is more
than feven times larger and heavier than the
Verfailles elephant. By comparing the growth
of this animal to that of man, we fhall find, that
an infant, being commonly thirty-one inches
high, that is, one half of its height, at the age of
two years, and taking its full growth at twenty
years, the elephant, which grows till thirty, ought
to acquire the half of his height in three years.
In the fame manner, if we would form a judgment of the enormous mafs of the elephant, we
fhall find, that, the volume of a man's body being
fuppofed to be two cubic feet and a half, the
body of an elephant of fourteen feet long, three
feet thick, and a proportional breadth, would be
fifty times as large; and, confequently, that an
elephant ought to weigh as much as fifty men*.

' I faw,

---

* Peirère, in his life of Gaffendi, fays, that an elephant,
which he caufed to be weighed, was three thoufand five hundred pounds. This elephant feems to have been very fmall;

‘ I faw,’ fays le P. Vincent Marie, ‘ fome ele-
‘ phants which were fourteen and fifteen * feet
‘ high, with a proportional length and thicknefs.
‘ The male is always larger than the female.
‘ The price of thefe animals augments in propor-
‘ tion to their fize, which is meafured from the
‘ eye to the extremity of the back; and, after ex-
‘ ceeding certain dimenfions, the price rifes like
‘ that of precious ftones †.’ ‘ The Guiney ele-
‘ phants,’ Bofman remarks, ‘ are ten, twelve, or
‘ thirteen feet high ‡; and yet they are incom-
‘ parably fmaller than thofe of the Eaft Indies;
‘ for the hiftorians of that country give more
‘ cubits to the height of the latter than the for-
‘ mer has feet §.’ ‘ I faw,’ faid Edward Terry,
‘ elephants of thirteen feet in height, and many
‘ people affirmed, that they had feen elephants
‘ fifteen feet high ‖.’

From thefe, and many other authorities which
might be enumerated, we may conclude, that the
ordinary ftature of the elephant is from ten to
eleven feet; that thofe of thirteen and fourteen
are very rare; and that the fmalleft, when they

for, according to the calculation I have made in the text, the dimenfions of which I rather under-rated, he would have weighed at
leaft eight thoufand pounds.

   * Thefe are probably Roman feet.

   † Voyage aux Indes Orientales du P. Vincent Marie, chap. xi.
p. 396.

   ‡ Thefe are probably Rhenifh feet.

   § Voyage en Guinée de Guillaume Bofman, p. 244.

   ‖ Voyage to the Eaft-Indies by Edward Terry. *Note,* Thefe
are perhaps Englifh feet.

acquire

acquire their full growth in a state of liberty, are
at least nine feet. These enormous masses of
matter fail not, however, as formerly remarked,
to move with great quickness. They are supported by four members, which, instead of
legs, resemble massy columns of fifteen or eighteen inches diameter, and from five to six feet
high. These legs, therefore, are twice as long
as those of a man. Hence, though the elephant
should make but one step, while a man makes
two, it would outstrip him in the chase. The
ordinary walk of the elephant is not quicker
than that of a horse *; but, when pushed, he af-
sumes a kind of amble, which, in fleetness, is
equivalent to a gallop. He performs with prompt-
ness, and even with freedom, all direct movements; but he wants facility in oblique or re-
trograde motions. It is generally in narrow and
hollow places, where the elephant can hardly
turn, that the Negroes attack him, and cut off
his tail, which they value above all the rest of
the body. He has great difficulty in descending
steep declivities, and is obliged to fold his hind
legs †, that, in going down, the anterior part of
his body may be on a level with the posterior,
and to prevent being precipitated by his own
weight. He swims well, though the form of his
legs and feet seem to indicate the contrary. But,

* Notes of M. de Buffy, communicated by the Marquis de
Montmirail.

† Notes of M. de Buffy.

as the capacity of his breaſt and belly is large, as
the ſize of his lungs and inteſtines is enormous,
and as all the great parts of his body are filled
with air, or matters lighter than water, he ſinks
not ſo deep as other animals. He has, therefore,
leſs reſiſtance to overcome, and, conſequently, is
enabled to ſwim more quickly with ſmaller efforts of his limbs. Of courſe, he is of great uſe
in the paſſage of rivers. When employed on theſe
occaſions *, beſide two pieces of cannon which
admit three or four pound balls, he is loaded
with great quantities of baggage, independent
of a number of men fixed to his ears and his
tail. When thus loaded, he enters the river, and
ſwims ſo much below the water that no part of
his body is ſeen except his trunk, which he
raiſes in the air for the benefit of reſpiration.

Though the elephant generally feeds on herbs
and tender wood, and though prodigious quantities of this aliment are neceſſary to afford a
ſufficient number of organic particles to nouriſh
ſo vaſt a body, he has not ſeveral ſtomachs, like
moſt animals who live on the ſame ſubſtances.
He has but one ſtomach, does not ruminate,
is formed rather like the horſe, than the ox
and other ruminating animals. The want of a
paunch is ſupplied by the largeneſs and length
of his inteſtines, and particularly of the colon,
which is two or three feet in diameter, by fifteen
or twenty in length. The ſtomach is much

* Notes of M. de Buſſy.

ſmaller

ſmaller than the colon, being only three and a
half or four feet long, and only one, or one and
a half in its largeſt diameter. To fill ſuch capacious veſſels, it is neceſſary that the animal,
when not furniſhed with nouriſhment more ſubſtantial than herbage, ſhould eat almoſt perpetually. Wild elephants, accordingly, are almoſt
continually employed tearing up trees, gather-
ing leaves, and breaking young wood; and the
domeſtic elephants, though ſupplied with great
quantities of rice, fail not to collect herbs whenever they have an opportunity. However great
the appetite of the elephant, he eats with moderation, and his taſte for cleanlineſs is ſuperior to
the calls of hunger. His addreſs in ſeparating
with his trunk the good leaves from the bad,
and the care which he takes in ſhaking them till
they are perfectly clear of inſects and ſand, afford great pleaſure to the ſpectator *. He is
fond of wine, aquavitæ, arrack, &c. By ſhow-
ing him a veſſel filled with any of theſe liquors,
and promiſing him it as the reward of his labours, he is induced to exert the greateſt efforts,
and to perform the moſt painful taſks. He
ſeems to love the ſmoke of tobacco; but it ſtu-
pifies and intoxicates him. He abhors all bad
ſmells; and has ſuch a terror at the hog, that
the cry of that animal makes him fly †.

* Notes of M. de Buffy.

† The Verſailles elephant had ſuch a terror and averſion at
ſwine, that the cry of a young hog made him fly to a great diſtance.
This antipathy has been remarked by Ælian.

　　　　　　　　　To

To complete the idea of the nature and intelligence of this fingular animal, I fhall here
add fome notes communicated to me by the
Marquis de Montmirail, prefident of the royal
academy of fciences, who has been fo obliging
as not only to colleĉt, but to tranflate every
thing regarding quadrupeds from fome Italian
and German books with which I am unacquainted. His zeal for the advancement of
knowledge, his exquifite difcernment, and his
extenfive knowledge in natural hiftory, entitle
him to the higheft marks of diftinĉtion; and
the reader will find how often I fhall have occafion to quote him in the fubfequent parts of
this work. ' The elephant is ufed in dragging
' artillery over mountains; and it is on fuch
' occafions that his fagacity is moft confpicuous.
' When the oxen, yoked to a cannon, make an
' effort to pull it up a declivity, the elephant
' pufhes the breach with his front, and, at each
' effort, he fupports the carriage with his knee,
' which he places againft the wheel. He feems
' to underftand what is faid to him. When his
' conduĉtor wants him to execute any painful
' labour, he explains the nature of the opera-
' tion, and recites the reafons which ought to
' induce him to obey. If the elephant fhows a
' repugnance to what is exaĉted of him, the
' Cornack, which is the name of the conduĉtor,
' promifes to give him arrack, or fome other
' thing that he likes. But it is extremely dan-
' gerous

' gerous to break any promife that is made to
' him: Many cornacks have fallen victims to in-
' difcretions of this kind. On this fubject, a fact,
' which happened at Decan, deferves to be re-
' lated, and though it has the appearance of in-
' credibility, it is, notwithftanding, perfectly true.
' An elephant out of revenge killed his cornack.
' The man's wife, who beheld the dreadful
' fcene, took her two infants and threw them at
' the feet of the enraged animal, faying, *Since
' you have flain my hufband, take my life alfo, as
' well as that of my children.* The elephant in-
' ftantly ftopped, relented, and, as if ftung with
' remorfe, took the eldeft boy in its trunk,
' placed him on its neck, adopted him for its
' cornack, and would never allow any other
' perfon to mount it.

' If the elephant is vindictive, he is not un-
' grateful. A foldier at Pondicherry was accuf-
' tomed to give a certain quantity of arrack to
' one of thefe animals every time he got his pay;
' and, having one day intoxicated himfelf, and,
' being purfued by the guard, who wanted to
' put him in prifon, he took refuge under the
' elephant, and fell faft afleep. The guard in
' vain attempted to drag him from this afylum;
' for the elephant defended him with its trunk.
' Next day the foldier having recovered from
' his intoxication, was in dreadful apprehenfions
' when he found himfelf under the belly of an
' animal fo enormous. The elephant, which
' unqueftion-

' unqueftionably perceived his terror, careffed
' him with its trunk.

'The elephant is fometimes feized with a
' kind of madnefs, which deprives him of all
' tractability, and renders him fo formidable,
' that it is often neceffary to kill him. The
' people try to bind him with large iron
' chains, in the hope of reclaiming him.
' But, when in his ordinary ftate, the moft a-
' cute pains will not provoke him to hurt thofe
' who have never injured him. An elephant,
' rendered furious by the wounds it had re-
' ceived at the battle of Hambour, ran about the
' field making the moft hideous cries. A foldier,
' notwithftanding the alarms of his comrades,
' was unable, perhaps on account of his wounds,
' to fly. The elephant approached, feemed a-
' fraid of trampling him under his feet, took him
' up with its trunk, placed him gently on his
' fide, and continued its route.'

Thefe notes I have tranfcribed verbatim.
They were communicated to the Marquis de
Montmirail by M. de Buffy, who refided ten
years in India, and performed many important
fervices to the ftate. He had feveral elephants
under his own charge, often rode upon them,
and had daily opportunities of obferving many
others, which belonged to his neighbours. Hence
thefe notes, as well as all the others quoted under the name of M. de Buffy, merit every degree of credit. The members of the royal
academy

academy of fciences have alfo left us fome facts
which they learned from thofe who had the
management of the elephant at Verfailles, and
which deferve a place in this work. 'The ele-
'phant feemed to know when it was mocked
'by any perfon; and remembered the affront
'till an opportunity of revenge occurred. A man
'deceived it by pretending to throw fome-
'thing into his mouth: The animal gave him
'fuch a blow with its trunk as knocked him
'down, and broke two of his ribs. After which,
'it trampled on him with its feet, broke one of
'his legs, and bending down on its knees, en-
'deavoured to pufh its tufks into his belly; but
'they luckily run into the ground on each fide
'of his thigh, without doing him any injury.
'A painter wanted to draw the animal in an
'unufual attitude, with its trunk elevated, and
'its mouth open. The painter's fervant, to
'make it remain in this pofition, threw fruits
'into its mouth, but generally made only a
'faint of throwing them. The elephant was
'enraged, and as if it knew that the painter
'was the caufe of this teazing impertinence, in-
'ftead of attacking the fervant, it eyed the
'mafter, and fquirted at him fuch a quantity of
'water from its trunk as fpoiled the paper on
'which he was drawing.

'This elephant generally made lefs ufe of its
'ftrength than its addrefs. With great eafe
'and coolnefs, it loofed the buckle of a large
'double

' double leathern ftrap, with which its leg was
' fixed; and, as the domeftics had wrapt the
' buckle round with a fmall cord, and tied many
' knots on it, the creature deliberately loofed
' the whole, without breaking either the cord
' or the ftrap. One night, after difengaging itfelf
' in this manner from its ftrap, it broke up the
' door of its lodge with fuch dexterity as not to
' waken the keeper.   From thence it went into
' feveral courts of the menagery, forcing open
' doors, and throwing down the walls when the
' doors were too narrow to let it pafs.   In this
' manner it got accefs to the apartments of
' other animals, and fo terrified them, that they
' fled into the moft retired corners of the inclo-
' fure.'

In fine, that nothing may be omitted which
can contribute to throw light upon the natural and acquired faculties of an animal fo
fuperior to all others, we fhall add fome facts,
extracted from the moft refpectable and unfuf-
picious travellers.

' Even the wild elephant,' fays le P. Vincent
Marie, ' has his virtues.   He is generous and
' temperate ; and, when rendered domeftic, he
' is efteemed for gentlenefs and fidelity to his
' mafter, friendfhip to his governour, &c.   If
' deftined to the immediate fervice of princes,
' he recognifes his good fortune, and maintains
' a gravity of demeanour correfponding to the
' dignity

' dignity of his office. If, on the contrary, lefs
' honourable labours are affigned to him, he
' turns melancholy, frets, and evidently difco-
' vers that he is humbled and depreffed. In
' war, during the firft onfet, he is fiery and
' impetuous. When furrounded with hunters,
' he is equally brave. But, after being van-
' quifhed, he lofes all courage. He fights with
' his tufks, and dreads nothing fo much as to
' lofe his trunk, which, from its confiftence, is
' eafily cut..... I fhall only add, that the
' elephant is mild, attacks no perfon without
' being injured, feems to love fociety, is parti-
' cularly fond of children, whom he careffes,
' and appears to difcern the innocence of their
' manners.'

' The elephant,' fays Pyrard*, ' is an animal
' of fo much knowledge and judgment, that,
' befide his infinite utility to man, he may be
' faid to enjoy a certain portion of reafon. When
' about to be ridden, he is fo obedient and well
' trained, that he accommodates his behaviour
' to the quality of the perfon he ferves. He
' bends down, and affifts his mafter to mount
' with his trunk..... He is fo tractable, that
' he will perform any thing that is required of
' him, provided he be treated with gentlenefs....
' He does every thing he is defired, careffes
' thofe who ride on him,' &c.

* Voyage de François Pyrard, tom. ii. p. 366.

' By

' By giving elephants,' fay the Dutch voyagers *, ' whatever is agreeable to them, they
' are foon rendered as tame and fubmiffive as
' men. They may be faid to be deprived of the
' ufe of language only. . . . . . They are proud
' and ambitious; but they are fo grateful for be-
' nefits received, that as a mark of refpect, they
' bow their heads in paffing the houfes where
' they have been hofpitably received. . . . They
' allow themfelves to be led and commanded by
' a child †; but they love to be praifed and ca-
' reffed. They quickly feel an injury or an af-
' front; and the guilty perfon fhould be on his
' guard; for he may reckon himfelf happy if
' they content themfelves with fquirting water
' upon him with their trunks, or fimply throw-
' ing him into a mire.'

' The elephant,' P. Philippe remarks ‡, ' makes
' a near approach to the judgment and reafoning
' of man. When compared with the apes, they
' appear to be ftupid and brutal animals. The
' elephants are fo extremely modeft, that they
' will not copulate in the prefence of any per-
' fon; and if, by accident, any man perceives
' this operation, they infallibly refent it, &c. . . .
' Their falute is performed by bending the
' knees, and lowering the head; and, when their

* Voyage de la Compagnie des Indes de Hollande, tom. i.
p. 413.
† Idem, tom. vii. p. 31.
‡ Voyage d'Orient du P. Philippe de la Très-Sainte-Tri-
nité, p. 366.

' mafter

' mafter wants to mount them, they affift him
' with great dexterity. When a wild elephant
' is taken, the hunters tie his feet, and one ac-
' cofts and falutes him, makes apologies for
' binding him, protefts that no injury is meant,
' tells him, that, in his former condition, he of-
' ten wanted food, but, that, henceforward, he
' fhall be well treated, and that every promife
' fhall be performed to him, &c. The hunter
' no fooner finifhes this foothing harangue, than
' the elephant follows him like a tamed lamb.
' We muft not, however, conclude from hence,
' that the elephant underftands language, but
' only, that, having a very ftrong difcerning
' faculty, he diftinguifhes efteem from contempt,
' friendfhip from hatred, and all the other emo-
' tions which men exhibit to him ; and for this
' reafon he is more eafily tamed by arguments
' than by blows. . . . . . . With his trunk he
' throws ftones very far, and very ftraight, and
' alfo ufes it for pouring water on his body when
' bathing.'

   ' Of five elephants,' Tavernier remarks [*],
' which the hunters had taken, three efcaped,
' though ropes and chains were thrown round
' their bodies and limbs. The natives told us
' the following moft aftonifhing ftory, if it could
' be credited. When an elephant, they faid,
' has once been caught in a pitfall, and efcapes
' from the fnare, he becomes extemely diffi-

* Voyage de Tavernier, tom. iii. p. 238.

' dent,

' dent, breaks off a large branch with his trunk,
' and ftrikes the ground every where before he
' fets down his feet, in order to difcover by the
' found whether there are any concealed holes
' by which he may be entrapped a fecond time.
' For this reafon, the hunters who related this
' ftory defpaired of being able, without much
' difficulty, to retake the three elephants which
' had made their efcape. . . . . . Each of the
' two elephants which had been feized were
' placed betwen two tame ones, and furrounded
' by fix men with burning torches, who fpoke
' to the animals, and, prefenting food to them,
' faid, in their language, *take this, and eat it.*
' The food confifted of fmall bunches of hay,
' pieces of black fugar, and boiled rice mixed
' with pepper. When the wild elephant re-
' fufed to do what he was ordered, the men
' ordered the tame elephants to beat him, which
' they performed, the one ftriking him on the
' front and head, and, if the captive animal at-
' tempted to defend himfelf, the other ftruck
' him on the fide; fo that the poor creature knew
' not where he was, and foon found himfelf ob-
' liged to obey.'

' I have frequently remarked,' fays Edward
Terry *, ' that the elephant performs many ac-
' tions which feem to proceed more from rea-
' fon than from inftinct. He does every thing
' that his mafter commands : If he wants to ter-

* Voyage to the Eaft Indies, by Edward Terry, p. 15.

' rify

' rify any perfon, he runs upon him with every
' appearance of fury, and, when he comes near,
' ftops fhort, without doing him the fmalleft
' injury. When the mafter choofes to affront
' any man, he tells the elephant, who collects
' water and mud with his trunk, and fquirts it
' upon the object pointed out to him. The
' trunk is compofed of cartilage, hangs between
' the tufks, and is by fome called his *hand*, be-
' caufe, on many occafions, it anfwers the fame
' purpofes as the human hand. . . . The Mogul
' keeps fome elephants who ferve as execution-
' ers to criminals condemned to death. When
' the conductor orders one of thefe animals to
' difpatch the poor criminals quickly, he tears
' them to pieces in a moment with his feet.
' But, if defired to torment them flowly, he
' breaks their bones one after another, and
' makes them fuffer a punifhment as cruel as
' that of the wheel.'

We might quote many other facts equally
curious and interefting. But we fhould foon
exceed the limits we have prefcribed to ourfelves
in this work. We fhould not even have given
fo long a detail, if the elephant had not been,
in many refpects, the chief animal in the brute
creation, and who, of courfe, merited the greateft
attention.

M. Daubenton has made feveral ufeful remarks on the nature and qualities of ivory, and
has reftored to the elephant thofe prodigious

tufks and bones which have been attributed to
the mammouth. I acknowledge that I was long
doubtful with regard to this point. I had often
compared thefe enormous bones with the fkeleton of nearly a full grown elephant preferved in
the Royal Cabinet: And, as before compofing
their hiftory, I could not perfuade myfelf that
there exifted elephants fix or feven times larger
than the one whofe fkeleton I had fo often examined, and, as the large bones had not the
fame proportions with the correfponding bones
of the elephant, I believed, with the generality
of naturalifts, that thefe huge bones belonged to
a much larger animal, the fpecies of which had
been loft or annihilated. But it is certain, from
the facts formerly mentioned, that there are elephants fourteen feet high, and, confequently,
(as the maffes are as the cubes of the height,) fix
or feven times larger than that whofe fkeleton
is in the Royal Cabinet, and which was not
above feven, or feven and a half feet high. It is
likewife certain, that age changes the proportions of bones, and that adult animals grow confiderably thicker, though their ftature does not
increafe. In fine, it is certain, from the teftimonies of travellers, that there are elephants' tufks,
each of which weighs more than a hundred and
twenty pounds *. From all thefe facts, it is apparent,

---

* Mr. Eden informs us, that he meafured feveral elephants'
tufks, which he found to be nine feet long; that others were

as

parent, that the prodigious bones and tufks above taken notice of, are really the tufks and bones of the elephant. Sir Hans Sloane* fays the fame thing; but brings no proof of the fact. M. Gmelin affirms it ftill more pofitively †, and gives

as thick as a man's thigh; and that fome of them weighed ninety pounds. It is faid, that, in Africa, fome tufks have been found, each of which weighed a hundred and twenty-five pounds. . . . . The Englifh voyagers brought from Guiney the head of an elephant, which Mr. Eden faw in the poffeffion of Mr. Judde: It was fo large, that the bones and cranium alone, without including the tufks, weighed about two hundred pounds; from which it was computed, that the whole parts of the head, taken in their entire ftate, would have weighed five hundred pounds; *Hift. Gen. des Voyages, tom.* i. *p.* 223.—Lopes amufed himfelf in weighing feveral tufks of the elephant, each of which amounted to about two hundred pounds; *Idem, tom.* v. *p.* 79.—The magnitude of elephants may be eftimated by their tufks, fome of which have been found to weigh two hundred pounds; *Drake's Voyage, p.* 104. ——In the kingdom of Loango, I purchafed two tufks, which belonged to the fame animal, and each of them weighed 2 hundred and twenty-fix pounds; *Voyage de la Compagnie des. Indes de Hollande, tom.* iv. *p.* 319.——At the Cape of Good Hope, the elephant's teeth are very large, and weigh from fixty to a hundred pounds; *Defcript. du Cap de Bonne-efperance, par Kolbe, tom.* iii. *p.* 12.

* Hift. de l'Acad. des Sciences, année 1727, p. 1.

† In Siberia, there are prodigious quantities of bones found in different places under the ground. This part of Natural Hiftory is both curious and important: I have therefore col-lected all the facts I could learn upon this fubject. Peter the Great, who was a patron of naturalifts, gave orders to his fubjects, in the year 1722, that, wherever any bones of the mammouth were difcovered, the other bones belonging to the animal fhould be diligently fought for, and the whole fent to Peterfburg. Thefe orders were publifhed in all the towns of

Siberia,

gives fome curious facts on the fubject, which
deferve to be here related. But M. Daubenton
appears

Siberia, and, among others, in Jakutzk, where, after this pub-
lication, a Slufchewoi, called *Wafilei Oltafow*, entered into a
written obligation before Michaele Petrowitfch Ifmailow, cap-
tain-lieutenant of the guard, and Woywode of the place, to
travel into the interior cantons of Lena, in order to fearch for
the bones of the mammouth; and he was difpatched thither
on the 23d of April the fame year. The following year, another addreffed the Chancery of Jakutzk, and reprefented, that
he had travelled along with his fon toward the fea, in queft of
the bones of the mammouth, and that; oppofite to Surjatoi
Nofs, about two hundred verfts from that place and the fea, he
found, in a turfy foil, which is common in thefe diftricts, the
head of a mammouth, with one of the horns adhering to it;
and in the neighbourhood there was another horn of the fame
animal, which had probably fallen off while the creature was
alive; that, at a little diftance, they drew out of the earth another head, with the horns, of an unknown animal; that this
head refembled that of an ox, only it had horns above its nofe;
that, on account of an accident which befel his eyes, he was
obliged to leave thefe heads where they were; and that, having heard of his Majefty's orders, he now begged to be fent
off with his fon toward Vft-janfkoje, Simowie, and the fea. His
demand was complied with, and they were inftantly difpatched.
A third Slufchewoi of Jakutzk reprefented to the chancery, in
1724, that he made a voyage on the river Jelon; that he was
happy enough to difcover, in a fteep bank of this river, a frefh
head of the mammouth, with the horn and all its parts; that
he drew it out of the earth, and left it where he could find it
again; and that he begged to be fent off with two men accuftomed to fuch refearches. The woywode accordingly confented.
The Coffack foon after fet out on his journey, and found the
head, and all its parts, except the horns; for there remained
only the half of one horn, which he brought, along with the
head, to the Chancery of Jakutzk. Some time after, he brought
two horns of the mammouth, which he alfo found on the river
Jelon.

The

appears to be the firſt who has put the matter
beyond all doubt, by accurate menſurations,
exact

The Coſſacks of Jakutzk were extremely happy to find, under the pretext of going in queſt of the bones of the mammouth,
an opportunity of making ſuch agreeable voyages. They were
furniſhed with five or ſix poſt horſes, when one would have been
ſufficient, and they could employ the reſt in carrying various
articles of merchandize. Such an advantage was a great en-
couragement to adventurers. . . . . . A Coſſack of Jakutzk,
called *Jwanſelſku*, petitioned the Chancery to be ſent to the
Simowies of Alaſeiſch and Kowymiſch, in queſt of theſe kind
of bones, and of true cryſtal. He had already ſojourned in
theſe places, had collected many curious objects, and actually
ſent to Jakutzk ſome of theſe bones. Nothing ſeemed more
important than this expedition; and the Coſſack was diſpatched
on the 21ſt day of April 1725.
Naſar-Koleſchow, commiſſary of Indigirſk, in the year 1723,
ſent to Jakutzk, and from that to Irkutzk, the bones of a ſingular head, which, according to my information was two
arſchines, bating three wherſchok, in length, one arſchine high,
and armed with two horns and a tuſk of the mammouth. This
head arrived at Irkutzk on the 14th day of October 1723;
and I found the hiſtory of it in the chancery of that town. I
was alſo aſſured, that the ſame man afterwards ſent a horn of
the mammouth.
Theſe facts, collected from different ſources, regard, in general, the ſame ſpecies of bones, namely, 1. All the bones in
the Imperial cabinet of Peterſburg, under the name of *Mammouth bones, will be found, upon examination, to have a perfect reſemblance to thoſe of the elephant.* 2. From what has been above
related, it appears, that there have been found in the earth,
heads of an animal totally different from an elephant, and
which, particularly in the figure of the horns, reſembled the
head of an ox more than that of an elephant. Beſides, this
animal could not be ſo large as an elephant; and I have ſeen
a head of it at Jakutzk, which had been ſent from Anadir-
ſkoi-Oſtrog, and was, according to my information, perfectly
ſimilar to that found by Portn-jagin. I myſelf had one from

llainſkoi-

exact comparifons, and reafonings derived from
the

Ilainſkoi-Oſtròg, which I ſent to the Imperial cabinet at Peterſburg. In fine, I learned, that, on the banks of Niſchnaja-
Tunguſka, ſimilar heads are not only found every where diſperſed,
but likewiſe other bones which unqueſtionably belong not to
the elephant, ſuch as ſhoulder bones, oſſa ſacra, oſſa innominata,
hip-bones, and leg bones, which probably belonged to the ſame
animal to which the above head ought to be attributed, and
which ſhould by no means be excluded from the ox kind. I
have ſeen leg and hip-bones of this ſpecies, concerning which
I have nothing particular to remark, except that they appeared to be extremely ſhort in proportion to their thickneſs.
Thus in Siberia, two kinds of bones are found in the earth,
of which none were formerly eſteemed, but thoſe which perfectly reſembled the tuſks of the elephant. But, after the imperial order, the whole began to be examined ; and, as the
firſt gave riſe to the fable of the mammouth, the laſt have
alſo been indiſcriminately ranked under the ſame claſs. Neither muſt we believe, with Iſbrand-Ides, and the followers of
his reveries, that it is only in the mountains which extend from
the river Ket to the North-eaſt, and, conſequently, likewiſe
in the environs of Mangaſca and Jakutzk, where the elephants
bones are to be found : For they appear not only through all
Siberia, not excepting its moſt ſouthern diſtricts, as in the ſuperior cantons of the Irtiſch, Toms, and Lena, but are diſperſed
in different parts of Ruſſia, and even in many places of Germany, where they are called, with much propriety, by the
name of *foſſil ivory* ; for they have a perfect reſemblance to elephants' teeth, except that they are in a corrupted ſtate. In
temperate climates, theſe teeth are ſoftened and converted into
foſſil ivory ; but in countries frequently frozen, they are generally found very freſh. From this circumſtance, the fable,
that theſe and other bones are often found beſmeared with
blood, might eaſily ariſe. This fable has been gravely related
by Iſbrand-Ides, and, after him, by Muller, (Mœurs et Uſages
des Oſtiaques, dans *le Recueil des Voyages au Nord, p.* 382.) who
have been copied by others with equal confidence as if there
had been no room for doubt : And as one fiction begets
another, the blood pretended to be found on theſe bones has
produced

the extensive knowledge he has acquired in the science of comparative anatomy.

produced the notion, that the mammouth is an animal which lives in Siberia below the ground, where it sometimes dies, and is buried under the rubbish. All this has been invented with the view to account for the blood pretended to be found on these bones. Muller gives a description of the mammouth. This animal, says he, is four or five yards high, and about thirty feet long. His colour is grayish; his head is very long, and his front very broad. On each side, precisely under the eyes, there are two horns, which he can move and cross at pleasure. In walking, he has the power of extending and contracting his body to a great degree. His paws, in thickness, resemble those of the bear. Isbrandes-Ides is candid enough to acknowledge, that he never knew any person who had seen the mammouth alive. . . . . The heads and other bones, which correspond with those of the elephant, unquestionably once constituted real parts of that animal. To this abundance of elephants' bones we cannot refuse our assent; and I presume, that the elephants, to avoid destruction in the great revolutions which have happened in the earth, have been driven from their native country, and dispersed themselves wherever they could find safety. Their lot has been different. Some longer, and others shorter after their death, have been transported to great distances by some vast inundation. Those, on the contrary, who survived, and wandered far to the North, must necessarily have fallen victims to the rigours of the climate. Others, without reaching so great a distance, might be drowned, or perish with fatigue. . . . . The largeness of these bones ought not to astonish us. The tusks are sometimes four arschines long, and six inches in diameter, (M. de Strahlenberg says they have been seen nine inches in diameter,) and the largest weigh from six to seven puds. I mentioned, in another place, that fresh tusks have been taken from the elephant, which were ten feet long, and weighed a hundred, a hundred and forty-six, a hundred and sixty, and a hundred and sixty-eight pounds. . . . . . There are pieces of fossil ivory which are yellowish, or grow yellow in the

courso

SUPPLEMENT.

FROM comparing the male and female elephants, the former of which we saw in the year
1771, and the latter in 1773, it appears, that, in
general, the parts of the female are groffer and
more flefhy. Her ears, indeed, are proportionally fmaller than thofe of the male: But her
body is more fwollen, her head larger, and her
members more rounded.

Like all other animals, the female elephant is
more gentle than the male. Our female even
careffed people with whom fhe was unacquainted. But the male is often formidable: The one
we faw in 1771 was fiercer, lefs affectionate, and

course of time; others are brown like cocoa nuts, and more
luftrous; and others are of a blackifh blue colour. The tufks
which have not been much affected with the froft in the earth,
and have remained fome time expofed to the air, are fubject to
become more or lefs yellow or brown, and affume other colours,
according to the fpecies of humidity with which the air is impregnated. M. de Strahlenberg alfo remarks, that pieces of thefe
corrupted teeth are fometimes of a bluifh black colour. . . . . .
For the intereft of Natural Hiftory, it were to be wifhed, that,
with regard to the other bones found in Siberia, we knew the
animal to which they belong; but there is little hope of accom-
plifhing this purpofe; *Relation d'un Voyage a Kamtfchatka, par
M. Gmelin, imprime en* 1735 *a Peterfbourg, en Langue Ruffe.* The
tranflation of this article was firft communicated to me by M. de
l'Ifle, of the Academy of Sciences, and afterwards by the Marquis de Montmirail.

5

more

more ungovernable than this female. In a ftate of repofe, the genitals of the male appear not externally: His belly feems to be perfectly fmooth; and it is only at the time of difcharging urine, that the extremity of the penis comes out of the fheath. This male elephant, though equally young with the female, was, as formerly remarked, more difficult to manage. He endeavoured to lay hold of people who approached too near, and often tore their clothes. Even his governors were obliged to act with caution; but the female obeyed with complacence and alacrity. The only time fhe exhibited marks of difpleafure was when her keepers forced her into a covered waggon, in order to be carried from one town to another. When they wanted her to enter, fhe refufed to advance, and they could only accomplifh their purpofe by pricking her behind. Irritated by this ill treatment, and being unable to turn herfelf in her prifon, fhe had no other method of revenge but to fill her trunk with water, and throw it in torrents upon thofe who had teazed her.

I remarked, in the hiftory of the elephant*, that thefe animals probably did not copulate in the manner of other quadrupeds; becaufe the pofition of the organs in both fexes feemed to require that the female, in order to receive the male, fhould lie on her back. This conjecture, which appeared to be plaufible, is not true; for

* See above, p. 59.

the

the following teftimony of M. Marcel Bles, an eye-witnefs, deferves full credit.

‘ Having perceived that the Count de Buffon,
‘ in his excellent work, is deceived with regard
‘ to the copulation of the elephants, I know, that,
‘ in feveral parts of Afia and Africa, thefe ani-
‘ mals, efpecially during the feafon of love, re-
‘ main always in the moft inacceffible places of
‘ the forefts; but, in the ifland of Ceylon, where
‘ I lived twelve years, the land being every where
‘ inhabited, they cannot fo eafily conceal them-
‘ felves; and, having often examined them, I
‘ perceived that the female organ is fituated near-
‘ ly under the middle of the belly, which would
‘ lead us to think, with M. de Buffon, that the
‘ males cannot cover the females in the manner
‘ of other quadrupeds. However, there is only
‘ a flight difference of fituation. When they in-
‘ clined to copulate, I perceived that the female
‘ bowed down her head and neck, and leaned
‘ her two fore legs, which were alfo bended, up-
‘ on the root of a tree, as if fhe meant to pro-
‘ ftrate herfelf on the ground; and the two hind
‘ legs remained erect, which gave the male an
‘ opportunity of embracing her as other quadru-
‘ peds do. I can likewife affirm, that the fe-
‘ males go with young about nine months.
‘ Moreover, the elephants never copulate, unlefs
‘ when in a ftate of freedom. In the feafon of
‘ love, the males are ftrongly chained for four
‘ or five weeks, during which time, they dif-
‘ charge

'charge vaft quantities of femen, and are fo fu-
'rious, that their cornacks or governours can-
'not come near them without danger. The ap-
'proach of the rutting feafon is eafily known ;
'for fome days before it happens, an oily liquor
'flows from a fmall hole on each fide of the
'head. The domeftic female, on thefe occa-
'fions, fometimes makes her efcape, and joins
'the wild males in the woods. Some days af-
'terward, her cornack goes in queft of her, and
'calls her by her name till fhe comes. She fub-
'mits to him with complacence, and allows her-
'felf to be conducted home, and fhut up in the
'ftable. It was from cafes of this kind that it
'was difcovered that the females bring forth
'about the end of nine months.'

The firft remark with regard to the mode of
copulating, feems to be unqueftionable, fince M.
Marcel Bles affures us, that he has feen the elephants perform the operation. But, as to the
time of geftation, which he limits to nine months,
we ought to fufpend our judgment, becaufe all
travellers affirm, that the female elephant is
believed to go with young no lefs than two years.

THE RHINOCEROS*.

NEXT to the elephant, the Rhinoceros is the ftrongeft quadruped. He is at leaft twelve feet long; from the extremity of the muzzle

* The rhinoceros has one large horn, fometimes two, placed near the end of the nofe; it is fometimes three feet and a half long, black, and fmooth. The upper lip is long, hangs over the lower, ends in a point, is very pliable, and ferves to collect its food, and deliver it into the mouth. The noftrils are placed tranfverfely. The ears are large, erect, and pointed. The eyes are fmall and dull. The fkin is naked, rough, or tuberculated, and lies about the neck in vaft folds. There is another fold from the fhoulders to the fore legs, and another from the hind part of the back to the thighs. The fkin is fo thick and fo ftrong as to turn the edge of a fcimitar and refift a mufket ball. The tail is flender, flatted at the end, and covered on the fides with very ftiff, thick, black hairs. The belly hangs low. The legs are fhort, ftrong, and thick. The hoofs are divided into three parts, each pointing forward; *Pennant's Synopf. of Quad. p. 75.*

Though the name of this animal be entirely Greek, it was unknown to the ancient Greeks. Ariftotle takes no notice of it. Strabo is the firft Greek, and Pliny the firft Roman author who mentions it. The rhinoceros probably did not frequent that part of India into which Alexander had penetrated, though he met with great numbers of elephants; for it was about three hundred years after Alexander, that Pompey firft brought this animal to Europe.

Rhinocerote in Italian; *Abada* in Portuguefe; *Linfcot, Navig. in Orient. pars* ii. *p.* 44. *Abada* in India and Java; *Bontius' Ind. Orient. p.* 50. *P. Philippe, p.* 371. *Purchas's Pilgrim, vol.* ii. *p.* 1001. 1773. *Borri Hift. Cochin-china, p.* 797. *Du Haldes's China,*

Plate CLXVI.

A.Bell Sculp.

ELEPHANT.

muzzle to the origin of the tail, and the circumference of his body is nearly equal to his length *.
                                                    In

China, *vol.* i. *p.* 120. *Faunul. Sinenf. Chiengtuenden* and *Elker-
kedon* in Perfia; *Pietro della Valle*, tom. iv. *p.* 245. *Chardin*, tom.
iii. *p.* 45. *Arou barifi*, according to Thevenot; *Relation de Divers
Voyages*, *p.* 20.

Rhinoceros; *Plin. lib.* viii. *c.* 20. *Gefner. Quad. p.* 842. *Raii
Synopf. p.* 122. *Klein. Quad. p.* 26. *Grew's Muf. p.* 29. *Worm.
Muf. p.* 336. *Briffon. Quad. p.* 78. *Phil. Tranf. Abrid. vol.* ix.
p. 93. *Kolben, vol.* ii. *p.* 101.

Rhinoceros unicornis; *Linn. Syf. Nat. p.* 104. *Edwards's
Gleanings of Natural Hift. p.* 221.

Rhinoceros, a ρις et κερας. *Naricornis* Catelani. It is called
Noemba in Java; *Tuabba, Nabba*, at the Cape of Good Hope;
Nozorozec, Zebati, in Poland; and *Gomala* in India.

* I have in my poffeffion a figure of a rhinoceros, drawn
by an officer of the Shaftefbury Eaft India veffel in the year
1737. The figure correfponds very well with mine. The animal died in the paffage from the Eaft Indies to Britain.
This Officer had written the following note at the bottom of
the figure. ‘ His back was about feven feet high. His colour
‘ refembled that of a hog, whofe fkin is beginning to dry
‘ after wallowing in the mire. He had three hoofs on each
‘ foot. The folds of his fkin lay backward on each other. Be-
‘ tween thefe folds were harboured infects, millepeds, fcorpions,
‘ fmall ferpents, &c. He was not above three years old when
‘ his figure was drawn. His penis, when extended, fpread
‘ out in the form of a flower de luce.’ In a corner of the plate
I have given a figure of the penis. As this figure was communicated to me by Dr. Tyfon, I had not an opportunity of con-
fulting the author, whether thefe noxious infects, which he
fays take up their abode in the folds of the animal’s fkin, were
feen by himfelf, or whether he only related what had been
told him by the Indians. I acknowledge that the fact appears
very fingular; *Edwards's Gleanings, p.* 25. *Note*, This laft fact
is not only doubtful, but that of the animal’s age, compared
with his largenefs, appears to be falfe. We faw a rhinoceros
                                                         of

In magnitude, therefore, he makes a near approach to the elephant; and he appears to be much lefs, only becaufe his legs are proportionally fhorter than thofe of the elephant. But he differs ftill more from the elephant in his natural powers and intelligence; for Nature has beftowed on him nothing that elevates him above the ordinary rank of quadrupeds. He is deprived of all fenfibility in his fkin; neither has he hands to enable him to improve by the fenfe of touching; and inftead of a trunk, he has only a moveable lip, to which all his means of dexterity or addrefs are limited. His chief fources of fuperiority over other animals confifts in his ftrength, his magnitude, and the offenfive weapon on his nofe, which is entirely peculiar to him. This weapon is a very hard horn, folid throughout its whole extent, and fituated more advantageoufly than the horns of ruminating animals, which defend only the fuperior parts of the head and neck. But the horn of the rhinoceros preferves from infult the muzzle, the mouth, and the face. For this reafon, the tiger will rather attack the elephant, whofe trunk he lays hold of, than the rhinoceros, whom he dare not face, without running the rifk of having his bowels torn out; for

of, at leaft, eight years of age, which exceeded not five feet in height. Mr. Parfons faw one of two years, which was not higher than a heifer, which may be computed at about four feet. How, then, could the rhinoceros above taken notice of be only three years old, if it was feven feet high?

the

the body and limbs of the rhinoceros are covered
with a fkin fo impenetrable, that he fears neither
the claws of the tiger or lion, nor the fword or
fhot of the hunter. His fkin is blackifh, being
of the fame colour, but thicker and harder than
that of the elephant, and is not fenfible to the
ftings of flies. He can neither extend nor
contract his fkin, which is rolled up into large
folds at the neck, the fhoulders, and the crupper,
in order to facilitate the motion of his head
and limbs, which laft are maffy, and terminated
by large feet, armed with three great toes. His
head is proportionably longer than that of the
elephant; but his eyes are ftill fmaller, and feldom above half open. The upper, which projects over the under lip, is moveable, and can
be ftretched out about fix or feven inches in
length; and it is terminated by a pointed appendix, which gives this animal a power of collecting herbage in handfuls, as the elephant does
with its trunk. This mufcular and flexible lip
is a kind of hand or imperfect trunk; but it
enables the creature to feize any object with force,
and to feel with fome dexterity. Inftead of thofe
long ivory tufks which conftitute the armour of
the elephant, the rhinoceros has a formidable
horn, and two ftrong incifive teeth in each jaw.
Thefe teeth, of which the elephant is deprived,
are fituated at a great diftance from each other,
one in each angle of the jaw. The under jaw is
fquare before; and there are no other incifive

teeth

teeth in the anterior part of the mouth, which is covered by the lips. But befide the four cutting teeth, in the four corners of the mouth, there are twenty-four grinders, fix on each fide of the two jaws. He holds his ears always erect: In figure they refemble thofe of the hog; but they are proportionally fmaller. The ears are the only parts of the body on which there are hairs, or rather briftles. The extremity of the tail, like that of the elephant, is garnifhed with a bufh of large, folid, hard briftles.

Dr. Parfons, a celebrated phyfician in London, to whom the republic of letters is much indebted for many valuable difcoveries in natural hiftory, and to whom I owe the higheft acknowledgments for the marks of efteem and friendfhip with which he has been pleafed to honour me, publifhed, in the year 1743, a hiftory of the rhinoceros, from which I fhall the more willingly make extracts, becaufe every compofition of that gentleman merits the attention and confidence of the public.

Though the rhinoceros was frequently exhibited in the Roman fpectacles, from the days of Pompey to thofe of Heliogabalus; though he has often been tranfported into Europe in more modern times; and though Bontius, Chardin, and Kolben, have drawn figures of him both in India and Africa; yet fo ill was he reprefented and defcribed, that he was very imperfectly known till the errors and caprices of thofe who had

had publiſhed figures of him were detected by inſpection of the animals which arrived in London in the years 1739 and 1741. The figure given by Albert Durer was the firſt, and the leaſt conformable to Nature; yet it was copied by moſt naturaliſts, ſome of whom loaded it with prepoſterous drapery and foreign ornaments. That of Bontius is more ſimple and correct; but the inferior part of the legs is improperly repreſented. That of Chardin, on the contrary, gives a pretty good idea of the feet, and the folds of the ſkin; but, in other reſpects, it has no reſemblance to the animal. That of Camerarius is no better; neither is that drawn from the rhinoceros exhibited at London in the year 1685, and which was publiſhed by Carwitham in the 1739. In fine, the figures on the ancient pavement of Præneſte, and on Domitian's medals, are extremely imperfect; but they have the merit of not being deformed by the imaginary ornaments repreſented in the figure drawn by Albert Durer. Dr. Parſons has taken the trouble of drawing this animal himſelf* in three different views,

* One of our learned philoſophers, M. de Mours, has made ſome remarks on this ſubject, which muſt not be omitted. ‘ The ‘ figure,' ſays he, ‘ of the rhinoceros which Dr. Parſons has ad-‘ ded to his Memoir, and which he drew from the life, is ſo dif-‘ ferent from that engraved at Paris in the year 1749, from a ‘ rhinoceros exhibited at the fair of Saint-Germain, that it is ‘ difficult to recogniſe them to be the ſame animal. That of ‘ Dr. Parſons is ſhorter, and the folds of the ſkin are fewer in

views, before, behind, and in profile. He has
likewise drawn the male organs of generation,
the

‘ number, lefs marked, and fome of them placed in a different
‘ pofition. The head, particularly, has hardly any refemblance
‘ to that of the Saint-Germain rhinoceros. We cannot, however,
‘ entertain a doubt with regard to the accuracy of Dr. Parfons.
‘ The reafons of fuch remarkable differences muft be fought for
‘ in the age and fex of the two animals. That of Dr. Parfons
‘ was drawn from a male rhinoceros, which exceeded not the
‘ age of two years. That which I have here added, was drawn
‘ from a picture of the celebrated M. Oudry, a moft diftinguifh-
‘ ed animal painter. He painted from the life, and of the na-
‘ tural fize, the Saint-Germain rhinoceros, which was a female,
‘ and at leaft eight years old; I fay at leaft eight years; for we
‘ fee by an infcription written on the bottom of a wooden
‘ print, entitled, *A true portrait of a living rhinoceros exhibited at
‘ the fair of Saint-Germain in Paris*, that this animal, when taken,
‘ in 1741, in the province of Affem belonging to the Mo-
‘ gul, was three years old: And, eight lines lower, it is faid,
‘ that the animal was only one month old when fome Indians
‘ entangled it with ropes, after having flain the mother by their
‘ fpears and darts. Hence it muft have been at leaft eight
‘ years of age, and might be ten or twelve. This difference of
‘ age is probably the reafon of the remarkable differences be-
‘ tween Dr. Parfons’s figure and that of M. Oudry, whofe pic-
‘ ture, executed by the order of the King, was exhibited in the
‘ painter’s hall. I fhall only remark, that M. Oudry has made
‘ the horn of his rhinoceros too long; for I examined the ani-
‘ mal with great attention, and I find that this part is better
‘ reprefented in the wooden print. The horn of the prefent fi-
‘ gure was drawn after this print, and the reft is copied from
‘ M. Oudry’s picture. The animal which it reprefents was
‘ weighed, about a year before, at Stouquart, in the dutchy of
‘ Wittemberg, and its weight was at that time five hundred
‘ pounds. It eat, according to the relation of Captain Dowemot
‘ Wan-dermeer, who conducted it to Europe, fixty pounds of
‘ hay, and twenty pounds of bread, every day. It was very
‘ tame, and furprifingly agile, confidering the enormity of its
‘ mafs, and its unwieldy afpect.’ Thefe remarks, like all thofe
of

the fingle and double horns, as well as the tail, from other rhinocerofes, whofe parts are preferved in the cabinets of Natural Hiftory.

The rhinoceros which came to London in the year 1739, was fent from Bengal. Though not above two years of age, the expence of his food and journey amounted to near one thoufand. pounds fterling. He was fed with rice, fugar, and hay. He had daily feven pounds of rice, mixed with three pounds of fugar, and divided into three portions. He had likewife hay and green herbs, which laft he preferred to hay. His drink was water, of which he took large quantities at a time. He was of a peaceable difpofition, and allowed all parts of his body to be touched. When hungry or ftruck by any perfon, he became mifchievous, and, in both cafes, nothing appeafed him but food. When enraged, he fprung forward, and nimbly raifed himfelf to a great height, pufhing, at the fame time, his head furioufly againft the walls, which he performed with amazing quicknefs, notwithftanding his heavy afpect and unwieldy mafs. I often obferved, fays Dr. Parfons, thefe movements produced by rage or impatience, efpecially in the mornings before his rice and fugar were brought to him. The vivacity and promptitude of his movements, Dr. Parfons adds, led

of M. de Mours, are judicious and fenfible. See the figure in his French tranflation of the Philofophical Tranfactions, ann. 1743.

me

me to think, that he is altogether unconquerable, and that he could eafily overtake any man who fhould offend him.

This rhinoceros, at the age of two years, was not taller than a young cow that has never produced. But his body was very long and very thick. His head was difproportionally large. From the ears to the horn there is a concavity, the two extremities of which, namely the upper end of the muzzle, and the part near the ears, are confiderably raifed. The horn, which was not yet above an inch high, was black, fmooth at the top, but full of wrinkles directed backward at the bafe. The noftrils are fituated very low, being not above an inch diftant from the opening of the mouth. The under lip is pretty fimilar to that of the ox; but the upper lip has a greater refemblance to that of the horfe, with this advantageous difference, that the rhinoceros can lengthen this lip, move it from fide to fide, roll it about a ftaff, and feize with it any object he wifhes to carry to his mouth. The tongue of this young rhinoceros was foft, like that of a calf *. His eyes had no vivacity: In

---

* Moft voyagers and all naturalifts, both ancient and modern, tell us, that the tongue of the rhinoceros is very rough, and its papillæ fo fharp, that with the tongue alone, he tore the flefh from a man's body even to the bones. This fact, which is every where related, appears to be very fufpicious and ill imagined; becaufe the rhinoceros does not eat flefh, and animals, in general, which have rough tongues, are feldom carnivorous.

figure,

figure, they refembled thofe of the hog, and
were fituated lower, or nearer the noftrils, than
in any other quadruped. His ears are large,
thin at the extremities, and contracted at their
origin by a kind of annular rugofity. The neck
is very fhort, and furrounded with two large
folds of fkin. The fhoulders are very thick,
and, at their juncture, there is another fold of
fkin, which defcends upon the fore legs. The
body of this young rhinoceros was very thick,
and pretty much refembled that of a cow about
to bring forth. Between the body and crupper
there is another fold, which defcends upon the
hind legs. Laftly, another fold tranfverfely furrounds the inferior part of the crupper, at fome
diftance from the tail. The belly was large, and
hung near the ground, particularly its middle
part. The legs are round, thick, ftrong, and
their joint bended backwards. This joint, which,
when the animal lies, is covered with a remarkable fold of the fkin, appears when he ftands.
The tail is thin, and proportionally fhort; that
of the rhinoceros fo often mentioned exceeded
not fixteen or feventeen inches in length. It
turns a little thicker at the extremity, which is
garnifhed with fome fhort, thick, hard hairs.
The form of the penis is very extraordinary.
It is contained in a prepuce or fheath, like that
of the horfe; and the firft thing that appears in
the time of erection, is a fecond prepuce, of a
flefh-colour, from which there iffues a hollow

G 3   tube,

tube, in the form of a funnel cut and bordered somewhat like a flower de luce*, and constitutes the glans and extremity of the penis. This anomalous glans is of a paler flesh-colour than the second prepuce. In the most vigorous erection, the penis extends not above eight inches out of the body; and it is easily procured by rubbing the animal with a handful of straw when he lies at his ease. The direction of this organ is not straight, but bended backward. Hence he throws out his urine behind; and, from this circumstance, it may be inferred, that the male covers not the female, but that they unite with their cruppers to each other. The female organs are situated like those of the cow, and she exactly resembles the male in figure and grossness of body. The skin is so thick and impenetrable, that, when a man lays hold of any of the folds, he would imagine he is touching a wooden plank of half an inch thick. When tanned, Dr. Grew remarks, it is excessively hard, and thicker than the hide of any other terrestrial animal. It is every where covered more or less with incrustations in the form of galls or tuberosities, which are pretty small on the top of the neck and back, but become larger on the sides. The largest are on the shoulders and crupper, and are still pretty large on the thighs and legs, upon which they are spread all round, and even on the feet. But, between the folds, the

* Phil. Transf. No. 470. pl. 111. Edwards's Gleanings.

skin

skin is penetrable, delicate, and as soft to the touch as silk, while the external part of the fold is equally hard with the rest. This tender skin between the folds is of a light flesh-colour; and the skin of the belly is nearly of the same colour and consistence. These galls or tuberosities should not be compared, as some authors have done, to scales. They are simple indurations of the skin only, without any regularity in their figure, or symmetry in their respective positions. The flexibility of the skin in the folds enables the rhinoceros to move with facility his head, neck, and members. The whole body, except at the joints, is inflexible, and resembles a coat of mail. Dr. Parsons remarks, that this animal listened with a deep and long continued attention to any kind of noise; and that, though he was sleeping, eating, or obeying any other pressing demands of nature, he raised his head and listened till the noise ceased.

In fine, after giving this accurate description of the rhinoceros, Dr. Parsons examines whether the rhinoceros, with a double horn, exists; and, having compared the testimonies of the ancients and moderns, and the remains of this variety in the collections of natural objects, he, with much probability, concludes, that the rhinoceroses of Asia have commonly but one horn, and that those of Africa have generally two.

It is unquestionably true, that some rhinoceroses have but one horn, and that others have

two.

two *. But it is not equally certain that this
variety is conftant, and depends on the climate
of Africa or India ; or that this difference is alone
fufficient to conftitute two diftinct fpecies. It
appears that the rhinocerofes with one horn
have this excrefcence always longer than thofe
with two. There are fingle horns of three and
a half, and perhaps of above four feet in length,
by fix or feven inches diameter at the bafe. Some
double horns are two feet long †. Thefe horns
are commonly of a brown or olive colour;
though there are inftances of their being gray,
and even white. They have only a flight concavity in form of a cup under the bafe, by which
they are fixed to the fkin of the nofe. The reft
of the horn is folid, and harder than common
horn. It is with this weapon that the rhinoce-

* Kolben afferts pofitively, and as if he had been an eye-
witnefs, that the firft horn of the rhinoceros is upon the nofe,
and the fecond upon the front, in a right line with the firft;
that the latter, which is brown, never exceeds two feet in
length ; and that the fecond is yellow, and feldom longer
than fix inches ; *Defcript du Cap de Bonne Efperance, tom.* iii.
p. 17.—But we have already mentioned double horns, the
fecond differing very little from the firft, which was two
feet long, and both were of the fame colour. Befides, it
appears to be certain, that they are never at fuch a diftance
from each other, as this author has placed them; for the
bafis of the two horns, preferved in the cabinet of Sir Hans
Sloane, were not three inches afunder.

† Urfus cornu gemino ; *Martial. Spectac. ep.* 22. *Phil. Tranf.
Abrid. vol.* ix. *p.* 100. *vol.* xi. *p.* 910. *Phil. Tranf. vol.* lvi. *p.* 32.
tab. 2. *Flacourt, Hift. Madag. p.* 395. *Lobo Abyff. p.* 230.
Rhinoceros bicornis ; *Linn. Syft. Nat. p.* 104.

ros is said to attack and sometimes mortally wound the largest elephants, whose tall legs give the rhinoceros an opportunity of striking, with his snout and horn, their bellies, where the skin is most tender and penetrable. But, if he misses his first blow, the elephant throws him on the ground and kills him.

The horn of the rhinoceros is more esteemed by the Indians than the ivory of the elephant, not on account of its real utility, though they make several toys of it with the chisel and turner's lathe, but on account of certain medicinal qualities they ascribe to it*. The white horns, being

* Sunt in regno Bengalen rhinocerotes Lusitanis *Abadas* dicti, cujus animalis corium, dentes, caro, sanguis, ungulæ, et cæteræ ejus partes, toto genere resistunt venenis; qua de causa in maximo pretio est apud Indos.—In those parts of Bengal which border on the Ganges, the rhinoceroses or unicorns, there called *Abades*, are very common, and numbers of their horns are brought to Goa. They are about two palms in circumference at the base, gradually taper to a point, and serve the animal as a defensive weapon. They are of an obscure colour, and the cups made of them are highly esteemed, especially if they have the power of counteracting poisonous liquors; *Voyage du P. Philippe*, p. 371.—Every part of the rhinoceros's body is medicinal. His horn is a powerful antidote against all kinds of poison; and the Siamese make a great article of traffic with it among the neighbouring nations. Some of them are sold for more than a hundred crowns. Those which are of a bright gray colour, and spotted with white, are most valued by the Chinese; *Hist. Nat. de Siam, par Nic. Gervaise*, p. 34.—The horns, teeth, toes, flesh, skin, blood, and even their urine and excrements, are in great request among the Indians, as powerful remedies for different diseases; *Voyage de la Compagnie des Indes de Hollande*, tom. i. p. 417.—

being rareft, are in great requeft. Among the prefents fent by the King of Siam to Lewis XIV. in the year 1686*, were fix horns of the rhinoceros. In the royal cabinet we have twelve, of different fizes; and one of them, though cut, is three feet eight inches and a half long.

The rhinoceros, without being ferocious, carnivorous, or even extremely wild, is, however, perfectly untractable †. He is nearly among large, what the hog is among fmall animals, rafh and brutal, without intelligence, fentiment, or docility. He feems even to be fubject to paroxyfms of fury, which nothing can appeafe;

417.—His horn is placed between the two noftrils; it is very thick at the bafe, and terminates in a fharp point: It is of a greenifh brown colour, and not black, as fome authors maintain. When very gray or approaching to white, it brings a high price. But it is always dear, on account of the value put on it by the Indians; *Idem, tom.* vii. *p.* 277.

* Among the prefents fent by the King of Siam to France, in the year 1686, were fix rhinocerofes horns, which were greatly valued over all the Eaft. The Chevalier Vernati has written from Batavia to Britain, that the horns, teeth, toes, and blood of the rhinoceros, are antidotes, and that they are as much ufed in the Indian pharmacopœia as the theriaca in that of Europe; *Voyage de la Compagnie des Indes de Hollande, tom.* vii. *p.* 484.

† Chardin fays, (*tom.* iii. *p.* 45.) that the Abyffinians tame the rhinoceros, and train him to labour, like the elephants. This fact feems to be extremely fufpicious: No other author mentions it; and it is well known, that, in Bengal, Siam, and other fouthern parts of India, where the rhinoceros is, perhaps, ftill more common than in Æthiopia, and where the natives are accuftomed to tame the elephants, he is regarded as an irreclaimable animal, of which no domeftic ufe can be made.

for

for the one which Emanuel King of Portugal
fent to the Pope in the year 1513, deftroyed the
veffel in which they were tranfporting him*;
and the rhinoceros, which we lately faw in Paris, was drowned in the fame manner in its
voyage to Italy. Like the hog, thefe animals are
fond of wallowing in the mire. They love
moift and marfhy grounds, and never quit the
banks of rivers. They are found in Afia and
Africa, in Bengal †, Siam ‡, Laos ‖, Mogul §,
Sumatra **, at Java in Abyffinia ††, in Æthiopia ‡‡, in the country of the Anzicos ‖‖, and as
far as the Cape of Good Hope §§. But, in general, the fpecies is not numerous, and much
lefs diffufed than that of the elephant. The female produces but one at a time, and at confiderable intervals. During the firft month, the

* Philofophical Tranfactions, No. 470.

† Voyage du P. Philippe, p. 371.—Voyage de la Compagnie
des Indes de Hollande, tom. i. p. 417.

‡ Hiftoire Naturelle de Siam, par Gervaife, p. 33.

‖ Journal de l'Abbé de Choify, p. 339.

§ Voyage de Tavernier, tom. iii. p. 97.—Voyage d'Edward
Terri, p. 15.

** Hiftoire Generale des Voyages, par M. l'Abbé Prevôt,
tom. ix. p. 339.

†† Voyage de la Compagnie des Indes de Hollande, tom vii.
p. 277.

‡‡ Voyage de Chardin, tom, iii. p. 45.—Relation de Thevenot, p. 10.

‖‖ Hiftoire Generale des Voyages, par M. l'Abbé Prevôt,
tom. v. p. 91.

§§ Voyage de Franc. le Guat. tom. ii. p. 145.—Defcription
du Çap de Bonne-efperance, par Kolbe, tom. iii. p. 15 et fuiv.

young

young rhinoceros exceeds not the fize of a large dog *. When recently brought forth, it has no horn †, though the rudiments of it appear in the fœtus. At the age of two years, the horn exceeds not an inch in length ‡. and, at the age of fix, it is from nine to ten inches long ‖ : Now, as fome of thefe horns are known to be near four feet in length, it appears that they continue to grow during the half, or perhaps during the whole of the animal's life, which muft be confiderably long, fince the rhinoceros defcribed by Dr. Parfons had only acquired about one half of its height at the age of two years; from which we may conclude, that this animal, like man, fhould live feventy or eighty years.

Without the capacity of becoming ufeful, like the elephant, the rhinoceros is equally hurtful by his voracity, and particularly by the great wafte he makes in the cultivated fields. He is of no ufe till he is flain. His flefh is reckoned

---

* We have feen a young rhinoceros which was not larger than a dog. It followed its mafter every where, and drank the milk of the buffalo. But it lived only three weeks. The teeth were beginning to appear; *Voyage de la Compagnie des Indes de Hollande, tom.* vii. *p.* 483.

† In two young rhinocerofes, nothing but a prominence was obferved on the place where the horns were to arife, though the animals were then as large as an ox. But their legs are very fhort, efpecially thofe before, which are fhorter than the hind legs; *Voyage de Pietro della Valle, tom.* iv. *p.* 245.

‡ Phil. Tranf. No. 470.

‖ Id. ibid.

excellent

excellent by the Indians and Negroes*; and Kolbe says he often eat it with pleasure. His skin makes the hardest and best leather in the world †; and not only his horn, but all the other parts of his body, and even his blood ‡, urine, and excrements, are esteemed to be antidotes against poison, or remedies for particular diseases. These antidotes or remedies, extracted from different parts of the rhinoceros, are of equal use in the Indian Pharmacopœia as the theriaca in that of Europe ‖. Most of the virtues ascribed to both are probably imaginary: But how many objects are in the highest repute, which have no value but in the opinions of men?

The rhinoceros feeds on the grossest herbs, as thistles and thorny shrubs, which he prefers to the soft pasture of the best meadows §. He is fond

---

* The Indians eat the flesh of the rhinoceros, and reckon it excellent. They even derive advantage from his blood, which they collect with care as a remedy for diseases in the breast; *Hist. Nat. de Siam, par Gervaise, p.* 35.

† His skin is of a fine gray colour, approaching to black, like that of the elephant; but it is rougher and thicker than that of any other animal. . . . The skin is covered every where, except on the neck and head, with small knots or tubercles, &c.; *Voyage de Chardin, tom.* iii. *p.* 45.

‡ Voyage de Mandelslo. tom. ii. p. 350.

‖ Voyage de la Comp. des Indes de Hollande, tom. vii. p. 484.

§ This animal feeds upon plants, and prefers brushwood, broom, and thistles. But of all plants he is fondest of a shrub which resembles the juniper, and is called the *rhinoceros shrub.* Great quantities of it grow on heathy lands and on the mountains;

fond of the fugar cane, and likewife eats all kinds of grain. Having no appetite for flefh, he neither difturbs the fmall nor fears the large animals, but lives in peace with all, not excepting the tiger, who often accompanies the rhinoceros, without daring to attack him. This peaceful difpofition renders the combats between the elephant and the rhinoceros very fufpicious: Such combats muft at leaft be rare, fince there is no motive to war on either fide. Befides, no antipathy has ever been remarked between thefe animals. They have been known, even in a ftate of captivity, to live peaceably together, without difcovering any marks of refentment or antipathy *. Pliny, I believe, is the firft author who mentions thefe combats between the elephant and rhinoceros. It appears that thefe animals were compelled to fight at the Roman fpectacles †; and from hence, probably, the idea was formed, that, when in their natural

mountains; *Defcript. du Cap de Bonne-efperance, par Kolbe, tom.* iii. *p.* 17.

* The Dutch hiftory, entitled *l'Ambaffade de la Chine,* gives a falfe defcription of this animal, efpecially when it exhibits the rhinoceros as the chief enemy of the elephant; for the rhinoceros I am mentioning was kept in the fame ftable with two elephants, and I have feveral times feen them near each other without difcovering the fmalleft antipathy. An Æthiopian ambaffador had brought this animal as a prefent; *Voyage de Chardin, tom.* iii. *p.* 45.

† The Romans took pleafure in making the rhinoceros and elephant fight at their public fhews; *Singular. de la France Antarctique, par André Thevet, p.* 41.

ftate

ſtate of liberty, they fight in the ſame manner. But every action without a motive is unnatural; it is an effect without a cauſe, which cannot happen but by accident.

The rhinoceroſes aſſemble not, nor march in troops like the elephants. They are more ſolitary and ſavage; and it is, perhaps, more difficult to hunt, and to overcome them. They never attack men *, unleſs they are provoked, when they become furious and formidable. Their ſkin is ſo hard as to reſiſt ſabres, lances, javelins, and even muſket balls†. The only penetrable parts of the body are the belly,

* The rhinoceros never attacks any perſon, nor becomes furious, unleſs he is provoked, and then his ferocity is tremendous; he grunts like a hog, and overturns trees and every thing that comes in his way; *Voyage de la Compagnie des Indes de Hollande, tom.* vii. *p.* 278.

† His ſkin is thick, hard, and rough. . . It is even impenetrable by the ſabres of the Japaneſe, and coats of arms, bucklers, &c. are made of it; *Id. Ibid. p.* 483.—The rhinoceros ſeldom attacks man, unleſs when provoked, or the perſon wears a red habit. In both theſe caſes, he becomes furious, and overturns every thing that oppoſes him. When theſe animals attack a man, they ſeize him by the middle of the body, and toſs him up with ſuch force, that he is killed by the fall. . . . However enraged he may be, it is eaſy to avoid his approach: He is, indeed, very ſwift; but he turns with great difficulty. Beſides, according to my information, he ſees only what is before him. Hence, when he comes within a few paces, we have only to ſtep to a ſide; for he then loſes ſight of us, and it is very difficult for him to return in queſt of us. I have experienced this fact, having more than once ſeen him advance toward me with all his fury; *Deſcript. du Cap de Bonne-eſperance, par Kolbe, tom.* iii. *p.* 17.

the

the eyes, and about the ears*. Hence the hunters, inftead of attacking him face to face, follow him at a diftance by the tracks of his feet, and watch till he lies down to fleep. We have, in the royal cabinet, a fœtus of a rhino-ceros, which was extracted from the body of the mother, and fent to us from the ifland of Java. By the memoir which accompanied this fœtus, we are informed, that twenty-eight hun-ters having affembled to attack the mother, they followed her at a diftance for fome days, de-taching one or two of their number, from time to time, in order to reconnoitre her fituation; that, by this means, they furprifed her when afleep, and filently approached fo near, that the whole twenty-eight mufkets were difcharged at once into the lower part of her belly.

From the defcription given by Dr. Parfons, it appears that this animal has an acute and very attentive ear. We are likewife affured that his

---

* It is difficult to kill him; and men never attack him without danger of being torn to pieces. Thofe who are ac-cuftomed to hunt the rhinoceros find means, however, to de-fend themfelves from his fury; for he is fond of marfhy grounds; they obferve when he repairs thither, and, con-cealing themfelves among the bufhes oppofite to the direction of the wind, they watch till he lies down either to fleep or to wallow, that they may have an opportunity of fhooting him near the ears, where alone he can receive a mortal wound. They place themfelves againft the wind; becaufe the fcent of the rhinoceros is fo acute, that he never approaches any object he perceives till the fmell of it reaches his noftrils; *Hift. Nat. de Siam, par Gervaife, p.* 35.

fenfe

sense of smelling is excellent. But it is said, that his eyes are not good, and that he sees such objects only as are before him *. The extreme minuteness of his eyes, their low, oblique, and deep situation, the dullness, and the small degree of motion they seem to possess, tend to confirm this fact. His voice, when he is in a state of tranquillity, is blunt, and resembles the grunting of a hog; but, when enraged, it becomes sharp, and is heard at a great distance. Though he lives on vegetables only, he does not ruminate. Hence it is probable, that, like the elephant, he has but one stomach, and capacious bowels, which supply the place of many stomachs. His consumption of food, though considerable, is not near so great as that of the elephant; and it appears, from the density and un-

---

* See the preceding note.—The eyes of the rhinoceros are very small, and he sees only forward. When he walks, or pursues his prey, he proceeds always in a direct line, forcing, overturning, and piercing through every obstruction that falls in his way. Neither bushes, nor trees, nor thickets of brambles, nor large stones, can turn him from his course. With the horn on his nose, he tears up trees, raises stones high in the air, and throws them behind him to a considerable distance, and with a great noise: In a word, he overthrows every object which he can lay hold of. When he is enraged, and meets with no obstruction, lowering his head, he plows the ground, and throws large quantities of earth over his head. He grunts like a hog: His cry, when in a state of tranquillity, does not reach far; but, when in pursuit of his prey, it may be heard at a great distance; *Descript. du Cap de Bonne Esperance, par Kolbe.*

interrupted

interrupted thickness of his skin, that he also loses much less by perspiration.

SUPPLEMENT.

I Have seen a second rhinoceros, which was lately brought to the royal menagery. In the month of September 1770, if the people who conducted it can be credited, the animal was only three months old. But, I am persuaded, that it was at least two or three years of age; for its body, including the head, was already eight feet two inches long, five feet six inches high, and eight feet two inches in circumference. A year afterward, its body was lengthened seven inches; so that on the 28th day of August 1771, it was eight feet nine inches, including the length of the head, five feet nine inches high, and eight feet nine inches in circumference. On the 12th day of August 1772, the length of the body, comprehending the head, was nine feet four inches, the height of the crupper six feet four inches, and that of the withers only five feet eleven inches. Its skin had the colour and appearance of an old elm tree, spotted in some places with black and gray, and in others doubled into deep furrows, which formed a kind of scales. It had only one horn, the

colour

colour of which was brown, and its fubftance folid and hard. The eyes are fmall and prominent, the ears large, and pretty fimilar to thofe of an afs. The back, which was hollow, or depreffed, feemed to be covered with a natural faddle. The legs were fhort and very thick. The feet were rounded behind, and divided before into three hoofs. The tail refembled that of an ox, and was garnifhed with black hairs at the extremity. The penis lay along the tefticles, and erected itfelf for the difcharge of urine, which the animal threw out to a great diftance. The point of it was alfo very remarkable, forming a cavity like the mouth of a trumpet. The fheath from which it iffues is flefhy, and of a vermilion colour, like the penis itfelf. This flefhy fubftance, which formed the firft tube, came out of a fecond fheath compofed of fkin, as in other quadrupeds. The tongue is fo hard and rough, that it tears off the fkin of any perfon whom it licks; hence this animal eats large thorns, without feeling any pain. The rhinoceros requires one hundred and fixty pounds of food every day. His flefh is much relifhed by the Indians and Africans, and efpecially by the Hottentots. If trained when young, he might be rendered domeftic, and, in this ftate, he would multiply more eafily than the elephant.

' I could never difcover the reafon (M. P. re-
' marks) why in Afia the rhinoceros is allowed

' to

' to remain in a wild ſtate, while in Abyſſinia he
' is rendered domeſtic, and is employed in car-
' rying burdens *.'

   ' M. de Buffon,' ſays Mr. Bruce, ' conjeĉtured
' that there were, in the interior parts of Africa,
' rhinoceroſes with two horns. This conjeĉture
' is fully verified ; for all the rhinoceroſes I ſaw
' in Abyſſinia had two horns. The firſt, that is,
' the one neareſt the noſe, is of the common
' form ; the ſecond is ſharp at the point, and
' always ſhorter than the firſt. Both ſpring at
' the ſame time; but the firſt grows more quickly,
' and exceeds the other in ſize, not only during
' the time of growth, but during the whole life
' of the animal †.'

   On the other hand, M. Allamand, a very able
naturaliſt, wrote to M. Daubenton a letter, dated
at Leyden, Oĉtober 31, 1766, in the following
terms :

   ' I recolleĉt a remark of M. Parſons, in a
' paſſage quoted by M. de Buffon : He ſuſpeĉted
' that the rhinoceroſes of Aſia have but one
' horn, and that thoſe of the Cape of Good
' Hope have two. I ſuſpeĉt the very oppoſite :
' The heads of the rhinoceroſes which I received
' from Bengal and other parts of India, had al-
' ways double horns, and all thoſe which came

* Defenſe des Recherches ſur les Americains, p. 95.
† Note communicated by Mr. Bruce to M. de Buffon.

' from

Plate CLXVII.

RHINOCEROS.

' from the Cape of Good Hope had but one
' horn.'

This laſt paſſage proves what we have formerly remarked, that the rhinoceroſes with
double horns form a variety in the ſpecies, a
particular race, which is found equally in Aſia
and Africa.

The CAMEL * and DROME-DARY **.

THE names *Camel* and *Dromedary* fignify not two different fpecies, but only two diftinct races of the camel, which have fubfifted long

* There are two fpecies of the camel, the Bactrian camel, and the Arabian camel or dromedary. They have no cutting teeth in the upper jaw. The upper lip is divided, like that of the hare; and they have fix cutting teeth in the lower jaw.—The Bactrian camel has two bunches on the back, a fmall head, fhort ears, and a long flender, bending neck. The height, to the top of the bunches, is fix feet fix inches. The hair is foft, longeft about the neck, under the throat, and about the bunches. The colour of the hair on the protuberances is dufky, on the other parts it is a reddifh afh-colour. The tail is long, the hairs on the middle is foft, and coarfe, black, and long on the fides. The hoofs are fmall; the feet flat, divided above, but not through. The bottom of the feet is exceffively tough, yet pliant. There are fix callofities on the legs, one on each knee; one on the infide of each fore-leg, on the upper joint; one on the infide of the hind-leg, at the bottom of the thigh; another on the lower part of the breaft, the places that the animal refts on when it lies down; *Pennant's Synopf. of Quad. p.* 60.

In Greek, Καμηλος Βακτρος; in Latin, *Camelus*; in Italian, *Camelo*; in Spanifh, *Camelo*; in German, *Koemel*; in Hebrew, *Gamal*; in Chaldean, *Gamala*; in ancient Arabic, *Gemal*; in modern Arabic, *Gimel*; in French, *Chameau*. From thefe denominations, it appears, that the name of this animal has been adopted into modern languages, with little variation, from the ancient Hebrew, Chaldean, and Arabic.

Camelus

long previous to the records of hiſtory. The
chief, and perhaps the only ſenſible character by
which theſe two races are diſtinguiſhed, is, that
the camel has two bunches on the back, and the
dromedary but one. The latter is alſo ſomewhat
ſmaller and weaker than the camel. But both

Camelus Bactrianus; *Ariſt. Hiſt. Anim. lib.* ii. *cap.* 1.—*Plin.
lib.* viii. *cap.* 18.—*Geſner. Icon. Quad. p.* 22.—*Proſp. Alpin. Hiſt.
Nat. Ægypt. tom.* ii. *p.* 224. *tab.* 13.

Camel called Becheti; *Leo, Afric. p.* 338.

Camelus duobus in dorſo tuberibus, ſeu Bactrianus; *Raii Synopſ. Quad. p.* 145.

Camelus Bactrianus, tophis dorſi duobus; *Linn. Syſt. Nat.
p.* 90.—*Klein. Quad. p.* 41.

Perſian camel; *Ruſſel's Aleppo, p.* 57.

** The Arabian camel, or dromedary, has but one bunch on
the back. In all other reſpects it is like the preceding, and is
equally adapted for riding or carrying loads; *Pennant's Synopſ. of
Quad. p.* 62.

In Greek, Δρομας, or rather *Camelus Dromas*; for dromas is
only an adjective derived from *dromos*, which ſignifies *ſwiftneſs*,
and *camelus dromas* is equivalent to the *ſwift running camel:*
In modern Latin, *Dromedarius*; in the Levant, *Maibary*, according to Doctor Shaw.

Camelus Arabicus; *Ariſt. Hiſt. Anim. lib.* ii. *cap.* 1.—*Plin.
lib.* viii. *cap.* 18.

Camelus dromas; *Geſner. Quad. p.* 159. *Icon. Quad. p.* 23.
Proſp. Alpin. Hiſt. Ægypt. tom. i. *p.* 223. *tab.* 12.

Camelus unico in dorſo gibbo, ſeu dromedarius; camel or
dromedary; *Raii Synopſ. Quad. p.* 143. *Klein. Quad. p.* 42.

Camel called *Hugiun*; *Leo, Afric. p.* 338.

Camelus dromedarius, topho dorſi unico; *Linn. Syſt. Nat.
p.* 90.

Chameau; *Mem. pour ſervir à l'Hiſt. des Animaux, part.* i. *p.* 69.
pl. 7.

Camel with one bunch; *Pocock's Travels, vol.* i. *p.* 207.
Shaw's Travels, p. 239. *Ruſſel's Hiſt. of Aleppo, p.* 56. *Plaiſted's
Journal, p.* 82.

of

of them intermix and produce; and the individuals which proceed from this croffing of the races, are the moft vigorous, and preferred to all others *. Thefe mongrels form a fecondary race, which multiply among themfelves, and likewife mix with the primary races. Hence, in this fpecies, as well as in thofe of other domeftic animals, there are many varieties, the moft general of which proceed from the influence of

* The Perfians have feveral kinds of camels. Thofe with two bunches they call *Bughur*, and thofe with one, *Schuttur*. Of thefe laft there are four kinds. Thofe called, from their excellence, *Ner*, that is *male*, which proceed from a mixture of a dromedary, or a camel with two bunches, and a female with one bunch, which is called *Maje*, are never allowed to be covered by others, and are fo highly efteemed, that fome of them fell for a hundred crowns. They carry loads of nine or ten hundred pounds, and are moft indefatigable. When in feafon, they eat little, foam at the mouth, grow enraged, and bite. To prevent them from hurting their keepers, the Perfians put muzzles on their mouths, which are called *agrab*. The camels which proceed from this kind degenerate much, and become weak and indolent. It is for this reafon that they are called *Jurda Kaidem* by the Turks, and fell at thirty or forty crowns only.

The third kind, called *Lohk*, are not fo good as the *Bughur*. When in feafon, they foam not, but pufh out from under their throat a red bladder, which they again retract with their breath, raife their heads, and often fwell. They fell at fixty crowns, and are by no means fo ftrong as the other kinds. Hence the Perfians, when they fpeak of a valiant man, fay that he is a *Ner*, and a poltroon is called *Lohk*. A fourth kind are called by the Perfians *Schuturi Baad*, and by the Turks *Jeldovefi*, that is, *Wind camels*. They are fmaller, but more fprightly than the other kinds; for, inftead of walking, like ordinary camels, they trot and gallop as well as horfes; *Voyage d'Olearius, tom.* i. *p.* 550.

different

different climates. Ariſtotle * has marked the
two principal races with much propriety; the
firſt, or the one with two bunches, under the
name of the *Bactrian camel* †, and the ſecond
under that of the *Arabian camel.* The firſt are
called *Turkiſh camels* ‡, and the other *Arabian
camels.* This diſtinction ſtill ſubſiſts; but, as
many parts of Aſia and Africa are now diſco-

* Camelus proprium inter cæteros quadrupedes habet in
dorſo, quod tuber appellant, ſed ita ut Bactrianæ ab Arabiis
differant; alteris enim bina, alteris ſingula tubera habentur;
Ariſt. Hiſt. Anim. lib. ii. *cap.* 1.—Theodore Gaza, whoſe tranſlation I have uniformly followed when I quote from Ariſtotle, appears to have rendered this paſſage in an ambiguous manner; *Alteris enim bina, alteris ſingula tubera habentur,* ſignifies only that ſome have two, and others but one bunch;
while the Greek text mentions expreſsly, that the Arabian
camels have but one, and the Bactrian camels two bunches.
Pliny likewiſe, who, in this article, as well as in many others,
copies Ariſtotle, has tranſlated this paſſage much better than
Gaza; *Cameli Bactriani et Arabici differunt, quod illi bina habent
tubera in dorſo, hi ſingula;* Plin. Hiſt. Nat. lib. viii. cap. 18.

† Bactriana is a province of Aſia, which now includes
Turkeſtan, the country of the Uſbecks, &c.

‡ We went to Mount Sinai upon camels, becauſe there is
no water on this road, and other animals cannot travel without drinking. . . . But the Arabian camels, which are ſmall,
and different from thoſe of Cairo, who come from Sour, and
other places, can travel three or four days without drink. . .
They travel from Cairo to Jeruſalem, not only upon theſe
ſmall Arabian camels, but upon a larger kind, which are called
Turkiſh camels; Voyage de Pietro della Valle, tom. i. *p.* 360. *et* 408.
— In Barbary, the dromedary is called *Maihari;* and is
not ſo common in Barbary as in the Levant. . . . . This
ſpecies differs from the ordinary camel, by having a rounder
and handſomer body, and only one ſmall bunch on the back;
Shaw's Travels.

vered,

vered, which were unknown to the ancients, it appears, that the dromedary is incomparably more numerous, and more generally diffused, than the camel. The latter is found only in Turkeſtan*, and ſome other places of the Levant †. But, in Arabia, the dromedary is more common than any other beaſt of burden. It is likewiſe very numerous in all the northern parts of Africa ‡, from the Mediterranean ſea to the river Niger ‖. It is alſo found in

* The Academy having ordered the miſſioners ſent to China, in quality of King's mathematicians, to obtain information concerning ſome particulars in the hiſtory of the camel, the Perſian ambaſſador gave the following anſwers to the queries put to him by M. Conſtance: 1. That, in Perſia, there were camels with two bunches on the back; but that they came originally from Turkeſtan, and belong to the race of thoſe which the King of the Moors had brought from that country, the only known part of Aſia where this kind exiſts; and that thoſe camels were highly eſteemed in Perſia, becauſe their two bunches render them more proper for carriages. 2. That theſe bunches are not formed by a curvature of the back-bone, which is here as low as in any other part, but are only excreſcences of a glandulous ſubſtance, ſimilar to that which compoſes the udders of other animals; and that the interior bunch is about ſix inches high, and the poſterior an inch lower; *Mem. pour ſervir a l'Hiſt. des Animaux, part.* i. *p.* 80.

† The camels of the Calmuck Tartars are pretty large and ſtrong; but they have all two bunches; *Relation de la Grande Tartarie, p.* 267.

‡ Camelus animal blandum ac domeſticum maxima copia in Africa invenitur, præſertim in deſertis Lybiæ, Numidiæ, et Barbariæ; *Leon. Afric. Deſcript. Africæ, vol.* ii. *p.* 748.

‖ The Moors have numerous flocks of camels upon the banks of the Niger; *Voyage au Senegal, par M. Adanſon, p.* 36.

Egypt,

Egypt*, in Perfia, in South Tartary †, and in the northern parts of India. Thus the dromedary occupies immenfe territories, and the camel is confined within narrow limits. The firft inhabits dry and hot regions, the fecond, countries which are lefs dry and more temperate; and the whole fpecies, including both varieties, feems to be limited to a zone of three or four hundred leagues in breadth, extending from Mauritania to China; for, on either fide of this zone, it has no exiftence. This animal, though a native of warm climates, dreads thofe which are exceffively hot. The fpecies terminates where that of the elephant commences; and it can neither fubfift under the burning heat of the Torrid Zone, nor under the mild air of the Temperate. It feems to be an original native of Arabia‡;

for

---

* Audio vero in Ægypto longe plura quam quater centum millia camelorum vivere; *Profp. Alp. Hift. Nat. Egypt. part.* i. *pag.* 226.

† Delectantur etiam Tartari Buratfkoi re pecuaria, maxime camelis, quorum ibi magna copia eft, unde complures a caravannis ad Sinam tendentibus redimuntur, ita ut optimus camelus duodecim vel ad fummum quindecim rubelis haberi poffit; *Noviffima Sinica hiftoriam noftri temporis illuftratura, &c. edente G. G. L. pag.* 166.——Tartary abounds in cattle, and particularly in horfes and camels; *Voyage Hiftorique de l'Europe, tom.* vii. *p.* 204.

‡ Arabia is the native country of camels; for, though they are found in all places into which they have been carried, and even multiply in thefe places; yet there is no part of the earth where they are equally numerous; *Voyage du P. Philippe, p.* 369.——Tanta apud Arabes eft camelorum copia,

ut

for this is not only the country where they are
moft numerous, but where they thrive beft.
Arabia is the drieft country in the world, and
where water is moft rare. The camel is the moft
fober of all animals, and can pafs feveral days
without drink *. The foil is almoft every where
dry and fandy. The feet of the camel are adapted
for walking on fands, and the animal cannot
fupport itfelf on moift and flippery ground †.
                                                  This

ut eorum pauperrimus decem ad minus camelos habeat?
Multique funt quorum quifque quatuor centum ac mille etiam
numerare poffit ; *Profp. Alpin. Hift. Egypt. pag.* 226.

  * Without the affiftance of camels, it would be extremely
difficult to traverfe the vaft deferts of Solyma, where neither
bird, wild beaft, herbage, nor even a mufhroom can be found,
and where nothing is to be feen but mountains of fand, rocks,
and camel's bones. Thefe animals fometimes pafs fix or feven
days without drinking, which I fhould never have believed,
if I had not feen the fact verified; *Relation du Voyage de Poncet
et Ethiopie*; *Lettres Edifiantes, recueil* iv. *p.* 259.———In going
from Aleppo to Ifpahan, by the great defert, we travelled
near fix days without finding water, which, added to the
three preceding, make the nine days I formerly mentioned,
during which our camels had no drink; *Voyage de Tavernier,
tom.* i. *p.* 202.

  † Camels cannot walk upon fat or flippery ground. They
are only fit for fandy places; *Voyage de Jean Ovington, tom.* i.
p. 222.—There are chiefly two kinds of camels, the one proper
for warm countries, the other for cold. The camels of very
warm countries, as thofe which come from Ormus, and as
far as Ifpahan, cannot walk when the ground is moift and
flippery; for, by the fpreading of their hind legs, they are in
danger of tearing open their bellies: They are fmall, and
carry loads of only fix or feven hundred pounds. . . . . . The
camels of colder countries, as thofe from Tauris to Conftan-
                                                  tinople,

This foil produces no pasture; the ox is also wanting; and the camel supplies his place.

When we consider the nature and structure of these animals, we cannot be deceived with regard to their native country, which must be suited to their frame and temperament, especially when these are not modified by the influence of other climates. In vain have attempts been made to multiply them in Spain*; in vain have they been transported to America. They have neither succeeded in the one country nor in the other; and, in the East Indies, they are not found beyond Surat and Ormus. We mean not to say absolutely, that they cannot subsist and produce in India, Spain, and America, and even in colder countries, as those of France, Germany, &c. †. By keeping them, during the winter, in warm stables; by feeding them well, and treating them with care; by not employing them in labour, and not allowing them to go out for

tinople, are large, and commonly carry burdens of one thousand pounds. They draw themselves out of miry ground; but, when the earth is fat and slippery, they are obliged to go, sometimes to the number of a hundred, at each other's sides, in order to pass over it; *Voyage de Tavernier, tom.* i. *p.* 161.

* Camels are frequently seen in Spain. They are sent, by the governours of places, from the frontiers of Africa. But they never live long there; because the country is too cold for them; *L'Afrique de Marmol, tom.* i. *p.* 50.

† M. le Marquis de Montmirail informs me, that he was assured that the King of Poland had, in the neighbourhood of Dresden, camels and dromedaries which multiplied.

exercise,

exercife, but in fine weather, their lives might
be preferved, and we might even hope to fee
them produce. But fuch productions are rare
and feeble; and the parents themfelves are weak
and languid. In thefe climates, therefore, they
lofe all their value, and, inftead of being ufeful,
they coft their owners much expence in the
rearing. But, in their native country, they conftitute the fole riches of their mafters *. The
Arabians regard the camel as a prefent from heaven, a facred animal †, without whofe affiftance
they could neither fubfift, carry on trade, nor
travel. Camel's milk is the common food of the
Arabians. They alfo eat its flefh that of the
young camel being reckoned highly favoury. Of
the hair of thofe animals, which is fine and foft,
and which is completely renewed every year ‡,
                                                  the

* Ex camelis Arabes divitias ac poffeffiones æftimant; et
fi quando de divitiis principis aut nobilis cujufdam fermo fiat,
poffidere aiunt tot camelorum, non aureorum, millia; *Leon.
Afric. Defcript. Africæ, vol.* ii. *p.* 748.

† Camelos, quibus Arabia maxime abundat, animalia fancta
ii appellant, ex infigni commodo quod ex ipfis indigenæ acci-
piunt; *Prof. Alpin. Hift. Egypt. pars* i. *p.* 225.

‡ In fpring, the hair of the camel falls off fo entirely, that
he refembles a fcalded hog. He is then fmeared all over with
pitch, to defend him from the flies. The hair of the camel is
a fleece fuperior to that of any other domeftic animal. In
thefe countries, it is made into very fine ftuffs, and, in Europe,
hats are made of it, by mixing it with beaver's hair; *Voyage de
Chardin, tom.* ii. *p.* 28.—In the fpring, the whole hair falls from
the camel in lefs than three days. The fkin is completely
naked, and then the flies become extremely troublefome,
                                                  againft

the Arabians make stuffs for clothes, and other furniture. With their camels, they not only want nothing, but have nothing to fear *. In one day, they can perform a journey of fifty leagues into the desert, which cuts off every approach from their enemies. All the armies of the world would perish in pursuit of a troop of Arabs. Hence they never submit, unless from choice, to any power. Figure to yourselves a country without verdure, and without water, a burning sun, an air always parched, sandy plains, mountains still more adust, which the eye runs over without perceiving a single animated being; a dead earth, perpetually tossed with the winds, and presenting nothing but bones, scattered flints, rocks perpendicular or overturned; a desert totally void, where the traveller never breathes under a shade, where nothing accompanies him, nothing recalls the idea of animated nature; absolute solitude,

---

against which there is no other remedy but besmearing the whole body with pitch; *Voyage de Tavernier*, tom. i. p. 162.— Præter alia emolumenta quæ ex camelis capiunt, vestes quoque et tentoria ex iis habent; ex eorum enim pilis multa fiunt, maxime vero pannus, quo et principes oblectantur; *Prosp. Alpin. Hist. Ægypt. pars* i. p. 226.

* The camels constitute the wealth, the safety, and the strength of the Arabs; for, by means of their camels, they carry all their effects into the deserts, where they have nothing to fear from the invasion of enemies; *L'Afrique d'Ogilvy, p.* 12.—Qui porro camelos possident Arabes steriliter vivunt ac libere, utpote cum quibus in desertis agere possint; ad quæ, propter ariditatem, nec reges, nec principes pervenire valent; *Leon. Afric. Descript. Africæ, vol.* ii. *p.* 749.

more

more dreadful than that of the deepeſt foreſts; for to man, trees are, at leaſt, viſible objects: More ſolitary and naked, more loſt in an unlimited void, he every where beholds ſpace ſurrounding him as a tomb: The light of the day, more diſmal than the darkneſs of night, ſerves only to give him a clearer view of his own wretchedneſs and impotence, and to conceal from his view the barriers of the void, by extending around him that immenſe abyſs which ſeparates him from the habitable parts of the earth; an abyſs, which, in vain, he ſhould attempt to traverſe; for hunger, thirſt, and ſcorching heat, haunt every moment that remains to him between deſpair and death.

The Arab, however, by the aſſiſtance of his camel, has learned to ſurmount, and even to appropriate, theſe frightful intervals of Nature. They ſerve him for an aſylum, they ſecure his repoſe, and maintain his independence. But man never uſes any thing without abuſe? This ſame free, independent, tranquil, and even rich Arab, inſtead of regarding his deſerts as the ramparts of his liberty, pollutes them with his crimes. He traverſes them to carry off ſlaves and gold from the adjacent nations. He employs them for perpetrating his robberies, which unluckily he enjoys more than his liberty; for his enterpriſes are almoſt always ſucceſsful. Notwithſtanding the vigilance of his neighbours, and the ſuperiority of their ſtrength, he eſcapes their purſuit, fuit, and carries off, with impunity, all that he ravages from them. An Arab, who gives himself up to this kind of terreſtrial piracy, is early accuſtomed to the fatigues of travelling, to want of ſleep, and to endure hunger, thirſt, and heat. With the ſame view, he inſtructs, rears, and exercifes his camels. A few days after their birth *, he folds their limbs under their belly, forces them to remain on the ground, and, in this ſituation, loads them with a pretty heavy weight, which is never removed but for the purpofe of replacing a greater. Inſtead of allowing them to feed at pleaſure, and to drink when they are dry, he begins with regulating their meals, and makes them gradually travel long journeys, diminiſhing, at the ſame time, the quantity of their aliment. When they acquire ſome ſtrength, they are trained to the courſe. He excites their emulation by the example of horſes, and, in time, renders them equally ſwift, and more robuſt †.

In

* The young camels, ſoon after birth, are obliged to lie on the ground, with their four legs folded under their belly, for fifteen or twenty days, in order to inure them to this poſture They never lie in another poſition. To learn them temperance and abſtinence, they are then allowed very little milk; and, by this practice, they are trained to continue eight or ten days without drinking: And, as to victuals, it is aſtoniſhing that ſo large an animal ſhould live on ſo ſmall a quantity of food; *Voyage de Chardin, tom.* ii. *p.* 28.

† The dromedary is particularly remarkable for ſwiftneſs. The Arabs ſay, that he can travel as far in one day as one of their beſt horſes can do in eight or ten. The *Bekb*, who conducted us to Mount Sinai, was mounted on one of theſe camels,

In fine, after he is certain of the ftrength, fleet-nefs, and fobriety of his camels, he loads them both with his own and their food, fets off with them, arrives unperceived at the confines of the defert, robs the firft paffengers he meets, pillages the folitary houfes, loads his camels with the booty, and, if purfued, he is obliged to accelerate his retreat. It is on thefe occafions that he un-folds his own talents and thofe of the camels. He mounts one of the fleeteft *, conducts the troop, and makes them travel night and day, without almoft either ftopping, eating, or drink-ing, and, in this manner, he eafily performs a journey of three hundred leagues in eight days †.

During

and often amufed us with the great fleetnefs of the animal on which he rode. He quitted our caravan to reconnoitre an-other, which was fo diftant, that we could hardly perceive it, and returned to us in lefs than a quarter of an hour; *Shaw's Travels.*—A kind of camels are reared in Arabia for the purpofes of the courfe. They trot fo fleetly, that a horfe cannot keep up with them, unlefs at a gallop; *Voyage de Chardin, tom.* ii. *p.* 28.

* The dromedaries are fo fleet that they march thirty-five or forty leagues a day, and continue at this rate for eight or ten days through the defert, and eat extremely little. They are ufed by the Arabs of Numidia and the Lybian Africans as poft horfes, when a long journey is neceffary; they likewife mount thefe animals in the time of combat; *L'Afrique de Marmol, tom.* i. *p.* 49.—The true dromedary is much lighter and fwifter than the other camels; he can travel a hundred miles in a day, and continue at the fame rate, acrofs the deferts, with very little food, for feven or eight days; *L'Afrique d'Ogilby, p.* 12.

† The dromedaries are fmaller, more flender, and fleeter than

During this period of motion and fatigue, his camels are perpetually loaded, and he allows them, each day, one hour only for repofe, and a ball of pafte. They often run in this manner nine or ten days, without finding water*; and when, by chance, there is a pool at fome diftance, they fcent the water half a league off †. Thirft makes them double their pace, and they drink

---

than the other camels, and are ufed only for carrying men. They have a fine foft trot, and eafily accomplifh forty leagues a-day. The rider has only to keep a firm feat; and fome people, for fear of falling, are tied on; *Relation de Thevenot, tom.* i. *p.* 312.

* The camel can difpenfe with drinking during four or five days. A fmall quantity of beans and barley, or rather fome morfels of pafte made of flour, are fufficient for his daily nourifhment. This fact I often experienced in my journey to Mount Sinai. Though each of our camels carried feven quintals, we travelled ten, and fometimes fifteen hours a day, at the rate of two and a half miles every hour; *Shaw's Travels.* —Adeo fitim cameli tolerant, ut potu abfque incommodo diebus quindecim abftinere poffint. Nociturus alioquin fi camelarius triduo abfoluto equam illis porrigat, quod fingulis quinis aut novenis diebus confueto more potentur vel urgente neceffitate quindenis; *Leon. Afric. Defcript. Africæ, vol.* ii. *p.* 749. —The patience with which the camels fuffer thirft is truly admirable. The laft time I travelled the deferts, which the caravan did not clear in lefs than fixty-five days, our camels were once nine days without drink; becaufe, during all this time, we found no water; *Voyage de Tavernier, tom.* i. *p.* 162.

† We arrived at a hilly country: At the foot of the hills were large pools. Our camels, which had paffed nine days without drink, fmelled the water at the diftance of half a league. They inftantly began their hard trot, which is their mode of running, and, entering the pools in troops, they firft troubled the water, &c. *Tavernier, tom.* i. *p.* 202.

as

as much at once as ferves them for the time that is paft, and as much to come; for their journeys often laft feveral weeks, and their abftinence continues an equal time.

In Turkey, Perfia, Arabia, Egypt, Barbary, &c. all the articles of merchandize are carried by camels *. Of all carriages, it is the cheapeft and moft expeditious. The merchants and other paffengers unite in a caravan, to prevent the infults and robberies of the Arabs. Thefe caravans are often very numerous, and are always compofed of more camels than men. Each camel is loaded in proportion to his ftrength; and, when overloaded †, he refufes to march, and continues lying till his burden is lightened. The large camels generally carry a thoufand, or

---

* The camels are very commodious for carrying baggage and merchandize at a fmall expence.———Their fteps, as well as their journeys, are regulated.———Their food is cheap; for they live on thiftles, nettles, &c.———They fuffer drought two or three days; *Voyage d'Olearius, tom.* i. *p.* 552.

† When about to be loaded, at the command of their conductor they inftantly bend their knees. If any of them difobey, they are immediately ftruck with a ftick, or their necks are pulled down; and then, as if conftrained, and complaining in their own manner, they bend their knees, put their bellies on the earth, and remain in this pofture till they are loaded and defired to rife. This is the origin of thofe large callofities on the parts of their bellies, limbs, and knees, which reft on the ground. If over-burdened, they give repeated blows with their heads to the perfon who oppreffes them, and fet up lamentable cries. Their ordinary load is double that which the ftrongeft mule can carry; *Voyage du P. Philippe, p.* 369.

even

even twelve hundred * pounds weight, and the
fmalleft from fix to feven hundred †. In thefe
commercial travels, their march is not haftened:
As the route is often feven or eight hundred
leagues, their motions and journeys are regulated. They walk only, and perform about
from ten to twelve leagues each day. Every
night they are unloaded, and allowed to pafture
at freedom. When in a rich country or fertile meadow, they eat, in lefs than an hour ‡,
as much as ferves them to ruminate the whole
night, and to nourifh them during twenty-four
hours. But they feldom meet with fuch paf-

* Some camels can carry loads of fifteen hundred pounds.
But they are never burdened in this manner, unlefs when the
merchants approach the places where the impofts on goods are
levied, which they mean partly to evade, by laying as much on
one camel as was carried before by two. But, with this
great load, they travel not above two or three leagues a day;
Voyage de Tavernier, tom. ii. *p.* 335.

† In the Eaft, the camel is called *a land fhip*, on account
of the great load he carries, which, for large camels, is generally twelve or thirteen hundred pounds; for there are two
kinds, *the northern* and *the fouthern*, as they are denominated
by the Perfians. The latter, who travel only from the Perfic
Gulf to Ifpahan, are much fmaller than the others, and carry
only about feven hundred pounds; but they bring as much
if not more profit to their mafters, becaufe their food hardly
cofts any thing. They march loaded in this manner, pafturing
along the road, without bridle or halter; *Voyage de Chardin,*
tom. ii. *p.* 27.

‡ Victum cameli parciffimum, exiguique fumptus ferunt, et
magnis laboribus robuftiffime refiftunt. ———— Nullum animal illius
molis citius comedit; *Profp. Alpin. Hift. Egypt. p.* 225.

tures;

tures; neither is this delicate food neceffary for them. They even feem to prefer wormwood, thiftles*, nettles, broom, caffia †, and other prickly vegetables to the fofteft herbage. As long as they find plants to browfe, they eafily difpenfe with drink ‡.

Befides, this facility of abftaining long from drink proceeds not from habit alone, but is rather an effect of their ftructure. Independent of the four ftomachs, which are common to ruminating animals, the camels have a fifth bag, which ferves them as a refervoir for water. This fifth ftomach is peculiar to the camel. It is fo large as to contain a vaft quantity of water, where it remains without corrupting, or mixing with the other aliments. When the animal is preffed with thirft, and has occafion for water to macerate his dry food in ruminating, he makes part of this water mount into his

---

* When the camels are unloaded, they are allowed to go in queft of briars or brambles.———Though the camel is a large animal, he eats little, and is content with what he finds. He fearches particularly for thiftles, of which he is very fond; *Voyage de Tavernier, tom.* i, *p.* 162.

† Cameli pafcentes fpinam in Egypto acutam, Arabicamque etiam vocatam Acaciam, in Arabia Petrea, atque juncum odoratum in Arabia deferta, ubivis abfynthi fpecies aliafque herbas et virgulta fpinofa quæ in defertis reperiuntur; *Profp. Alpin. Hift. Egypt. part.* i. *p.* 226.

‡ When the camel is loaded, he lies on his belly, and never allows a greater burden to be put on his back than he is able to carry. If he finds herbage to eat, he can pafs feveral days without drink; *L'Afrique d'Ogilby, p.* 12.

paunch,

paunch, or even as high as the œfophagus, by a fimple contraction of certain mufcles. It is by this fingular ftructure that the camel is enabled to pafs feveral days without drinking, and to take at a time a prodigious quantity of water, which remains in the refervoir pure and limpid, becaufe neither the liquors of the body, nor the juices of digeftion, can mix with it.

If we reflect on the diffimilarities in this animal from other quadrupeds, we cannot doubt that his nature has been confiderably changed by conftraint, flavery, and perpetual labour. Of all animals, the camel is the moft ancient, the completeft, and the moft laborious flave. He is the moft ancient flave, becaufe he inhabits thofe climates where men were firft polifhed. He is the moft complete flave, becaufe, in the other fpecies of domeftic animals, as the horfe, the dog, the ox, the fheep, the hog, &c. we ftill find individuals in a ftate of nature, and which have never fubmitted to men. But the whole fpecies of the camel is enflaved; for none of them exift in their primitive ftate of liberty and independence. Laftly, he is the moft laborious flave, becaufe he has never been nourifhed for pomp, like moft horfes, nor for amufement, like moft dogs, nor for the ufe of the table, like the ox, the hog, and the fheep; becaufe he has always been made a beaft of burden, whom men have never taken the trouble of yoking in machines, but have regarded the body of the animal as a

living

living carriage which they may load, or overload,
even during fleep; for, when hurried, the load
is fometimes not taken off, but he lies down to
fleep under it; with his legs folded *, and his
body refting on his ftomach.   Hence thefe animals perpetually bear the marks of fervitude and
pain.   Upon the under part of the breaft, there
is a large callofity as hard as horn, and fimilar
ones on the joints of the limbs.   Though thefe
callofities are found on all camels, they exhibit a
proof that they are not natural, but produced by
exceffive conftraint and painful labour; for they
are often filled with pus †. The breaft and legs,
therefore, are deformed by callofities; the back
is ftill more disfigured by one or two bunches.
The callofities, as well as the bunches, are perpetuated by generation.   As it is obvious, that
the firft deformity proceeds from the conftant
practice of forcing thefe animals, from their ear-
lieft age ‡, to lie on their ftomach, with their limbs
folded

---

* In the night, the camels fleep on their knees, and ruminate what they have eaten during the day; *Voyage du P. Philippe*,
p. 269.

† Having opened the callofities on the legs to examine their
ftructure, which is a medium between fat and ligament, we
found, in a fmall camel, that fome of them contained a collection
of thick pus. The callofity on the fternum was eight inches
long, fix broad, and two thick. In it likewife we found a great
deal of pus; *Mem. pour fervir à l'Hift. des Animaux, part.* i.
p. 74.

‡ As foon as the camel is brought forth, his four legs are
folded under his body. After which, he is covered with a
cloth, which hangs down to the ground, and on the borders
of

folded under the body, and, in this fituation, to bear both the weight of their own bodies, and that of the loads laid on their backs, we ought to prefume that the bunch or bunches have alfo originated from the unequal preffure of heavy burdens, which would naturally make the flefh, the fat, and the fkin, fwell; for thefe bunches are not offeous, but compofed of a flefhy fubftance fimilar to that of a cow's udder*. Hence the callofities and bunches fhould be equally regarded as deformities produced by continual labour and bodily conftraint; and, though at firft accidental and individual, they are now become permanent and common to the whole fpecies. We may likewife prefume, that the bag which contains the water, and is only an appendix to the paunch, has been produced by an unnatural extenfion of this vifcus. The animal, after fuffering thirft for a long time, by taking at once as much, and perhaps more water than the ftomach could eafily contain, this membrane would be gradually extended and dilated; in the fame manner as we have feen the ftomach of a fheep extend in proportion to the quantity of its aliment. In fheep fed with grain, the ftomach is very fmall;

---

of which a quantity of ftones are laid, to prevent him from rifing, and in this pofition he remains fifteen or twenty days. He is ferved with milk but very fparingly, in order to accuftom him to drink little; *Voyage de Tavernier, tom.* i. *p.* 161.

* The flefh of the camel is infipid, efpecially that of the bunch, the tafte of which refembles that of a fat cow's udder; *L'Afrique de Marmol, tom.* i. *p.* 50.

but

but becomes very large in thofe fed with herbage alone.

Thefe conjectures would be either fully confirmed or deftroyed, if we had wild camels to compare with the domeftic. But thefe animals no where exift in a natural ftate, or, if they do, no man has obferved or defcribed them. We ought to fuppofe, therefore, that every thing good and beautiful belongs to Nature, and that whatever is defective and deformed in thefe animals proceeds from the labour and flavery impofed on them by the empire of man. Thefe inoffenfive creatures muft fuffer much; for they utter the moft lamentable cries, efpecially when overloaded. But, though perpetually oppreffed, their fortitude is equal to their docility. At the firft fignal*, they bend their knees and lie down to be loaded †, which faves their conductor the trouble

* The camels are fo obedient to their mafters, that, when he wants to load or unload them, by a fingle word or fignal, they inftantly lie down on their bellies. Their food is fcanty, and their labour great; *Cofmog. du Levant, par Thevet, p.* 74.— They are accuftomed to lie down to be loaded, by having their legs folded under them when very young; and their obedience is fo prompt as to excite admiration. Whenever the caravan arrives at the place of encampment, all the camels which belong to one mafter range themfelves fpontaneoufly in a circular form, and lie down on their four legs; fo that, by loofing a cord which binds the bales, they gently fall down on each fide of the animal. When the time of loading arrives, the camels come and lie down between the bales, and, after they are fixed, rife foftly with their load. This exercife they perform in a fhort time, and without the fmalleft trouble or noife; *Voyage de Tavernier, tom.* i. *p.* 160.

† The camels, when about to be loaded, lie down on their

four

trouble of raifing the goods to a great height. As foon as they are loaded, they rife fpontaneoufly, and without any affiftance. One of them is mounted by their conductor, who goes before, and regulates the march of all the followers. They require neither whip no fpur. But, when they begin to be tired, their courage is fupported, or rather their fatigue is charmed, by finging, or by the found of fome inftrument*. Their conductors relieve each other in finging ; and, when they want to prolong the journey†, they give the

---

four legs, and then rife with their burden ; *Voyage de la Boulaie-le-Gouz, p.* 255.—The camels lie down to be loaded or unloaded, and rife when defired ; *Relation de Thevenot, tom.* i. *p.* 312.

* The camels rejoice at the harmonious found of the voice, or of fome inftrument. . . . . The Arabs ufe timbrels, becaufe whipping does not make the animals advance. But mufic, and particularly that of the human voice, animates and gives them coorage ; *Voyage d'Olearius, tom.* i. *p.* 552.— When their conductor wants to make his camels perform extraordinary journeys, inftead of chaftifing, he encourages them with a fong ; and, though they had formerly ftopt, and refufed to proceed farther, they now go on cheerfully, and quicker than a horfe when pufhed with the fpur ; *L'Afrique de Marmol, tom.* i. *p.* 47.—The mafter conducts his camels by finging, and, from time to time, blowing his whiftle. The more he fings, and the louder he blows, the animals march the quicker ; and, when he ceafes to fing, they ftop. Their conductors relieve each other by finging alternately, &c. *Voyage de Tavernier, tom.* i. *p.* 163.

† It is remarkable, that the camels learn to march by a kind of finging ; for they proceed quickly or flowly, according to the found of the voice. In the fame manner, when their mafters want an extraordinary journey performed, they know

the animals but one hour's reft; after which, refuming their fong, they proceed on their march for feveral hours more, and the finging is continued till they arrive at another refting-place, when the camels again lie down; and their loads, by unloofing the ropes, are allowed to glide off on each fide of the animals. Thus they fleep on their bellies in the middle of their baggage, which, next morning, is fixed on their backs with equal quicknefs and facility as it had been detached the evening before.

The callofities and tumours on the breaft and legs, the contufions and wounds of the fkin, the complete falling off of the hair, hunger, thirft, and meagernefs, are not the only inconveniences to which thefe animals are fubjected : To fuffer all thefe evils they are prepared by caftration, which is a misfortune greater than any other they are obliged to undergo. One male is only left for eight or ten females*; and the labouring camels are generally geldings. They are unqueftionably weaker than unmutilated males; but they are more tractable, and at all feafons ready for fer-vice. While the former are not only unma-nageable, but almoft furious†, during the rut-

ting

know the tunes which the animals love beft to hear; *Voyage de Chardin, tom.* ii. *p.* 28.

* The Africans geld all their camels which are deftined to carry burdens, and only one entire male is left for ten females; *L'Afrique de Marmol, tom.* i. *p.* 48.

† In the rutting feafon, the camels are extremely trouble-fome. They fret and foam, and bite every perfon who ap-proaches

ting feafon, which lafts forty days *, and returns
annually in the fpring †. It is then faid, that
they foam continually, and that one or two red
veficles, as large as a hog's bladder, iffue from
their mouths ‡. In this feafon, they eat little,
attack and bite animals, and even their own maf-

proaches them, and for that reafon they are muzzled; *Relation de Thevenot, tom.* i. *p.* 222.—When the camels are in feafon,
thofe who have the charge of them are obliged to muzzle
them, and to be much on their guard; for the animals are
mifchievous, and even furious; *Voyage de Jean Ovington, tom.* i.
p. 222.

* The camels, in the feafon of love, are dangerous. This
feafon continues forty days, and, when paft, they refume their
ordinary mildnefs; *L'Afrique de Marmol, tom.* i. *p.* 49.

† The male camels, which, in all other feafons, are extremely gentle and tractable, become furious in the fpring,
which is the time of their copulating. Like the cats, the
camels generally perform this operation during the night.
The fheath of their penis then lengthens, as happens to all
animals which lie much on their bellies. At all other times,
it is more contracted and inclined backward, that they may
difcharge their urine with more eafe; *Shaw's Travels.*—In
the month of February, the camels come in feafon, and the
males are fo furious that they foam inceffantly at the mouth:
Voyage de la Boulaie-le-Goux, p. 256.

‡ When the camel is in feafon, he continues forty days without eating or drinking; and he is then fo furious, that, unlefs
prevented, he bites every perfon who comes near him. Where-
ever he bites, he carries off the piece; and from his mouth
there iffues a white foam, accompanied with two bladders,
which are large, and blown up like the bladder of a hog;
Voyage de Tavernier, tom. i. *p.* 161.—The camels, when in feafon,
live forty-two days without food; *Relat. de Thevenot, tom.* ii.
p. 222.— ' Veneris furore diebus quadraginta permanent famis
' patientes;' *Leon. Afric. vol.* ii. *p.* 748.—In the rutting feafon,
which lafts five or fix weeks, the camel eats much lefs than at any
other time; *Voyage de Chardin, tom.* ii. *p.* 28.

ters,

ters, to whom, at all other times, they are very submissive. Their mode of copulating differs from that of all other quadrupeds; for the female, instead of standing, lies down on her knees, and receives the male in the same position that she reposes, or is loaded *. This posture, to which the animals are early accustomed, becomes natural, since they assume it spontaneously in coition. The time of gestation is near twelve months †, and, like all large quadrupeds, the females bring forth only one at a birth. Her milk is copious and thick; and, when mixed with a large quantity of water, affords an excellent nourishment to men. The females are not obliged to labour, but are allowed to pasture and

---

* When the camels copulate, the female lies down in the same manner as when she is about to be loaded. Some of them go thirteen months with young; *Relation de Thevenot, tom.* ii. *p.* 23.—The female receives the male lying on her belly; *Voyage de Jean Ovington, p.* 223.—It is remarkable, that, when these animals copulate, the females lie on their bellies in the same manner as when they are loading. The time of their gestation is from eleven to twelve months; *Voyage de Chardin, tom.* ii. *p.* 28.—It is true, that the females go with young twelve months: But those who assert, that, during the time of coition, the male turns his crupper to the female, are deceived. This error proceeds from the circumstance of his discharging his urine backward, by placing the penis between the two hind legs. But, in copulating, the female lies on her belly, and receives the male in that position; *Voyage de Olearius, tom.* i. *p.* 553.

† The females go with young near twelve months, or from one spring to the following; *Shaw's Travels.*

produce

produce at full liberty*. The advantages derived from their produce and their milk †, are perhaps fuperior to what could be drawn from their work. In fome places, however, moft of the females are caftrated ‡, in order to fit them for labour; and it is alleged, that this operation, inftead of diminifhing, augments their ftrength, vigour, and plumpnefs. In general, the fatter camels are, they are the more capable of enduring great fatigue. Their bunches feem to proceed from a redundance of nourifhment; for, during long journeys, in which their conductor is obliged to hufband their food, and where they often fuffer much hunger and thirft, thefe bunches gradually diminifh, and become fo flat, that the place where they were is only perceptible by the length of the hair, which is always longer on thefe parts than on the reft of the back. The meagernefs of the body augments in proportion as the bunches decreafe. The Moors, who tranfport all articles of merchandife from Barbary and Numidia, as far as Æthiopia, fet out with their camels well laden, and when they are very fat

---

* Camelos fœminas intactas propter earum lac fervant, eas omni labore folutas vagari permittentes per loca fylveftria pafcentes, &c. *Profp. Alpin. Hift. Ægypt. part. i. p.* 226.

† Of the camel's milk, fmall cheefes are made, which are very dear, and highly efteemed among the Arabs; *Voyage du P. Philippe, p.* 370.

‡ The males are caftrated; and the females fometimes undergo a fimilar operation, which renders them ftronger and larger; *Wotton, p.* 82.

and vigorous*; and bring back the fame animals fo meager, that they commonly fell at a low price to the Arabs of the Defert, to be again fattened.

We are told by the ancients, that camels are in a condition for propagating at the age of three years †. This affertion is fufpicious; for, in three years, they have not acquired one half of their growth ‡. The penis of the male, like that of the bull, is very long, and very flender ‖. During erection, it ftretches forward, like that of all other quadrupeds; but, in its ordinary ftate, the fheath is drawn backward, and the urine is difcharged from between the hind legs §; fo

that

___

* When the camels begin their journey, it is neceffary that they fhould be fat; for, when this animal has travelled forty or fifty days without having barley to eat, the fat of the bunches begins to diminifh, then that of the belly, and, laftly, that of the limbs; after which he is no longer able to carry his load. . . . The caravans of Africa, which travel to Æthiopia, never think of bringing back their camels; becaufe they tranfport no heavy goods from that country; and, when they arrive, they fell their meager animals; *L'Afrique de Marmol, tom.* i. *p.* 49.—Camelos macilentos, dorfique vulneribus faucios, vili pretio Defertorum incolis faginandos divendunt; *Leon. Afric. Defcript. Africæ, vol.* ii. *p.* 479.

† Incipit mas et fœmina coire in trimatu; *Arift. Hift. Anim. lib.* v. *cap.* 14.

‡ In the year 1752, we faw a female camel of three years of age. . . . She had not acquired above one half of her ftature; *Hift. Nat. des Animaux, par Mef. Arnault de Nobleville et Salerne, tom.* iv. *p.* 126. *et* 130.

‖ Though the camel is a large animal, his penis, which is at leaft three feet long, is not thicker than the little finger of a man; *Voyage d'Olearius, tom.* i. *p.* 554.

§ The camels difcharge their urine backward. Perfons unacquainted

that both males and females urine in the same manner. The young camel sucks his mother twelve months *; but, when designed to be trained, in order to render him strong and robust in the chase, he is allowed to suck and pasture at freedom during the first years, and is not loaded, or made to perform any labour, till he is four years of age †. He generally lives forty and sometimes fifty years ‡, and the duration of his life is thus proportioned to the time of his growth. There is no foundation for what has been advanced by some authors, that he lives one hundred years.

By considering, under one point of view, all the qualities of this animal, and all the advantages derived from him, it must be acknowledged that he is the most useful creature which was ever subjected to the service of man. Gold and silk constitute not the true riches of the East. The camel is the genuine treasure of Asia. He is more valuable than the elephant; for he may be said to perform an equal quantity of labour at a

unacquainted with this circumstance, are liable to have their clothes foiled with urine; *Cosmographie du Levant, par Thevet, p. 74.*—The camel discharges his urine backward; *Voyage de Villamont, p.* 688.

* Separant prolem a parente anniculam; *Arist. Hist. Anim. lib.* vi. *cap.* 26.

† The camels called *Hegin* by the Africans, are the largest; but they are never loaded till they are four years old; *L'Afrique de Marmol, tom.* i. *p.* 48.

‡ Camelus vivit diu, plus enim quam quadraginta annos; *Arist. Hist. Anim. lib.* vi. *cap.* 26.

twentieth

twentieth part of the expence. Befides, the whole fpecies are fubjected to man, who propagates and multiplies them at pleafure. But he has no fuch dominion over the elephants, whom he cannot multiply, and the individuals of which he conquers with great labour and difficulty. The camel is not only more valuable than the elephant, but he is perhaps equal in utility to the horfe, the afs, and the ox, when their powers are united. He carries as much as two mules, though he eats as little, and feeds upon herbs equally coarfe, as the afs. The female furnifhes milk longer than the cow *. The flefh of young camels is as good and wholefome † as veal. Their hair is finer ‡ and more in requeft than the beft wool. Even their excrements are ufeful; for fal ammoniac is made of their urine, and their dung

---

* Parit in vere, et lac fuum ufque eo fervat quo jam conceperit; *Arif. Hif. Anim. lib.* vi. *cap.* 26.—Fœmina poft partum interpofito anno coit; *Id. lib.* v. *cap.* 14.

† The Africans and Arabs fill their pots and tubs with camels flefh, which is fried with greafe, and preferved in this manner during the whole year for their ordinary repafts; *L'Afrique de Marmol, tom.* i. *p.* 50.—Præter alia animalia quorum carnem in cibo plurimi faciunt, cameli in magno honore exiftunt; in Arabum principum caftris cameli plures unius anni aut biennes mactantur, quorum carnes avide comedunt, eafque odoratas, fuaves, atque optimas effe fatentur; *Prof. Alpin Hif. Ægypt. part.* i. *p.* 226.

‡ Socks are made of the camel's hair; and, in Perfia, fine girdles are made of it; fome of which, efpecially when white, coft two *tomans*, becaufe camels of this colour are rare; *Relation de Thevenot, tom.* ii. *p.* 223.

ferves

ferves for litter* to themfelves, as well as to horfes, with which people frequently travel † in countries where no hay or ftraw can be had. In fine, their dung makes excellent fewel.   It burns freely ‡, gives as clear and nearly as hot a flame as dry wood, and is of great ufe in the deferts, where not a tree is to be found, and where, for want of combuftible materials, fire is as fcarce as water §.

SUPPLEMENT.

HAVING little to add to what has been faid with regard to the camel and dromedary, we

* Their own dung ferves them for litter. For this purpofe it is expofed to the fun during the day, which dries it fo completely, that it crumbles down into a kind of powder, which is carefully fpread for litter; *Relation de Thevenot*, *p.* 73.

† The ancients tell us, without any foundation, that the camels have a great antipathy to horfes.   I could not learn, fays Olearius, why Pliny, after Xenophon, fhould advance, that camels have an averfion to horfes.   When I mentioned it to the Perfians, they laughed at me. . . .   There is hardly a caravan in which there are not camels, horfes, and affes, all lodged promifcuoufly together, without difcovering the fmalleft averfion or animofity againft each other; *Voyage d'Olearius,* *tom.* i. *p.* 553.

‡ The camels dung left by fome caravans, which had gone before us, generally ferved us for fewel; for, after being ex-pofed a day or two to the fun, it is eafily inflamed, and burns as clear and with as ftrong a heat as dried wood or charcoal; *Shaw's Travels.*

§ Hift. Nat. des Animaux, par Meff. Arnault de Nobleville et Salerne, tom. iv. p. 313.

fhall

fhall content ourfelves with quoting a paffage from M. Niebuhr's defcription of Arabia, p. 144.

'In the country of Iman, moft of the camels 'are of a middle ftature, and of a bright brown 'colour; fome of them, however, are large, 'heavy, and of a deep brown colour. When 'about to copulate, the female lies down on her 'legs; and her fore legs are tied, to pre- 'vent her from rifing. The male fits on his 'pofteriors like a dog, with his two fore feet 'refting on the ground. He feems to be colder 'and more indifferent than any other animal; 'for he often requires to be teazed a long time 'before the ardour of love is excited. When 'the operation is finifhed, the female is fuddenly 'raifed and forced to walk. The fame thing, 'it is faid, takes place in Mefopotamia, Natolia, 'and probably every where elfe.'

I remarked, that camels had been tranfported to the Canaries, Antilles, and Peru; but that they had not fucceeded in any part of the New World. Dr. Brown, in his Hiftory of Jamaica, affirms, that he faw dromedaries there, which the Englifh, in former times, had tranfported thither in great numbers, and that, though they ftill fubfift, they are of little ufe; becaufe the inhabitants are ig- norant of the proper manner of feeding and treating thefe animals. They, however, multi- ply in all thefe climates, and I doubt not but they might produce even in France. We fee from the Gazette of June 9, 1775, that M. Brin-
kenof

kenof having made a male and female camel copulate in his territories near Berlin, obtained, on the 24th day of March 1775, after a period of twelve months, a young camel, which was healthy and vigorous. This fact confirms what I faid concerning the production of dromedaries and camels at Drefden; and I am perfuaded, that, if we had Arabian fervants, who know how to manage thefe animals, we might foon render this fpecies domeftic, which I confider as the moft ufeful of all quadrupeds.

The BUFFALO *, the BONASUS †, the URUS ‡, the BISON ‖, and the ZEBU §.

THE buffalo, though now common in Greece, and domestic in Italy, was unknown both to the ancient Greeks and Romans; for he

has

---

* This animal has no name either in Greek or Latin. In modern Latin, *Bubalus, Buffelus*; in Italian, *Bufalo*; in German, *Buffel*; at Congo, according to Dapper, *Empakaſſa*, or *Pakaſſa*; and at the Cape of Good Hope, according to Kolbe, *Gu-Arobo*.

Bos bubalus, cornibus reſupinatis, intortis, antice planis; *Linn. Syſt. Nat. p.* 99.

Buffelus vel Bubalus vulgaris; *Johnſton de Quad p.* 38. *tab.* 20.

Buffle; *Kolbe Deſcript. du Cap de Bonne-Eſperance, tom.* iii. *p.* 25. *pl. at p.* 54. *fig.* 3. *Note,* I have here quoted Johnſton and Kolbe ſolely becauſe the figures they have given of the buffalo are not ſo bad as thoſe of other authors.

† Bonaſus quoque e ſylveſtribus cornigeris enumerandus eſt; *Ariſt. Hiſt. Anim. lib.* ii. *cap.* 1. . . . . Sunt nonnulla quæ ſimul biſulca ſunt, et jubam habeant et cornua bina, orbem inflexu mutuo colligentia, gerant, ut bonaſus, qui in Pœonia terra et Media gignitur; *Idem. Ibid.* . . . Bonaſus etiam interiora omnia bubus ſimilia continet; *Idem. lib.* ii. *cap.* 16. . . . Bonaſus gignitur in terra Pœonia, monte Meſſapo, qui Pœoniæ et Mediæ terræ collimitium eſt, et Monapios a Pœonibus appellatur, magnitudine tauri, ſed corpore quam bos latiore: Brevior enim et in latera auctior eſt. Tergus diſtentum ejus locum ſeptem accubantium occupat; cætera, forma bovis ſimilis eſt, niſi quod cervix jabata armorum tenus ut equi eſt,

ſed

Plate CLXVIII.

DROMEDARY.

Plate CLXIX.

A Bell Sculpt.

CAMEL.

has no name in the languages of thefe people. Even the word *Buffalo* indicates a foreign origin; for it has no root either in Greek or Latin. In a word, this animal is a native of the warm regions

fed villo molliore quam juba equina et compofitiore; color pili totius corporis flavus, juba prolixa et ad oculos ufque demiffa et frequenti colori inter cinereum et rufum, non qualis equorum quos partos vocant eft, fed villo fupra fqualidiore, fubter lanario. Nigri aut admodum rufi nulli funt. Vocem fimilem bovi emittunt; cornua adunca in fe flexa et pugnæ inutilia gerunt, magnitudine palmari, aut paulo majora, amplitudine non multo arêtiore quam ut fingula femi-fextarium capiant nigritie proba. Antiæ ad oculos ufque demiffæ, ita ut in latus potius quam ante pendeant. Caret fuperiore dentium ordine, ut bos et reliqua cornigera omnia. Crura hirfuta atque bifulca habet; caudam minorem quam pro fui corporis magnitudine, fimilem bubulæ. Excitat pulverem et fodit, ut taurus. Tergore contra iêtus prævalido eft. Carnem habet guftu fuavem: Quamobrem in ufu venandi eft. Cum percuffus eft, fugit, nifi defatigatus nufquam confiftit. Repugnat calcitrans et proluviem alvi vel ad quatuor paffus projiciens, quo præfidio facile utitur, et plerumque ita adurit, ut pili infeêtantium canum abfumantur. Sed tunc ea vis eft in fimo, cum bellua excitatur et metuit: Nam fi quiefcit, nihil urere proteft. Talis natura et fpecies hujus animalis eft. Tempore pariendi univerfi in montibus enituntur; fed priufquam fœtum edant, excremento alvi circiter eum locum in quo pariunt, fe quafi vallo circumdant et muniunt, largam enim quandam ejus excrementi copiam hæc bellua egerit; *Idem. lib. ix. cap.* 45. *Traduêtion de Theodore Gaza.*

Bos bonafus, cornibus in fe flexis, juba longiffima; *Linn. Syf. Nat. p.* 99.

‡ Urus; *Caii Jul. Cæf. Comment. lib.* vi. *c.* 5. The *aurochs* cf the Germans.

‖ Bifon jubatus Plinii et aliorum.

Bos bifon, cornibus divaricatis, juba longiffima, dorfo gibbofo; *Linn. Syf. Nat. p.* 99.

regions of Africa and the Indies, and was not transported and naturalized in Italy till about the seventh century. The moderns have improperly applied to him the name *bubalus*, which, indeed, denotes an African animal, but very different from the buffalo, as might be shewn from many passages of ancient authors. If the bubalus were to be referred to a particular genus, he should rather belong to that of the antilope than to that of the ox. Belon, having seen at Cairo a small ox with a bunch on its back, which differed from the buffalo and common ox, imagined that it might be the bubalus of the ancients. But, if he had carefully compared the characters given by the ancients to the bubalus, with those of this small ox, he would have discovered his error. Besides, we are enabled to speak of it with certainty ; for we have seen it alive ; and, after comparing the description we have given of it with that of Belon, we cannot hesitate in pronouncing it to be the same animal. It was exhibited at the fair of Paris in the year 1752, under the name of *zebu*, which we have adopted to denote this animal, because it is a particular race of the ox, and not a species of the buffalo or bubalus.

§ Petit bœuf d'Afrique ; *Obs. de Belon*, *p.* 118. where there is a figure of it.

Guabex in Barbary, according to Marmol ; *Bekker el Wasb*, that is *wild ox*, among the Arabs ; *Shaw's travels*.

Ariftotle,

Ariftotle, when treating of oxen, mentions not the common ox, but only remarks, that, among the *Arachotas* in India, there are wild oxen, which differ from the domeftic kind as much as the wild boar differs from the common hog. But, in another place, as quoted above in the notes, he gives a defcription of a wild ox in Pœonia, a province bordering on Macedonia, which he calls *bonafus*. Thus the common ox and the bonafus are the only animals of this kind mentioned by Ariftotle ; and, what is fingular, the bonafus, though fully defcribed by this great philofopher, was unknown to the Greek and Latin naturalifts who wrote after him ; for they have all copied him verbatim on this fubject : So that, at prefent, we only know the name *bonafus*, without being able to diftinguifh the animal to which it ought to be applied. If we confider, however, that Ariftotle, when fpeaking of the wild oxen of temperate climates, mentions the bonafus only, and that, on the contrary, the Greeks and Latins of after-ages take no notice of the bonafus, but point out thefe wild oxen under the appellations of *urus* and *bifon*, we will be induced to think that the bonafus muft be either the one or the other of thefe animals ; and, indeed, by comparing what Ariftotle has faid of the bonafus, with what we know concerning the bifon, it is probable that thefe two names denote the fame animal. The urus is firft mentioned by Julius Cæfar ; Pliny and Paufanias are alfo

the

the firſt who announced the biſon. From the
time of Pliny, the name *bubalus* has been indiſcriminately applied to the urus or the biſon.
Confuſion always augments as time advances.
To the bonaſus, bubalus, urus, and biſon, have
been added the *catopleba*, the *thur*, the bubalus
of Belon, the Scottiſh and American biſons; and
all our naturaliſts have made as many different
ſpecies as they have found names. Here truth is
ſo environed with darkneſs and error, that it will
be difficult to elucidate this part of natural hiſtory, which the contrariety of evidence, the variety
of deſcriptions, the multiplicity of denominations, the diverſity of places, the differences of
languages, and the obſcurity of time, ſeemed to
have condemned to perpetual darkneſs.

I ſhall firſt give my opinion on this ſubject,
and afterwards produce the proofs of it.

1. The animal we call *buffalo* was unknown
to the ancients.

2. The buffalo, now domeſtic in Europe, is
the ſame as the domeſtic or wild buffalo of India and Africa.

3. The *bubalus* of the Greeks and Romans
is neither the buffalo nor the ſmall ox of Belon,
but the animal deſcribed in the Memoires of
the *Barbary cow*, and which we call *bubalus*.

4. The ſmall ox of Belon, which we have
ſeen, and diſtinguiſhed by the name *zebu*, is
only a variety of the common ox.

5. The

5. The *bonasus* of Ariftotle is the fame animal with the bifon of the Latins.

6. The *bifon* of America might proceed originally from the European bifon.

7. The *urus* or *aurochs* is the fame animal with the common bull in its natural and wild ftate.

8. The bifon differs from the aurochs by accidental varieties only; and, confequently, it is, as well as the aurochs, of the fame fpecies with the domeftic ox; fo that I think I fhall be able to reduce all the denominations, and all the pretended fpecies both of ancient and modern naturalifts, to three, namely, the ox, the buffalo, and the bubalus.

Some of the propofitions I am about to lay down, will, I doubt not, appear to be mere affertions, particularly to thofe who have been accuftomed to ftudy the nomenclators of animals, or have attempted to give lifts of them. There are none of thefe affertions, however, which I am not able to prove. But before entering into critical difcuffions, each of which requires particular propofitions, I fhall relate the facts and remarks which led me into this refearch; and as they have fatisfied myfelf, I hope they will be equally fatisfactory to others.

Domeftic animals differ, in many refpects, from wild animals. Their nature, their fize, and their form are more fluctuating, and fubject to greater changes, efpecially in the external

I parts

parts of the body. The influence of climate, which acts powerfully upon all Nature, exerts itself with greater efficacy upon captive than upon free animals. Food prepared by the hand of man, which is often ill chosen, and sparingly administered, joined to the inclemency of a foreign sky, produce, in the progress of time, alterations so deeply engraven that they become constant, and are transmitted to posterity. I pretend not to maintain, that this general cause of change is so powerful as to alter essentially the nature of beings, whose constitution is so permanently fixed as that of animals. But it transforms and masks their external appearance; it annihilates some parts, and gives rise to others; it paints them vith various colours; and, by its action on the temperament of the body, it has an influence on the dispositions, instincts, and other internal qualities. The modification of a single part, in a machine so perfect as that of an animal body, is sufficient to make the whole feel the effects of the alteration. It is for this reason that our domestic animals differ nearly as much in dispositions and instincts, as in figure, from those which enjoy their natural state of freedom. Of this the sheep affords a striking example. This species, in its present condition, could not exist without the care and defence of man; it is also much changed, and very inferior to its original species. But, not to depart from our chief object, we see how many alterations the ox has undergone,

undergone, from the combined effects of climate, food, and management, in a wild, and in a domeſtic ſtate.

The bunch which ſome oxen carry between their ſhoulders, both in a domeſtic and wild ſtate, is the moſt general and moſt remarkable variety. This race of oxen are denominated *biſons;* and, it has been imagined, till now, that they were of a different ſpecies from the common ox. But, as we are certain that theſe animals produce with the common kind, and that the bunch diminiſhes from the firſt generation, and diſappears in the ſecond or third, it is evident, that this bunch is only an accidental and variable character, which prevents not the bunched ox from belonging to the ſame ſpecies with our ox. Now, in the deſert parts of Europe, there were, in ancient times, wild oxen, ſome of them with bunches, and others without bunches. Hence this variety ſeems to be natural, and to proceed from the abundance and more ſubſtantial quality of the food ; for we remarked, when treating of the camels, that, when meager and ill fed, they have not even the leaſt veſtige of a bunch. The ox without a bunch was called *vrochs* and *turochs* in the language of the Germans, and, in the ſame language, the bunched ox was called *viſen.* The Romans, who knew neither of theſe wild oxen till they ſaw them in Germany, adopted their German names. From *vrochs* they made *vrus,* and from *viſen, biſon.* They never
imagined

imagined that the wild ox defcribed by Ariftotle, under the name of *bonafus*, could be one or other of thefe oxen whofe names they had Latinized.

The length of the hair is another difference between the aurochs and bifon. The neck, the fhoulders, and the throat of the bifon, are covered with very long hair. But, in the aurochs, all thefe parts are covered with fhort hair, fimilar to that on the reft of the body, except the front, which is covered with crifped hair. This difference of the hair, however, is ftill more accidental than that of the bunch, and depends likewife on the food and the climate, as we have proved under the articles Goat, Sheep, Dog, Cat, Rabbit, &c. Thus, neither the bunch, nor the difference in the length of the hair, are fpecific characters, but accidental varieties only.

A more extenfive variety than the other two arifes from the figure of the horns; to which character naturalifts have afcribed more importance than it deferves. They have not confidered, that, in our domeftic cattle, the figure, the fize, the pofition, the direction, and even the number of the horns, vary fo greatly, that it is impoffible to afcertain what is the real model of Nature. In fome cows, the horns are much crooked, and hang fo low as to be almoft pendulous; in others, they are more erect, longer, and more elevated. There are entire races of ewes with fometimes two, fometimes four horns; and

there

there are races of cows without horns. Thefe external, or, as they may be called, acceffory parts of the body, are as fluctuating as the colours of the hair, which, in domeftic animals, are varied and combined in every poffible manner. This difference in the figure and direction of the horns, which is fo frequent, ought not, therefore, to be regarded as a diftinctive character of fpecies. It is, however, the only character which our naturalifts have adopted in their fpecies; and, as Ariftotle, in his defcription of the bonafus, fays, that its horns bended inwards, they have, from this confideration alone, and without having ever feen the individual, feparated it from the reft, and made it a diftinct fpecies. In this variation of the horns of domeftic animals, we have confined our remarks to cows and ewes; becaufe the females are always more numerous than the males; and we every where fee thirty cows or ewes for one bull or ram.

The mutilation of animals by caftration feems to injure the individual only, and to have no influence on the fpecies. It is certain, however, that this practice reftrains Nature on the one hand, and weakens her on the other. A fingle male, obliged to ferve thirty or forty females, muft be enfeebled; befides, the ardour of love is unequal. It is cool in the male, who exerts himfelf beyond the bounds of Nature, and too ardent in the female, whofe enjoyment is limit-

ed

ed to an inftant. Of courfe, the offspring muft
be chiefly tinctured with the feminine qualities;
more females will be produced than males; and
even the males will partake more of the mother
than the father. This is unqueftionably the
reafon why more girls than boys are brought
forth in thofe countries where the men have a
great number of wives. On the contrary, in all
countries where the men are allowed but one
wife, more males are produced than females. It
is true, that, in domeftic animals, the fineft males
are felected to become the fathers of an offspring
fo numerous. The firft productions from thefe
males will be ftrong and vigorous. But, in proportion to the number of copies taken from the
fame mould, the original impreffion of Nature
will be deformed, or at leaft rendered lefs perfect. The race muft, therefore, degenerate, and
become more feeble. This, perhaps, is the reafon why more monfters are produced among
domeftic than wild animals, where the number
of males is equal to that of the females. Befides,
when one male is obliged to ferve many females,
they have not the liberty of following their own
tafte. They are deprived of that gaiety, and
thofe foft emotions which proceed from fponta-
neous pleafures. The fire of their love is half
extinguifhed; and they languifh, waiting for
the cold approaches of a male whom they have
not felected, who is often not accommodated to
them, and who always flatters lefs than one that
is

is obliged to carefs, in order to obtain a preference. Thefe melancholy and taftelefs amours muft give rife to productions equally difmal and infipid ; beings who never have that courage, fpirit, and ftrength, which Nature can only beftow on each fpecies, by leaving all the individuals in full poffeffion of their powers, and, above all, of the liberty of choice in the intermixture of the fexes. We learn from the example of horfes, that croffed races are always the moft beautiful. We ought not, therefore, to confine our female cattle to a fingle male of their own country, who already has too much refemblance to his mother, and who, confequently, inftead of improving, continues to degrade the fpecies. Man, in this article, prefers his convenience to every other advantage. We never think of improving or of embellifhing Nature ; but we fubmit to her operations, that we may enjoy her in a more arbitrary manner. The males conftitute the glory of each fpecies. They have more courage, fire, and obftinacy. A great number of males in our flocks would render them lefs tractable, and more difficult to manage. In thofe flaves of the moft abject kind, it is even neceffary to deprefs every head that offers to exalt itfelf.

To thefe caufes of degeneration in domeftic animals, we muft ftill add another, which alone has produced more changes than all the combined force of the others; I mean, the conftant

tranfportation

tranſportation of thoſe animals from climate to climate. The ox, the ſheep, the goat, have been carried to every habitable part of the globe. Theſe ſpecies have been ſubjected to the influence of every climate, and have received impreſſions from every ſoil and every ſky; ſo that it has become extremely difficult, amidſt the number of changes they have undergone, to recogniſe thoſe which are leaſt removed from the prototype of Nature.

Having pointed out the general cauſes of the varieties among domeſtic animals, I ſhall now exhibit the particular proofs of what I advanced concerning the oxen and buffalos.

1. I remarked, *that the animal we now know by the name of buffalo, was unknown to the ancient Greeks and Romans.* This poſition is evident; for in none of their authors is there any deſcription, or even name, which can be applied to the buffalo. Beſides, we learn from the annals of Italy, that the firſt buffalo was tranſported thither about the end of the ſixth century *.

2. *The buffalo, now domeſtic in Europe, is the ſame with the wild or domeſtic buffalo of India and Africa.* Of this no other proof is neceſſary than a compariſon of our deſcription of the buffalo, which was made from the live animal, with the notices given by travellers of the buffalos in Perſia †, Mogul ‡, Bengal ‖,

---

* Ann. 595. Voyage de Miſſon, tom. iii. p. 54.　† Voyage de Tavernier, tom. i. pag. 41. et 298.　‡ Relation de Thevenot, page 11.　‖ Voyage de l'Hullier, page 50.

Egypt *, Guiney †, and the Cape of Good Hope ‡. It is eafy to perceive, that, in all thefe countries, this animal is the fame, and differs from our buffalo only by very flight varieties.

3. *The bubalus of the Greeks and Latins is neither the buffalo, nor the fmall ox of Belon, but the animal defcribed in the Memoirs of the Academy of Sciences, under the name of the Barbary Cow.* The following facts will prove this pofition. Ariftotle ‖ ranks the bubalus with the ftag and fallow deer, and not with the ox §. In another place he mentions the bubalus along with the roe deer; and remarks, that he makes a bad defence with his horns, and that he flies from all ferocious animals. Pliny **, fpeaking of the wild oxen of Germany, fays, that it is only from ignorance that the vulgar give the

* Defcript. de l'Egypte, par Maillet, tom. ii. p. 121.

† Voyage de Bofman, pag. 437.

‡ Defcription du Cap de Bonne-efperance; par Kolbe; tom. iii. p. 25.

‖ Genus id fibrarum cervi, damæ, bubali fanguini deeft; *Arift. Hift. Anim. lib.* iii. *cap.* 6.

§ Bubalis etiam capreifque interdum cornua inutilia funt: Nam etfi contra nonnulla refiftant, et cornibus fe defendant, tamen feroces pugnacefque belluas fugiunt; *Idem, de Part. Animal. lib.* iii. *cap.* 11.

** Germania gignit infignia boum ferorum genera, jubatos bifontes, excellentique vi et velocitate uros, quibus imperitum vulgus *bubalorum* nomen impofuit; cum id gignat Africa; vituli potius cervive quadam fimilitudine; *Plin. Hift. Nat. lib.* viii. *cap.* 15.

name

name of *bubalus* to thefe oxen; for the bubalus is an African animal, which refembles, in fome meafure, a calf or a ftag. Hence the bubalus is a timid creature, his horns are ufelefs to him, and, to avoid the affaults of ferocious animals, he has no other refource but flight; of courfe, he is nimble, and is related, by his figure, both to the cow and the ftag. All thefe charaċters, none of which apply to the buffalo, are combined in the animal whofe figure was fent by Horatius-Fontana to Aldrovandus *, and of which the Gentlemen of the Academy † have likewife given a figure and defcription, under the name of the *Barbary cow*; and they agree with me in thinking, that it is the bubalus of the ancients ‡. The zebu, or fmall ox of Belon, has none of the charaċters of the bubalus; for the zebu differs as much from the bubalus as the ox from the antilope; and Belon is the only naturalift who regarded this fmall ox as the bubalus of the ancients.

4. *The fmall ox of Belon is only a variety of the common ox.* This pofition may be eafily proved by fimply referring to the figure of the animal given by Belon, Profper Alpinus, and Edwards, and to our own defcription of it. We have feen it alive: Its conduċtor told us, that it came from

---

* Aldrov. de Quad. Bifulc. p. 365.

† Mem. pour fervir à l'Hift. des Animaux, part. ii. p. 24.

‡ This animal fhould rather be regarded as the bubalus of the ancients, than the fmall African ox defcribed by Belon; *Id. ibid. p.* 26.

Africa,

Africa, where it was called *zebu*; that it was domeftic, and was ufed for riding. It is, indeed, a
very mild and even a careffing animal. Its figure, though thick and fquat, is agreeable. It
has, however, fo perfect a refemblance to the ox,
that I can give no better idea of it, than by re-
marking, that if a handfome bull were viewed
through a glafs which diminifhed objects one
half, this contracted figure would be that of the
zebu.

The defcription I made of this animal, in
the year 1752, is inferted below in the note *.

It

* This fmall ox has a perfect refemblance to that of Belon.
Its crupper is round, and plumper than that of the common
ox. It is fo gentle and familiar, that it licks the hand like a
dog, and careffes every perfon who approaches. It is a very
beautiful animal; and its intelligence feems to be equal to its
docility. We were informed by its conductor, that it was
brought from Africa, and that its age was twenty-one
months. Its colour was white, mixed with yellow and a little
red. All the legs were white. The hair on the fpine of the
back, for about a foot wide, is black, and the tail of the fame
colour. In the middle of this black band, there is on the
crupper a fmall white ftreak, the hairs of which ftand erect
like briftles. It had no mane, and there was very little
hair on the tuft. The hair of the body is very fmooth
and fhort. It was five feet feven inches in length, from the
end of the muzzle to the origin of the tail, five feet one inch
in circumference behind the fore legs, five feet fix inches at
the middle of the body, and five feet one inch above the
hind legs. The circumference of the head, taken before the
horns, was two feet ten inches, and that of the muzzle, taken
behind the noftrils, was one foot three inches. The fiffure
of the mouth, when fhut, was eleven inches. The noftrils
were two inches long by one broad; and from the end of the

muzzle

It corresponds very well with the figure and description * given by Belon, which I have also

muzzle to the eye measured ten inches. The eyes were distant from each other about six inches; and from their posterior angle, to the aperture of the ears, measured four inches. The ears were situated behind and a little to one side the horns, and were near seven inches long, and nine inches in circumference at the base. The distance between the horns was little more than four inches; they were one foot two inches in length, six inches in circumference at the base, and, at half an inch from the points, only an inch and a half. They were of the ordinary colour of horn, and black near the extremities, which were distant from each other one foot seven inches. The bunch, which consisted entirely of flesh, was seven inches in perpendicular height. The colour of the hair which covered it was blackish, and an inch and a half long. The tail, to the end of the vertebræ, was little more than two feet long; but, including the hair which hangs down to the ground, it was two feet ten inches and a half. The longest hairs of the tail measured one foot three inches. The testicles were a foot and a half distant from the anus. It had four paps, situated like those of the bull.

* This is a very small bull; it is thick, fat, smooth, and well shaped. . . . It was already old, though its body was not so large as that of a stag; but it was more squat, and thicker than a roebuck, and so neat and compact in all its members, that it was extremely agreeable to behold. . . . Its feet resembled those of the ox; and its legs were short and squat. Its neck is thick and short, and the dewlap very small. It has the head of an ox; and the horns rise from a bone on the top of the head. They are black, much notched, like those of the Gazelle, or Barbary antilope, and formed like a crescent. . . It has the ears of a cow; its shoulders are plump, and a little elevated; its tail is long, and covered with black hair. It has the appearance of an ox, only it is not so tall. . . We have here given a figure of it.—Belon adds, that this small ox was brought to Cairo from Azamia, a province of Asia, and that it is also found in Africa; *Obf. de Belon, fol.* 118.

inserted,

Inferted, that the reader may have an opportunity of comparing them. Profper Alpinus *, who defcribes this animal, and gives a figure of it, fays that it is found in Egypt. His defcription agrees with mine, and alfo with Belon's. The only differences between the three are in the colour of the horns and hair. The zebu of Belon was yellow on the belly, brown on the back, and had black horns. That of Profper Alpinus was red, marked with fmall fpots, with horns of the ordinary colour. Ours was of a pale yellow, almoft black on the back, with horns of the fame colour as thofe of a common ox. In the figures of Belon and Profper Alpinus, the bunch on the back is not fufficiently marked. The oppofite error takes place in the figure which Mr. Edwards † has lately given of this animal, from a drawing communicated to him by Sir Hans Sloane; for the bunch is too large. Befides, the figure is incomplete; for it feems to have been drawn from a very young animal, whofe horns were only beginning to fhoot. It came, fays Mr. Edwards, from the Eaft Indies, where thefe fmall oxen are ufed as we do horfes. From all thefe hints, and likewife from the varieties in the colour, and the natural mildnefs of this animal, it is apparent, that it belongs to the bunched race of oxen, and has derived its origin from a domeftic ftate, in which the fmalleft in-

* Profp. Alpin. Hift. Nat. Egypt. p. 233.
† Nat. Hift. of Birds, p. 200.

　　　　　dividuals

dividuals have been chofen for a breed ; for, in general, we find, that the bunched oxen in a domeſtic ſtate, like our own domeſtic kind, are ſmaller than thoſe in a wild ſtate. Theſe facts ſhall afterwards be fully confirmed by the teſtimonies of travellers.

5. *The bonaſus of Ariſtotle is the ſame animal with the biſon of the Latins.* This propoſition cannot be proved, without a critical diſcuſſion, with which I ſhall not fatigue the reader *. Geſner, who was a man of literature as well as a naturaliſt, and who thought, as I do, that the bonaſus might probably be the biſon, has examined the notices given of the bonaſus by Ariſtotle with more care than any other perſon ; he has, at the ſame time, corrected ſeveral erroneous expreſſions in Theodore Gaza's tranſlation ; which errors, however, have been ſervilely copied by all the ſucceeding naturaliſts. From theſe aſſiſtances, and by rejecting from the remarks of Ariſtotle whatever is obſcure, contradictory, or fabulous, the following ſeems to be the reſult. The bonaſus is a wild ox of Pœonia, and is equally large, and of the ſame figure with the domeſtic ox. But his neck, from the ſhoulders to the eyes, is covered with long

* Here it is neceſſary to compare what Ariſtotle has ſaid of the bonaſus *(Hiſt. Anim. lib.* ix. *cap.* 45.) with what he elſewhere remarks, *(lib. de Mirabilibus)* and likewiſe the particular paſſages in his *Hiſt. Anim. lib.* ii. *c.* 1. *and* 16. and alſo to read Geſner's diſſertation on this ſubject ; *Hiſt. Quad. p.* 131.

hair,

hair, which is fofter than the mane of a horfe.
He has the voice of an ox. His horns are fhort,
and bended down round the ears. His legs are
covered with long hair, as foft as wool; and his
tail is fhort in proportion to his fize, though in
every other refpect it is fimilar to that of the
ox. Like the bull, he has the habit of raifing
the duft with his feet. His fkin is hard, and
his flefh tender and good. From thefe charac‐
ters, which are all that can be collected from
the writings of Ariftotle, we fee how nearly
the bonafus approaches to the bifon. Every
article, indeed, correfponds, except the form
of the horns, which, as was formerly remarked,
varies confiderably in animals that belong to
the fame fpecies. We have feen horns bend‐
ed in the fame manner, which were taken from
a bunched ox of Africa; and we fhall afterwards
prove, that this bunched ox is nothing but the
bifon. What I now advance may likewife be
confirmed by the teftimonies of ancient authors.
Ariftotle calls the bonafus a Pœonian ox;
and Paufanius *, fpeaking of the Pœonian bull,
fays, in two different places, that thefe bulls are
bifons. He likewife tells us, that the Pœonian
bulls, which he faw at the Roman fhews, had
very long hair on the breaft, and about the
jaws. Laftly, Julius Cæfar, Pliny, Paufanius,
Solinus, &c. when fpeaking of wild oxen, men‐
tion the aurochs and the bifon, but take no no‐

* Paufan. in Beoticis et Phocicis.

tice

tice of the bonafus. We muſt, therefore, ſuppoſe that, in the courſe of four or five centuries,
the ſpecies of bonafus has been loſt, unleſs we
allow that the terms *bonaſus* and *biſon* denote
only the ſame animal.

6. *The biſon of America might proceed originally from the European biſon.* The foundation of this opinion has already been laid in
our diſſertation on the animals peculiar to the
two Continents *. It was from the experiments of M. de la Nux that we derived much
information on this ſubject. From him we
learn, that the biſons, or bunched oxen of India
and Africa, produce with the European bulls
and cows, and that the bunch is only an accidental character, which diminiſhes in the firſt
generation, and totally diſappears in the ſecond
or third. Since the Indian biſons are of the
ſame ſpecies with our oxen, and, of courſe,
have the ſame origin, is it not natural to extend
this origin to the American biſon? In ſupport
of this ſuppoſition, every thing ſeems to concur.
The biſon appears to be a native of cold and
temperate regions. His name is derived from
the German language. The ancients tell us, that
he was found in that part of Germany which
borders upon Scythia†; and there are ſtill biſons in the northern parts of Germany, in Poland,

---

* See vol. v. of this work.

† Pauciſſima Scythia gignit animalia, inopia fructus, pauca con-
termina illi Germania, inſignia tamen boum ferorum genera, jubatos biſontes; *Plin. Hiſt. Nat. lib.* viii. *cap.* 15.

and

and in Scotland. Hence they might pafs to America, or come from that country, as they are animals common to both Continents. The only difference between the European and American bifons is, that the latter are fmaller. But even this difference is a farther proof that they belong to the fame fpecies; for it was formerly remarked, that, in general, both the domeftic and wild animals, which have fpontaneoufly paffed, or been tranfported into America, have uniformly diminifhed in fize. Befides, all the characters, not excepting the bunch and the long hair on the anterior parts of the body, are the fame in the American and European bifons. Hence thefe animals muft be regarded as not only of the fame fpecies, but as proceeding from the fame race *,

7. *The urus, or aurochs, is the fame animal with the common bull in its natural and wild ftate.* This pofition is evident from the figure of the aurochs, and its whole habit of body, which are perfectly fimilar to thofe of our do-

---

* Several perfons of note have reared fmall oxen and wild cows, which are found in Carolina, and in other countries as far fouth as Pennfylvania. Thefe fmall oxen are tamed; but they ftill retain fo much of their natural ferocity, that they pierce through every hedge which oppofes their paffage. Their heads are fo ftrong, that they overturn the pallifades of their inclofures, to come at the cultivated fields, where they do much mifchief; and, as foon as a paffage is opened, they are followed by the whole flock of domeftic cattle. Thefe two kinds couple together, and have given rife to an intermediate kind; *Voyage de Pierre Kalm, p.* 350.

meftic

meftic bull. The aurochs, like every other
animal that enjoys liberty, is only larger and
ftronger. The aurochs is ftill found in fome
northern provinces: The young aurochs have
fometimes been carried off from their mothers,
and, after being reared to maturity, they produced with our domeftic bulls and cows *.
Hence thefe animals muft unqueftionably belong to the fame fpecies.

8. *Laftly, the bifon differs from the aurochs
by accidental varieties only; and, confequently,
it is, as well as the aurochs, of the fame fpecies
with the domeftic ox.* The bunch, the length
and quality of the hair, and the figure of the
horns, are the fole characters by which the bifon can be diftinguifhed from the aurochs. But
we have feen the bunched oxen produce with
the common domeftic kind; we likewife know,
that the length and quality of the hair, in all
animals, depend on the nature of the climate;
and, we have remarked, that, in the ox, fheep,
and goat, the form of the horns is various and
fluctuating. Thefe differences, therefore, are
by no means fufficient to conftitute two diftinct
fpecies: And, fince our domeftic cattle produce
with the bunched Indian oxen, they would likewife undoubtedly produce with the bifon or
bunched ox of Europe. Among the almoft in-
numerable varieties of thefe animals in different

---

* Epift. ant. Schmebergenis, ad Gefnerum, *Hift. Quad.*
p. 141.

climates, there are two primitive races, both of which have long continued in a natural ftate, the bifon or bunched ox, and the aurochs, or ox without a bunch. Thefe races have fub-fifted either in a wild or domeftic ftate, and have been diffufed, or rather tranfported by men into every climate of the globe. All the domeftic oxen without bunches have proceeded originally from the aurochs, and all the bunch-ed oxen have been derived from the bifon. To obtain a juft idea of thefe varieties, we fhall give an enumeration of them as they exift in different parts of the world.

To begin with the north of Europe; the fmall bulls and cows of Iceland *, though they belong to the fame race with our oxen, are deprived of horns. The magnitude of thefe animals depends more on the abundance and quality of their paf-ture, than on the nature of the climate. The Dutch † bring meager cattle from Denmark, which fatten prodigioufly in their rich meadows, and give a great quantity of milk. Thefe Da-nifh cattle are much larger than ours. The cows and bulls of the Ukraine, where the pafture is excellent, are reckoned to be the largeft in Eu-

---

* Iflandi domeftica animalia habent vaccas, fed multæ funt mutilæ cornibus; *Dithmar Blefken. Ifland. p.* 49.

† About the month of February, vaft numbers of meager cows are brought from Denmark, which the Dutch peafants turn into their meadows. They are much larger than thofe of France; and each of them yields from eighteen to twenty Paris pints of milk a day; *Voyage Hift. de l'Europe, tom.* v. *p.* 77.

rope,

rope *, and are of the fame race with the common kind. In Switzerland, where the tops of the
firſt mountains are covered with verdure and
flowers, and are ſolely deſtined for the feeding
of cattle, the oxen are nearly double the ſize of
thofe in France, where they are commonly
fed upon grofs herbage, which is deſpiſed by
the horſes. During winter, bad hay and leaves
are the common food of our oxen; and, in
ſpring, when they ſtand in need of being re-
cruited, they are excluded from the meadows.
Hence they ſuffer more in ſpring than in winter; for they then hardly receive any thing in
the ſtable, but are conducted into the highways,
into fallow grounds, or into the woods, and are
always kept at a diſtance from fertile land ; ſo
that they are more fatigued than nouriſhed.
Laſtly, in ſummer, they are permitted to go
into the meadows, which are then eat up, and
parched with drought. During the whole year,
therefore, thefe animals are never ſufficiently
nouriſhed, nor receive food agreeable to their
nature. This is the ſole caufe which renders
them weak, and of a ſmall ſize; for, in Spain,
and in ſome diſtricts of our provinces, where
the paſture is good, and reſerved for oxen alone,
they are much larger and ſtronger.

* In the Ukraine, the paſture is ſo excellent, that the cattle
are much larger than in any other part of Europe. It requires a man above the common ſtature to be able to lay his hand
on the middle of an ox's back; *Relat. de la Grande Tartarie,*
p. 227.

In

In Barbary *, and moſt parts of Africa, where the lands are dry, and the paſture poor, the oxen are ſtill ſmaller, the cows give much leſs milk than ours, and moſt of them loſe their milk with their calves. The ſame remark applies to ſome parts of Perſia †, of Lower Æthiopia ‡, and of Great Tartary ‖; while, in the ſame countries, and at no great diſtances, as in Cal-

* In the kingdom of Tunis and Algiers, the oxen and cows, generally ſpeaking, are not ſo large as thoſe of England. After being well fattened, the largeſt of them ſeldom weigh above five or ſix hundred pounds. The cows give very little milk, and it commonly dries up when their calves are taken from them; *Shaw's Travels.*——Boves domeſtici, quotquot in Africæ montibus naſcuntur, adeo ſunt exigui, ut aliis collati, vituli biennes appareant, monticolæ tamen illos aratro exercentes tum robuſtos, tum laboris patientes aſſerunt; *Leon. Afric. Africæ Deſcript. tom.* ii. *p.* 753.——The cows of Guiney are dry and meager. . . . Their milk is ſo poor and ſcanty, that twenty or thirty of them are hardly ſufficient to ſerve the General's table. Theſe cows are very ſmall and light; one of the beſt of them, when full grown, weighs not above two hundred and fifty pounds, though, in proportion to its ſize, it ought to weigh one half more; *Voyage de Boſman, p.* 236.

† The people of Caramania, at a little diſtance from the Perſic gulph, have ſome goats and cows; but their horned cattle are not ſtronger than calves, or Spaniſh bulls of a year old; and their horns exceed not a foot in length; *Ambaſſade de Silva Figueroa, p.* 62.

‡ In the province of Guber in Æthiopia, a number of large and ſmall cattle are reared; but their cows are not larger than our heifers; *L'Afrique de Marmol, tom.* iii. *p.* 66.

‖ At Kraſnojarſk, the Tartars have a number of cattle; but a Ruſſian cow gives twenty times as much milk as one of theirs; *Voyage du Gmelin à Kamtſchatka.*

muck

muck Tartary *, in Upper Æthiopia †, and, in Abyſſinia ‡, the oxen are of a prodigious ſize. Hence this difference depends more on the quantity of food, than on the temperature of the climate. In the northern and temperate, as well as in the warm regions, we find, at very inconſiderable diſtances, large or ſmall oxen, according to the quantity and quality of the paſture they have to feed upon.

The race of aurochs, or of the ox without a bunch, occupies the frozen and temperate zones, and is not much diffuſed over the ſouthern regions. The race of the biſon, or bunched ox, on the contrary, occupies all the warm climates. In the whole continent of India ||, in the eaſtern

and

* The oxen, in the provinces occupied by the Calmuck Tartars, are ſtill larger than thoſe of the Ukraine, and taller than in any other part of the world; *Relat. de la Grande Tartarie*, *p.* 228.

† In Upper Æthiopia,, the cows are as large as camels, and without horns ; *L'Afrique de Marmol, tom.* iii. *p.* 157.

‡ The riches of the Abyſſinians conſiſt chiefly in cows. . . . The horns of the oxen are ſo large, that they hold twenty pints. They are uſed by the Abyſſinians for pitchers and bottles; *Voyage de Abyſſinie du P. Lobo, tom.* i. *p.* 57.

|| The oxen which draw coaches in Surat are white, of a good ſize, and have two bunches like thoſe of certain camels. They run and gallop like horſes, and are garniſhed with ſplendid houſing, and a number of ſmall bells fixed to their necks. When the animals are in motion, the bells are heard at a conſiderable diſtance, and their noiſe in the ſtreets is very agreeable, Theſe coaches are uſed not only in the cities of India, but in travelling through the country; *Voyage de Pietro della Valle, tom.* vi. *p.* 273.—The carriages of the Mogul are

and southern islands *, throughout all the regions of Africa †, from Mount Atlas to the Cape
of

are a kind of coaches with two wheels. They are drawn by
oxen, which, though naturally heavy and flow in their movements, acquire, by long habit, such a dexterity in drawing these
carriages, that no other animal can outrun them. Moſt of theſe
oxen are very large, and have a bunch between their ſhoulders,
which riſes to the height of ſix inches; *Voyage de Jean Ovington, tom.* i. *p.* 258.—The oxen of Perſia are like our own, except on the frontiers of India, where they have a bunch on
the back. Few oxen are eaten in this country: They are
reared chiefly for labouring the ground, or for carrying burdens. Thoſe employed in carrying loads are ſhod, on account of the ſtony mountains they have to paſs; *Voyage de
Chardin, tom.* ii. *p.* 28.—The oxen of Bengal have a kind of
bunch on the back. We found them as fat and as well
taſted as in any other country. The largeſt and beſt ſell at
two rixdollars only; *Voyage de la Compagnie des Indes de Hollande, tom.* iii. *p.* 270.—The oxen of Guzarat are ſhaped like
ours, except that they have a bunch between the ſhoulders;
Voyage de Mandelſlo, tom. ii. *p.* 234.

* In the iſland of Madagaſcar, an immenſe number of oxen
are reared: They are very different from thoſe of Europe,
each of them having a bunch of fat on their backs, in the form
of a wen, which has made ſome authors alledge that they
are ſuckled by camels. There are three kinds, namely, thoſe
which have horns, thoſe which have pendulous horns attached
to the ſkin, and thoſe which have no horns, but only a ſmall
oſſeous eminence, in the middle of their front, covered with
ſkin. The laſt kind fail not, however, to combat other bulls,
by ſtriking their bellies with their heads. They all run like
our ſtags, and have longer legs than thoſe of Europe; *Voyage
de Flacourt, p.* 3.—The oxen in the iſland of Johanna, near the
Moſambique coaſt, differ from ours. They have a fleſhy creſcent between the neck and back. This portion of fleſh is
preferred to the tongue, and is as well taſted as the marrow;
Graſſe's Travels, p. 42.

† The oxen of Aguada-Sanbras are likewiſe larger than
thoſe of Spain. They have bunches, but no horns; *Premier
Voyage*

of Good Hope *, there are almoft no oxen without bunches. It even appears that this race,
which is diffufed over all the warm countries,
has feveral advantages over the other; for, like
the bifon, from which they have proceeded,
thefe bunched oxen have fofter and more gloffy
hair than ours, whofe hair, like that of the aurochs, is hard, and thinly fpread over the body.
They are likewife fwifter, more proper for fup-
plying the place of the horfe †, and, at the fame
time,

Voyage aes Hollandois aux Indes Orientales, tom. i. *p.* 218.—The
Moors have numerous flocks on the banks of the Niger. . . . .
Their oxen are much thicker, and have longer legs than thofe
of Europe. They are remarkable for a large flefhy wen,
which rifes between their fhoulders more than a foot high.
This wen is a delicious morfel; *Voyage au Senegal, par M. Adanfon, p.* 57.

* At the Cape of Good Hope, there are three kinds of oxen,
which are all large, and very fwift. Some of them have a
bunch on the back; others have pendulous horns; and others have
horns like thofe of the European kind; *Voyage de Francois le Guat,
tom.* ii. *p.* 147.

† As the oxen in India are perfectly gentle, many people
travel on them as we do on horfes. Their common pace is
foft. Inftead of a bit, a fmall cord is paffed through the cartilage of their noftrils, which is tied to a larger cord, and
ferves as a bridle; and this bridle is fixed to a bunch on the
fore part of the back, which is wanting in our oxen. They
are faddled like horfes, and, when pufhed, move as brifkly.
Thefe animals are ufed in moft parts of India; and no other
are employed in drawing carts and chariots. They are fixed
to the end of the beam by a long yoke, which is placed on
the necks of the two oxen; and the driver holds the rope to
which the cord that paffes through the noftrils is tied; *Relation de Thevenot, tom.* iii. *p.* 151.—This Indian Prince was feated
on

time, not fo ftupid and indolent as our oxen. They are more tractable and intelligent *, and have more of thofe relative feelings from which advantage may be derived. They are likewife treated with more care than our beft horfes. The refpect the Indians entertain for

on a chariot drawn by two white oxen, with fhort necks, and bunches on their fhoulders; but they were as fwift and alert as our horfes; *Voyage d'Olearius, tom.* i. *p.* 458.—The two oxen which were yoked to my coach coaft near 600 rupees. This price need not aftonifh the reader; for fome of thefe oxen are very ftrong, and perform journeys of fixty days, at the rate of from twelve to fifteen leagues a day, and always at a trot. When one half of the day's journey is finifhed, each of them is fupplied with two or three balls of the fize of a penny loaf, made of flour knedded with butter and black fugar; and, at night, their common food is chick-peas bruifed, and fteeped for half an hour in water; *Voyage de Tavernier,* *p.* 36.—Some of thefe oxen follow the horfes at a fmart trot. The fmalleft are the moft nimble. The Gentoos, and particularly the Banians and merchants of Surat, ufe thefe oxen for drawing their carriages. It is remarkable, that, notwith-ftanding their veneration for thefe animals, the people fcruple not to employ them in fuch laborious fervices; *Groffe's Travels,* *p.* 253.

* In the country of Camandu in Perfia, there are many oxen entirely white, with fmall blunt horns, and bunches on their backs. They are very ftrong, and carry heavy burdens. When about to be loaded, they lie down on their knees like the camels, and rife again when the goods are properly faftened. To this practice they are trained by the natives; *Defcription de l'Inde, par Marc. Paul, liv.* i. *chap.* 22.——The European labourers prick their oxen with a goad, in order to make them advance. But, in Bengal, their tails are only twifted. Thefe animals are extremely tractable. When loading, they are inftructed to lie down, and to rife with the burdens on their backs; *Lett. Edif. recueil* ix. *p.* 422.

thefe

thefe animals is fo great*, that it has degenerated into fuperftition, which is the ultimate
ftep of blind veneration. The ox, being the
moft ufeful animal, has appeared to them to
merit the greateft reverence. This venerable
object they have converted into an idol, a kind
of beneficent and powerful divinity; for every
thing we refpect muft be great, and have the
power of doing much good, or much evil.

Thefe bunched oxen vary perhaps more than
ours in the colour of the hair and the figure
of their horns. The moft beautiful are white,
like thofe of Lombardy †. Some of them
have no horns; the horns of others are very
high, and in others they are almoft pendulous.
It even appears that this firft race of bifons, or
bunched oxen, fhould be divided into two fecondary races, the one large, and the other
fmall, which laft comprehends the zebu. Both

---

* The Queen is attended with the ladies of fafhion, and
the pavement or roads through which fhe paffes are ftrewed
with the dung of the cows formerly mentioned. Thefe people have fuch a veneration for their cows, that they are allowed
to enter the King's palace, and are never ftopped on their paffage,
wherever they choofe to go. The King and all the nobles give
place to thefe cows, as well as to the bulls and oxen, with every
poffible mark of refpect and veneration; *Voyage de Francois Pyrard, tom*. i. *p*. 449.

† All the cattle of Italy are gray or white; *Voyage de Bur-
net, part*. ii. *p*. 12.——The oxen of India, and efpecially thofe
of Guzarat and of Cambaya, are generally white, like thofe of
Milan; *Groffe's Travels, p*. 253.

are

are found nearly in the fame climates *, and are equally gentle and eafily managed. Both have fine hair, and bunches on their backs. This bunch is only an excrefcence, a flefhy wen, which is equally tender and good as the tongue of an ox. The bunches of fome oxen weigh from forty to fifty pounds †, and thofe of others are much fmaller ‡. In fome, the horns are prodigioufly large. In the royal cabinet, there are fpecimens of them of three feet and a half in length, and feven inches in diameter at the bafe. We are affured by feveral tra-

---

* The oxen of India are of different fizes, fome large, others fmall, and others of a middle fize. But, in general, they travel well, fome of them making journeys of fifteen leagues a day. Some of them are near fix feet high; but thefe are rare. There is another kind called *dwarfs*, becaufe they exceed not three feet in height. The latter, like the others, have a bunch on their backs, run very faft, and are ufed for drawing fmall carts. The white oxen are extremely dear. I have feen two, which belonged to the Dutch, each of which coft two hundred crowns. They were indeed very beautiful and ftrong; and the chariot in which they were yoked had a magnificent appearance. When the people of fafhion have fine oxen, they take great care of them. The tips of their horns are ornamented with copper rings. They are covered with clothes, in the fame manner as horfes. They are daily curried, and fed with great attention; *Relat. d'un Voyage par Thevenot, tom.* iii. *p.* 252.

† At Madagafcar, there are oxen whofe bunch weighs thirty, forty, fifty, and even fixty pounds; *Voyage à Madagafcar, par de V. Paris, p.* 245.

‡ The oxen have a bunch near the neck, which is larger and fmaller in different individuals; *Relat. de Thevenot, tom.* ii. *p.* 223.

vellers,

vellers, that they have feen horns which could
contain fifteen and even twenty pints of water.

Throughout all Africa *, the large cattle are
never caftrated ; and this operation is not much
practifed in India †. When the bulls are caftrated, the tefticles are not cut off, but compreffed.
Though the Indians keep a great number of
thefe animals for drawing their carriages and
plowing the ground, they do not rear fo many
as we do. As, in all warm countries, the cows
give little milk, as the natives are unacquainted
with butter or cheefe, and, as the flefh of the
calves is not fo good as in Europe, the inhabitants
do not greatly multiply horned cattle. Befides,
in all the fouthern provinces of Africa and
Afia, being more thinly peopled than thofe of
Europe, there are a number of wild oxen,
which are taken when young. They tame
fpontaneoufly, and fubmit, without refiftance,
to all kinds of domeftic labour. They become
fo tractable, that they are managed with as much
eafe as horfes : The voice of their mafter is fufficient to direct their courfe, and to make them
obey. They are fhod ‡, curried, careffed, and
fupplied

* Along the coaft of Guiney, we fee bulls and cows only ;
for the negroes underftand not the practice of caftration;
Voyage de Bofman, p. 236.

† When the Indians caftrate their bulls, it is not by in-
cifion, but by the compreffion of ligatures, which prevents the
nourifhment of the parts; *Groffe's Travels, p. 253.*

‡ As the roads in the province of Afmer are very ftony,
the oxen are fhod before they fet out on long journeys.
They

supplied abundantly with the best food. These animals, when managed in this manner, appear to be different creatures from our oxen, which only know us from our bad treatment. The goad, blows, and hunger, render them stupid, refractory, and feeble. If we had a proper knowledge of our own interest, we would treat our dependents with greater lenity. Men of inferior condition, and less civilized, seem to have a better notion than other people of the laws of equality, and of the different degrees of natural equity. The farmer's servant may be said to be the peer of his master. The horses of the Arab, and the oxen of the Hottentot, are favourite domestics, companions in exercises, assistants in every labour, and participate the habitation, the bed, and the table of their masters. Man, by this communication, is not so much degraded as these brutes are exalted and humanized. They acquire affectionateness, sensibility, and intelligence. There they perform every thing from love, which they do here from fear. They do more; for as their nature is improved by the gentleness of their education, and the perpetual attention bestowed on them,

They are thrown on the ground by ropes fixed to their feet. When in this situation, their four feet are placed on a machine made of two cross sticks. At the same time, two thin, light pieces of iron are fixed to each foot, and cover not above one half of the hoof. They are fixed by three nails, above an inch in length, which are rivetted on the opposite side; *Relat. de Thevenot, tom.* iii. *p.* 150.

they

they become capable of performing actions which approach to the human powers. The Hottentots * train their oxen to war, and employ them nearly in the same manner as the Indians employ the elephants. These oxen are instructed to guard the flocks †, which they

conduct

* The Hottentots have oxen which they employ successfully in their combats. These animals are called *Backeleys*, from the word *backeley*, which, in the Hottentot language, signifies *war*. In all their armies there are considerable troops of those oxen, which are easily governed, and which are let loose by the chief, when a proper opportunity occurs. They instantly dart with great impetuosity on the enemy. They strike with their horns, kick, overturn, and trample under their feet every thing that opposes their fury. Hence, of not quickly turned back, they run ferociously into the ranks, which they soon put into the utmost disorder, and thus prepare an easy victory for their masters. The manner in which these animals are trained and disciplined, reflects much honour on the genius and ability of the Hottentots; *Voyage du Cap de Bonne-Esperance, par Kolbe, tom.* i. *p.* 160.

† These backeleys are likewise of great use in guarding the flocks. When pasturing, at the smallest signal from the keeper, they bring back and collect the wandering animals. They also run with fury upon strangers, which makes them a great security against the attacks of the *buschies*, or robbers of cattle. Every *Kraal* has at least six of these backeleys, which are chosen from among the fiercest oxen. When one of them dies, or becomes unserviceable by age, another is selected from the flock to succeed him. The choice is made by one of the oldest Kraals, who is supposed to distinguish the animal that will be most easily instructed. This noviciate is associated with one of the most experienced backeleys; and he is taught to follow his companion, either by blows, or by other means. In the night, they are tied together by the horns, and are likewise kept in the same situation during part of the day, till the young ox is completely trained to be a vigilant defender of the flock. These backeleys, or

keepers

conduct with dexterity, and defend them from
the attacks of ftrangers and ferocious animals.
They are taught to diftinguifh friends from enemies, to underftand fignals, and to obey their
mafter's voice. Thus the moft ftupid of men are
the beft preceptors to brutes. How does it happen, that the moft enlightened man, inftead of
managing his fellow creatures, has fo much
difficulty in conducting himfelf?

Thus the bifons, or bunched oxen, are diffufed over all the fouthern parts of Africa and
Afia. They vary greatly in fize, in colour,
in the figure of the horns, &c. On the contrary, in all the northern regions of thefe two
quarters of the world, and in the whole of
Europe, including the adjacent iflands, as far as
the Azores, there are only oxen without
bunches *, which derive their origin from the
aurochs.

keepers of the flocks, know every inhabitant of the *Kraal,*
and fhew the fame marks of refpect for all the men, women,
and children, as a dog does for thofe who live in his mafter's
family. Hence, thefe people may approach their cattle with the
utmoft fafety; for the backeleys never do them the fmalleft
injury. But, if a ftranger, and particularly an European,
fhould ufe the fame freedom, without being accompanied
with a Hottentot, his life would be in the greateft danger.
Thefe backeleys, which pafture all around, would foon run
upon him at full gallop, and, if not protected by the fhepherds,
by fire arms, or by fuddenly climbing a tree, his deftruction is inevitable. In vain would he have recourfe to
fticks or ftones: A backeley is not to be intimidated by fuch
feeble weapons; *Defcription du Cap de Bonne-Efperance, par Kolbe,
part.* i. *chap.* 20. *p.* 307.

* The oxen of Tercera are the largeft and fineft in Europe. Their horns are very large. They are fo gentle and
tame,

aurochs. And, as the aurochs, which is our ox in a wild ftate, is larger and ftronger than the domeftic kind, the bifon, or wild ox with a bunch, is likewife ftronger and larger than the Indian domeftic ox. He is alfo fometimes fmaller; but the fize depends folely on the quantity of food. In Malabar*, Canara, Abyffinia, and Madagafcar, where the meadows are fertile and fpacious, the bifons are of a prodigious fize. In Africa, and in Arabia Petrea †, where the ground is dry and fterile, the zebus or bifons are of a fmall fize.

Oxen without bunches are fpread over all America. They were fucceffively tranfported

tame, that, from a flock confifting of more than a thoufand, a fingle animal, upon its name being called by the proprietor, (for every individual has its peculiar name, like our dogs,) inftantly runs to him; *Voyage de la Compagnie des Indes de Hollande, tom.* i. *p.* 490.——See alfo *Le Voyage de Mandelflo, tom.* i. *p.* 478.

* In the mountains of Malabar and Canara, there are wild oxen fo large, that they approach the ftature of the elephant; while the domeftic oxen of the fame country are fmall, meager, and fhort lived; *Voyage du P. Vincent-Marie, chap.* 12.

† I faw at Mafcati, a town of Arabia Petrea, another fpecies of mountain ox, with gloffy hair, as white as that of the ermine. It was fo handfomely made, that it rather refembled a ftag than an ox. Its legs, indeed, were fhorter; but they were fine and nimble. The neck was fhort. The head and tail refembled thofe of the common ox, but were better fhaped. The horns are black, hard, ftraight, beautiful, about three or four palms in length, and garnifhed with rings which feem as if they had been turned in a lathe; *Voyage du P. Vincent-Marie, chap.* 12.

thither

thither by the Spaniards and other Europeans. These oxen have greatly multiplied, but have become smaller in these new territories. This species was absolutely unknown in South America. But, in all the northern regions, as far as Florida, Louisiana, and even in the neighbourhood of Mexico, the bisons, or bunched oxen, were found in great numbers. These bisons, which formerly inhabited the woods of Germany, of Scotland, and other northern countries, have probably passed from the Old to the New Continent. Like all the other animals, their size has diminished in America; and according as they lived in climates more or less cold, their hair became longer or shorter. In Hudson's Bay, their beard and hair are longer and more bushy than in Mexico; and, in general, their hair is softer than the finest wool *. We cannot hesitate in pronouncing these bisons of the New Continent to be the same species with those of the Old. They have preserved all the principal characters, as

* The wild oxen of Louisiana, instead of hair, are covered with wool as fine as silk, and all curled. It is longer in winter than in summer, and is much used by the inhabitants. On their shoulders they have a pretty high bunch. Their horns are very fine, and are used by the hunters for carrying their powder. Between the horns, and toward the top of the head, there is a tuft of hair so thick, that a pistol bullet, though discharged ever so near, cannot penetrate it. I tried the experiment myself. The flesh of these oxen is excellent, as well as that of the cow and calf; its flavour and juice are exquisite; *Mem. sur la Louisiane, par M. Dumont, p. 75.*

the

the bunch on the fhoulders, the long hair under the muzzle and on the anterior parts of the body, and the fhort legs and tail: And, upon comparing what has been faid of them by Hernandez *, Fernandez †, and all the other travellers and hiftorians of the New World ‡, with what has been delivered concerning the European bifon, by ancient and modern naturalifts ‖, we will be convinced that they are not animals of different fpecies.

Thus the wild and domeftic ox of Europe, Afia, Africa, and America, the bonafus, the aurochs, the bifon, and the zebu, are animals of the fame fpecies, which, according to the differences of climate, of food, and of treatment, have undergone the various changes above defcribed. The ox is not only the moft ufeful animal, but moft generally diffufed; for it has been found every where, except in South America §. Its
conftitution

---

* Hernand. Hift. Mex. p. 587.

† Fernand. Hift. Nov. Hifp. p. 10.

‡ Singularités de la France Antarctique, par Thevet, p. 148.
—Memoir fur la Louifiane, par Dumont, p. 75.—Defcription de la Nouvelle France, par le P. Charlevoix, tom. iii. p. 130.
—Lettres Edif. xi. recueil, p. 318, et xxiii. recueil, p. 238.
—Voyage de Robert Lade, tom. ii. p. 315.—Dernieres decouvertes dans l'Amerique feptentrionale, par M. de la Salle, p. 104. &c. &c.

‖ Plin. Hift. Nat. lib. viii.—Gefner. Hift. Quad. p. 128.—Aldrov. de Quad. Bif. p. 253.—Rzacinfky, Hift. Nat. Polon, p. 214. &c.

§ The bunched ox, or wild bifon, appears to have inhabited the northern parts of America only, as Virginia, Florida,

conftitution is equally adapted to the ardours of the South, and the rigours of the North. It appears to be very ancient in all climates. It is domeftic in civilized nations, and wild in defert countries, or among unpolifhed people. From its own refources, it fupports itfelf in a ftate of nature, and never lofes thofe qualities which render it ferviceable to man. The young wild calves which are carried off from their mothers in India and Africa, foon become as gentle as thofe of the domeftic race. This conformity in natural difpofitions is a ftill farther proof of the identity of the fpecies. Mildnefs of charaĉter in thefe animals indicates a phyfical flexibility in the form of their bodies; for in every fpecies, whofe difpofitions are gentle, and who have been fubjeĉted to a domeftic ftate, there are more varieties than in thofe who, from an inflexibility of temper, have remained favage.

---

rida, the country of the Illionois, Louifiana, &c.; for, though Hernandez calls it the *Mexican bull*, we learn from a paffage of Antonio de Solis, that this animal was a ftranger in Mexico, and that it was kept in the menagery of Montezuma with other wild beafts which were brought from New Spain. ‘ In ‘ a fecond court, we faw all the wild beafts of New Spain. ‘ They were kept in ftrong wooden cages. But nothing fur- ‘ prifed us fo much as the appearance of the Mexican bull, ‘ which is a rare animal, and has the camel’s bunch on its ‘ fhoulders, the narrow and meager flank of the lion, a bufhy ‘ tail and mane, and the horns and cloven foot of the bull. ‘ . . . . . This kind of amphitheatre appeared to the Spa- ‘ niards worthy of a great Prince;’ *Hift. de la Conquête du Mexique, par Antonio de Solis, p. 519.*

If

If it be afked, whether the aurochs or the bifon be the primitive race of oxen, a fatisfactory anfwer may be obtained by drawing conclufions from the facts already related. The bunch of the bifon, as formerly remarked, is an accidental character only, which is effaced by the commixture of the two races. The aurochs, or ox without a bunch, is, therefore, the moft powerful and predominant race. Were it otherwife, the bunch, inftead of difappearing, would extend, and fubfift in all the individuals proceeding from a mixture of the two races. Befides, this bunch of the bifon, like that of the camel, is not fo much a production of nature, as an effect of labour, and a badge of flavery. In all ages, and in every country, the oxen have been obliged to carry burdens. Their backs, by conftant and often exceffive loads, have been deformed; and this deformity was afterwards tranfmitted by generation. There remained no oxen without this deformity, except in thofe countries where they were not employed in carrying burdens.

Throughout all Africa and the Eaft, the oxen are bunched; becaufe, at all periods, they have carried loads on their fhoulders. In Europe, where they are employed in the draught only, they have not undergone this deformed change, which is probably occafioned, in the firft place, by the compreffion of the loads, and, in the fecond, by a redundance of nourifhment; for it difappears when the animal is meager and ill fed.

fed. Domeſtic oxen with bunches might eſcape, or be abandoned in the woods, where their poſterity would inherit the ſame deformity, which, inſtead of diſappearing, would augment by the abundance of food peculiar to all uncultivated countries; ſo that this ſecondary race would ſpread over all the deſert lands of the North and South, and paſs, like the other animals which can ſupport the rigours of cold, into the New Continent. The identity of the ſpecies of the biſon and aurochs is ſtill farther confirmed from this circumſtance, that the biſons of North America have ſo ſtrong an odour of muſk, that they have been called *muſk oxen* by moſt travellers *; and, at the ſame time, we learn, from the teſtimony of ſpectators †, that the aurochs, or wild

* Fifteen leagues from the river Danoiſe, is the river called *Sea-wolf*, both in the neighbourhood of Hudſon's Bay. In this country, there is a ſpecies of ox called the *muſk ox*, from his ſtrong odour of muſk, which, in certain ſeaſons, renders his fleſh uneatable. Theſe animals have very fine wool, which is longer than that of the Barbary ſheep. I had ſome of it ſent me to France in the year 1708, of which I made ſtockings, which were as fine as thoſe of ſilk. . . . . Theſe oxen, though ſmaller than ours, have larger and longer horns. Their roots join on the top of the head, and deſcend on the ſide of the eyes as low as the throat; then the tips mount up in the form of a creſcent. I have ſeen two of them which weighed together ſixty pounds. Their legs are ſo ſhort, that the wool always trails on the ground where they walk, which renders them ſo unſhapely, that it is difficult, at a diſtance, to know at which end the head is placed; *Hiſt. de la Nouvelle France, par le P. Charlevoix, tom.* iii. *p.* 132.—See alſo *Le Voyage de Robert Lade, tom.* ii. *p.* 315.

† Ephem. German. decad. ii. ann. 2. obſerv. 7.

OX

ox of Pruffia and Livonia, has the fame fcent of mufk.

Of all the names, therefore, prefixed to this article, which, both by ancient and modern naturalifts, are reprefented as fo many diftinct fpecies, there remain only the buffalo and the ox. Thefe two animals, though very fimilar, both domeftic, often living under the fame roof, and fed in the fame paftures, though at liberty to intermix, and frequently ftimulated to it by their keepers, have uniformly refufed to unite. They neither copulate nor produce together. Their natures are more remote from each other than that of the afs and horfe : They even feem to have a mutual antipathy; for we are affured, that cows will not fuckle young buffaloes, and that female buffaloes refufe to fuckle calves. The difpofition of the buffalo is more obftinate and untractable than that of the ox. He is lefs obedient, more violent, and fubject to humours more frequent and more impetuous. All his habits are grofs and brutal. Next to the hog, he is the dirtieft of domeftic animals; for nothing is more difficult than to drefs and keep him clean. His figure is grofs and forbidding. His afpect is wild and ftupid. He ftretches out his neck in an awkward, ignoble manner, and carries his head fo ungracefully, that it generally hangs down toward the ground. He bellows hideoufly, and with a ftrong and deeper tone than that of the bull. He has meager limbs, a naked

tail,

tail, a dark countenance, and a skin as black as his hair. He differs chiefly from the ox by this black colour of his skin: It appears under the hair, which is not close. His body is thicker and shorter than that of the ox, his legs longer, his head proportionally smaller, his horns less round, being black and compressed; and he has a tuft of curled hair on his front. His skin is also thicker and harder than that of the ox. His flesh is black and hard, and has not only a bad taste, but a most disagreeable odour*. The milk of the female buffalo is not so good as that of the cow; but she yields it in much greater quantity †. In warm countries, most cheeses are made of the buffalo's milk. The flesh of young buffaloes, though fed with milk, is not good. The skin is of more value than the rest of

* In travelling from Rome to Naples, we are sometimes regaled with crows and buffaloes, and are happy to find them. The flesh of the buffalo is black, hard, and stinking, and none but poor people and the Jews of Rome are in the habit of eating it; *Voyage de Misson*, tom. iii. *p.* 54.

† In entering Persia, by the way of Armenia, the first place worthy of notice is called the *Three Churches*, at the distance of three leagues from Erivan. In this country, there are vast numbers of buffaloes, which serve the inhabitants for ploughing their lands. The females yield a great quantity of milk, of which butter and cheese are made. Some females give daily twenty-two pints of milk; *Voyage de Tavernier, liv.* i. *tom.* i. *p.* 41.—The female buffaloes go with young twelve months, and often give twenty-two pints of milk a-day, of which so great quantities of butter are made, that, in some of the villages on the Tigris, we saw from twenty to twenty-five barks loaded with butter, to be sold along both sides of the Persic Gulf; *Id. ib.*

the

the animal, the tongue of which alone is good
for eating. The ſkin is ſolid, pretty flexible,
and almoſt impenetrable. As theſe animals are
larger and ſtronger than oxen, they are employed with advantage in different kinds of labour.
They are made to draw, and not to carry burdens. They are directed and reſtrained by means
of a ring paſſed through their noſe. Two buffaloes yoked, or rather chained, to a chariot,
draw as much as four ſtrong horſes. As they
carry their neck and head low, the whole weight
of their body is employed in drawing; and their
maſs much ſurpaſſes that of a labouring horſe.

The height and thickneſs of the buffalo are
ſufficient indications that he originated from
warm climates. The largeſt quadrupeds are
produced in the Torrid Zone of the Old Continent; and the buffalo, in the order of magnitude,
ſhould be ranked next to the elephant, the rhinoceros, and the hippopotamus. The camelopard and the camel are taller but thinner; and
the whole are equally natives of the ſouthern
regions of Aſia and Africa. Buffaloes, however,
live and produce in Italy, in France, and in
other temperate countries. Thoſe kept in the
royal menagery have produced twice or thrice.
The female brings forth but one at a birth, and
goes with young about twelve months; which
is a ſtill farther proof of the difference of this
ſpecies from that of the cow, whoſe time of
geſtation is only nine months. It appears, likewife,

wife, that thefe animals are more gentle and lefs brutal in their native country; and that, the warmer the country, their difpofition is the more docile. In Egypt *, they are more tractable than in Italy, and in India † than in Egypt. The Italian buffaloes have alfo more hair than thofe of Egypt, and the Egyptian than thofe of India ‡. Their fur is by no means clofe;

---

* The buffaloes are numcrous in Egypt. Their flefh is good; and they are not fo ferocious as thofe of Europe. Their milk is of great ufe, and produces excellent butter; *Defcrip. l'Egypte, par Maillet, p. 27.*

† In the kingdom of Aunan and Tonquin, the buffaloes are very tall, and have high fhoulders. They are alfo robuft, and fuch excellent labourers, that one alone is fufficient to draw a plough, though the coulter enters very deep into the ground. Their flefh is not difagreeable; but that of the ox is better and more commonly ufed; *Hift. de Tonquin, par le P. de Rhodes, p. 51.*

‡ At Malabar, the buffalo is larger than the ox. He is fhaped nearly in the fame manner. His head is longer and flatter. His eyes are larger, and almoft entirely white. His horns are flat, and often two feet long. His legs are thick and fhort. He is ugly, and almoft without hair. He walks flowly, and carries heavy burdens. Like the cows, they go in flocks; and their milk produces butter and cheefe. Their flefh is good, though lefs delicate than that of the ox. They are excellent fwimmers, and traverfe the moft rapid rivers. We have feen them tamed. But the wild buffaloes are extremely dangerous; for they tear men to pieces, or crufh them with a fingle ftroke of their heads. They are lefs to be feared in the woods than in any other fituation; for their horns often entangle among the branches, which gives thofe time to fly who are purfued. The fkin of thefe animals is ufed for a number of purpofes; and even pitchers are made of it to keep water and other liquors. Thofe on the Malabar coaft are almoft all wild; and ftrangers are not prohibited from hunting and eating them; *Voyage de Dellon, p. 110.*

becaufe

becaufe they belong to warm climates; and the large animals, in general, of thefe countries, have little or no hair.

In Africa and India, there are vaft quantities of wild buffaloes, which frequent the banks of rivers and extenfive meadows. Thefe wild buffaloes go in flocks *, and make great havock in the cultivated fields. But they never attack men, unlefs when they are wounded. They are then extremely dangerous †; for they run ftraight upon the enemy, overturn him, and trample him under their feet. They are, however, afraid at the fight of fire ‡, and they ab-

hor

---

* There are fuch numbers of wild buffaloes in the Philippine ifles, that a good hunter, with a horfe and a fpear, may kill thirty of them in a day. The Spaniards kill the buffalo for his fkin, and the Indians for his flefh; *Voyage de Gemelli Careri, tom.* v. *p.* 162.

† We are told by the Negroes, that, when they fhoot at the buffaloes, without wounding them mortally, they dart with fury on the hunters, and trample them to death. . . . The Negroes watch where the buffaloes affemble in the evening, climb a large tree, from which they fire upon them, and defcend not till the animals are dead; *Voyage de Bofman, p.* 437.

‡ At the Cape of Good Hope, the buffaloes are larger than thofe of Europe. Inftead of being black, like the latter, they are of a dark red colour. Upon the front, there is a rude tuft of curled hair. Their whole body is well proportioned, and they advance their head very much forward. Their horns are very fhort, and hang down on the fide of their neck; the tips bend inward, and nearly join. Their fkin is fo hard and firm, that it is difficult to kill them without a good firelock. Their flefh is neither fo fat nor fo tender as that of ordinary oxen. The buffalo, at the Cape, turns furious at the fight of a red garment, or upon hearing a gun difcharged

hor a red colour. We are affured by Aldrovandus, and feveral other naturalifts and travellers, that no perfon dare clothe himfelf in red, in countries frequented by the buffalo. I know not whether this averfion to fire and a red colour be general among the buffaloes; for it is only fome of our oxen which are enraged at the fight of red clothes.

The buffalo, like all the large animals of warm climates, is fond of wallowing, and even of remaining in the water. He fwims well, and boldly croffes the moft rapid rivers. As his legs are longer than thofe of the ox, he runs more fwiftly. The Negroes of Guiney, and the Indians of Malabar, where the buffaloes are very numerous, are fond of hunting them. They never attack thefe animals openly, but watch for them on the tops of trees, or lie hid in the thickets through which the buffaloes cannot pafs on account of their horns. Thefe people efteem the flefh of the buffalo, and draw great profits from his fkin and horns, which are harder and better than thofe' of the ox.

The animal called *empacaffa* or *pacaffa* at Congo, though very imperfectly defcribed by travel-

charged over him. On thefe occafions, he cries in a hideous manner, ftrikes with his feet, turns up the earth, and rurs with fury againft the man who has fhot, or wears a red garment. Neither fire nor water can ftop his courfe. Nothing but a high wall, or fome fimilar obftacle, is capable of reftraining him; *Defcript. de Bonne-efperance, par Kolbe, tom.* iii. *chap.* 11. *p.* 25.

lers,

lers, appears to me to be the buffalo; and the animal mentioned under the name of *empabanga* or *impalunca*, in the fame country, is, perhaps, the bubalus, whofe hiftory fhall be given along with that of the gazelles or antilopes.

SUPPLEMENT.

THE ox and bifon are two diftinct races of the fame fpecies. Though the bifon uniformly differs from the ox by the bunch on his back, and the length of his hair, he fucceeds very well in the Ifle of France : His flefh is much better than that of the European oxen; and after fome generations, his bunch vanifhes entirely. His hair is fmoother, his limbs are more flender, and his horns longer than thofe of the common ox. I faw, fays M. de Querhoënt, bifons brought from Madagafcar, which were of an aftonifhing fize *.

The bifon, of which we here give a figure, and which we faw alive, was taken, when young, in the forefts of the temperate parts of North America. It was brought to Holland, and purchafed by a Swede, who tranfported it from town to town in a large cage, where it was

---

* Note communicated by M. le Vicomte de Querhoënt.

firmly

firmly fixed by the head with four ropes. The enormous mane which furrounds its head is not hair, but a flowing wool, divided into locks, like an old fleece. This wool is very fine, as well as that which covers the bunch, and the anterior part of the body. The parts which appear naked in the engraving, are only fo at a certain time of the year, which is rather in fummer than in winter; for, in the month of January, all parts of the body were almoft equally covered with a fine, clofe, frizled wool, under which the fkin was of a footy colour; but, on the bunch, and all the other parts which are covered with lon-ger wool, the fkin is tawny. This bunch, which confifts entirely of flefh, varies according to the plight of the animal. To us he appeared to dif-fer from the European by the bunch and the wool only. Though under much reftraint, he was not ferocious, but allowed his keepers to touch and carefs him.

It would appear, that there were formerly bi-fons in the north of Europe. Gefner even, af-ferts, that, in his time, they exifted in Scotland. Having inquired into this fact, I was informed, by letters both from Scotland and England, that no remembrance or veftige of them could be traced in that country. Mr. Bell, in his travels from Ruffia to China, mentions two fpecies of oxen which he faw in the northern parts of Afia; one of which was the aurochs, or wild ox, and is

the

the fame race with our oxen; and the other,
which we have denominated, after Gmelin, the
Tartarian, or *Grunting Cow*, appeared to be the
fame fpecies with the bifon.   After comparing
this grunting cow with the bifon, I found an
exact coincidence in all the characters, except the
grunting, inftead of bellowing.   But I appre-
hend, that this grunting is not conftant and general, but contingent and particular, fimilar to
the deep interrupted voice of our bulls, which
is never fully exhibited but in the feafon of love.
Befides, I was informed, that the voice of the
bifon, whofe figure I have reprefented, was never
heard, and that though confiderably hurt, it did
not complain, which induced his mafter to think
that it was mute: And it is probable that its
voice would be developed by grunting or interrupted founds, when in full poffeffion of freedom and in prefence of a female, the animal's
fpirits were excited by love.

It is fingular, that the bifons, or bunched oxen,
whofe race appears to be extended in the Old
Continent, from Madagafcar and the point of
Africa, and from the extremity of the Eaft Indies
as far as Siberia, and that, in the New Continent, though they are found from the country
of the Ilionois to Louifiana, and even Mexico,
they fhould never have paffed the ifthmus of Pa-
nama; for there are no bifons in any part of
South America, though the climate is perfectly
agreeable

agreeable to their nature, and the European oxen have multiplied there as well as in any other part of the globe.

At Madagafcar, the beft kind of bulls and cows were brought thither from Africa, and have a bunch on their backs. The cows yield fo little milk, that a fingle Dutch cow would give fix times as much. In this ifland, there are wild bifons, which wander in the forefts. The flefh of thefe bifons is not equal to that of our oxen *. In the fouthern parts of Afia, we likewife find wild oxen. The natives of Agra hunt thefe animals on the mountain of Nerwer, which is furrounded with wood. This mountain is fitu-ated on the road from Surat to Golconda. Thefe wild cattle are generally beautiful, and fell very dear †.

The zebu feems to be a miniature of the bi-fon, whofe race, as well as that of the ox, has undergone great variations, efpecially in fize. The zebu, though an original native of very warm regions, is capable of exifting and multi-plying in temperate climates. ' I faw,' fays Mr. Colinfon, ' a great number of thefe animals in ' the Duke of Richmond's, and alfo in the Duke ' of Portland's parks, where they every year ' bring forth calves, which are extremely beau-' tiful. The fathers and mothers were brought

* Voyage de François le Guat, tom. ii. p. 71.
† Voyage de Thevenot, tom. iii. p. 113.

' from

' from the Eaſt Indies. The bunch on the
' ſhoulder is twice as large in the male as in the
' female, whoſe ſtature exceeds that of the male.
' The young zebu ſucks its mother like other
' calves; but, in our climate, the milk of the
' mother ſoon dries up, and the ſuckling of the
' young is completed by the milk of another
' female. The Duke of Richmond ordered one
' of theſe animals to be ſlain; but its fleſh was
' not ſo good as that of the ox *.'

Among the oxen without bunches, there are
alſo ſmall individuals, which, like the zebu, may
conſtitute a particular race. Gemelli Careri, in
his journey from Iſpahan to Schiras, ſaw two
ſmall cows, which the Baſhaw of the Province
had ſent to the King, and which exceeded not
the ſize of calves. Though fed ſolely on ſtraw,
they were very fat †. In general, it appears,
that the zebus, or ſmall biſons, as well as our little
oxen, are more fleſhy and fatter than the biſons
and oxen of the common ſize.

With regard to the buffaloes, we have little to
add. It ſhall only be remarked, that, though
they cannot uſe their horns, they are made to
fight lions and tigers in the Mogul's country.
Theſe animals are very numerous in all warm
climates, eſpecially in marſhy countries, and in

* Letter from the late Mr. Colinſon to M. de Buffon, dated
at London, December 30, 1764.
† Voyage de Gemelli Careri, tom. ii. p. 338.

the

the neighbourhood of rivers. Water, and a moift foil, feem to be ftill more neceffary to them than the warmth of a climate *. It is for this reafon that none of them are found in Arabia, where almoft the whole country is dry. The wild buffaloes are hunted, but with much caution; for they are exceedingly dangerous, and, when wounded, run againft men with great fury. As to the domeftic buffaloes, Niebuhr remarks, that, in fome places, as at Bafra, it is the practice, when milking the female, to thruft the hand, as far as the elbow, into the vagina, becaufe this operation makes her yield a greater quantity of milk †. This fact appears not to be probable; but the female buffalo, like fome of our cows, may forcibly retain her milk, and this gentle kind of titillation may relax the contraction of her teats.

At the Cape of Good Hope, the body of the buffalo is of the fame fize with our ox; but he has fhorter legs, and a larger head. He is a very formidable animal. He frequents the borders of the woods, and, as his fight is not good, he remains there with his head placed near the ground, in order the better to diftinguifh objects among the roots of the trees. When he per-

---

* I formerly remarked, that the buffaloes might fucceed in France. Attempts have lately been made to propagate them in Brandenbourg, near Berlin; *Gazette de France, June* 9, 1775.

† Defcript. de l'Arabie, par M. Niebuhr, p. 145.

ceives

ceives any difagreeable object near him, he darts fuddenly upon it, making, at the fame time, a moft hideous bellowing ; and it is very difficult on thefe occafions to efcape his fury. He is not fo much to be dreaded in the open fields. His hair is red, and black in fome places. They appear often in numerous flocks *.

* Note communicated by the Vicomte de Querhoënt to M. de Buffon.

Plate CLXX.

A.Bell sculp.

BUFFALO.

Plate CLXXI.

BISON.

The MOUFLON*, and other SHEEP.

THE weakeſt ſpecies of uſeful animals were firſt reduced to a domeſtic ſtate. The ſheep and goat were ſubjugated before the horſe, the

* The Siberian goat has large horns bending back, cloſe at their baſe, diſtant at their points, with circular rugæ. Theſe animals vary in ſize and colour. The ſkin of the one the Britiſh muſeum did me the favour of accepting, was covered with pale ferruginous hair, on the ſides ſhort, on the top of the neck longer, and a little erect. Along the lower ſide of the neck, and on the ſhoulders, the hair was fourteen inches long. Beneath, the hair was a ſhort wool. On the knees there was a bare ſpot, as if by kneeling to lie down. The tail was very ſhort; and the horns were twenty-five inches long, eleven in girth in the thickeſt place, and one foot ſeven inches diſtant from point to point.—The horns of the females are much leſs than thoſe of the males; *Pennant's Synopſ. of Quad. p.* 18.

Mouflon is derived from the Italian word *Muſione*, the name of this animal in the iſlands of Corſica and Sardinia; in Greek, μουϊμων, according to Strabo; in Latin, *Muſmon* or *Muſimon*; in Siberia, *Stepnie-barani*, that is, *wild ſheep*, according to Gmelin; and, among the Mogul Tartars, *Argali*.

Muſmon; *Plin. lib.* viii. *c.* 49. Ophion; *Id. lib.* xxviii. *c.* 9: *lib.* xxx. *c.* 15.

Tragelaphus; *Belon. Obſ. p.* 54. *Raii Synopſ. Quad. p.* 82. *Klein, Quad. p.* 20. The coat of the tragelaphus, ſays Belon, is ſimilar to that of the he-goat; but he has no beard. His horns, which do not ſhed, reſemble thoſe of a ſhe-goat; but they are ſometimes twiſted like thoſe of a ram. He has the muzzle, front, and ears of a ſheep; and his ſcrotum is likewiſe

pendu-

the ox, or the camel. They were likewife more
eafily tranfported from one climate to another.
From this fource, all the varieties among thefe
fpecies, as well as the difficulty of diftinguifhing
the genuine ftock of each, have proceeded. We
formerly proved, that our domeftic fheep, in
their prefent condition, could not fubfift without the fupport of man *; from which it is apparent, that Nature never produced them as
they exift at prefent, but that they have degenerated under our care. We muft, therefore,
fearch among the wild animals for thofe which
make the neareft approach to the fheep. We muft
compare them with the domeftic fheep of foreign
countries, examine the different caufes which

pendulous and large. His thighs, under the tail, are white,
and the tail is black. Upon the breaft and throat the hair
is fo long that he feems to have a beard. The hairs upon
the fhoulders and breaft are long and black. He has two
gray fpots, one on each fide of the flanks. His noftrils are
black; and his muzzle, as well as the under part of his belly,
are white.—*Note,* This defcription of the tragelaphus by Belon agrees, in every effential character, with that we have given
of the moufflon.

Mufmon, feu mufimon; *Gefner, Hift. Quad. p.* 823.

Hircus cornibus fupra rotundatis, infra planis, femicircu-
lum referentibus. . . . . Le chamois de Siberie; le chevre
du Levant; *Briffon, Quad. p.* 46.

Rupicapra cornibus arietinis, Argali; *Nov. Com. Petrop. tom.* iv.
p. 49. 388. *tab.* 8.

Fifhtall, Lerwee; *Shaw's Travels, p.* 243.

Capra Ammon, cornibus arcuatis, femicircularibus, fubtus
planiufculis, palearibus laxis, pilofis, gula imberbi; *Linn. Syft.
Nat. p.* 97.

* See above, article *Sheep,* vol. III.

might

might introduce changes into the species, or make it degenerate, and endeavour, as in the case of the ox, to recall all these varieties, and all these pretended species, to one primitive race.

Our sheep, in its present state, exists no where but in Europe, and some of the temperate provinces of Asia. When transported into warm countries, as Guiney *, it loses its wool, and is covered with hair: Its fertility is diminished, and the taste of its flesh is altered. In very cold countries it cannot subsist. But, in cold climates, and particularly in Iceland, we find a race of sheep with several horns, a short tail, and hard thick wool, under which, as in most nor-

---

* Ovis Africana pro vellere lanoso pilis brevibus hirtis vestita; hoc genus vidimus in vivario regio, Westmonasteriensi, S. Jacobi dicto; quoad formam corporis externam ovibus vulgaribus persimile, verum pro lana ei pilus fuit. . . . . Specie a nostratibus differre non fidenter affirmaverim; fortasse quemadmodum homines in Nigritarum regionibus pro capillis lanam quandam obtinent, ita vice versa pecudes hæ pro lana pilos; *Ray, Syn. Quad. p. 75.*——In the kingdom of Congo, in Loango, and Cabinda, the sheep, instead of soft wool, are covered with coarse hair, similar to that of dogs. The extreme heat of the air, which dries up all the oily humours, is the cause of this coarseness. I made the same observation with regard to the Indian sheep; *Voyage de J. Ovington, tom. i. p. 60.*——The sheep are pretty numerous along the coast of Guiney, and yet they are very dear. They have the same figure with those of Europe, except that they are one half smaller, and, instead of wool, are covered with hair of an inch long. . . The flesh has not the smallest appearance of that of the European sheep, being extremely dry, &c.; *Voyage de Bosman, p. 237.*

them

thern animals, there is a layer of softer, finer, and more bushy wool. In warm countries, on the contrary, the sheep have generally short horns and a long tail, some of which are covered with wool, others with hair, and others with a mixture of wool and hair. The first of these warm country sheep, which is commonly called the *Barbary sheep* *, or the *Arabian sheep* †, resembles the domestic kind in every respect, except the tail ‡, which is so loaded with fat,

---

* Persia abounds in sheep and goats. Some of these sheep, which are called *Barbary*, or *broad-tailed sheep*, have a tail that weighs above 30 pounds. It is a heavy burden to the poor animals, and still more so, as it is narrow at the origin, and broad at the extremity. Some of them are so heavy, that the animals are unable to trail them; and the shepherds are obliged to fix boards with two wheels under the tail, to preserve it from galling, &c.; *Chardin, tom.* ii. *p.* 28.

† Ovis laticauda Arabica; *Raii Synopf. Quad. p.* 74. Most naturalists call this animal the *Arabian sheep*. It is not, however, an original native of Arabia, nor does it belong to the Arabian race of sheep. But they are very numerous in South Tartary, Persia, Egypt, Barbary, and in all the Eastern coasts of Africa.

Aries laniger, cauda latissima. . . . Ovis laticauda. La brebis à large queue; *Brisson. Quad. p.* 50. *Linn. Syst. Nat. p.* 97. *Nov. Com. Petrop. tom.* v. *p.* 347. *tab.* 8.

‡ Neque his arietibus ullum ab aliis discrimen præterquam in cauda quam latissimam circumferunt. . . Nonnullis libras decem aut viginti cauda pendet, cum sua sponte impinguantur; verum in Ægypto plurimi farciendis vervecibus intenti, furfure hordeoque faginant; quibus adeo crassescit cauda ut seipsos dimovere non possint; verum qui eorum curam gerunt caudam exiguis vehiculis alligantes gradum promovere faciunt; vidi hujusmodi caudam libras octuaginta pondera re. *Leon. Afric. Descript. Afric. vol.* ii. *pag.* 253.

that

that it is often more than a foot broad, and weighs above twenty pounds. Besides, there is nothing remarkable in this animal but its tail, which it carries as if a cushion were fixed to its thighs. Among this race of sheep, there are some whose tails are so long* and heavy, that they are obliged to be supported by a small wheel machine, to enable the animals to walk. In the Levant, this sheep is covered with very fine wool; but, in warm countries, as Madagascar, and the Indies †, it is covered with hair. The redundance of fat, which, in our sheep, fixes about the kidneys, descends, in these animals, upon the vertebræ of the tail: The other parts of their bodies are less loaded with fat than our fed wedders. This variety should be attributed to the food, the climate, and the care of men; for those broad or long tailed sheep are domestic like ours, and even require more care and management. This race is much more diffused than that of the ordinary kind. It is common

---

* Ovis Arabica altera; *Raii Synopf. Quad.* p. 74. Aries laniger cauda longiffima.——Ovis longicauda; *Briffon. Quad.* p. 76. *Note*, Ray and Briffon have made two diftinct fpecies of thefe broad and long tailed fheep. But Linnæus has properly reduced them to one.

† The ifland of Madagafcar produces fheep with tails fo large that they weigh twenty pounds. They are loaded with fat, which does not melt, and their flefh is very delicate. The wool of thefe fheep is like goat's hair; *Voyage de Flacourt*, p. 3.—— The flefh of the wedders and young females has an excellent favour; *Idem*, p. 151.

in

in Tartary *, Perſia †, Syria ‡, Egypt, Barbary, Æthiopia §, Moſambique ||, Madagaſcar **, and the Cape of Good Hope ††.

In

* The ſheep of Tartary, like thoſe of Perſia, have large tails, which conſiſt entirely of fat, and weigh from twenty to thirty pounds. Their ears are pendulous, and their noſe flat; *Voyage d'Olearius, tom.* i. *p.* 321.——The ſheep of Eaſt Tartary have tails which weigh from ten to twelve pounds. Theſe tails conſiſt of ſolid fat, which has an excellent reliſh. The bones of the vertebræ are not larger than thoſe of our ſheep; *Relation de la Grande Tartarie, p.* 187.——The ſheep of Calmuck Tartary have their tails concealed in a cuſhion of many pounds weight; *Id. p.* 267.

† A ſingle tail of ſome of the Perſian ſheep weighs from ten to twelve pounds, and yields five or ſix pounds of fat. Its figure is the reverſe of that of our ſheep, being broad at the extremity, and ſmall at the origin; *Voyage de Tavernier, tom.* ii. *p.* 379.

‡ In Syria, Judea, and Egypt, the tails of the ſheep are ſo large, that I have ſeen one of them weigh above thirty-three pounds, though the animals were not larger than the ſheep of Berri, but much handſomer, and had finer wool; *Voyage de Villamont, p.* 629.

§ In Æthiopia, there are ſheep whoſe tails weigh more than twenty-five pounds.——Others have tails a fathom long, and twiſted like a vine branch; *Drake's Voyage, p.* 85.

|| Sunt ibi oves quæ una quarta parte abundant; integram enim ovem ſi quadrifide ſecaveris præciſe quinque partibus pienarie conſtabit; cauda ſiquidem quam habent tam lata, craſſa, et pinguis eſt, ut ob molem reliquis par ſit; *Hug. Lintſcot. Navig. part.* ii. *p.* 19.

** The iſland of Madagaſcar abounds in cattle.——The tails of the rams and ewes are ſo large, that we ſaw one which weighed twenty-eight pounds; *Voyage de Pyrard, tom.* i. *p.* 37.

†† In the ſheep at the Cape of Good Hope there is nothing remarkable, except the length and thickneſs of the tail, which

In the iflands of the Archipelago, and particularly in Crete, there is a race of domeftic fheep, of which Belon has given a figure and defcription under the name of *ftrepficheros* *. This fheep is of the fame fize with the common kind. Like the latter, it is covered with wool, and differs from them only by having erect horns chamfered in the form of a fcrew.

In fine, we find in the warmer countries of Africa and India, a race of large fheep with coarfe hair, fhort horns, pendulous ears, with a kind of dewlap which hangs under the neck. This fheep is called by Leo Africanus and Marmol, *adimain* †; and it is known to the naturalifts under the name of the *Senegal fheep* ‡, the

---

which commonly weighs from fifteen to twenty pounds. The Perfian fheep, though fmaller, have ftill larger tails. I have feen fome of this race at the Cape, whofe tails weighed at leaft thirty pounds; *Defcript. du Cap de Bonne-Efperance, par Kolbe, tom.* ii. *p.* 97.

* In Crete, and particularly on Mount Ida, there is a race of fheep, which go in large flocks, and are called *ftriphocheri.* They refemble the common kind in every thing but their horns, which, inftead of being twifted, are ftraight and chamfered like a fcrew ; *Obferv. de Belon, p.* 15.

† *Adimain,* animal domefticum arietem forma refert.—— Aures habet oblongas et pendulas. Lybici his animalibus pecoris vice utuntur.————Ego quondam juvenili fervore ductus horum animalium dorfo infidens ad quartam miliarii partem delatus fui ; *Leon. Afric. Defcript. Afric. vol.* ii. *p.* 752. See alfo *l'Afrique de Marmol, tom.* i. *p.* 59.

‡ The wedders, or rather the rams of Senegal, for none of them are caftrated, are a diftinct and ftrongly marked fpecies. They have nothing of the common kind but the head and

the *Guiney fheep* *, the *fheep of Angola*, &c. It is domeftic, like the other kind, and fubject to the fame varieties. We have given figures of two of thefe fheep, which, though they differ in particular characters, have fo many re-

---

tail. From the coarfenefs of their hair, they feem to be allied to the goat. ———— It appears that wool would be incommodious to the fheep in very warm climates; and that Nature has changed it into hair of a moderate length, and pretty thin; *Voyage au Senegal, par M. Adanfon, p.* 36.

African fheep. ————It is meager, very long legged, and tall, with fhort horns and pendant ears. It is covered with fhort hair, inftead of wool, and has wattles on its neck. Perhaps it is the *adimain* of Leo Africanus, *p.* 341. which he fays furnifhes the Lybians with milk and cheefe. It is of the fize of an afs, and fhaped like a ram; *Pennant's Synopf. of Quad. p.* 12.

* Aries Guineenfes, five Angolenfis; *Marcgrav. p.* 234. *Raii Synopf. Quad. p.* 75.

Aries Pilofus, pilis brevibus veftitus, juba longiffima, auriculis longis pendulis.————Ovis Guineenfis. La brebis de Gunée; *Briffon. Regn. Anim. p.* 77.

Ovis Guineenfis, auribus pendulis, palearibus laxis, pilofis, occipite prominente; *Linn. Syft. Nat. p.* 98.

Sheep of Sahara; *Shaw's Travels, p.* 241.

Carnero, or Bell wedder; *Della Valle, Trav. p.* 91.

The Guiney fheep differ from the European kind. They are generally longer legged, and have no wool, but fhort, foft hair, like that of a dog. The rams have long manes, which fometimes hang down to the ground, and cover their necks from the fhoulders to their ears, which are pendulous. Their horns are knobbed, pretty fhort, fharp, and bended forward. Thefe animals are fat; their flefh is good, and well flavoured, efpecially when they feed on the mountains or along the fea coafts; but it fmells of tallow when they pafture on marfhy grounds. The ewes are exceedingly prolifi.———— They always bring forth two lambs at a time; *Voyage de Defmarchais, tom.* i. *p.* 141.

femblances,

femblances, that we muſt pronounce them to belong to the ſame race. Of all the domeſtic kinds, this race appears to approach neareſt to a ſtate of nature. It is larger, ſtronger, nimbler, and, conſequently, more capable of ſubſiſting as a wild animal. But, as it is only found in very warm climates, and cannot endure cold, and as, even in its native climate, it ſubſiſts not in a wild ſtate, but is domeſtic, and requires the aid of man, it cannot be regarded as the primitive ſtock from which all other ſheep have derived their origin.

In conſidering domeſtic ſheep, therefore, relative to the order of climate, we have, 1. The northern ſheep with ſeveral horns, and whoſe wool is extremely coarſe. The ſheep of Iceland, Gothland, Muſcovy *, and other parts of the north of Europe, have all coarſe hair, and ſeem to belong to the ſame race.

2. Our ſheep, whoſe wool is very fine and beautiful in the mild climates of Spain and Perſia, but which, in very warm countries, turns coarſe. We have already remarked the conformity between the influence of the climates of Spain and of Chorazan, a province of Perſia,

* Twenty Sileſian ſhepherds arrived at Peterſburg, and were afterwards ſent to Cazan to ſhear the ſheep, and to teach the Muſcovites the mode of preparing wool.——— But this did not ſucced; and the chief cauſe of its failure was ſaid to be owing to the coarſeneſs of the wool, the ſheep and goats having always intermixed and produced together; *Nouv. Mem. ſur l'Etat de la Moſcovie, tom.* i. *p.* 290.

upon

upon the hair of goats, cats, and rabbits: It acts in the same manner upon the wool of sheep, which is very fine in Spain, and still finer in that part of Persia *.

3. The large tailed sheep, whose wool is very fine in temperate countries, such as Persia, Syria, and Egypt; but, in warmer climates, it is converted into hair more or less coarse.

* At Meschet in the country of Chorazan, on the frontiers of Persia, lamb skins formerly constituted a great article of commerce. The fleeces were of a beautiful silver gray colour, all curled, and finer than silk: Those sheep which come from the mountains to the south of this city, and from the province of Kerman, afford the finest wool in Persia; *Relation de la Grande Tartarie, p.* 187.—The greatest part of this fine wool is furnished by the province of Kerman, which is the ancient Caramania; and the best kind comes from the mountains adjacent to the town, which has the same name with the province. It is singular, that when the sheep of these places have eat the new herbage from January to May, the fleeces fall entirely off, and leave the animals as bare as scalded pigs; so that there is no occasion for shearing them as in France. When the fleeces are collected, they are beat or threshed; by which operation the coarser part separates and leaves nothing but the fine.———This wool is never dyed: It is naturally of a bright brown or a gray ash colour, and very little of it is white; *Voyage de Tavernier, tom.* i. *p.* 130.———The wedders of the Usbeck and Beschac Tartars have long, grayish wool, curled at the ends into small white rings, which have the appearance of pearls. These fleeces are more esteemed than the flesh; because, next to the sable, they are the most valuable furs used in Persia. The animals are fed with great care, and generally in the shade. When obliged to be exposed to the open air, they are covered like our horses. The tail of these wedders is small, like that of the common kind; *Voyage d'Olearius, tom.* i. *p.* 547.

4. The

.4. The ftrepficheros or Cretan fheep. They refemble ours in every article but the horns, which are erect and chamfered in a fpiral form.

5. The *adimain*, or large fheep of Senegal and India, which are covered with hair more or lefs fhort and coarfe, in proportion to the heat of the climate. All thefe fheep are only varieties of the fame fpecies, and would unqueftionably produce with each other; fince we know from experience that the he-goat, whofe fpecies is more remote, produces with our ewes. But, though thefe five or fix races of domeftic fheep are all varieties of the fame fpecies, entirely produced by difference of climate, food, and management; yet none of them appears to be the primitive ftock or fource of all the reft. None of them is fufficiently ftrong or nimble to refift the carnivorous animals, or to efcape from them by flight. All of them equally require care and protection. Hence the whole fhould be re-garded as degenerate races, formed by the hand of man, and multiplied for his ufe. While he nourifhed, cultivated, and increafed thefe domeftic races, he would neglect, injure, and deftroy the wild race, which being ftrong and lefs tract-able, would, of courfe, be more incommodious and lefs ufeful to him. The individuals of this race, therefore, would be fmall, and limited to fuch defert or thinly inhabited places as could afford them fubfiftence. Now, in the mountains of Greece, in the ifland of Cyprus, Sardinia, and Corfica, and in the deferts of Tartary, we find

the

the animal called *mouflon*, which feems to be the primitive ftock of all the different varieties of fheep. It lives in a ftate of nature, and fubfifts and multiplies without the aid of man. It refembles, more than any other wild animal, all the domeftic kinds, and it is ftronger, fwifter, and more vivacious than any of them. It has the head, front, eyes, and face of the ram. It likewife refembles him in the figure of the horns, and in the whole habit of the body. In fine, it produces with the domeftic fheep*, which alone is fufficient to prove that it belongs to the fame fpecies, and is the primitive ftock from which all the other varieties have originated. The only difference between the mouflon and our fheep is, that the former is covered with hair, inftead of wool. Now, we have already feen, that, in domeftic fheep, wool is not an effential character, but only a production of temperate climates; fince, in warm countries, thefe fame fheep lofe their wool, and are covered with hair; and, in very cold regions, their wool is as coarfe as hair. Hence it is by no means furprifing, that the primitive wild fheep, which muft have been expofed to heat and cold, and

---

* Eft et in Hifpania, fed maxime Corfica, non maxime abfimile pecori (fcilicet ovili) genus mufmonum, caprino villo, quam pecoris velleri propius: Quorum e genere et ovibus natos prifci umbros vocarunt; *Plin. Hift. Nat. lib.* viii. *cap.* 49. From this paffage we learn, that the mouflon has at all times produced with the fheep. The ancients called all the mongrels animals of this race, *umbri, imbri,* or *ibri.*

muft

muſt have multiplied without ſhelter in the
woods and deſerts, ſhould not be covered with
wool, which it would ſoon loſe among the thickets, and its nature would be changed·by the
continual action of the air and temperance of
the ſeaſons. Beſides, when the he-goat copulates
with the domeſtic ewe, the produce is a kind of
mouflon ; for the lamb is covered with hair, and
is not an unfertile mule, but a mongrel, which
riſes up toward the primitive ſpecies, and ſeems
to indicate that the goat and our domeſtic ſheep
have ſomething common in their origin : And,
as we know from experience, that the he-goat
eaſily produces with the ewe, but that the ram
is incapable of impregnating the ſhe-goat, it is
evident, that, among theſe animals, while in a
domeſtic ſtate, the goat is the predominant ſpecies. Thus, our ſheep is a ſpecies much more
degenerated than that of the goat ; and it is extremely probable, that, if the ſhe-goat were ſerved with a mouflon, inſtead of a domeſtic ram,
ſhe would produce kids which would approach
to the ſpecies of the goat, as the lambs produced
by the he-goat and ewe riſe toward the original
ſpecies of the ram.

I am aware of objections to this doctrine from
thoſe ſyſtematic naturaliſts, who found all their
knowledge of natural hiſtory upon ſome particular
characters ; and, therefore, ſhall endeavour to prevent them. The firſt character, they will ſay, of
the ram, is to carry wool, and the firſt character of
the

the goat is to be covered with hair. The second
character of the ram is to have horns bended in
a circular form, and turned backward, and that
of the he-goat is to have them straight and
erect. Thefe, they will affirm, are the effential
and infallible marks by which fheep and goats
will always be diftinguifhed; for they muft acknowledge, that every other article is common
to both. None of them have cutting teeth in the
upper jaw; but each of them has eight in the
under jaw. In both, the canine teeth are wanting;
their hoofs are equally divided, and their horns
are fimple and permanent. Both have their paps
fituated in the region of the belly; and both
feed upon herbage. Their internal ftructure is
ftill more fimilar; for it appears to be the very
fame. The number and form of their ftomachs,
the ftructure and difpofition of their inteftines,
the fubftance of the flefh, the qualities of the fat
and feminal liquor, the times of geftation and
growth, and the duration of their lives, are exactly the fame. There remain, therefore, only the
wool and the horns by which thefe two fpecies
can be diftinguifhed. But, it has already been
fhown, from facts, that wool is not fo much a
natural fubftance, as a production of climate,
aided by the care of man. The fheep of warm
and of cold countries, and wild fheep, have no
wool. Befides, in very mild climates, the goats
may be faid to have wool inftead of hair;
for that of the Angora goat is finer than the

I   wool

wool of our wedders. This character, therefore, is not effential, but purely accidental, and
even equivocal; for it may equally belong to
thefe two fpecies, or be wanting altogether, according to the difference of the climates. That
of the horns appears to be ftill lefs certain; for
they vary in number, fize, figure, and direction.
In our domeftic fheep, the rams have generally
horns, and the ewes have none. I have feen
fheep not only with two, but with four horns.
Thofe of the North and of Iceland have fometimes eight. In warm countries, the rams have
only two fhort horns, and often want them, like
the ewes. In fome, the horns are fmooth and
round; in others, they are flat and chamfered.
The points, inftead of being bended backward,
are fometimes turned outward, forward, &c. This
character, therefore, is not more conftant than
the former; and, confequently, it is not fufficient to conftitute different fpecies *. Neither can
the

---

* Linnæus, with great propriety, inftead of fix fpecies,
has made fix varieties only of domeftic fheep. 1. Ovis ruftica
cornuta. 2. Anglica mutica, cauda fcrotoque ad genua pendulis.
3. Hifpanica cornuta, fpira extrorfum tracta. 4. Polycerata e Goth-
landia. 5. Africana pro lana pilis brevibus hirta. 6. Laticauda
platyura Arabica; Linn. Syft. Nat. p. 97. All thefe fheep are only
varieties, to which this author fhould have added the adimain
or Guiney fheep, and the ftrepficeros of Crete, inftead of
making them two different fpecies. In the fame manner, if
he had feen the mouflon, and had known that it produced
with the fheep, or had only confulted the paffage of Pliny concerning the mouflon, he would never have ranked it with the
goat,

the thickneſs or length of the tail anſwer this purpoſe ; ſince it may be conſidered as an artificial member, which, by great care and abundance of good nouriſhment, may be enlarged at pleaſure. Beſides, among our domeſtic races, as in certain Britiſh ſheep, there are ſome which have tails longer than the common kind. Our modern naturaliſts, however, truſting ſolely to the differences in the horns, the wool, and the largeneſs of the tail, have made ſeven or eight diſtinct ſpecies out of the ſheep-kind. The whole of theſe we have reduced to one. And this reduction ſeems to be ſo well founded, that there is little proſpect of its being overturned by future obſervations.

In compoſing the hiſtory of wild animals, we found it convenient to examine them one by one, without any regard to genus, but, in the domeſtic animals, on the contrary, it was neceſſary not only to adopt, but to increaſe the number of genera ; becauſe in Nature there exiſt only individuals, and ſucceſſions of individuals, that is, ſpecies. Men have had no influence on independent animals ; but they have greatly altered and modified the domeſtic kinds. We have, therefore, eſtabliſhed phyſical and real genera,

goat, but with the ſheep. Briſſon has not only placed the mouflon and ſtrepſicheros, which he calls *hircus laniger*, among the goats, but he has made four diſtinct ſpecies of domeſtic ſheep covered with wool, beſide the domeſtic ſheep of warm countries covered with hair, and the broad and long tailed ſheep. All theſe ſeven we have reduced to a ſingle ſpecies.

very

very different from thofe metaphyfical and arbitrary ones, which have no exiftence but in idea.
Thefe phyfical genera are, in reality, compofed
of all the fpecies, which, by our management,
have been greatly variegated and changed; and,
as all thofe fpecies, fo differently modified by the
hand of man, have but one common origin in
Nature, the whole genus ought to conftitute but
a fingle fpecies. In writing, for example, the
hiftory of tigers, we have admitted as many fpecies as are really found in different parts of the
earth; becaufe we are certain that man has never introduced any changes among thefe untractable and ferocious animals, who fubfift at prefent in the fame manner as they were originally
produced by Nature. The fame remark applies
to all free and independent animals. But, in
compofing the hjftory of oxen and fheep, we
have reduced all the varieties of the oxen to one
ox, and all the varieties of the fheep to one fheep;
becaufe it is equally certain that Man, and not
Nature, has produced the different kinds which
we have enumerated. Every thing concurs in
fupporting this idea, which, though clear in itfelf, may not, perhaps, be fufficiently underftood.
That all the oxen produce together, we are affured by the experiments of M. de la Nux, Ment-
zelius, and Kalm: That all the fheep produce
with one another, with the mouflon, and even
with the goat, I know from my own experience.
All the varieties of oxen, therefore, form but one

9   fpecies;

fpecies; and all the fheep, however numerous their varieties, conftitute only another fpecies.

I am obliged, by the importance of the fub-ject, to repeat, that Nature is not to be judged of by particular minute characters, and that by thefe the differences of fpecies are not to be determined; that methodical diftributions, inftead of throwing light on the hiftory of animals, render it ftill more obfcure, by a fruitlefs multiplication of denominations, and of fpecies; by forming arbitrary genera, which Nature never knew; by confounding real beings with creatures of imagination; by giving falfe ideas of the effential characteriftics of fpecies; and by mixing or feparating them in an arbitrary manner, without fkill, and often without having examined or even feen the individuals. It is for this reafon that our nomenclators perpetually deceive themfelves, and publifh nearly as many errors as lines. Of this we have already given fo many examples, that nothing but the blindeft and moft obftinate prejudice can poffibly refift the evidence they afford. On this fubject M. Gmelin talks very fenfibly, when treating of the animal under confideration *.

We

* 'The *argali,* or *ftepnie-baranl,* which occupy,' fays he, ' the fouthern mountains of Siberia, from the river Irtis, as far as Kamtfchatka, are extremely vivacious animals; and this vivacity feems to exclude them from the clafs of fheep, and to rank them with that of the ftags. I fhall here give a fhort defcription of them, from which it will appear, that

neither

We are convinced, as M. Gmelin remarks, that we can never acquire a knowledge of Nature,

neither fprightlinefs, nor inactivity, neither the wool nor hair with which an animal is covered, neither crooked nor ftraight horns, neither permanent horns nor thofe which fall off annually, are marks fufficiently characteriftic to diftinguifh claffes. Nature loves variety; and I am perfuaded, that, if we knew better how to manage our fenfes, they would often lead us to more effential characters, with regard to the differences of animals, than we generally derive from reafon, which feldom apprehends thofe marks but in a fuperficial manner. In this animal, the external form of the head, neck, and tail, correfponds with that of the ftag. His vivacity, alfo, as formerly remarked, is fo great, that he feems to be ftill more wild than the ftag. The individual I faw, though reputed to be only three years old, ten men durft not attack. The largeft of this fpecies are about the fize of a fallow deer. The one I examined meafured, from the ground to the top of the head, a Ruffian ell and a half in height. His length, from the root of the horns, was an ell and three quarters. The horns rife above and very near the eyes, and juft before the ears. They firft bend backward and then forward in a circular form. The tips turn upward and outward. The horns, from the root to the middle, are furrowed, but afterward become fomewhat fmoother. It is probably from the figure of the horns that the Ruffians have called this animal the *wild sheep*. If we can truft the natives of thefe provinces, his whole ftrength lies in his horns. They fay that the rams of this fpecies fight by ftriking each other with their horns; and, when any of them are knocked off, the aperture of the bafe is fo large, that the young foxes frequently take fhelter in the cavity. It is not difficult to eftimate the force neceffary to break off one of thefe horns, fince they, as long as the animal lives, continue to augment both in thicknefs and in length; and the part of the head alfo from which they fpring becomes always harder. It is faid, that a well grown horn, comprehending the curvatures, meafures two ells in length; that it weighs between thirty

and

ture, but by a judicious ufe of our fenfes, by feeing, examining, comparing, and, at the fame time,

and forty Ruffian pounds; and that, at the bafe, it is feven or eight inches in diameter. The horns of the one I faw were of a whitifh yellow colour; but they turn browner and blacker as the animal advances in years. He carries his ears, which are pointed and tolerably large, very erect. The hoofs are divided, and the fore legs are three quarters of an ell long, and the hind legs ftill longer. When the animal ftands erect on a plain, his fore legs are always fully extended and ftraight, and thofe behind are crooked; and this curvature feems to diminifh in proportion to the inequality of the ground over which he paffes. On the neck there are fome pendulous folds. The colour of the body is grayifh mixed with brown. Along the back, there is a yellowifh or rather reddifh line; and the fame colour appears behind, on the infide of the legs, and on the belly, where it is a little paler. This colour continues from the beginning of Auguft till the fpring, at the approach of which thefe animals caft their hair, and become every where more red. They caft their hair a fecond time about the end of July. This defcription applies to the males. The females are always fmaller; and though they have fimilar horns, they are fmaller and thinner, and even acquire not thicknefs with age. The horns are nearly ftraight, have no furrows, and much refemble thofe of our caftrated he-goats.

In the internal parts, they refemble other ruminating animals. The ftomach is compofed of four different cavities, and the gall-bladder is confiderably large. Their flefh is good, and has nearly the fame tafte with that of the roebuck. The fat is delicious, according to the teftimony of the Kamtfchatkan nations. They feed upon herbage. They couple in autumn, and bring forth one or two lambs in the fpring.

By the hair, the tafte of the flefh, the figure and vivacity of this animal, it belongs to the clafs of the ftag. By the permanent horns, it is excluded from this clafs. The circular horns give it fome refemblance to the fheep. It is diftinguifhed from that animal by its vivacity and want of wool. Its hair, its abode upon high rocks, and its frequent combats, make

time by denying ourfelves the liberty of fabricating methodical diftributions, contemptible fyftems, in which animals are claffed which the authors never faw, and knew nothing more of them than their names, which are often ambiguous, obfcure, and mifapplied. The falfe employment of thefe names confounds ideas in a farrago of words, and drowns truth in a torrent of error. We are likewife convinced, after examining the mouflon alive, and comparing him with Gmelin's defcription, that the argali is the fame animal. We formerly remarked, that this animal was found in Europe, and in pretty warm countries, fuch as Greece *, the ifland of Cyprus †, Sardinia,

make it approach to the goats. But the crooked horns, and the want of a beard, exclude it from this clafs. Should we not rather regard this animal as conftituting a particular clafs, and recognife it as the *mufimon* of the ancients? In a word, it has a ftrong refemblance to Pliny's defcription of the mufimon, and ftill more to that given by the learned Gefner;" *Relation d'un Voyage par Terre à Kamtfchatka, par Gmelin*. This curious relation is written by a man of good fenfe, and much verfed in natural hiftory.

* The tragelaphus of Belon is unqueftionably our mouflon; and we perceive, from his remarks, that he faw, defcribed, and drew a figure of this animal in Greece, and that it is found in the mountains between Macedonia and Servia.

† In the Ifland of Cyprus, there are rams denominated by the ancient Greeks, according to Strabo, *mufmones*, and called by the prefent Italians *mufione*. Inftead of wool, they are covered with hair, like that of goats; or rather their fkin and hair differ little from thofe of the ftag. Their horns refemble thofe of rams; but they are bent backward. They are as tall and as large as a middle fized ftag. They run with

nia, and Corfica *. But it is ftill more numerous in the fouthern mountains of Siberia, under
a climate rather cold than temperate, where it
even appears to be larger, ftronger, and more
vigorous. Hence it might equally fupply the
north and the fouth : Its offspring might be rendered domeftic. After fuffering long the hard-
fhips of this ftate, it would degenerate ; and,
according to the differences of climate and treatment, would affume relative chara&ters, and new
habits of body, which, being afterward tranfmitted by generation, gave rife to our domeftic
fheep, and all the other races formerly enumerated.

SUPPLEMENT.

WE have given the figure of a ram which was
fhown at the fair of St. Germain, in the year

great fwiftnefs; but they never quit the higheft and moft rugged
mountains. Their flefh is good and favoury. . . . . . The
fkins of thefe animals are dreffed, and fent to Italy, where
they go by the name of *cordoani* or *corduani* ; *Defcript. des
Ifles de l'Archipel, par Dapper, p.* 50.

* His in infulis (Sardinia et Corfica) nafcuntur arietes qui
pro lana pilum caprinum producunt, quos mufmones vocitant;
Strabo, lib. v.—Nuper apud nos Sardus quidam vir non illi-
teratus Sardiniam affirmavit abundare cervis, apris, ac damis,
et infuper animali quod vulgo muflonem vocant, pelle et pilis
(pilis capreæ, ut ab alio quodam accepi, cætera fere ovi fimile)
cervo fimile ; cornibus arieti, non longis fed retro circa aures
reflexis, magnitudine cervi mediocris, herbis tantum vivere,
in montibus afperioribus verfari, curfu velociffimo, carne venati-
onibus expedita; *Gefner, Hift. Quad. p.* 823.

1774,

1774, under the name of the *ram of the Cape of Good Hope*. This fame ram was exhibited, the year preceding, under the denomination of the *Mogul ram with a thick tail*. But we learned that it was purchafed at Tunis; and we think it is the fame with the Barbary fheep formerly reprefented, from which it differs only by the fhortnefs of its tail, which is alfo flatter, and broader in the upper part. The head is likewife proportionally thicker, and refembles that of the Indian ram. The body is well covered with wool, and the legs are fhort, even when compared with thofe of our fheep. The figure and fize of the horns differ little from thofe of the Barbary fheep. We have called it the *ram of Tunis*, to diftinguifh it from the other; but we are perfuaded that they both belong to the fame country of Barbary, and that they are very nearly of the fame race.

We have likewife given the figure of a ram, which was exhibited at the fair of Saint-Germain, in the year 1774, under the name of the *morvant of China*. This ram is remarkable for a kind of mane on his neck, and for long hairs which hang down from his throat, and form a kind of cravat. Thefe hairs are a mixture of red and gray, hard to the touch, and about ten inches long. The hairs of the main are red, not very thick, extend as far as the middle of the back, and are of the fame colour and confiftence with thofe on the throat; but they are fhorter, and mixed with fome brown and black hairs. The wool which covers the body is a little curled, and foft at the extremity ; but near the fkin of the animal it is ftraight and hard : In general, it is about three inches long, and of a bright yellow colour. The legs are of a deep red, and the head is fpotted with different fhades of yellow. The greateft part of the tail is yellow and white, and in figure refembles that of a cow, being well furnifhed with hair toward the extremity. This ram ftands lower on his legs than the common kinds, and he refembles the Indian ram more than any other. His belly is very large, and not above fourteen inches nine lines raifed from the ground. M. de Seve, who defcribed this animal, adds, that, from the groffnefs of the belly, this ram had the appearance of a pregnant ewe. The horns are nearly the fame with thofe of our rams. But the hoofs are not prominent, and they are longer than thofe of the Indian ram.

We formerly remarked, and now repeat, that the mouflon is the primæval ftock of all the other fheep, and that his conftitution is fufficiently robuft to enable him to fubfift in cold, temperate, and warm climates. The wild rams of Kamtfchatka, fays M. Steller, have the air of a goat and the hair of a rain deer. Their horns are fo large, that fome of them weigh from twenty-five to thirty pounds. Spoons and other utenfils are made of them. Thefe rams are as active and nimble as roebucks. They inhabit

the

Plate CLXXII.

MUFFLON.

Plate CLXXIII.

ICELAND RAM.

Plate CLXXIV.

ICELAND EWE.

Plate CLXXV.

BARBARY WEDDER.

Plate CLXXVI.

INDIAN RAM.

Plate CLXXVII.

A.Bell Sculp.

INDIAN RAM.

Plate CLXXVIII.

A. Bell Sculp.

INDIAN EWE.

Plate CLXXIX.

A.Bell Sculp.

RAM of TUNIS.

Plate CLXXX.

A.Bell Sculp.

MORVANT

the precipices of the moft rugged mountains. Their flefh is exceedingly delicate ; but they are hunted chiefly for the fake of their furs.

I believe that few of the genuine mouflons now exift in Corfica. The frequent wars which happened in that ifland have probably accomplifhed their deftruction. But, in the figure of their prefent races of fheep, we ftill find marks of the former exiftence of the mouflon. In the month of Auguft 1774, we faw a Corfican ram, which belonged to the Duc de Vrilliére. It excceded not the fize of a French fheep. It was white, low on its legs, and had long hair difpofed in locks. It had four large horns, the upper two being more bulky than the under, and they had rugofities like thofe of the mouflon.

THE AXIS[*].

THIS animal being known only under the vague names of *Sardinian hind* and *Stag of the Ganges*, we have preserved the appellation given to it by Belon †, which he borrowed from Pliny,

---

[*] Deer with slender trifurcated horns; the first branch near the base, and the second near the top, each pointing upwards. It is of the size of the fallow deer, of a light gray colour, and the body is beautifully marked with white spots. Along the lower part of the sides-next the belly, is a line of white. The tail, which is as long as that of a fallow deer, is red above, and white beneath; *Pennant's Synops. of Quad.* p. 51.

Axis; *Plinii, lib.* viii. *cap.* 21. *Belon. Obs.* p. 119. *Raii Synops. Quad.* p. 88.

Speckled deer; *Nieuhoff. Voy.* p. 262.

Biche de Sardaigne; *Mem. pour servir à l'Hist. des Animaux,* part. ii p. 73. *tab.* 45.

† " In the court of this castle, there were a male and a female of a kind of *stag* or *fallow deer*, which we should never have recognised, if we had not suspected that it was the *axis* mentioned by Pliny, (*lib.* viii. *cap.* 21.) in the following words; *In India . . . . et feram nomine Axim, hinnuli pelle, pluribus candidioribusque maculis, sacram Libero Patri.* Both of them wanted horns, and, like the fallow deer, had a long tail that hung as low as the hocks, by which we knew that they were not stags; and, in fact, at first sight, we thought they were fallow deer. But, upon a closer examination, we rejected this opinion. The female is smaller than the male; and their skin was variegated with round, white spots. The ground colour of the body was yellowish, and white on the belly. In this article they differ from the camelopard; for the ground colour of the camelopard is white, and the spots are reddish. Their voice is clearer than that

Pliny, both becaufe the characters correfpond
with Pliny's axis, and the name has never been
applied to any other quadruped; and, therefore,
we are in no danger of falling into error or confufion; for a generic denomination, accompanied with an epithet derived from the climate, is
not a name, but a phrafe by which an animal may
be confounded with others of its own genus, as
the prefent animal with the ftag, though, perhaps, it is different both in fpecies and in climate. The axis is one cf the fmall number of
ruminating animals which carry horns, like thofe
of the ftag. He has the ftature and fwiftnefs of
the fallow deer. But, what diftinguifhes him
from both, he has the horns of the ftag, and the
figure of the fallow deer; his whole body is
marked with white fpots, elegantly difpofed, and
feparate from each other; and, laftly, he is a
native of warm climates *. But the hair of the
ftag

that of the ftag; for, having heard them bray, we were certain
that they could neither be fallow deer nor ftags, and, therefore, believed them to be the *axis* of the ancients; *Belon, Obferv.*
p. 119.

* This animal was in the royal menagery, under the name
of the *Ganges ftag*. From this denomination, as well as from the
paffages of Pliny and Belon, it appears that he is a native
of warm countries. The teftimonies of travellers, which we
are about to quote, confirm this fact, and at the fame time
prove, that the common fpecies of the ftag is not much
diffufed beyond the temperate climates. ' I never faw,' fays
le Maire, ' ftags at Senegal with horns like thofe of France;'
Voyage de le Maire, p. 190.—' In the peninfula of India, on this
' fide the Ganges, there are ftags whofe bodies are all inter-

' fperfed

ſtag and fallow deer is generally of a uniform
colour, and they are very numerous in cold and
temperate regions, as well as in warm climates.

The gentlemen of the Academy of Sciences
have given a figure and a deſcription of the internal parts of this animal *; but they have ſaid
little concerning its external form, and nothing
relative to its hiſtory. They have ſimply called
it the *Sardinian hind*, probably becauſe it was
brought to the royal menagery under that name.
But we have no evidence of this animal's being
a native of Sardinia. It is mentioned by no
author as exiſting wild in this iſland: On the contrary, we ſee, from the paſſages already quoted,
that it is found in the warmeſt countries of Aſia.
Hence the denomination of *Sardinian hind* has
been falſely applied : That of *Ganges ſtag* would
have been more proper, if it had belonged to the

---

* ſperſed with white ſpots ;' *Voyage de la Compagnie des Indes de
Hollande, tom.* iv. *p.* 423.—' At Bengal, we find ſtags which
' are ſpotted like tigers ;' *Voyage de Luillier, p.* 54.

* The height of theſe hinds, from the top of the back to
the tail, was two feet eight inches. The neck was a foot long,
and the hind legs three feet. Their hair was of four colours ;
namely, yellow, white, black, and gray. It was white on the
belly and on the inſide of the thighs and legs. The back was
a yellowiſh brown, and the flanks were of a dun yellow, or
Iſabella colour. Theſe ground colours were variegated with
white ſpots of different figures. Along the back were two
rows of ſpots in a ſtraight line ; the other ſpots were ſcattered
without any order. On each ſide of the flanks there was a
white line. The neck and head were gray ; the tail was all white
below, black above, and the hair of it was ſix inches long ;
Mem. pour ſervir à l'Hiſt. des Animaux, part. ii. *p.* 73.

ſtag

ftag fpecies, becaufe that part of India, through
which the Ganges runs, appears to be its native
country. It feems, however, to be likewife
found in Barbary *, and it is probable that the
fpotted fallow deer of the Cape of Good Hope
is the fame animal †.

We formerly remarked, that no fpecies‡ made
fo near an approach to another, as the fallow
deer to the ftag. The axis, however, feems to
form an intermediate fhade between the two.
It refembles the fallow deer in the fize of the
body, the length of the tail, and in a kind of
livery which it perpetually wears: There is no
effential difference but in the horns, which want
brow antlers, and refemble thofe of the ftag.
The axis, therefore, may be a variety only, and
not a different fpecies from that of the fallow
deer; for, though it is a native of the warmeft
countries of Afia, it eafily fubfifts and multiplies
in Europe. There are flocks of them in the menagery of Paris. They produce among themfelves with equal facility as the fallow deer.

* The Arabs call a fpecies of fallow deer *Bekker-el-Wafb*,
which has the horns of a ftag, but is not fo large. Thofe
which I faw had been taken in the mountains near Sgigata,
and appeared to be of a mild and tractable difpofition. The
female had no horns, &c.; *Shaw's Travels*.

† We faw, at the Cape of Good Hope, a kind of fpotted
fallow deer, which were fomewhat fmaller than thofe of Europe. . . . Their fpots were white and yellow. They always
go in flocks; *Defcript. du Cap de Bonne-efperance, par Kolbe,*
tom. i. *p.* 120.

‡ See the article *Fallow Deer*, vol. iv. of this work.

They

They have never been obferved, however, to intermix with the fallow deer, nor with the ftags, which has led us to prefume that they are not a variety either of the one or of the other, but a diftinct intermediate fpecies. But, as no decifive experiments have been made on this fubject, as no neceffary means have been ufed to oblige thefe animals to join, we do not affert pofitively that they belong to different fpecies.

We have already feen, under the article *ftag* and *fallow deer*, how liable thefe animals are to varieties, efpecially in the colour of their hair. The fpecies of the fallow deer and ftag, without being numerous in individuals, are very much diffufed. Both are found in either Continent, and both are fubject to a great number of varieties, which feem to form permanent races. The white ftags, whofe race is very ancient, fince they are mentioned by the Greeks and Romans, and the fmall brown ftags, which we have called *Corfican ftags*, are not the only varieties of this fpecies. In Germany, there is another race, known in that country under the name of *Brandbirtz ** , and by our hunters under that of the *ftag of Ardennes*. This ftag is larger than the common kind, and differs from the others not

---

* Alterum cervi genus, ignotius, priore majus, pinguius, tum pilo denfius et colore nigrius; unde Germanis a femiufti ligni colore *Brandbirtz* nominatur: Hoc in Mifenæ faltibus Boëmiæ vicinis reperitur; *Fabricius, apud Gefner, Hift. Quad. p.* 297.

only

only by its deeper and almoft black colour, but by long hair between the fhoulders and on the throat. This kind of mane and beard give him fome relation, the firft to the horfe, and the fecond to the he-goat. The ancients beftowed on this ftag the compound names of *hippelaphus* and *tragelaphus*. As thefe denominations have occafioned many critical difcuffions, in which the moft learned naturalifts by no means agree, and as Gefner *, Caius, and others, tell us that the *hippelaphus* was the rain deer, we thought it proper here to give the reafons which induce us to think differently, and lead us to believe, that the hippelaphus of Ariftotle is the fame animal with the tragelaphus of Pliny, and that both thefe names equally denote the ftag of Ardennes.

Ariftotle † gives to his hippelaphus a kind of mane upon the neck and top of the fhoulders, a beard

---

* Gefner. Hift. Quad. p. 491 et 492.

† Quinetiam hippelaphus fatis jubæ fummis continet armis, qui a forma equi et cervi, quam habet compofitam, nomen accepit, quafi equicervus dici meruiffet. . . . Tenuiffimo jubæ ordine a capite ad fummos armos crinefcit. Proprium equicervo villus qui ejus gutturi, modo barbæ, dependet. Gerit cornua utrinque, excepta fœmina, ... et pedes habet bifculcos. Magnitudo equicervi non diffidet a cervo. Gignitur apud Arachotas, ubi etiam boves fylveftres funt, qui differunt ab urbanis, quantum inter fues urbanos et fylveftres intereft. Sunt colore atro, corpore robufto, rictu leviter adunco; cornua gerunt refupinatiora. Equicervo cornua funt *Capræ* proxima; *Arift. Hift. Anim. liv.* ii. *cap.* i. *Nota,* Theodore Gaza, whofe Latin verfion we have quoted, has falfely tranflated Δορκας *capra,* inftead of *caprea.* Hence the word *caprea* fhould be fubftituted for *capræ,* that is, the *roe deer,* in

beard under the throat, horns to the male similar to those of the roebuck, and no horns to the
female. He says, that the hippelaphus is as large
as the stag, and is produced among the Arachotas,
a people of India, where there are also wild oxen,
whose bodies are very robust, their skin black,
their muzzle elevated, and their horns bended
more backward than those of the domestic ox.
It must be acknowledged, that Aristotle's characters of the hippelaphus will apply almost
equally well to the rain deer and to the stag of
Ardennes. They have both long hair upon the
neck and shoulders, and likewise on the throat,
which forms a kind of beard upon the gullet, and
not on the chin. But the hippelaphus, which
is of the size of the stag only, differs in this particular from the rain deer, which is much larger;
but, what appears to decide this question, the rain
deer, being an animal peculiar to cold countries,
never existed among the Arachotas. This country of the Arachotas is one of the provinces
which Alexander over-ran in his expedition into
India. It is situated beyond Mount Caucasus,

place of the *she-goat*. The wild oxen, here mentioned by
Aristotle, appear to be buffaloes. The short description he has
given of them, the climate, their resemblance to the ox, and
their black colour, have made this philosopher believe that
they differed not more from the domestic oxen, than the wild
boar from the common hog. But, as we formerly remarked,
the buffalo and ox are two distinct species. If the ancients
have bestowed no particular name on the buffalo, it is because
this animal was a stranger to them, because their knowledge
of him was imperfect, and they regarded him as a wild ox,
which differed from the domestic ox by some slight varieties only.

between

between Perſia and India. This warm country
never produced rain deer; for they cannot ſubſiſt in temperate countries, and are found only
in the northern regions of both Continents. The
ſtags, on the contrary, have no particular attachment to the north; for they are very numerous
both in temperate and warm climates. Hence
the hippelaphus of Ariſtotle, which is found
among the Arachotas, and in the ſame countries
with the buffalo, is unqueſtionably the ſtag of
Ardennes, and not the rain deer.

Now, if we compare what Pliny has ſaid of
the tragelaphus, with what Ariſtotle has advanced concerning the hippelaphus, and both with
nature, we will perceive that the tragelaphus is
the ſame animal with the hippelaphus, and conſequently the ſame with our ſtag of Ardennes.
Pliny remarks *, that the tragelaphus belongs to
the ſpecies of ſtag, and differs from him only by
the beard and the hair on its ſhoulders. Theſe
characters are poſitive, and can apply only to the
ſtag of Ardennes; for Pliny, in another place,
mentions the rain deer under the name of *Alca.*
He adds, that the tragelaphus is found in the
neighbourhood of Phaſis, which ſtill farther
agrees with the ſtag, and not with the rain deer.
We may, therefore, ſafely pronounce, that the
tragelaphus of Pliny, and the hippelaphus of
Ariſtotle, both denote the animal which we call

* Eadem eſt ſpecie (cervi videlicet) barba tantum, et armorum
villo diſtans quem *tragelaphon* vocant, non alibi quam juxta Phaſin
amnem, naſcens; *Plin. Hiſt. Nat. lib.* viii. *cap.* 33.

the

the *ſtag of Ardennes*; and that the axis of Pliny is the animal commonly denominated the *Ganges ſtag.* Though names have no influence upon nature, the explication of them is of great uſe to thoſe who ſtudy her productions.

S U P P L E M E N T.

IN the year 1765, the Duke of Richmond had in his parks a number of that ſpecies of the fallow deer, commonly known by the name of *Ganges ſtags,* and which I have called *axis.* Mr. Colinſon aſſures me, that they propagated with the ordinary kind of fallow deer.

' They live ſpontaneouſly,' he remarks, ' with ' the fallow deer, and form not ſeparate flocks. ' It is more than ſixty years ſince this ſpecies ' exiſted in England, where they had been tranſ-' ported before the white and black fallow deer, ' and even before the ſtag, which laſt, I ſuppoſe, ' was brought from France; becauſe, previous ' to that period, there were in England only the ' common fallow deer, and the Scottiſh roebuck. ' But, beſide this firſt ſpecies, we have now the ' axis, the black, the yellow, and the white fal-' low deer. The mixture of all theſe colours ' has produced moſt beautiful varieties *.'

In the year 1764, we had a male and female Chineſe fallow deer at the menagery of Verſailles.

* Lettre de M. Colinſon à M. de Buffon.

In

Plate CLXXXI.

AXIS

Plate CLXXXII.

FEMALE AXIS

In height, they exceeded not two feet four inches.
The body and tail were of a dark brown colour,
and the belly and limbs of a bright yellow.
The legs were fhort, the horns large and garnifhed with antlers. This fpecies, though fmaller
than the common fallow deer, and even than
the axis, is perhaps a variety only of the latter,
though it has no white fpots ; but inftead of
thefe white fpots, it had, in fome places, large
yellow hairs, which had a confiderable effect
upon the brown colour of the body. In fine, the
colour of the female was the fame as that of the
male ; and, it is probable, that the race might not
only be perpetuated in France, but that it might
even intermix with the axis, efpecially as both
thefe animals are natives of the eaftern regions
of Africa.

The ZEBU, or DWARF OX *.

THIS small ox was mentioned above under the article Buffalo, p. 164. But as,
since that article was printed, a zebu has been
brought to the royal menagery, we are now in a
condition to speak of it with more certainty,
and to give a figure of it drawn from the life,
with a more perfect description than the former
one.

* The zebu from which the following description was taken,
was not larger than a calf of five weeks old. We knew
it, however, to be an adult, and at least seven or eight years
of age, by inspection of its teeth. It arrived at the menagery
of Versailles in the month of August 1761, and its horns were
then as large as they are now in the year 1763. They are
five inches three lines long, and four inches three lines in circumference at the base. They are black at the points, and in
every other respect resemble those of the common ox. It has
a bunch on the withers, four inches and a half high, and its
circumference at the base is sixteen inches. In other articles,
it differs not in figure from our ox, except that its legs and
feet are proportionally smaller, and its ears longer.

The tuft of hair above the coronet is black. The legs and
upper part of the tail are yellowish. The under part, and the
long hairs at the point of the tail, are white, and a foot in
length. The rest of the body is variegated with black and
brown spots, of different dimensions, and slightly tinged with a
reddish colour.

" Dwarf ox, with horns almost close at their base, broad
and flat at the beginning, receding in the middle, and standing erect. It is larger than a roebuck, less than a stag, and
compact, and well made in all its limbs. Its hair is shining,
and of a tawny colour. Its legs are short, neck thick, and

shoulders

one. I have alfo learned, from frefh inquiries, that the zebu is probably the fame animal which is called the *lant* *, or *dant* †, in Numidia, and feveral other northern provinces of Africa, where it is very common; and that the name *dant*, which folely pertains to the animal under confideration, has been tranfported from Africa to America, and given to an animal which has no refemblance to the former but in the fize of its body, and belongs to a very different fpe-

fhoulders a little elevated. The tail is terminated with long hairs, twice as coarfe as thofe of a horfe. It is only a variety of the Indian ox;" *Pennant's Synopf. of Quad. p. 9.*

Un moult beau petit bœuf d'Afrique; *Belon, p. 119.*

Bos cornibus aure brevioribus, dorfo gibbo, juba nulla; *Linn. Syft. Nat. p. 99..*

* *Lant* bovem fimilitudine refert, minor tamen cruribus et cornibus elegantius; colorem album gerit, unguibus nigerrimis; tantæque velocitatis ut a reliquis animalibus, præterquam ab equo Barbarico, fuperari nequeat. Facilius æftate capitur quod arenæ æftu curfus velocitate ungues dimoveantur, quo dolore affeftus curfum remittit, &c.; *Leonis Afric. Africæ Defcript. vol. ii. p. 751.*

† The dant, which the Africans call *lampt*, is of the figure of a fmall ox, but its legs are fhort.———It has black horns, which bend round, and are fmooth. Its hair is whitifh, and its hoofs are black and cloven. It is fo fwift that no animal, unlefs the Barbary horfe, can overtake it. Thefe animals are faid to be more eafily taken in fummer; becaufe, by the force of running, their hoofs are worn among the burning fands, and the pain occafioned by this circumftance makes them ftop fhort, like the ftags and fallow deer of thefe deferts. There are numbers of thefe dants in the deferts of Numidia and Lybia, and particularly in the country of the Morabitains. Of their fkins the natives make excellent fhields, the beft of which are proof againft arrows.

cies.

cies. This American dant is the tapir or the maipouri ; and, to prevent the African dant, which
is our zebu, from being confounded with the
tapir, we fhall give the hiftory of the latter in
the fubfequent article.

Plate CLXXXIII.

ZEBU.

Plate CLXXXIV.

TAPIR.

THE TAPIR*.

THIS is the largeſt animal of the New World, where, as formely remarked, animated Nature ſeems to be contracted, or rather

* The tapir has the fore hoofs divided into four, and the hind hoofs into three parts. The noſe extends far beyond the under jaw, is ſlender, and forms a ſort of proboſcis; it is capable of being contracted or extended at pleaſure, and its ſides are ſulcated. The extremities of both jaws end in a point, and there are ten cutting teeth in each. Between them and the grinders, there is vacant ſpace, and there are ten grinders in each jaw. The ears are erect, the eyes ſmall, and the body ſhaped like a hog. The back is arched, the legs ſhort, and the hoofs ſmall, black, and hollow. The tail is very ſmall. The animal grows to the ſize of a heifer of half a year old. The hair is ſhort; when young, it is ſpotted with white, when old, it is of a duſky colour; *Pennant's Synopſ. of Quad. p. 82.*

Tapir is the Braſilian name of this animal.

Tapira; *Voyage de la Riviere des Amazones, par Condamine, p. 163.*

Tapierette Braſilienſibus; *Marcgr. et Piſo.*

Tapirouſſou; *Voyage au Braſil par Lery, p. 154.*

This animal, which is not only found in Braſil, but in Guiana and Peru, is called *Maipouri* in the Galibi language upon the Guiana coaſt, and *vagra* at Peru; *Condamine, ibid.*

Maipouri or manipoure; *Hiſt. de la France Equin. par Barrere, p. 160.*

Anta; *Marcgrave, Braſil. p. 229. Piſo, Braſil. p. 101. Nieuhoff's Voy. p. 23. Raii Synopſ. Quad. p. 126. Klein. Quad. p. 36.*

Q 2   Danta;

rather not to have had time fufficient to acquire her full dimenfions.   Inftead of the huge
maffes produced by the ancient lands of Afia,
inftead of the elephant, rhinoceros, hippopotamus, camelopard, and camel, all the creatures
of thefe new lands are modelled upon a fmall
fcale.   The tapirs, the lamas, the pacos, and the
cabiais are twenty times fmaller than the animals of the Old World to which they fhould
refpectively be compared.   Here matter is not
only ufed with a niggardly hand, but even forms
are imperfect, and feem to have failed, or been
neglected.   Almoft the whole animals of South
America, which alone can be regarded as peculiar to the New World, have neither tufks,
horns, nor tails.   Their figure is awkward; their
bodies and members are ill proportioned; and
fome of them, as the ant-eaters, the floth, &c. are
fo miferably formed, that they have hardly the
powers of moving, or of eating their food.   With

Danta; *Condamine,* 163. *Relat. de la Riviere des Amazones,
par Chrift. Acuna, tom.* ii. *p.* 157. *Hift. de Paraguai, par Charlevoix, tom.* i. *p.* 32. *Hift. Nat. des Indes, par Jofeph Acofta,
p.* 204.

Ante; *Herrera, Defcript. des Indes Occidentales, p.* 25. *Hift.
des Indes, par Maffée, p.* 69.

Beori; *Hift. Gen. des Voyages, par M. l'Abbé Prevot, tom.* ii.
p. 636.

Elephant hog; *Wafer's Voy. in Dampier, vol.* iii. *p.* 400.

Mountain cow; *Dampier, vol.* ii. *p.* 102.

Sus acquaticus multifulcus; *Barrere, Hift. Fr. Equin. p.* 160.

Species of hippopotamus, or river horfe; *Bancrafi's Guiana,
p.* 127.

                                             much

much difficulty they drag out a painful and lan-
guiſhing life in the ſolitudes of the deſert, and
cannot ſubſiſt in inhabited regions, where man
and the ſtronger animals would ſoon deſtroy
them.

The tapir is of the ſize of a ſmall cow, or
zebu ; but has neither horns nor tail. His legs
are ſhort, and his body arched. When young,
he is ſpotted like the ſtag ; and afterwards his
hair becomes of an uniform deep brown colour.
His head is large, and terminates like that of the
rhinoceros, in a long trunk. He has ten cutting teeth and an equal number of grinders in
each jaw, a character which ſeparates him entirely from the ox kind, and from all other ruminating animals. As we have only ſome ſkins
of this animal, and a drawing ſent us by M. Condamine, we cannot do better than tranſcribe the
deſcriptions of him made from the life by Marcgrave * and Barrere, ſubjoining, at the ſame
time,

---

* *Tapiierete* Braſilienſibus, Luſitanis *anta*. Animal quadrupes, magnitudine juvenci ſemeſtris ; figura corporis quodammodo ad porcum accedens, capite etiam tali, verum craſ-
ſiori, oblongo, ſuperius in acumen deſinente ; promuſcide
ſuper os prominente, quam validiſſimo nervo contrahere et
extendere poteſt ; in promuſcide autem ſunt fiſſuræ oblongæ ;
inferior oris pars eſt brevior ſuperiore. Maxillæ ambæ an-
terius faſtigiatæ, et in qualibet decem dentes inciſores ſuperne
et inferne ; hinc per certum ſpatium utraque maxilla caret
dentibus, ſequuntur dein molares grandes omnes, in quolibet
latere quinque, ita ut haberet viginti molares et viginti inciſores. Oculos habet parvos porcinos, aures obrotundas, ma-

Q 3 juſculas,

time what has been said concerning him by travellers, and historians. The tapir seems to be
a gloomy melancholy animal *. He comes
abroad

jusculas, quas versus anteriora surrigit. Crura vix longiora
porcinis, et crassiuscula; in anterioribus pedibus quatuor ungulas,
in posterioribus tres; media inter eas major est in omnibus
pedibus; in prioribus pedibus tribus, quarta parvula exte-
rius est adjuncta: Sunt autem ungulæ nigricantes, non solidæ sed
cavæ, et quæ detrahi possunt. Caret cauda, et ejus loco proces-
sum habet nudum pilis, conicum, parvum more *Cutian* (Agouti).
Mas membrum genitale longe exserere potest, instar cerco-
pitheci: Incedit dorso incurvato ut *Capybara* (Cabiai). Cutem
solidam habet instar alcis, pilos breves. Color pilorum in ju-
nioribus est umbræ lucidæ, maculis variegatus albicantibus
ut capreolus; in adultis fuscus sive nigricans sine maculis. Animal interdiu dormit in opacis silvis latitans. Noctu aut mane
egreditur pabuli causa. Optime potest natare. Vescitur gra-
mine, arundine saccharifera, brassica, &c. Caro ejus comeditur,
sed ingrati saporis est; *Marcgr. Hist. Brasil. p. 229.*———The
tapir or *maypouri* is an amphibious animal, being oftener
in the water than on the land, to which he resorts from time
to time, in order to browse the more tender herbage. His
hair is very short, and interspersed with black and white bands,
which extend from the head to the tail. He makes a kind of
hissing or whistling noise; and seems to partake a little both
of the mule and the hog. We find *manipouris*, as they
are called by some people, in the river Ouyapok. His flesh
is coarse and ill tasted; *Barrere, Hist. Nat. de la France Equin.
p.* 160.

* *Tapiierete*, bestia iners et socors apparet, adeoque luci-
fuga ut in densis mediterraneis silvis interdiu dormire amet:
Ita ut, si detur animal aliquod, quod noctu tantum nunquam
vero de die venetur, hæc sane est Brasiliensis bestia, &c.; *Hist.
Nat. Brasil. p.* 101. ———During the day, the anta browses
herbage, and, in the night, he eats a kind of clay found in
the marshes, to which he retires when the sun sets. - The
antas are hunted during the night, and it is not a difficult
business.

abroad in the night only, and delights in the water, where he dwells oftener than on the land. He lives in the marshes, and never wanders to any great distance from the margins of rivers and lakes. When alarmed, pursued, or wounded, he plunges into the water *, remains long under it, and passes over a considerable space before he makes his appearance. These habits, which he possesses in common with the hippopotamus, have induced some naturalists to suppose that he belongs to the same species †. But these animals are as remote from each other in their natures, as the countries they inhabit. To be ascertained of this fact, we have only to compare the above descriptions with that we have given of the hippopotamus. Though both inhabit the water, the tapir does not feed upon fishes; and, though his mouth is armed with

business. These animals are hunted in their retreats, where they assemble spontaneously in flocks; and, as soon as they approach, the hunters run up to them with burning torches, with which they are so dazzled and confounded, that they overturn one another, &c.; *Hist. du Paraguai, par le P. Charlevoix, tom.* i. *p.* 33.——The antas conceal themselves during the day in their dens, and come out in the night to feed; *Descript. des Indes Occidentales, par Herrera, p.* 251.

* The manipouri is a kind of wild mule. We shot at one, but did not kill him. Unless the ball or arrow pierce his flanks, he generally escapes, particularly when water is near; for he instantly plunges into it, and quickly gains the opposite bank; *Lettres Edifiantes, recueil* xxiv. *Lettre du P. Fauche.*

† Hippopotamus amphibius pedius quadrilobis; habitat in Nilo. —Hippopotamus terrestris pedibus posticis trisulcis. Tapüerete habitat in Brasilia; *Linn. Syst. Nat. p.* 74.

twenty

twenty fharp cutting teeth *, he is not carnivorous. He lives upon plants and roots, and never ufes his weapons againft other animals. His
difpofitions are fo mild and timid, that he de-
clines all hoftilities, and flies from every danger.
Though his legs are fhort and his body heavy,
he runs very fwiftly, and he fwims ftill better
than he runs. The texture of his fkin † is fo
clofe and firm, that it often refifts a mufket
ball. His flefh is coarfe and infipid ; but it is
eaten by the Indians ‡. He is found in Brafil,
in Paraguay, in Guiana, in the country of the
Amazons ‖, and throughout all South America,
from the extremity of Chili to New Spain.

* Though the tapirouffou has fharp teeth, his only defence
is flight, and he is by no means dangerous. The Savages kill
him with arrows, or entrap him with fnares ; *Voyage de Lery,*
p. 152.

† The tapirouffou is in great requeft among the Savages,
on account of his fkin ; for, after drying it, they cut it into
round fhields as large as the bottom of a ton.—This fkin,
when dried, is fo hard that I believe no arrow can pierce it;
Idem.

‡ The flefh of the manipouri is coarfe, and has a difagreeable
tafte ; *Lettres Edifiantes, recueil* xxiv. *p.* 347.

‖ In the environs of the river of the Amazons, we find an
animal called *danta.* It is of the fize of a mule, which it refembles in colour and the figure of its body ; *Relation de la Riviere*
des Amazones, par Chrijt. d'Acuna, tom. ii. *p.* 177.————The elk,
which is found in fome of the woods near Quito, is not rare
in the Amazon woods, nor in thofe of Guiana. I here give
the name of *elk* to the animal which the Spaniards and Portuguefe
call the *danta ; Voyage de la Riviere des Amazones, par M. de la*
Condamine, p. 163.

OF NATURE.

FIRST VIEW.

NATURE is that fyftem of laws eftablifhed by the Creator for regulating the exiftence of bodies, and the fucceffion of beings. Nature is not a body; for this body would comprehend every thing. Neither is it a being; for this being would neceffarily be God. But Nature may be confidered as an immenfe living power, which animates the univerfe, and which, in fubordination to the firft and fupreme Being, began to act by his command, and its action is ftill continued by his concurrence or confent. This power is that portion of the divine power which manifefts itfelf to men. It is at once the caufe and the effect, the mode and the fubftance, the defign and the execution. Very different from human art, whofe productions are only dead works, Nature is herfelf a work perpetually alive, an active and never ceafing operator, who knows how to employ every material, and, though always labouring on the fame invariable plan, her power, inftead of being leffened, is perfectly inexhauftible. Time, fpace, and matter, are her means; the univerfe her object; motion and life her end.

The

The phænomena of the univerfe are the effects of this power. The fprings fhe employs are active forces, which time and fpace can only meafure and limit, but never deftroy; forces which balance, mix, and oppofe, without being able to annihilate each other. Some penetrate and tranfport bodies, others heat and animate them. Attraction and impulfion are the two principal inftruments by which this power acts upon brute matter. Heat and organic particles are the active principles fhe employs in the formation and expanfion of organized beings.

With fuch inftruments, what can limit the operations of Nature? To render her omnipotent, fhe wants only the power of creating and annihilating. But thefe two extremes of power the Almighty has referved to himfelf alone. To create and to annihilate, are his peculiar attributes. To change, to deftroy, to unfold, to renew, to produce, are the only privileges he has conferred on another agent. Nature, the minifter of his irrevocable commands, the depofitary of his immutable decrees, never deviates from the laws he has prefcribed to her. She alters no part of his original plan; and, in all her operations, fhe exhibits the zeal of the eternal Lord of the univerfe. This divine impreffion, this unalterable prototype of all exiftence, is the model upon which fhe operates; a model, all the features of which are expreffed in characters fo ftrongly marked, that nothing can poffibly efface;

face; a model which the number of copies or impreffions, though infinite, inftead of impairing, only renews.

Every thing, therefore, has been created, and nothing is annihilated. Nature vibrates between thefe two extremes, without ever reaching either the one or the other. Let us endeavour to lay hold of her in fome points of this vaft fpace which fhe has filled and pervaded from the beginning of ages.

What an infinity of objects; an immenfe mafs of matter, which would have been created in vain, if it had not been divided into portions, feparated from each other by fpaces a thoufand times more immenfe. Thoufands of luminous globes, placed at inconceivable diftances, are the bafes which fupport the fabric of the univerfe; and millions of opaque globes, which circulate round the former, conftitute the moving order of its architecture. Thefe great maffes are revolved, and carried through fpace, by two primitive forces, each of which acts continually; and their combined efforts produce the zones of the celeftial fpheres, and eftablifh, in the midft of vacuity, fixed ftations and determined routes or orbits. It is motion that gives rife to the equilibrium of worlds and the repofe of the univerfe.

The firft of thefe forces is equally divided; the fecond is diftributed in unequal proportions. Every atom of matter has the fame quantity of

attractive

attractive force; and a different quantity of impulsive force is assigned to each individual globe. Some stars are fixed and others wandering. Some globes seem to be destined for attracting, and others for impelling, or being impelled. There are spheres which have received a common impulsion in the same direction, and others a particular impulsion. Some stars are solitary, and others accompanied with satellites: Some are luminous, and others opaque masses. There are planets, the different parts of which successively enjoy a borrowed light, and comets, which lose themselves in the profundity of space, and return after many ages, to receive the influence of solar heat. Some suns appear and disappear, and seem to be alternately kindled and extinguished; others exhibit themselves for once, and then vanish for ever. Heaven is a country of great events; but the human eye is hardly able to perceive them. A sun which perishes, and destroys a world, or a system of worlds, has no other effect on our eyes than an ignis fatuus, which gives a transitory blaze, and appears no more. Man, limited to the terrestrial atom on which he vegetates, views this atom as a world, and sees worlds only as atoms.

The earth which man inhabits, hardly perceptible among the other globes, and totally invisible to the distant spheres, is a million of times smaller than the sun by which it is illuminated, and a thousand times smaller than some other planets, which are also subjected to the

power

power of the fun, and obliged to circulate around him. Saturn, Jupiter, Mars, the Earth, Venus, Mercury, and the Sun, occupy the fmall part of the heavens which we call *our Univerfe*. All thefe planets with their fatellites, moving with rapidity in the fame direction, and nearly in the fame plane, compofe a wheel of an immenfe diameter, whofe axis fupports the whole weight, and which, by the celerity of its own rotation, muft inflame and diffufe heat and light to every part of the circumference. As long as thefe movements continue, (and they will be eternal, unlefs the hand of the prime Mover interpofe, and exert as much force to deftroy, as was neceffary to create them,) the fun will burn, and fill all the fpheres of this univerfe with his fplendour: And as, in a fyftem, where all bodies attract each other, nothing can be loft, or remove without returning, the quantity of mattter remaining always the fame, this fertile fource of light and life can never be dried up or exhaufted; for the other funs, which likewife dart forth their fires continually, reftore to our fun as much light as they receive from him.

The comets, which are much more numerous than the planets, and, like the latter, depend on the power of the fun, prefs alfo on this common focus, and, by augmenting the weight, increafe the inflammation. They conftitute a part of our univerfe; for, like the planets, they are fubjected to the attraction of the fun. But, in their

projectile

projectile or impelled motions, they have nothing in common, either among themfelves, or
with the planets. Each circulates in a different
plane ; and they defcribe orbits in very different
periods of time ; for fome perform their revolutions in a few years, and others require feveral
centuries. The fun, revolving round his own
centre, remains, in other refpects, perfectly at
reft in the midft of the whole, and ferves, at the
fame time, as a torch, a focus, and an axis to all
the parts of this vaft machine.

It is by his magnitude alone that the fun remains immoveable, and regulates the motions of
the other globes. As the force of attraction is
proportioned to the mafs of matter, as the fun
is incomparably larger than any of the comets,
and contains a thoufand times more matter than
the largeft planet, they can neither derange him,
nor diminifh his influence, which, by extending
to immenfe diftances, reftrains the whole, and,
at fixed periods, recalls thofe which have ftretched fartheft into the regions of fpace. Some of
them, when they return, make fo near an approach to the fun, that, after cooling for ages,
they undergo an inconceivable degree of heat.
They are fubjected to ftrange viciffitudes from
thefe alternate extremes of heat and cold, as
well as from the inequalities of their motions,
which are fometimes prodigiously accelerated, and
at other times almoft infinitely retarded. When
compared with the planets, the comets may be
                                    confidered

confidered as worlds in diforder; for the orbits
of the planets are more regular, and their movements more equal; their temperature is always
the fame; they feem to be places of repofe,
where every thing being permanent, Nature is
enabled to eftablifh an uniform plan of operation, and to mature fucceffively all her various
productions. Among the planets, that which we
inhabit feems to enjoy peculiar privileges. Lefs
cold and lefs diftant than Saturn, Jupiter, and
Mars, it is alfo not fo much fcorched as Venus
and Mercury, which appear to be too near the
body of the fun. Befides, with what magnificence does Nature fhine upon the earth? A
pure light, which gradually ftretches from eaft
to weft, alternately gilds both hemifpheres of
this globe. It is furrounded with a light and
tranfparent element. A mild and fertile heat
animates and unfolds all the germs of exiftence; and they are nourifhed and fupported by
wholefeme waters. Various eminences, diftributed over the furface of the land, ftop and collect the moift vapours which float in the air, and
give rife to perpetual fountains. Immenfe cavities, deftined for the reception of thefe waters, feparate iflands and continents. The extent of the
fea is as great as that of the land. This is not
a cold and barren element. It is a new empire
equally rich, and equally peopled with the former. The limits of the waters are marked out
by the finger of God. If the fea encroaches on

the

the weſtern ſhores, it deſerts thoſe of the eaſt. This vaſt maſs of water, though naturally inactive, is agitated by the influence of the celeſtial bodies, which produces the regular motions of the flux and reflux. It riſes and falls with the courſe of the moon, and, when the action of the ſun and moon concurs, it riſes ſtill higher. Both theſe cauſes uniting during the time of the equinoxes, is the reaſon why the tides are then higheſt. This is the ſtrongeſt mark of our connection with the heavens. Theſe conſtant and general movements give riſe to variable and particular motions; to tranſportations of earth, which, falling to the bottom in the form of ſediment, produce mountains ſimilar to thoſe on the ſurface of the land; to currents, which, following the direction of thoſe chains of mountains, beſtow on them a figure whoſe angles correſpond, and, running in the midſt of the waves, as waters run on the land, are really ſea-rivers.

The air, ſtill lighter and more fluid than water, is likewiſe ſubject to a number of powers. Continual agitations are produced in it by the diſtant influence of the ſun and moon, by the immediate action of the ſea, and by the rarefaction and condenſation of heat and cold. The winds are its currents. They puſh and collect the clouds. They produce meteors, and tranſport to the arid ſurface of iſlands and continents the moiſt vapours of the ocean. They give riſe to ſtorms, and diffuſe and diſtribute

the

the fertile dew and rains. They difturb the movements of the fea, agitate the waters, ftop or precipitate the currents, elevate the waves, and raife tremendous tempefts : The troubled ocean rifes toward the heavens, and rolls on with noife and violence againft thofe immoveable barriers, which, with all its efforts, it can neither deftroy nor furmount.

The earth, elevated above the level of the ocean, is defended againft its irruptions. Its fur-face, enamelled with flowers, adorned with a verdure which is always renewing, and peo-pled with numberlefs fpecies of animals, is a place of perfect repofe, a delightful habitation, where man, deftined to aid the intentions of Nature, prefides over every other being. He alone is capable of knowledge, and dignified with the faculty of admiration : God, therefore, has made him the fpectator of the univerfe, and the witnefs of his perpetual miracles. The ray of divinity with which he is animated, makes him participate the myfteries of the Deity. It is by this light that he thinks and reflects, that he perceives and underftands the wonderful opera-tions of his Creator.

Nature is the external throne of the divine magnificence. Man, who contemplates her, rifes gradually to the internal throne of the Almighty. Formed to adore his Creator, he has dominion over every creature. The vaffal of heaven, the lord of the earth, he peoples, ennobles, and

enriches this lower world. Among living beings, he establishes order, subordination, and harmony. To Nature herself he even gives im-
bellishment, cultivation, extension, and polish.
He cuts down the thistle and the bramble, and
he multiplies the vine and the rose. View those
melancholy deserts where man has never resi-
ded. Over-run with briars, thorns, and trees
which are deformed, broken, corrupted, the seeds
that ought to renew and embellish the scene
are choaked and buried in the midst of rubbish
and sterility. Nature, who, in other situations,
assumes the splendour of youth, has here the appearance of old age and decrepitude. The earth,
surcharged with the spoils of its productions,
instead of a beautiful verdure, presents nothing
but a disordered mass of gross herbage, and of
trees loaded with parasitical plants, as lichens,
agarics, and other impure fruits of corruption:
All the low grounds are occupied with putrid and
stagnating waters; the miry lands, which are neither solid nor fluid, are impassable, and remain
equally useless to the inhabitants of the earth and
of the waters; and the marshes, which are covered with stinking aquatic plants, serve only to
nourish venomous insects, and to harbour impure animals. Between those putrid marshes
which occupy the low grounds, and the decayed
forests which cover the elevated parts of the
country, there is a species of lands, or savanna's,
that have no resemblance to our meadows.
There noxious herbs rise and choak the useful

kinds.

kinds. Inftead of that fine enamelled turf, which appears to be the down of the earth, we fee nothing but rude vegetables, hard prickly plants, fo interlaced together, that they feem to have lefs hold of the earth than of each other, and which, by fucceffively drying and fhooting, form a coarfe mat of feveral feet in thicknefs. There is no road, no communication, no veftige of intelligence, in thefe favage and defolate regions. Man, reduced to the neceffity of following the tract of wild beafts, when he wants to kill them, obliged to watch perpetually left he fhould fall a victim to their rage, terrified by their occafional roarings, and even ftruck with the awful filence of thofe profound folitudes, he fhrinks back, and fays:
' Uncultivated Nature is hideous and languifh-
' ing. It is I alone who can render her agreeable
' and vivacious. Let us drain thefe marfhes;
' let us animate thefe waters by converting them
' into brooks and canals; let us employ this ac-
' tive and devouring element, whofe nature was
' formerly concealed from us; let us fet fire to
' this cumberfome load of vegetables, and to thofe
' fuperannuated forefts, which are already half
' confumed; let us finifh the work by deftroy-
' ing with iron what could not be diffipated by
' fire. Inftead of rufhes, and water-lilies, from
' which the toad is faid to extract his poifon,
' we fhall foon fee the ranunculus, the truffle,
' and other mild and falutary herbs; flocks of
' fprightly cattle will browfe upon this land,

R 2   ' which

‘ which was formerly impaffable ; here they will
‘ find abundance of food, a never failing pafture,
‘ and they will continue to multiply and to re-
‘ ward us for our labours, and the protection
‘ we have afforded them. To complete the
‘ work, let the ox be fubjected to the yoke;
‘ let his ftrength and the weight of his body be
‘ employed in ploughing the ground, which ac-
‘ quires frefh vigour by culture. Thus will
‘ Nature acquire redoubled ftrength and fplen-
‘ dour from the fkill and induftry of man.’

How beautiful is cultivated Nature! How
pompous and brilliant, when decorated by the
hand of man! He himfelf is her chief ornament,
her nobleft production. By multiplying his
own fpecies, he increafes the moft precious of
her works. She even feems to multiply in the
fame proportion with him; for, by his art, he
brings to light every thing which fhe concealed
in her bofom. What a fource of unknown
treafures! Flowers, fruits, and grains matured
to perfection, and multiplied to infinity; the
ufeful fpecies of animals tranfported, propagated, and increafed without number; the noxious
kinds diminifhed, and banifhed from the abodes
of men; gold, and iron a more ufeful metal,
extracted from the bowels of the earth; torrents reftrained, and rivers directed and confined within their banks; even the ocean itfelf
fubdued, inveftigated, and traverfed from the
one hemifphere to the other; the earth every

where

where acceffible, and rendered active and fertile; the valleys and plains converted into fmiling meadows, rich paftures, and cultivated fields; the hills loaded with vines and fruits; and their fummits crowned with ufeful trees; the deferts turned into populous cities, whofe inhabitants fpread from its centre to its utmoft extremities; open and frequented roads and communications every where eftablifhed, as fo many evidences of the union and ftrength of fociety. A thoufand other monuments of power and of glory fufficiently demonftrate that man is the lord of the earth; that he has entirely changed and renewed its furface; and, that from the remoteft periods of time, he alone has divided the empire of the world between him and Nature.

He reigns however by the right of conqueft only. He enjoys rather than poffeffes; and preferves his privileges by perpetual vigilance and activity. If thefe are interrupted, every thing languifhes, alters, and returns to the abfolute dominion of Nature. She refumes her rights, effaces the operations of man, covers with mofs and duft his moft pompous monuments, which, in the progefs of time, fhe totally deftroys, and leaves him only the regret of having loft by his own fault, what his anceftors had acquired by their induftry. Thofe periods, when man lofes his empire, thofe barbarous ages in which every thing of value perifhes, commence with war, and are completed by famine and depopulation. Man, whofe ftrength confifts folely in the

union

union of numbers, and whose happiness is derived from peace, is yet mad enough to take up arms, and to fight, which are never failing sources of misery and ruin. Incited by insatiable avarice, and by blind ambition, which is still more insatiable, he renounces the feelings of humanity, turns all his strength against himself, and his whole desires centre in the destruction of his own species, which he soon accomplishes. After these days of blood and carnage, when the intoxicating fumes of glory are dispelled, he surveys with a melancholy eye, the earth desolated, the arts buried, nations dispersed, an enfeebled people, the ruin of his own happiness, and the annihilation of his real power.

Omnipotent GOD! *whose presence supports Nature, and maintains harmony among the laws of the universe; who, from thy immoveable throne in the Empirean, seest all the celestial spheres rolling under thy feet, without deviation or disorder; who, from the bosom of repose, renewest, at every instant, their vast movements, and who alone governest, in profound peace, an infinite number of heavens and of earths; restore, restore tranquillity to a troubled world* ! Let the earth be silent! Let the presumptuous tumults of war and discord be dispelled by the sound of thy voice! Merciful* GOD! *Author of all beings, thy paternal regards embrace every created object : But man is thy chief*

* This effusion was probably written before the termination of the last war between Britain and France.

favourite.

favourite, Thou hast illuminated his mind with a ray of thy immortal light; penetrate also his heart with a shaft of thy love: This divine sentiment, when universally diffused, will unite the most hostile spirits; man will no longer dread the aspect of man, and his hand will cease to be armed with murdering steel; the devouring flames of war will no more dry up the sources of generation; the human species, now weakened, mutilated, and prematurely mowed down, will germinate afresh, and multiply without number: Nature, groaning under the pressure of calamity, sterile, and abandoned, will soon resume, with accumulated vigour, her former fecundity; and we, beneficent GOD, we shall aid, cultivate, and incessantly contemplate her operations, that we may be enabled to offer thee, every moment, a fresh tribute of gratitude and admiration.

THE ZEBRA*.

WHETHER we confider fymmetry of fhape, or beauty of colours, the zebra is perhaps the moft elegant of all quadrupeds. In this animal, the figure and gracefulnefs of the horfe are united with the nimblenefs of the ftag. His robe is adorned with black and white belts or ribands, alternately difpofed, with fuch regularity and exact proportion, that Nature feems here to have employed the rule and the compafs. Thefe alternate bands of black and white are the more fingular, becaufe they are ftraight, parallel, and as nicely feparated as thofe of a ftriped ftuff. Befides, they extend not only over the body, but the head, thighs, legs, and even the

* The zebra has a fhort erect mane; the tail is furnifhed with long hairs at the end; and the whole body is beautifully ftriped, from the back to the belly, with lines of brown, on a very pale buff ground, It is the moft elegant of all quadrupeds; *Pennant's Synopf. of Quad. p. 2.*

It is called *Zebra, Zevera,* and *Sebra,* in Congo; and, according to Pyrard, *Efure* in Angola.

Pulcher onager; *Martial. Epig. lib.* xii. 101. *Oppian. Cyneg.* iii. 183.

Zebra; *Nieremberg. p.* 168. *Raii Synopf. Quad. p.* 64. *Klein. Quad. p.* 5. *Aldrovand. de Quad. Solid. p.* 416.

Le zebre, ou l'âne rayé; *Briffon. Quad. p.* 70.

Equus zebra, fafciis fufcis verficolor; *Linn. Syft. Nat. p.* 101.

Wild afs; *Kolben's Cape of Good Hope, vol.* ii. *p.* 112.

ears

ears and tail; fo that, at a diftance, the whole
body of the animal has the appearance of being
artificially adorned, in the moft elegant manner,
with ribbands. In the female, thefe bands are
alternately black and white, and black and yellow in the male. The fhades are always lively
and brilliant; and the hair is fhort, clofe, and
fine, the luftre of which augments the beauty of
the colours. The zebra, in general, is fmaller
than the horfe, and larger than the afs. Though
he has often been compared to thefe two animals, under the names of the *wild horfe* *, and
ftriped afs †, he is not a copy of either, but
fhould rather be regarded as their model, if in
Nature every fpecies were not equally original,
and had not an equal right to creation.

The zebra, therefore, is neither a horfe nor
an afs; for, though it has often been attempted,
we never learned that they intermixed and produced together. She-affes in feafon were prefented to the zebra which was in the menagery
of Verfailles in the year 1761. He difdained
them, or rather difcovered no emotion. He
however fported with them, and even mounted
them, but without difcovering any defire, or external fign. This coldnefs could be attributed
to no other caufe than an unfuitablenefs in the

---

* Equus ferus genere fuo; zebra; *Klein. de Quad. p.* 5.

† Infortunatum animal, quod tam pulchris coloribus præditum, *afini* nomen in Europa ferre cogatur. Vide Ludol-
phi Comment. p. 150. Ibique zebræ figuram.

natures

natures of the two animals; for the zebra was four years of age, and, in every other exercise, was fprightly and vigorous.

The zebra is not the animal mentioned by the ancients under the name of *onager.* In the Levant, in the eaftern parts of Afia, and in the north of Africa, there is a fine race of affes, which, like the moft beautiful horfes, originated in Arabia*. This race differs from the common kind by the largenefs of their body, the nimblenefs of their limbs, and the luftre of their hair. They are of one uniform colour, which is a beautiful moufe gray, with a black crofs on the back and fhoulders. Sometimes their colour is a brighter gray with a whitifh crofs †. Thefe African and Afiatic affes ‡, though more beautiful

---

* In Perfia there are two kinds of affes; thofe belonging to the country, which, like ours, are flow and ftupid, and ufed for carrying burdens only; and the Arabian affes, which are extremely handfome, and the moft excellent of the fpecies. They have fmooth hair, a high head, and nimble limbs. They are ufed folely for riding. . . . Like horfes, they are trained to amble; and their motion is extremely foft, and fo fleet, that it requires a gallop to keep up with them; *Voyage de Chardin, tom. ii. p. 37. Voyage de Tavernier, tom. ii. p. 20.*

† At Baffora, I faw a wild afs. Its figure differed not from that of the domeftic kind; but its colour was brighter, and, from the head to the tail, there was a band of whitifh hair. . . . In running, and in every other motion, it feemed to be much more nimble than the common kind; *Voyage de Pietra della Valle, tom. viii. p. 49.*

‡ The Moors, who come to Cape-Verd to traffick, carry their baggage and wares upon affes. Thefe animals were fo beautiful and fo fmooth fkinned, that it was with difficulty I

could

tiful than those of Europe, proceed equally from
the *onagri* or *wild asses*, which are still numerous in South and East Tartary *, in Persia, Syria; the islands of the Archipelago, and in Mauritania †. The onagers differ from the domestic asses by those qualities only which result
from freedom and independence: They are
stronger and more nimble, and they have more
courage and vivacity. The figure of their bodies

could recognise them to be asses. Those of Europe, I imagine, would be in the same condition, if their labour, and the
manner in which they are loaded, did not greatly disfigure
them. Their hair was of a beautiful, shining, mouse gray
colour, upon which the black band along the back and across
the shoulders had a fine effect. These asses are a little larger
than ours. Their head, however, is easily distinguishable from
that of the horse; especially the Barbary horse, which is a
native of this country, and of a still higher stature; *Voyage
au Senegal*, par M. Adanson, p. 118.—There are great numbers of wild asses in the deserts of Numidia and Lybia, and
the adjacent country. They are so fleet, that the Barbary
horses alone are able to overtake them in the course. As soon
as they see a man, they stop, fling up their heels, and cry;
and, when he is near, they run off. They are taken by various
kinds of snares. They go in troops to pasture and to
drink. Their flesh is very good; but it must be allowed
to cool two days after being roasted, on account of its strong
smell. We have seen a number of these animals in Sardinia; but they were smaller; *L'Afrique de Marmol*, tom. 1.
p. 53.

* The animal which the Mogul Tartars call *Czigithai*, and
which Messerschmid has denominated *mulus fœcundus Daur-
icus*, is the same with the *onager* or *wild ass*.

† We find many wild asses in the islands of Peine, and of
Levata or Lebinthos. . . . They are also found in the island
of Cythera, now called *Cerigo*; *Descript. des Isles de l'Archipel*,
par Dapper, p. 185. 378.

is

is the fame, though the hair is longer. This difference depends likewife on their condition; for our affes would have hair equally long, if they were not fhorn at the age of four or five months. The hair of a colt is at firft nearly as long as that of a young bear. The fkin of the wild afs is equally hard as that of the domeftic kind, and we are affured that it is full of fmall tubercles. The chagrin brought from the Levant, which we employ for various purpofes, is faid to be made of the wild afs's fkin.

But neither the onager, nor the fine affes of Arabia, can be regarded as the origin of the zebra fpecies, though they refemble it in figure and fwiftnefs. None of them exhibit that regular variety of colours, by which the zebra is fo eminently diftinguifhed. This beautiful fpecies is fingular, and very remote from all other kinds. It likewife belongs to a different climate from that of the onager, being only found in the eaftern and fouthern regions of Africa, from Æthiopia to the Cape of Good Hope *, and from thence

* At the Cape of Good Hope there are numbers of wild affes, which are the moft beautiful in the world. They are finely ftriped with black and white bands, and are very difficult to tame; *Relation du Chevalier de Chaumont, p.* 12 —The wild afs of the Cape is one of the moft beautiful animals I have ever feen. He is of the fize of an ordinary faddle horfe. His limbs are flender, and well proportioned, and his hair is foft and clofe. From the mane to the tail, a black band runs along the back, from which numbers of other bands of *different colours* proceed, and form circles by meeting under the belly.

thence as far as Congo *. He exists not in Europe, Asia, America, nor in any of the northern parts of Africa. Those mentioned by some voyagers

belly. Some of these circles are white, others yellow, and others chesnut; and their various shades run into each other in such a manner, as charms the eye of the spectator. His head and ears are also adorned with small bands of the same colours. Those on the mane and tail are mostly white, chesnut, or brown, and few of them yellow. He is so fleet that no horse in the world can be compared to him. Hence it is extemely difficult to catch him, and, when caught, he sells very dear. . . . I have often seen large troops of these animals. Father Tellez, Thevenot, and other authors, assert, that they have seen them tamed; but I never heard of their being tamed at the Cape. Several Europeans have ineffectually exerted all their skill and industry to accomplish this end; *Descript. du Cap de Bonne-Esperance, par Kolbe, tom.* iii. *p.* 25.

* At Pamba, in the kingdom of Congo, we find an animal called *zebre* by the natives, which exactly resembles a mule, except that it is prolific. Besides, its hair is wonderfully disposed; for, from the spine of the back to the belly, there are bands, of white, black, and yellow, about three inches broad, and arranged with the nicest proportion. These animals multiply greatly in this country; for they produce every year. They are extremely fleet and wild. If tamed, they might supply the place of the horse; *Drake's Voyage, p.* 106.—On the road to Loanda in the kingdom of Congo, there is an animal of the size and strength of a mule; but its hair is variegated with white, black, and yellow bands, which encircle the body from the spine of the back to the belly, and are so beautiful, and so regularly disposed, that they have the appearance of being drawn by a pencil. It is named *zebra; Relat. d'un Voyage de Congo, par les P. P. Michel-Ange de Galliné et Denys de Charly, Capucins, p.* 76.—In Congo, there is an animal called *sebra*, which every way resembles a mule, except in its power of producing. Its hair is very singular: From the ridge of the back to the belly, there are three bands

of

agers* to have been found in Brasil, had been
transported thither from Africa. Others, which
have been seen in Persia †, and in Turkey ‡, had
been

of different colours, &c. *Voyage de la Compagnie des Indes de
Hollande; tom.* iv. *p.* 320.

* When I arrived in Brasil, I saw two very rare animals,
which were of the figure and size of a small mule; yet they
are not mules; for they are fertile. The skin is extremely
beautiful, very smooth, short, and shining like velvet. The
hair is disposed into fine white and blacks bands, which run
in the most exact proportion over the whole body, ears, tail,
and other extremities. Moreover, these animals are very
fierce, and never can be fully tamed. They are called, in the
country from which they are brought, *esures*. They are
natives of Angola in Africa, from whence they were transported to Brasil, in order to be afterwards presented to the
King of Spain. Though they had been taken when very
young, and were a little tamed, no body durst approach them,
except their keeper. Some time before I arrived, one of
them had broke loose, and killed a groom. . . . Though
tied up very close, the keeper showed me several bites he had received from them. The skin of the animal is extremely beautiful;
Voyage de Pyrard, tom. ii. *p.* 376.

† The ambassadors from Æthiopia to the Mogul, must
give a present of a kind of mule, whose skin I was shown as
a great rarity. No tiger is so finely marked, no silken stuff
is striped with such variety, order, and proportion, as the skin
of this animal; *Hist. de la Revolution du Mogol, par Fr. Bernier,
tom.* i. *p.* 181.

‡ An ambassador from Æthiopia arrived at Cairo with
presents for the Grand Seignior. Among others, there was
an ass that had a most beautiful skin, provided it was natural,
of which I am uncertain, as I did not examine it. It had
a black line along the back, and all the rest of the body was
variegated with alternate bands of white and tawny. The
head was very long, and striped in the same manner with
the body. The ears were black, yellow, and white. The legs
were striped like the body, not lengthwise, but round in the
manner

been brought to thefe countries from Æthiopia.
In fine, almoft all thofe we have feen in Europe
came from the Cape of Good Hope. This point
of Africa is their native climate, where they are
very numerous, and where the Dutch have exerted every effort to tame and render them domeftic; but they have not hitherto been able
fully to accomplifh this purpofe. The zebra,
which was the fubject of our defcription, was
extremely wild when he arrived at the royal
menagery, and is not yet entirely tamed. They
have, however, brought him the length of being
mounted; but it requires great precaution.
Two men hold the bridle, while a third fits on
the animal's back. His mouth is extremely hard :
His ears are fo fenfible, that he flings whenever
they are touched, and, like a vicious horfe, he
is reftlefs, and as ftubborn as a mule. But the
wild horfe and the onager are perhaps equally
untractable; and it is extremely probable, that,
if the zebra were early accuftomed to obedience,
and to a domeftic ftate, he would become equally
gentle with the afs and horfe, and might fupply
the place of both.

manner of garters. The whole of thefe ftripes or bands were
difpofed with fuch fymmetry, that no tiger or leopard's fkin
could equal the beauty of this animal's fkin. Two fimilar
affes, belonging to the fame ambaffador, died on the road,
and he was carrying their fkins, together with the animal that fur-
vived, as a prefent to the Grand Seignior; *Relat. d'un Voyage,
par Thevenot, tom.* i. *p.* 473.

SUPPLEMENT.

THE afs, either in a domeftic or wild ftate, is found in almoft every warm and temperate climate of the Old Continent, and exifted not in the New when it was firft difcovered. But the fpecies, after being tranfported thither from Europe, has now fubfifted and multiplied greatly in America, during more than two centuries; fo that, at prefent, it is almoft equally diffufed over the four quarters of the globe. The zebra, on the contrary, which was brought to us from the Cape of Good Hope, feems to be a fpecies limited to the fouthern regions of Africa; though Lopez afferts, that the zebras are more frequent in Barbary than in Congo, and though Dapper relates that troops of them are found in the forefts of Angola.

This beautiful animal, which, both from the variety of its colours and the elegance of its figure, is fo fuperior to the afs, feems, notwithftanding, to be nearly of the fame fpecies; fince moft travellers give it the name of the *ftriped afs*, becaufe, at firft fight, they are ftruck with its fuperior refemblance, both in fize and figure, to the afs than to the horfe; for it was not with the fmall common affes that they compared the zebra, but with the largeft and moft beautiful of

the

the fpecies. I am ftill inclined to think, however, that the zebra approaches nearer to the
horfe than the afs; for his figure is fo elegant,
that though, in general, he is fmaller than the
horfe, the fimilarities between them, in 6ther refpects, are very apparent. To confirm this
opinion, it has been remarked, with fome degree
of furprife, that, in the neighbourhood of the
Cape of Good Hope, which appears to be the
native country of the zebra, there are horfes
fpotted on the back and belly with yellow, black,
red, and azure *. This particular argument is
fupported by the general fact, that, in all climates, the colour of the horfe varies more than
that of the afs. We pretend not to decide this
queftion; but we hope it will foon be determined. As the Dutch have lately tranfported great
numbers of thefe elegant animals, and have even
yoked them in the Stadtholder's chariot, it is probable, that, in a fhort time, we fhall receive information of every thing relating to their nature.
That induftrious nation cannot fail to make thefe
animals unite among themfelves, and perhaps
with horfes and affes, in order to produce direct
or baftard races. In Holland there are feveral
expert naturalifts who will perhaps fucceed better than we did in the multiplication of the zebra, upon which only a fingle experiment was
made at the royal menagery in the year 1761.
The male, which was four years of age, difdained

* Captain Robert's Voyage, tom. i. p. 94.

the fhe-affes, though in feafon, and no more
were prefented to him. Perhaps he was alfo
too young. Befides, he was not rendered familiar with the females, a neceffary preliminary
for fucceeding in the union of different fpecies,
which Nature feems to require even in the intercourfe of individuals of the fame fpecies.

The fertile mule of Tartary, called *czigithai*,
may perhaps be an animal of the fame fpecies
with the zebra; for there feems to be no difference between them, but in colour. Now, it is
well known that the differences in the colour
of the hair or feathers are extremely flight, and
depend on the influence of the climate. The
czigithai is found in the fouthern parts of Siberia, in Thibet, in Dauria, and in Tartary. Ger-
billon remarks, that thefe animals are common
in the country of the Mongoux and Kakas;
that they differ from domeftic mules; and that
they cannot be trained to bear burdens *. Muller and Gmelin affure us, that they are numerous in the country of the Tongufians, where
they are hunted like other game; that, in Siberia, toward Borsja, they are very plenty in dry
years; and he adds, that they refemble, in
figure, fize, and colour, a bright bay horfe, except that they have very long ears †, and a tail
like that of a cow. If thefe travellers who ex-

* Hift. Gen. des Voyages, tom. vi. p. 601.
† Voyage de M. Muller et Gmelin, tom. ii, p. 105. 107.

amined

amined the czigithai, had, at the fame time, compared it with the zebra, they would perhaps
have difcovered a greater number of relations
than we are apt to imagine. In the Peterfburgh
cabinet there are ftuffed fkins both of the zebra
and czigithai. Though thefe fkins differ in colour, they may belong to the fame, or a very
neighbouring fpecies. Time alone can remove
or confirm thefe conjectures. But, as all the
other animals of Africa are likewife found in
Afia, if the zebra and czigithai are not of the
fame fpecies, the zebra alone would be an exception to this general rule.

Befides, if the czigithai is not the fame with
the zebra, it may be the Afiatic animal called
onager or *wild afs*. The onager fhould not be
confounded with the zebra; but I am uncertain whether the fame remark is applicable to
the onager and czigithai; for, from comparing
the relations of travellers, it appears, that there
are different kinds of wild affes, of which the
onager is the moft remarkable. Perhaps the
horfe, the afs, the onager, and the czigithai,
conftitute four diftinct fpecies: And, on the
fuppofition that they are only three, it is ftill
uncertain whether the czigithai be an onager or
a zebra. The fwiftnefs of the onager is mentioned by travellers, who remark, that he runs
with fuch rapidity as to efcape the hunters,
though mounted on horfes; and they fay the
fame thing of the czigithai. However this

matter

matter ſtands, the horſe, the aſs, the zebra, and the czigithai, belong to the ſame genus, and conſtitute three or four branches of the ſame family; the two firſt of which have long been reduced to a domeſtic ſtate. We may therefore hope, that the two laſt may likewiſe be tamed, and prove a uſeful acquiſition to mankind.

Plate CLXXXV.

ZEBRA.

Plate CLXXXVI.

ZEBRA.

The HIPPOPOTAMUS*.

THOUGH the hippopotamus has been celebrated from the remoteſt antiquity; though
the ſacred writings mention him under the name
of *Behemoth*; and though his figure is engraved

---

* The hippopotamie has four cutting teeth in each jaw.
Thoſe in the middle are ſtraight and pointed forward, the
two middlemoſt the largeſt. It has four tuſks, thoſe in the
upper jaw are ſhort, and the lower very long, and truncated obliquely. The head is of an enormous ſize, and the mouth is
vaſtly wide. The ears are ſmall and pointed, and lined within
very thickly with ſhort fine hairs. The eyes and noſtrils
are ſmall in proportion to the bulk of the animal. On the
lips are ſome ſtrong hairs ſcattered in patches here and there.
The hair on the body is very thin, of a whitiſh colour, and
ſcarce diſcernable at firſt ſight. There is no mane on the neck,
as ſome writers feign, only the hairs on that part are rather
thicker. The ſkin is very thick and ſtrong, and of a duſky
colour. The tail is about a foot long, taper, compreſſed, and
naked. The hoofs are divided into four parts; but, notwithſtanding it is an amphibious animal, they are not connected
by membranes. The legs are ſhort and thick. In bulk,
it is ſecond only to the elephant. The length of a male has
been found to be ſeventeen feet, the circumference of the body
fifteen, the height near ſeven, the legs near three, the head above
three and a half, and the girth near nine; *Pennant's Synopſ.
of Quad. p.* 78.

In Hebrew, *Behemoth*; *Shaw's Travels, Suppl. p.* 87. *Bochart*; in
Greek, Ἱπποποταμος; *Ariſt. Hiſt. Anim. lib.* ii. *c.* 7.; in Latin,
Hippopotamus; in Italian, *Hippopotamo*; in the Egyptian language,
according to Zerenghi, *Foraſl'bar*, which ſignifies *ſea-horſe.*

Hippopotamus;

ed on the Egyptian obelifks, and on the Roman medals; yet he was very imperfectly known to the ancients. Ariftotle * fpeaks of this animal

in

Hippopotamus; *Belon. Obf. de la Nature de Poiffons, p.* 17. *Gefner. Quad. p.* 493. *Razivil Iter Hierofol. p.* 142. *Raii Synopf. Quad. p.* 123. *Fab. Columna. Aquat. p.* 28. *Aldrov. de Quad. Digit. vivip. p.* 181.

River-horfe; *Grew's Mufeum, p.* 14. *tab.* 1. *Ludolph. Æthiop. p.* 60.

Cheropotamus et hippopotamus; *Profp. Alp. Egyp. Hift. Nat. lib.* iv. *p.* 246. *tab.* 23.

Sea-ox; *Lobo Abyffin. p.* 105. *Kolben's Cape,* vol. ii. *p.* 129.

Sea-horfe; *Leo Afric. p.* 344. *Dampier's Voy.* vol. ii. *p.* 104. *Adanfon's Voy. p.* 133. *Moore's Voy. to Gambia, p.* 105. 188. 216.

River-paard; *Houttuyn. Nat. Hift.* vol. iii. *p.* 405. *tab.* 28.

Water-elephant; *Barbot, Voy. to Guiney, p.* 113. 173.

Hippopotamus amphibius, pedibus quadrilobis; *Linn. Syft. Nat. p.* 101. *Haffelquift. Iter, p.* 201. *Klein. Quad. p.* 34. *Briffon. Quad. p.* 83.

Hippopotamo; *La vera Defcriptione dell Hippopotamo, auctore Federico Zerenghi da Narni, medico Chirurgico in Napoli,* 1603, *p.* 67. *Note,* This defcription of the hippopotamus makes a part of an abridgement of furgery, compofed by the fame author, on the 65th page of which is the particular title above quoted. This fmall work, which is both original and excellent, is at the fame time fo rare, as not to be mentioned by any naturalifts. The figure was drawn from a female hippopotamus.

* Equo fluviatili, quem gignit Egyptus, juba equi, ungula qualis bubus, roftrum refimum. Talus etiam ineft bifulcorum modo; dentes exerti fed leviter; cauda apri, vox equi, magnitudo afini, tergoris craffitudo tanta ut ex eo venabula faciant, interiora omnia equi et afini fimilia; *Arift. Hift Anim. lib.* ii. *cap.* 7.——— Natura etiam equi fluviatilis ita conftat, ut vivere nifi in humore non poffit; *Idem. lib.* viii. *cap.* 24. *Note,* The hippopotamus has no mane like the horfe; and his hoofs are not divided into two, but into four. His tufks appear not

in the moſt ſuperficial manner; and in the
little he ſays, there are more errors than truth.
Pliny * copies Ariſtotle, and, inſtead of cor-
recting, adds to the number of his blunders. It
was not till about the middle of the ſixteenth
century that any preciſe information was obtained concerning this animal. Belon, being
then at Conſtantinople, ſaw a living hippopotamus, of which, however, he gives but an imperfect repreſentation; for the two figures which
he has added to his deſcription were not drawn
from the animal he ſaw, but were copied from
the reverſe of Adrian's medal, and from the
Egyptian Coloſſus at Rome. Hence the æra of
any exact knowledge concerning this animal
muſt be brought forward to the year 1603,
when Federico Zerenghi, a ſurgeon of Narni in
Italy, printed at Naples the hiſtory of two hippopotami which he had taken alive in a great
ditch dug on purpoſe in the neighbourhood of
the Nile, near Damietta. This little book was
written in Italian; and, though it be the only

---

on the outſide of the mouth. His tail is very different from
that of the wild boar; and he is at leaſt ſix times larger
than the aſs. Like other quadrupeds, he can live on land; for
the one deſcribed by Belon had lived two or three days without
entering the water. Hence Ariſtotle muſt have had very bad information concerning this animal.

* Pliny ſays, that the hippopotamus inhabits the ſea as well as
the rivers, and that he is covered with hair like the ſea-calf.
Note, This laſt fact is advanced without any foundation; for
it is certain that he has no hair on his ſkin, and that he was never
ſeen nearer the ſea than the mouths of rivers.

thing

thing original we have upon this fubject, it feems to have been totally neglected both by contemporary and fucceeding naturalifts. The defcription it contains of the hippopotamus is, at the fame time, fo good, and appears fo worthy of credit, that I fhall here give an extract and tranflation of it.

' With a view,' fays Zerenghi, ' of obtaining
' an hippopotamus, I ftationed men upon the
' Nile, who, having feen two of thefe animals go
' out of the river, made a large ditch in the way
' through which they paffed, and covered it with
' thin planks, earth, and herbage. In the even-
' ing, when returning to the river, they both fell
' into the ditch. I was immediately informed
' of the event, and haftened to the place along
' with my Janiffary. We killed both the ani-
' mals by pouring three fhot into each of their
' heads from a large arquebufe. They almoft
' inftantly expired, after uttering a cry which
' had more refemblance to the bellowing of
' a buffalo, than to the neighing of a horfe.
' This exploit was performed on the 20th day
' of July 1600. The following day, they were
' drawn out of the ditch, and carefully fkinned.
' The one was a male and the other a female.
' I caufed their fkins to be falted, and ftuffed
' with the leaves of the fugar-cane, in order to
' tranfport them to Cairo, where they were
' falted a fecond time with more attention and
' convenience. Each fkin required four hun-
' dred pounds of falt. On my return from
' Egypt,

' Egypt, in 1601, I brought thefe fkins to Venice,
' and from thence to Rome. I fhowed them
' to feveral intelligent phyficians. Doctor Je-
' rome Aquapendente and the celebrated Al-
' drovandus were the only perfons who recog-
' nifed them to be the fpoils of the hippopota-
' mus; and, as Aldrovandus's work was then
' printing, I allowed him to draw a figure from
' the fkin of the female, which he inferted in
' .his book.

   ' The fkin of the hippopotamus is very thick,
' and very hard; it is even impenetrable, un-
' lefs after being long fteeped in water. The
' mouth is not, as the ancients alledge, of a
' middle fize, but enormoufly large. Neither
' are his feet divided into two toes, but into
' four. His fize is not that of an afs; for
' he is much larger than the largeft horfe or
' buffalo. His tail refembles not that of a hog,
' but rather that of the tortoife, only it is in-
' comparably larger. His muzzle is not turned
' up, but refembles that of the buffalo, and is
' much larger. He has no mane, but only a
' few fhort fcattered hairs. He neighs not like
' a horfe; but his voice is a medium between
' the bellowing of a buffalo and the neighing
' of a horfe. He has no tufks which protrude
' out of the mouth; for, when the mouth is
' fhut, the teeth, though extremely large, are all
' concealed within the lips. . . . . The inha-
' bitants of this part of Egypt call him *foras*
' *l'bar*, which fignifies the *fea-horfe*. . . . Be-
' lon's

' lon's defcription is very erroneous : He gives
' to this animal the teeth of the horfe, which
' would lead us to think, contrary to his own
' affertions, that he had never feen it ; for the
' teeth of the hippopotamus are very large and
' very fingular. . . . To remove every uncer-
' tainty,' continues Zerenghi, ' I here give the
' figure of the female hippopotamus with all the
' dimenfions and proportions of the body and
' members, drawn exactly according to nature. ·

' The length of this hippopotamus, from the
' extremity of the upper lip to the origin of the
' tail, is nearly eleven feet two inches *.

' The circumference of the body is about ten
' feet.

' The height, from the fole of the foot to the
' top of the back, is four feet five inches.

' The circumference of the legs, near the
' fhoulders, is two feet nine inches, and, when
' taken lower, one foot nine inches and a half.

' The height of the legs, from the fole of the
' foot to the breaft, is one foot ten inches and a
' half.

' The length of the feet from the extremity
' of the nails, is about four inches and a half.'
Nota, I have here taken a mean between Zerenghi's two meafures for the length of the feet.

' The nails, or divifions of the hoof, are as
' long as they are broad, being two inches and
' two lines.

---

* This and the following meafures are all Paris feet and
inches.

' Each

' Each toe has a nail, and each foot four toes.
' The fkin, on the back, is near an inch, and
' that on the belly about feven lines thick.

' The fkin, when dried, is fo hard that a
' mufket ball cannot pierce it. The country
' people make large fhields of it, and likewife
' ufe it for thongs or whips. On the furface
' of the fkin there are a few fcattered whitifh
' hairs, which are not perceptible at firft fight.
' On the neck the hairs are longer, and all of
' them placed one by one, at greater or fmaller
' diftances from each other. But, on the lips,
' they form a kind of whifkers; for, in feveral
' places, ten or twelve of them iffue from the
' fame point. Thefe hairs are of the fame co-
' lour as the others, only they are harder, thicker,
' and fomewhat longer, though none of them
' exceeds half an inch in length.

' The length of the tail is eleven inches four
' lines : Its circumference, at the origin, is a
' little more than a foot, and, at the extremity,
' two inches ten lines.

' The tail is not round; but, from the middle
' to the point, it is flattened, like that of an eel.
' Upon the tail and the thighs there are fome
' round fcales, of a whitifh colour, and as large
' as lentiles. Thefe fmall fcales likewife appear
' on the breaft, the neck, and fome parts of the
' head.

' From the extremity of the lips to the be-
' ginning of the neck, the head is four feet four
' inches.

' The

' The circumference of the head is about five
' feet eight inches.

' The ears are two inches nine lines long,
' two inches three lines broad, a little pointed,
' and garnifhed in the infide with fine, fhort, thick
' hairs, of the fame colour as the others.

' The eyes, from one corner to the other, are
' two inches three lines ; and the eye-lids are
' diftant from each other one inch one line.

' The noftrils are two inches four lines long,
' and one inch three lines broad.

' The mouth opens to the width of one foot
' five inches four lines. It is of a fquare form,
' and furnifhed with forty-four teeth of differ-
' ent figures *. . . . . All thefe teeth are fo
' hard, that they ftrike fire with fteel. It is
' chiefly the enamel of the canine teeth which
' poffeffes this degree of hardnefs, the internal
' fubftance of the whole being fofter. . . . When
' the hippopotamus keeps his mouth fhut, no
' teeth appear without, but are all covered with
' the lips, which are extremely large.

' With regard to the figure of the hippopo-
' tamus, it appears to be a medium between
' thofe of the buffalo and hog, becaufe it par-
' ticipates of both, except the cutting teeth,

---

* In three heads of the hippopotamus, preferved in the
royal cabinet, there are only thirty-fix teeth. As thefe heads
are fmaller than that defcribed by Zerenghi, it may be prefumed that, in young hippopotami, all the grinders are not developed, and that adults have eight more.

' which

' which have no refemblance to thofe of either
' of thefe animals. The grinding teeth have
' fome fimilarity to thofe of the buffalo or horfe,
' though they are much longer. The colour
' of the body is dufky and blackifh. . . . We
' are affured that the hippopotamus produces
' but one at a time; that he lives upon fifhes,
' crocodiles, and even cadaverous flefh. He
' eats, however, rice, grain, &c. though, if we
' confider the ftructure of his teeth, it would
' appear that Nature had not deftined him for
' pafture, but for devouring other animals.'

Zerenghi finifhes his defcription by inform-
ing us, that all thefe meafures had been taken
from the female fubject, and that the male perfectly refembled her, except that, in all his
dimenfions, he was one third larger. It were to
be wifhed that the figure given by Zerenghi had
been equally good as his defcription: This animal, however, was not drawn from the life, but
from the fkin of the female. It likewife appears, that Fabius Columna took his figure from
the fame fkin, which was preferved in falt. But
Columna's defcription is not equal to that of
Zerenghi; and he even merits reproach for mentioning only the name, and not the work, of this
author, though it was publifhed three years before
his own. For example, Columna remarks, that,
in his time, (1603,) Federico Zerenghi brought
from Egypt to Italy an entire hippopotamus,
preferved in falt, though Zerenghi himfelf tells

us,

us, that he brought only the skin. Columna makes the body of his hippopotamus thirteen feet long *, and fourteen feet in circumference, and the legs three feet and a half in length; while, by the measures of Zerenghi, the body was only eleven feet two inches long, its circumference ten feet, the legs one foot ten inches and a half, &c. We can have no dependence, therefore, on Columna's description: Neither can he be excused by supposing that his description was taken from another subject; for it is evident, from his own words, that he described the smallest of Zerenghi's two hippopotami, since he acknowledges, that, some months afterwards, Zerenghi exhibited a second hippopotamus, which was much larger than the first. I have insisted upon this point, because no body has done justice to Zerenghi, though he merits the highest eulogiums. On the contrary, all naturalists, for these hundred

* Hippopotami a nobis conspecti ac dimensi corpus a capite ad caudam pedes erat tredecim, corporis latitudo sive diameter pedes quatuor cum dimidio, ejusdem altitudo pedes tres cum dimidio, ut planum potius quam carinosum ventrem habeat: Orbis corporis quantum longitudo erat: Crura a terra ad ventrem pedes tres cum dimidio: Ambitus crurum pedes tres; pes latus pedem; ungulæ singulæ uncias tres: Caput vero latum pedes duo cum dimidio, longum pedes tres; crassum ambitu pedes septem cum dimidio: Oris rictus pedem unum, &c. Perhaps the foot used by Columna was shorter than the Paris foot. But this circumstance will not justify him; for the body of his hippopotamus being thirteen feet long, its circumference ought to have been only eleven feet seven or eight inches, and not fourteen feet. The other proportions are equally erroneous; for they correspond not with those given by Zerenghi.

and

and fixty years, have afcribed to Fabius Columna what was due to Zerenghi alone; and, inftead of inquiring after the work of the latter, they have contented themfelves with copying and praifing that of Columna, though, with regard to this article, he is neither original, exact, nor even honeft.

The defcription and figures of the hippopotamus, which Profper Alpinus publifhed more than a hundred years after, are ftill worfe than thofe of Columna, having been drawn from ill preferved fkins; and M. Juffieu *, who wrote upon the hippopotamus in the year 1724, has only defcribed the bones of the head and feet.

By comparing thefe defcriptions, and efpecially that of Zerenghi, with the information derived from travellers †, it appears that the hippo-

potamus

---

* Mem. de l'Acad. de Sciences, ann. 1724, p. 209.

† In the river Nile there are *hippopotami* or *fea-horfes*. In the year 1658, one of them was taken at Girge. It was foon brought to Cairo, where I faw it in the month of February of the fame year; but it was dead. This animal was of a kind of tawny colour. Behind he refembled the buffalo; but his legs were fhorter and thicker. He was as tall as a camel. His muzzle refembled that of an ox; but his body was twice as large. His head was fimilar to that of a horfe, but larger. His eyes were fmall, his neck very thick, his ears fmall, his noftrils very large and open, his feet very large, almoft round, with four toes on each, like thofe of the crocodile, and his tail fmall. Like the elephant, he had little or no hair on the fkin. In the under jaw, he had four large teeth, about half a foot in length. Two of them were crooked, and as thick as the horns of an ox. At firft, he was miftaken for a

fea

potamus is an animal whofe body is longer, and as thick as that of the rhinoceros; that his legs are much fhorter *; that his head is not fo long, but larger in proportion to his body; that he has no horns, either on the nofe, like the rhinoceros, or on the head, like the ruminating animals. As the cry he utters when pained is compofed, according to ancient authors and modern travellers †, of the neighing of a horfe and the

fea buffalo. But I, and fome others, who had read defcriptions of this animal, knew it to be a fea horfe. It was brought dead to Cairo by the Janiffaries, who fhot it on land, where it had come to feed. They poured feveral fhots into it before it fell; for, as I formerly remarked, a mufket ball hardly pierces its fkin. But one ball entered its jaw, and brought it to the ground. None of thefe animals had been feen at Cairo for a long time; *Relat. d'un Voyage du Levant, par Thevenot, tom.* i. *p.* 491.

* The legs of the hippopotamus are fo fhort, that the belly of the animal, when he walks, is not more than four inches above the ground; *Belon des Poiffons, p.* 17.—*Crura e terra ad ventrem pedes tres cum dimidio*; Fabius Columna, p. 31. The teftimonies of Belon and Columna, with regard to the length of the legs, differ fo widely, that none of their dimenfions can be adopted. It muft be remarked, that the hippopotamus which Belon faw alive, was very young and very fat; that, of courfe, his belly muft have been large and pendulous; that, on the contrary, the fkin defcribed by Columna, which was the fame with that of Zerenghi, had been dried with falt, and, confequently, Columna could not be certain that the belly of the animal was not *round* but *flat*. Thus the meafures of Belon are too fhort for an adult hippopotamus, and thofe of Columna too long for a living one. Hence we may infer from both, that, in general, the belly of this animal is not above a foot and a half from the ground; and that, as Zerenghi remarks, its legs exceed not two feet in length.

† Vocem equinam edit, illius gentis relatione; *Profp. Alp. Egypt.*

the bellowing of a buffalo, his ordinary voice may perhaps refemble the neighing of a horfe, from which, however, he differs in every other refpect. If this be the cafe, we may prefume that the animal has obtained the name *hippopotamus*, which fignifies the *river-horfe*, folely from the fimilarity of his voice to that of a horfe; in the fame manner as the lynx, from his howling like a wolf, obtained the appellation of *lupus cervarius* *. The cutting, and particularly the canine teeth of the lower jaw, are very long, and fo hard and ftrong, that they ftrike fire with fteel †. This circumftance, it is probable,

---

Egypt. Hift. Nat. lib. iv. *p.* 248.—Merolla fays, that, in the river Zaira, there are river-horfes, which neigh like the common horfe; *Hift. Gen. des Voyages. par M. l'Abbé Prevoft, tom.* v. *p.* 95. —This animal has derived his name from his neighing like a horfe; *Recueil des Voyages de la Compagnie des Indes de Hollande, tom.* iv. *p.* 440.—The neigh of the hippopotamus differs little from that of a horfe; but it is fo loud as to be heard diftinctly at the diftance of more than a quarter of a league; *Voyage au Senegal, par M. Adanfon, p.* 73.

* See the article *Lynx*, vol. v. p. 206.

† Tutti i denti fono di foftantza cofi dura, che percoffovi fopra con un cortello, o accialino, buttano faville di foco in gran quantita, ma piu le zanne che gli altri; ma dentro non fono di tanto dura materia; *Zerenghi, p.* 72. . . . Dentes habebat in inferiore maxilla fex, quorum bini exteriores e regione longi femipedem, lati et trigoni uncias duas cum dimidio, per ambitum femipedem, aprorum modo parum retrorfum declives, non adunci, non exerti, fed admodum confpicui aperto ore. Intermedii vero parum a gingiva exerti trigona acie digitali longitudine, medium locum occupantes, veluti jacentes craffi, orbiculati, elephantini femipedem fuperant longitudine, atque aciem in extremis partibus planam

probable, gave rife to the fable of the ancients, that the hippopotamus vomited fire from his mouth. The fubftance of the canine teeth is fo white, fo fine, and fo hard, that it is preferable to ivory for making artificial teeth *. The cutting teeth, efpecially thofe of the under jaw, are very long, cylindrical, and chamfered. The canine teeth are alfo long, crooked, prifmatic, and fharp like the tufks of the wild boar. The grinders are fquare or oblong, like thofe of man,

parum detraɛlam. Maxillares vero utrinque feptem craffos latos breves admodum. In fuperna vero mandibula, *quam crocodili more mobilem habet*, qua mandit et terit, anteriores fex infunt dentes, fex imis refpondentes acie contrario modo adaptata, leviffima ac fplendida, eboris politi modo, claufoque ore conjunguntur, aptanturque imis, veluti ex illis recifi, ut planum plano infideat; verum omnium acies pyramidalis veluti oblique recifi calami modo, fed medii fuperiores non aciem inferiorum, at medium illorum in quo detraɛlio confpicitur rotunditatis, petunt; ac non incidere, fed potius illis terere poffe videtur. Molares totidem quot inferni, fed bini priores parvi exigui, atque rotundo ambitu, et ab aliis diftant, ut medium palatum inter dentes anteriores occupare videantur; inter maxillares dentes linguæ locus femipedalis remanebat. Dentium vero color eburneus parum pallens, fplendidus, diaphanus fere in acie videbatur; durities illorum filicea, vel magis cutelli quidem cofta non parva confpicientium admiratione ignis excitabantur favillæ, parum vel nihil tot percuffionibus figni remanente: Quapropter verifimile foret noɛlis tempore dentes terendo ignem ex ore evomiffe; *Fab. Columna, p. 32.*

* The fineft and whiteft teeth of the hippopotamus are found at Cape Mefurada in Africa. The dentifts prefer them to ivory for making artificial teeth; becaufe they are harder, whiter, and do not turn yellow fo foon; *Voyage de Defmarchais, tom. ii. p. 148.*

and

and fo large that a fingle tooth weighs more than three pounds. The largeft cutting and canine teeth are twelve * and fometimes fixteen inches long †, and each of them weighs from twelve to thirteen pounds ‡.

In fine, to give a juft idea of the magnitude of the hippopotamus, we fhall employ the meafures of Zerenghi, and augment them one-third; becaufe thefe meafures were taken from the female, which was one-third lefs than the male in all its dimenfions. This male hippopotamus was, of courfe, fixteen feet nine inches long, from the extremity of the muzzle to the origin of the tail, fifteen feet in circumference, and fix feet and a half high; and the legs were about two feet ten inches long. The head was three feet and a half in length, and eight feet and a

---

* Poft menfes aliquot alium (hippopotamum) longe majorem, *idem*, Federicus Zerenghi, Romæ nobis oftendit, cujus dentes aprini pedali longitudine fuerunt, proportione craffiores, fic et reliqua omnia majora.—This paffage, which finifhes Fabius Columna's defcription, proves that it was taken from the female or fmaller hippopotamus of Zerenghi, and that the largeft, of which he gives no defcription, was a male. It likewife proves that no dependence can be had on Columna's meafures; for he is no where exact but in the dimenfions of the teeth, becaufe they can neither contract nor lengthen; but a fkin dried in falt varies in all its dimenfions.

† I remarked, that thefe teeth, which were crooked in the form of an arch, were about fixteen inches long, and that, where thickeft, they were more than fix inches in circumference; *Dampier's Voyages, tom.* iii. *p.* 360.

‡ As to the river-horfes, I never faw any of them; but I purchafed fome of their teeth which weighed thirteen pounds; *Relation de Thevenot, p.* 19.

T 2

half

half in circumference. The opening of the mouth was two feet four inches; and the largest teeth were more than a foot long.

With such powerful arms, and such prodigious strength of body, the hippopotamus might render himself formidable to all other animals. But he is naturally mild *; besides, he is so heavy and slow in his movements, that he could not overtake any quadruped. He swims faster than he runs; and he pursues fishes, and preys upon them †. Though he delights in the water, and lives in it as freely as upon land; yet he has not, like the beaver or otter, membranes between his toes. The great size of his belly renders his specific gravity nearly equal to that of water, and makes him swim with ease. Besides, he continues long at the bottom of the water ‡, where

he

---

* Qui hippopotamum animal terribile et crudele esse putarunt, falsi mihi videntur. Vidimus enim nos adeo mansuetum hoc animal, ut homines minime reformidaret, sed benigne sequeretur. Ingenio tam miti est, ut nullo negocio cicuretur, nec unquam morsu lædere conatur. . . . . Hippopotamum e stabulo solutum exire permittunt, nec metuunt he mordeat. Rector ejus, cum spectatores oblectare libet, caput aliquot brassicæ capitatæ, aut melopeponis partem, aut fascem herbarum aut panem e manu sublimi protendit feræ: Quod ea conspicata tanto rictum hiatu diducit, ut leonis etiam hiantis caput facile suis faucibus caperet. Tum rector quod manu tenebat in voraginem illam seu saccum quempiam immittit. Manducat illa et devorat; *Bellonius de Aquatilibus.*

† The hippopotamus walks slowly on the banks of the rivers; but swims very quickly in the water. He lives upon fishes, and every thing he can seize; *Dampier, vol.* iii. *p.* 360.

‡ I have seen the hippopotamus descend to the bottom of

three

he walks as in the open air; and, when he comes out of it to pasture, he eats sugar canes, rushes, millet, rice, roots, &c. of which he consumes great quantities, and does much damage in the cultivated fields. But, as he is more timid on land than in the water, it is not difficult to drive him off. His legs are so short, that, when at a distance from water, he cannot escape by flight. When in danger, his only resource is to plunge into the water, and travel under it a great way before he again appears. When hunted, he generally flies; but, when wounded, he returns with fury, darts boldly against the boats, seizes them with his teeth, tears pieces off them, and sometimes sinks them *. ‘ I have ‘ known,’ says a traveller †, ‘ the hippopota- ‘ mus open his mouth, and set one tooth on the ‘ gunnel of a boat, and another on the second ‘ strake from the keel (which was more than ‘ four feet distant), and there bit a hole through ‘ the plank, and sunk the boat; and, after he ‘ had done, he went away shaking his ears. His ‘ strength is incredibly great; for I have seen ‘ him, in the wash of the shore, when the sea ‘ has tossed in a Dutchman’s boat with fourteen ‘ hogsheads of water in her, upon the said beast,

---

three fathoms water, and remain there more than half an hour, before he returned to the surface; *Id. ib.*

  * Hippopotamus cymbis insidiatur quæ mercibus onustæ secundo Nigro feruntur, quas dorsi frequentibus gyris agitatas demergit; *Leon. Afric. Descript. tom.* ii. *p.* 758.

  † Dampier, vol. ii. part ii. p. 105.

‘ and

‘ and left it dry on its back; and another sea
‘ came and fetched the boat off, and the beast
‘ was not hurt, as far as I could perceive. How
‘ his teeth grow in his mouth I could not fee;
‘ only that they were round like a bow, and
‘ about fixteen inches long; and in the biggeft
‘ part more than fix inches about. We made
‘ feveral fhot at him; but to no purpofe, for
‘ they would glance from him as from a wall.
‘ The natives call him *kittimpungo*, and fay he
‘ is *Telijfo*, which is a kind of god; for no-
‘ thing, they fay, can kill him: And, if they
‘ fhould do to him as the white men do, he
‘ would foon deftroy their canoes and fifhing
‘ nets. Their cuftom is, when he comes near
‘ their canoes, to throw him fifh; and then he
‘ paffeth away, and will not meddle with their
‘ fifhing craft. He doth moft mifchief when
‘ he can ftand on the ground; but, when afloat,
‘ hath only power to bite. As our boat once
‘ lay near the fhore, I faw him go under her,
‘ and with his back lift her out of the water, and
‘ overfet her with fix men aboard; but, as it
‘ happened, did them no harm. Whilft we lay
‘ in the road, we had three of them, which did
‘ trouble this bay every full and change, and
‘ two or three days after. The natives fay, they
‘ go together, two males and one female. Their
‘ noife is much like the bellowing of a large
‘ calf.’ Thefe facts are fufficient to give an idea
of the ftrength of this animal. Many fimilar

facts

facts are to be found in the General History of Voyages, by the Abbé Prevost, where we have a complete and judicious collection * of all that has been delivered by travellers concerning the hippopotamus.

The individuals of this species are not numerous, and seem to be confined to the rivers of Africa. Most naturalists tell us, that the hippopotamus is also found in India. But the evidence they have of this fact appears to be equivocal. Alexander's † letter to Aristotle would be the most positive, if we could be certain that the animals mentioned in it were really hippopotami; which to me seems very problematical; for, if they were, Aristotle must have told us, in his history of animals, that the hippopotamus was a native of India as well as of Egypt. Onesicritus ‡ and some old authors say, that the hippopotamus was found in the river Indus. But

---

* Hist Gen. des Voyages, tom. v. p. 95. 330.

† Humanas carnes hippopotamis pergratas esse, ex eis collegimus, quæ in libro Aristotelis de mirabilibus Indiæ habentur, ubi Alexander Macedo scribens ad Aristotelem inquit : ' Ducen-' tos milites de Macedonibus, levibus armis, misi per amnem ' nataturos; itaque quartam fluminis partem nataverunt, cum ' horrenda res visu nobis conspecta est, hippopotami inter ' profundos aquarum ruerunt gurgites, aptosque milites nobis ' flentibus absumpserunt. Iratus ego tunc ex eis, qui nos in ' insidias deducebant, centum et quinquaginta mitti in flumen ' jussi, quos rursus hippopotami justa dignos pœna confecerunt;' *Aldrov. de Quad. Digit. p.* 188 et 189.

‡ In India quoque reperitur hippopotamus, ut *Onesicritus* est autor, in amne Indo; *Hermolaus apud Gesner de Piscibus,* p. 417.

this

this fact has received no confirmation from modern travellers, at leaſt from ſuch of them as merit the greateſt degree of credit: They all agree*, that the hippopotamus is found in the Nile, and Senegal or Niger, the Gambia, the Zaira, the other great rivers and lakes of Africa †, eſpecially in the ſouthern and eaſtern regions of that country. None of them ſay poſitively that this animal exiſts in Aſia. Father Boym ‡ is the only one who ſeems to inſinuate that the hippopotamus is found in Aſia. But his relation appears to be ſuſpicious, and, in my opinion, only proves that this animal is common in Moſambique, and all the eaſtern parts of Africa. At preſent, the hippopotamus, which the ancients call the *horſe of the Nile*, is ſo rare in the lower Nile, that the inhabitants of Egypt are totally ignorant of the name §. He is equally unknown in all the nor-

thern

* Coſmographie du Levant, par André Thevet, p. 139.—Leonis Afric. Africæ Deſcript. tom. ii. p. 758.—L'Afrique de Marmol, tom. i. p. 51.; et tom. ii. p. 144.—Relation de Thevenot, tom. i. p. 491.—Relation de l'Ethiopie, par Poncel. Lettres Edif. 4. Recueil. p. 363.—Deſcription de l'Egypte, par Maillet, tom. ii. p. 126.—Deſcription du Cap de Bonne-Eſperance, par Kolbe, tom. iii. p. 30.—Voyage de Flacourt, p. 394.—Hiſtoire de l'Abyſſinie, par Ludoff. p. 43 et 44.—Voyage au Senegal, par M. Adanſon, p. 73. &c.

† Relation de l'Ethiopie, par Ch. Jacq. Poncel; Suite des Lettres Edifiantes, 4. Recueil. p. 363.

‡ Flora Sinenſis, a P. Michaële Boym, p. 1.—La Chine Illuſtrée, par d'Alquié, p. 258.

§ With regard to animals, the preſent inhabitants of Egypt know nothing of the hippopotamus; *Shaw's Travels.*—The hippopotamus is produced in Æthiopia . . . deſcends by the

Nile

thern parts of Africa, from the Mediterranean to the river Bambou, which runs at the foot of Mount Atlas. Hence the climate inhabited by the hippopotamus extends only from Senegal to Æthiopia, and from thence to the Cape of Good Hope.

As moſt authors mention the hippopotamus under the names of the *ſea-horſe*, or the *ſea-cow*, he has ſometimes been confounded with the latter, which inhabits only the Northern ſeas. It appears, therefore, to be certain, that the hippopotami, which the author of the Deſcription of Muſcovy ſays are found on the ſea-ſhore near Petzora, are nothing elſe than ſea-cows. Aldrovandus, therefore, merits reproach for adopting this opinion without examination, and maintaining that the hippopotamus is found in the North ſeas *; for he not only does not inhabit the

---

Nile into Upper Egypt .... deſolates the fields by devouring the grain, and particularly the Turkiſh wheat. ... He is very rare in Lower Egypt; *Deſcript. de l'Egypte, ſur le Mem. de M. de Maillet, par M. l'Abbé Maſcrier, tom.* ii. *p.* 126.

* Sed quod magis mirandum eſt, in mari quoque verſari ſcripſit *Plinius,* qui agens de animantibus aquaticis, communes amni, terræ, et mari *crocodilos* et *hippopotamos* prædicabat. Idicirco non *debemus admiratione capi,* quando legitur in deſcriptione *Moſcoviæ,* in *oceano adjacenti regionibus Petzoræ, equos marinos creſcere. Pariter* Odoardus-Barboſa, Portughenſis, in Cefala obſervavit multos equos marinos, a mari ad prata exire, denuoque ad mare reverti. Idem repetit *Edoardus-Vuot,* de hujuſmodi feris in mari Indico errantibus. Propterea habetur in primo volumine navigationum, multos quandoque naucleros in terram deſcendere, ut hippopotamos in vicinis prates paſcentis comprehendant; ſed ipſi ad mare fugientes

the North feas, but it appears that he is rarely found in the South feas. The teftimonies of Odoardus-Barbofa and Edward Wotton, quoted by Aldrovandus, and which feem to prove that the hippopotamus inhabits the Indian feas, are nearly as equivocal as that of the defcriber of Mufcovy; and, I am inclined to think, with M. Adanfon*, that, now at leaft the hippopotamus is found only in the great rivers of Africa. Kolbe †, who fays he faw feveral of them at the
Cape

---

fugientes eorum cymbas aggrediuntur, dentibus illas difrumpendo et fubmergendo, et tamen beftiæ lanceis, ob cutis duritiem, fauciari minime poterant; *Aldrov. de Quad. Digit. Vivip. p.* 181. *et feq.*

* In going up the Niger, we came to a quarter where the hippopotami or river-horfes are very common. This animal, which is the largeft of the amphibious kind, is found only in the rivers of Africa, and in no other part of the world. He is generally faid to be of the figure of an ox; and, indeed, he refembles that animal more than any other. But his legs are fhorter, and his head is enormoufly large. With regard to fize, the hippopotamus may be ranked after the elephant and rhinoceros. His jaws are armed with four tufks, by which he tears up the roots of trees, which ferve him for food. He cannot remain long under water without refpiring, which obliges him to raife his head, from time to time, above the furface, like the crocodile; *Voyage au Senegal, par M. Adanfon, p.* 73.

† If the epithet *fea* be applied to the hippopotamus or *feahorfe,* it is not becaufe he is a fpecies of fifh or lives always *in the fea.* He comes upon the dry land in queft of food, and he retires for fafety to the *fea* or to a *river.* Herbage is his ordinary food. When preffed with hunger, he comes out of the water, in which he lies always in an extended pofture. When he raifes his head above the water, he looks about on all fides to fee if there is any danger, and he fcents a man at a
confider-

Cape of Good Hope, affures us, that they plunge
equally into the fea and the rivers; and the fame
thing

confiderable diftance. If he perceives any thing, he plunges
again into the water, where he continues three hours without
moving. . . . He generally weighs from two thoufand five
hundred to three thoufand pounds. . . . The fea-horfe, both
in colour and fize, refembles the rhinoceros, only his legs are
fomewhat fhorter. His head, as Tellez remarks, (lib. 1.
cap. 8.) has a greater refemblance to that of the horfe, than
to that of any other animal; and, from this circumftance, he
has derived his name. His mouth is much larger than that
of the horfe, and, in this refpect, he approaches nearer the ox.
His noftrils are very large; and, when he rifes to the furface
of the river or fea, he fquirts the water out of them. His ears
and eyes are remarkably fmall. His legs are fhort, and of an
equal thicknefs throughout. His hoofs are not divided into
two, like thofe of the ox, but into four parts, on each of which
there are fpiral furrows. His tail is fhort like that of the elephant, with a few fhort hairs on it; and there is no hair on
the reft of the body.

The paps of the female hang, like thofe of the cow, between the hind legs; but they, as well as the teats, are very
fmall in proportion to the fize of the animal. I have often
feen the mothers fuckling their young, which were then as
large as fheep. . . . The fkin of the river-horfe is more than
an inch thick, and fo hard that it is difficult to kill him even
with mufket balls. The Europeans always aim at his head,
where the fkin is moft tender, and eafily pierced. This animal feldom receives a mortal wound in any other part of his
body.

The teeth of the under jaw are very remarkable. They are
four in number, two on each fide, one of them crooked and
the other ftraight. They are as thick as an ox's horn, about
a foot and a half long, and each of them weighs twelve pounds.
They are very white, and never turn yellow with age, as
ivory does. Hence they are more efteemed than the teeth of
the elephant.

The flefh of this animal, whether boiled or roafted, is moft
delicious.

thing is advanced by other authors. Though Kolbe is more exact than ufual in his defcription of this animal, yet it is doubtful whether he faw it fo frequently as he infinuates; for the figure he gives is ftill worfe than thofe of Columna, Aldrovandus, and Profper Alpinus, which were all drawn from ftuffed fkins. It is eafy to perceive, that the defcriptions and figures in Kolbe's works have not been taken on the fpot, nor drawn from nature. His defcriptions are written from memory, and moft of the figures have been copied from thofe of other naturalifts. The figure he has given of the hippopotamus has a great refemblance to the cheropotamus of Profper Alpinus *.

Hence Kolbe, when he tells us that the hippopotamus inhabits the fea, has perhaps copied Pliny, inftead of giving his own obfervations. Moft authors relate that this animal is only found in frefh water lakes, and in rivers, fometimes near their mouths, but oftener at great diftances from the fea. Some travellers are aftonifhed that the hippopotamus fhould have been called the *fea-horfe*; becaufe, as Merollo

delicious. It is fo highly valued at the Cape, as to fell at twelve or fifteen pence the pound. The fat fells as dear as the flefh: It is very mild and wholefome, and ufed inftead of butter, &c.; *Defcript. du Cap de Bonne-Efperance, par Kolbe, tom.* iii. *ch.* 3.

* *Note,* The figures of the cheropotami of Profper Alpinus, *lib.* iv. *cap.* xii. *tab.* 22. feem to have been drawn from ftuffed fkins of hippopotami, from which the teeth appear to have been extracted.

remarks,

remarks *, this animal cannot endure falt water. He generally remains in the water during the day, and comes out in the night to pafture. The male and female feldom feparate. Zerenghi caught a male and a female the fame day, and in the fame ditch. The Dutch voyagers tell us, that the female brings forth three or four young at a time. But this fact is rendered fufpicious by the very evidence which Zerenghi quotes. Befides, as the hippopotamus is of an enormous fize, like the elephant, the rhinoceros, the whale, and all other large animals, it muft produce but one at a time: This analogy feems to be more certain than the vague reports of travellers.

S U P P L E M E N T.

M. Le Chevalier Bruce affured me, that, in his travels through Africa, he faw a number of hippopotami in Lake Tzana, which is fituated in Upper Abyffinia, near the true fources of the Nile; and that, in this lake, which is at leaft fix leagues long by ten or twelve broad, the hippopotami are more numerous than in any other part of the world. He adds, that he faw fome of them which were twenty feet long, with very thick fhort legs.

* Hift. Gen. des Voyages, tom. v. p. 95.

Addition

*Addition to the Article Hippopotamus, by Pro-
feſſor Allamand, Editor of the Dutch Edition
of this Work.*

TO complete the defcription of the adult hippopotamus given by M. de Buffon, nothing is
wanting but a genuine figure of the animal. M.
de Buffon, who is always original, chofe not to
copy the figures publiſhed by different authors.
They are all too imperfect to be ufed; and,
with regard to the animal itfelf, he could not
poffibly procure it. Even in its native country,
it is very rare, and too large to be tranfmitted
without great expence and trouble. In the cabinet of natural curiofities in the univerfity of
Leyden, there is a ftuffed fkin of the hippopotamus, which had been fent from the Cape of
Good Hope. Though it had been tranfported
to Holland more than a century ago, it has
been fo well preferved, that it ftill exhibits an
exact reprefentation of the animal. It is fupported by rings of iron, and by pieces of wood
of fuch folidity, that drying has produced no
confiderable alterations. As it is probably the
only fpecimen of the kind in Europe, I am perfuaded that all lovers of natural knowledge will
thank me for enriching the magnificent work of
M. de Buffon with an exact engraving of it.
The figure I have given reprefents the ani-

6   mal

mal better than any that has hitherto been drawn, or, rather, it is the only figure we have of it; for, in all the others, the hippopotamus is not diftinguifhable, if we except that to be found in a Dutch book, concerning the Leviathan of Holy Writ, which was copied from the fame model; but the proportions of the animal are not accurately obferved.

It is unneceffary to add a defcription of this enormous animal, having no additions to what has been faid of it by M. de Buffon and M. Daubenton.

[As the figure of the young hippopotamus in the cabinet of the Prince of Conde differs from that which M. Allamand had engraved from the ftuffed fkin in the Leyden cabinet, and as it has a greater refemblance to a new figure given by Dr. Klockner from another fkin in the Prince of Orange's cabinet, I have here preferred the latter; and I fhall add fome remarks of the fame author, which were tranflated from the Dutch.]

Addition to M. de Buffon's Hiftory of the Hippopotamus, by Dr. Klockner of Amfterdam.

I Am furprifed that M. de Buffon takes no notice of a paffage in Diodorus Siculus, concerning the hippopotamus, efpecially as this ancient author

author remarks, that its voice refembled the neighing of a horfe, which perhaps induced him to give it the denomination of *hippopotamus* or *river-horfe*. M. de Buffon founded his opinion of this matter upon the teftimonies of ancient and modern authors. Diodorus Siculus ought to have held the firft rank among the former, fince he not only travelled into Egypt, but is juftly efteemed to be one of the beft hiftorians of antiquity. The following are the words of the paffage alluded to : ' The Nile pro-
' duces feveral animals, of which the crocodile
' and hippopotamus merit particular attention.
' . . . The latter is five cubits in length. His
' feet are cloven like thofe of the ruminating
' animals ; and in each jaw he has three tufks
' larger than thofe of the wild boar. The
' whole mafs of his body refembles that of the
' elephant. His fkin is harder and ftronger
' than, perhaps, that of any other animal. He
' is amphibious, and remains, during the day,
' under the water, where he moves and acts in
' the fame manner as if he were on land, which
' he vifits in the night, in order to feed on the
' herbage of the mountains. If this animal were
' more prolific, he would commit great devafta-
' tion in the cultivated fields of Egypt. The
' hunting of the hippopotamus requires a num-
' ber of men, who endeavour to pierce him with
' iron daggers. They attack him with feveral
' boats joined together, and ftrike with crooked
' harpoons.

' harpoons. To fome of thefe hooks they fix a
' rope, and then leave the animal to exhauft
' himfelf with ftruggling and the lofs of blood.
' His flefh is very hard, and of difficult dige-
' ftion *.'

This is perhaps the beft defcription of the hippopotamus to be found among the ancients;
for Diodorus commits not a fingle error, but
with regard to the number of the animal's toes.

*Obfervations on the Mode of preparing the Skin of
the Hippopotamus, now in the Prince of
Orange's Cabinet, by Dr. Klockner.*

I Received from the Hague, in a very dry
ftate, the fkin of this hippopotamus, with the
head inclofed within it. The fkin had been
firft falted, then dried, and afterwards the fkin
of a young hippopotamus (which is likewife in
the Prince's cabinet) fteeped in brine, was, in a
moift ftate, put into the adult fkin. After which,
the whole was packed up in coarfe cloth, and
tranfmitted from the Cape of Good Hope to
Holland. The fmall fkin and the head, of
courfe, produced a difagreeable odour of rancid
greafe, which attracted the infects, and they da-
maged the large fkin that was firft expofed to
their attacks.

* Diodor. Sicul, lib. i. p. 42. edit. Wefelingii.

When I diluted the head it fwelled greatly. The opening of the mouth was more than fixteen inches of Amfterdam meafure *. The upper and under lips were fufficiently large to cover all the animal's teeth, efpecially as the inferior canine teeth are crooked, and flip along the curvature of the fuperior, in the form of fciffars, and pafs into a focket formed by the fkin of the lip and the gums. Between the cutting teeth and the cylindrical grinders, as well as between the tongue and cutting teeth, there is a fmooth hard fkin; and the palate is full of notches or hollows. The tongue had been cut out. . . . The flefh on each fide of the head had alfo been removed; and the fat which remained was corrupted. The whole, however, was interfperfed with very ftrong mufcles, and the flefh about the two lips was red and white, or of the colour of an ox's tongue.

Immediately behind the inferior canine teeth, there is a protuberance, which, when the mouth is fhut, fills the fpace between the canine teeth and grinders. This opening, though filled, has contracted one half in drying, as well as the lips.

Under the ears, and around the auditory paffage, which is remarkably fmall, as well as in the orbits of the eyes, there was a great quantity of fat.

The ears are placed upon an eminence, and in fuch a manner as to form circular folds. The

* The Amfterdam foot is only ten inches five lines of the French foot.

elevation

elevation of the right ear was much diminifhed in drying; but it was confpicuous on the left.

We know that the ears of the hippopotamus are very fmall. But thofe of our fubject had been confiderably diminifhed by infects. The internal part of the ears is garnifhed with fine clofe hair; but there is a very little hair on the outfide.

The eyes muft have been very fmall; for the fockets were uncommonly fmall in proportion to the magnitude of the animal. The eyes I placed in my fubject are perhaps larger than nature; but, when I ufed fmaller ones, they did not feem to correfpond with the animal.

The noftrils flope downward, and have a fmall aperture. They are afterwards joined internally by a fmall crooked line. When the fkin was dry, it was difficult to perceive thefe tubes. I enlarged them a little before the fkin was again dried.

I muft here remark, that I only found thirty-two teeth in this hippopotamus, which accords not either with Zerenghi's or M. Daubenton's defcriptions. The firft fays, that he found forty-four teeth in his fubjects; and the fecond found thirty-fix in the head preferved in the Royal Cabinet. This difference excited my attention: But I could perceive no marks of teeth having fallen out, except one of the cutting teeth, which feemed to have been broken. There are four canine teeth placed perpendicularly, eight cutting teeth, four in the upper jaw, which are per-

pendicular,

pendicular, and four in the under jaw, placed horizontally, as may be feen in the figure. Befides, I found two grinders in each fide of the under jaw, and three teeth, placed before the grinders, which had the form of kayles. In each fide of the upper jaw, were three grinders, and two of thefe cylindrical teeth. Between thefe cylindrical teeth, there is a fpace of about half an inch.

[I muft here remark, fays the Count de Buffon, that the hippopotamus has commonly thirty-fix teeth, namely, four cutting teeth above, and four below, and two canine teeth and twelve grinders in each jaw. This obfervation has been verified by three heads, which have long remained in the Royal Cabinet, and by a fourth head, which was tranfmitted to me in the month of December 1775, by M. de Sartine, fecretary of ftate to the marine department. The laft grinder, at the bottom of the mouth, is much thicker, broader, and flatter on the edge, than the other five. But I am inclined to think that the number of grinders varies according to the age of the animal; and that, inftead of twenty-four, we may fometimes find twenty-eight, and even thirty-two, which, as Zerenghi remarks, would make forty-four in all.]

The upper and under lips, continues Dr. Klockner, are garnifhed, at confiderable diftances, with fmall tufts of hair, which, like pencils, proceed from one tube. I counted about twenty of them,

I exa-

I examined a section of one of these tubes with the microscope, and found seven roots issuing from one tube. These seven roots afterwards split, and each gave rise to several hairs, which formed a kind of pencil.

On the sides of the mouth, toward the lower part, I saw some fine hairs, which were placed nearer each other than the former.

Besides, I found here and there upon the body some scattered hairs; but there were none upon the legs, flanks, or belly.

The extremity and edges of the tail were garnished with pencils of hair, like the nose; but they were a little longer.

I could not discover the sex of this animal. Near the fundament there was a kind of triangular pinked aperture, about six inches wide, where I imagined the organs of generation had been situated; but, as no vestige of them remained, it was impossible to ascertain the sex.

The skin of the belly, near the hind legs, was an inch and nine lines thick: Here the insects had made a hole, which rendered it an easy matter to measure the thickness. The substance of the skin was white, cartilaginous, and coriaceous; and, at this place, it was well separated from the fat and flesh. Higher up, toward the back, a good deal of the skin had been pared off, with a view, no doubt, to render it lighter for carriage. It was for this reason that the skin

about

about the fpine exceeded not an inch in thicknefs.

The toes were furnifhed with nails. The fkin between the toes were very wide; and I believe that the feet of this animal, when alive, were rather flat than round. The heel, which is placed high and backward, appeared to be well adapted for fwimming. The hoof, though thick and hardened, was neverthelefs flexible.

The dimenfions of this animal were nearly the fame with thofe of Zerenghi's female hippopotamus, formerly defcribed.

I was told, that this hippopotamus had advanced a great way upon land in the territories of the Cape, and even near the place called the *Mountains of fnow*, when it was fhot by Charles Marais, a peafant of French extraction. This peafant brought the fkin to M. de Piettenberg, Governour of the Cape, who tranfmitted it to his Highnefs the Prince. I had the relation from a nephew of C. Marais, who refides in Amfterdam. According to the account given by this man, who had it from the mouth of Marais, the hippopotamus runs extremely fwift, both in marfhy places and on the firm ground. It is for this reafon that the peafants, though excellent hunters, dare not fire upon him but when he is in the water. They lie in wait for him about funfet, when the animal raifes his head above the water, and keeps his fmall ears in perpetual agitation, in order to hear if any noife is near. When

When any object of prey appears upon the water, he darts upon it like an arrow from a bow. While the hippopotamus is liftening in this manner, and floating on the furface of the water, the hunters endeavour to fhoot him in the head. The one whofe fkin I ftuffed was fhot between the eye and the right ear; and the young one, which is alfo in the Prince's cabinet, had been fhot, or ftruck with an harpoon, in the breaft, as appears from infpection. When he feels that he is wounded, he plunges below the water, and walks or fwims till he lofes both motion and life. Then, by means of about twenty oxen, he is dragged on fhore and diffected. An adult hippopotamus generally yields about two thoufand pounds of fat, which is falted and fent to the Cape, where it fells very dear. This fat or lard is extremely good, and in relifh excels all others. When preffed, it yields a mild oil, as white as cream. In Africa, it is recommended as a fovereign remedy for difeafes of the breaft. The quantity of lard derived from an individual, demonftrates that this animal is of a furprifing weight and magnitude.

Before finifhing my remark, I fhall here add fome particulars, regarding the natural hiftory of the hippopotamus, which are not to be found in the preceding defcription.

We have feen, that the hippopotamus probably derived his name from the refemblance of his voice to the neighing of a horfe. From the

U 4   moft

moft authentic accounts, however, it appears that his cry has a greater fimilarity to that of the elephant, or to the ftammering and indiftinct founds uttered by deaf perfons. Befide this cry, the hippopotamus, when afleep, makes a kind of fnorting noife, which betrays him at a diftance. To prevent the danger arifing from this circumftance, he generally lies among the reeds that grow upon marfhy grounds, and which it is difficult to approach.

I can no where find the remark of Marais, concerning the agility of this animal, confirmed. We are perpetually affured, on the contrary, that the hunters choofe rather to attack him on land than in the water, which indicates, that they are not afraid of his fwiftnefs. According to other hiftorians, his return to the river is cut off by trees and ditches; becaufe they know that he uniformly inclines to regain the water, where he has no other animal to fear, rather than to fight or fly upon land. The great fhark and the crocodile avoid the hippopotamus, and dare not engage with him.

The fkin of the hippopotamus is fo extremely hard on the back, the crupper, and the external parts of the thighs and buttocks, that neither arrows nor mufket balls can pierce it. But it is fofter and thinner on the infide of the thighs and belly, where the hunters endeavour to fhoot him, or to pierce him with a javelin. He is extremely tenacious of life; and, therefore, they

try

try to break his legs by large blunderbuffes, charged with iron wedges. When they fucceed, they are full mafters of the animal. The Negroes, who attack the fharks and crocodiles with long knives and javelins, are afraid of the hippopotamus, and would perhaps never attempt to combat him, unlefs they knew that they could outrun him. They believe, however, that this animal has a ftronger antipathy to the Whites than to the Blacks.

The female brings forth on land, where fhe fuckles her young, and foon teaches it to take refuge in the water, when the fmalleft noife is heard.

The Negroes of Angola, Congo, Elmina, and, in general, of the whole weft coaft of Africa, regard the hippopotamus as one of thofe inferior divinities which they call *Fetiches*. They fcruple not, however, to eat his flefh, when they can procure it.

I am uncertain whether I fhould here quote a paffage from P. Labat, where he fays that the hippopotamus, who is of a very fanguiferous temperament, knows how to let blood of himfelf. For this purpofe, he remarks, the animal fearches for a fharp-pointed rock, and rubs himfelf againft it, till he makes a fufficient aperture for the blood to flow. To promote the flux, he agitates his body; and when he thinks he has loft a fufficient quantity, he rolls in the mud in order

order to fhut up the wound. In this ftory there is nothing impoffible; but how could P. Labat difcover fuch a fingular operation?

Befide the ufes to which the fkin and teeth of the hippopotamus are applied, we are affured that the Indian painters employ the blood of this animal as one of their colours.

Plate CLXXXVII.

A. Bell Sculp.

HIPPOPOTAMUS.

The ELK * and the RAIN-DEER **.

THOUGH the elk and rain-deer are animals of different species, yet, as it would
be difficult to give the history of the one without

---

* The elk has horns with short beams spreading into large
and broad palms, one side of which is plain, the outmost furnished with several sharp snags. It has no brow antlers. The
largest horn I have seen is in the house belonging to the Hudson's Bay company, and weighed 56 pounds. The length is 33
inches, between tip and tip 34, and the breadth of the palm
13½. There is in the same place an excellent picture of an elk
which was killed in the presence of Charles XI. of Sweden,
and weighed 1229 pounds. It is a very deformed and seem-
ingly disproportioned beast. A young female, of about a
year old, was to the top of the withers 5 feet or fifteen hands.
The head alone was two feet, and the length of the whole
animal, from nose to tail, was about seven feet. The neck
was much shorter than the head, with a short, thick, upright
mane, of a light brown colour. The eyes were small, the
ears one foot long, very broad and slouching, and the nostrils
very large. The upper lip was square, hung greatly over
the lower, and had a deep sulcus in the middle, so as to appear
almost bifid. The nose was very broad. Under the throat
was a small excrescence, from whence hung a long tuft
of coarse black hair. The withers were very high, and the
fore-feet three feet three inches long. From the bottom of
the hoof to the end of the tibia was two feet four inches.
The hind legs were much shorter than the fore-legs. The
hoofs were much cloven; and the tail is very short, dusky
above, and white beneath. The general colour of the body

was

out encroaching on that of the other, we find it convenient to treat of them under one article. Most ancient, as well as modern authors, have confounded

was a hoary black, but more gray above the face than any where else. This animal was living last spring at the Marquis of Rockingham's house, at Parson's-green; *Pennant's Synops. of Quad. p.* 40.

In the Celtic language, *Elch*; in modern Latin, *Alce*; in Greek, αλκη; in German, *Hellend*, or *Ellend*; in Polish, *Loss*; in Swedish, *Oelg*; in Russ, *Lozxi*; in Norwegian, *Ælg*; in Chinese, *Han-ta-han*; in Canada, *Orignal*; in French, *Elan*.

Alce, machlis; *Plin. lib.* viii. *c.* 15. *Gesner, Quad. p.* 1. *Munster, Cosmog. p.* 883.

Cervus palmatus, alce vera et ligitima; *Klein. Quad. p.* 24.

Cervus cornibus ab imo ad summum palmatis; *Brisson. Quad. p.* 6. *Faunul. Sinens.*

Cervus alces, cornibus acaulibus palmatis, caruncula gutturali; *Linn. Syst. Nat. p.* 92.

Elk; *Raii Syn. Quad. p.* 86. *Scheffer. Lapl. p.* 133. *Bell's Trav. vol.* i. *p.* 5. 215. 322.

** The rain deer has large but slender horns, bending forward, the top palmated, brow antlers broad and palmated. Both sexes have horns; those of the female are less and with fewer branches. A pair from Greenland were three feet nine inches long, two feet and a half from tip to tip, and weighed nine pounds twelve ounces. The height of a full grown rain is four feet six inches. The space round the eye is always black. When it first sheds its coat, the hairs are of a brownish ash colour, and afterwards change to white. The hairs are very close set together, and, along the fore part of the neck, they are very long and pendent. The hoofs are large, and the tail short; *Pennant's Synops. of Quad. p.* 46.

The rain-deer was unknown to the Greeks. In French, *Rangier, Ranglier, le Renne*; in Latin, *Tarandus*; in Norwegian, *Reben*; in Lapland, *Boetsoi*; in German, *Reentbier*; in Swedish, *Rhen*; in Canada, *Caribou*; in modern Latin, *Rangifer.*
——In partibus magnæ Lapponiæ bestia est de genere cervorum.——Rangifer duplici ratione dicta; una quod in capito

confounded them, or exhibited them under equivocal denominations, which are equally applicable to both. The Greeks knew neither the elk nor the rain-deer; for Ariftotle * makes no mention of them : And, among the Latins, Julius Cæfar is the firft who employed the word *alce.* Paufanius †, who wrote about a century after

Cæfar,

pite ferat alta cornua velut quos quercinarum arborum ramos: Alia quod inftrumenta cornibus pectorique, quibus hiemalia plauftra trahit impofita *Rancha* et *Locha,* patrio fermone vocantur; *Olai Magni. Hift. de Gent. Sept. p.* 135.

Rangier or Ranglier; *Gafton de Foix apud du Fouilloux, p.* 90.

Tarandus, Rangifer; *Gefner, Quad. p.* 839. Icon. *Quad. p.* 57. *Aldrov. de Quad. Bifulc. p.* 859.

Cervus mirabilis; *Johnfton, de Quad. tab.* xxxvi. *Munfter Cofmog, p.* 1054.

Cervus rangifer; *Raii Synopf. Quad. p.* 88. *Klein. Quad. p.* 23.

Daim de Groenland; Edwards; *Hift. des Oifeaux, part.* i. *p.* 51.

Cervus cornuum fummitatibus omnibus palmatis; *Briffon, Regn. Anim. p.* 92.

Cervus Tarandus, cornubus ramofis, recurvatis, teretibus, fummitatibus palmatis; *Linn. Syft. Nat. p.* 93.

Rein-deer; *Schæffer. Suppl. p.* 82. 129. *Le Brun's Travels, vol.* i. *p.* 10. *Oeuvres de Maupertuis, tom.* iii. *p.* 198. *Voyage d'Othier, p.* 141. *Hift. Kamtfchatka, p.* 228. *Bell's Travels, vol.* i. *p.* 213. *Martin's Spitzberg. p.* 99. *Crantz's Greenland, vol.* i. *p.* 70. *Egede Greenl. p.* 60. *Dobb's Hudfon's Bay, p.* 20. 22. *Voyage au Hudf. Bay, tom.* ii *p.* 17.

Rheno; *Linn. Aman. Acad. p.* 4.

La Caribou; *Charlevoix, Hift. Nouv. France, tom.* v. *p.* 190.

* We have fhown, under the article *Axis,* that the hippelaphus of Ariftotle is not the elk.

† Argumento funt Æthiopici tauri et *alces* feræ Celticæ, ex quibus mares cornua in fuperciliis habent, fœmina caret.

Paufan.

Cæfar, is the firft Greek author in which the name Αλκη occurs; and Pliny *, who was nearly contemporary with Paufanias, has given fome
·obfcure

Panfan. in Eliacis ———— *Alce* nominata fera fpecie inter cer-vum et camelum eft; nafcitur apud Celtas; explorari invefti-garique ab hominibus animalium fola non poteft, fed obiter aliquando dum alias venantur feras, hæc etiam incidit. Sa-gaciffimam effe aiunt, et hominis odore per longinquum inter-vallum percepto, in foveas et profundiffimos fpecus fefe abdere. Venatores montem vel campum ad mille ftadia circundant, et contracto fubinde ambitu, nifi intra illum fera delitefcat, non alia ratione eam capere poffunt; *Idem. In Bæoticis.*

* Septentrio fert et equorum greges ferorum, ficut afino-rum Afia et Africa: Præter ea alcem, ni proceritas aurium et cervicis diftinguat, jumenta fimilem: Item notam in Scan-dinavia infula, nec unquam vifam in hoc orbe, multis tamen narratam, *machlin*, haud diffimilem illi, fed nullo fuffraginum flexu; ideoque non cubantem, fed acclivem arbori in fomno, eaque incifa ad infidias, capi; velocitatis memoratæ. Labrum ei fuperius prægrande: Ob id retrograditur in pafcendo, ne in priora tendens, involvatur; *Plin. Hift. Nat. lib. viii. cap.* 15.

———— Mutat colores et Schytarum tarandus. ———— Tarando magnitudo quæ bovi, caput majus cervino, nec abfimile; cornua ramofa; ungulæ bifidæ: Villus magnitudine ur-forum, fed cum libuit fui coloris effe, afini fimilis eft: Tergoris tanta duritia ut thoraces ex eo faciant. ———— Metuens latet, ideoque raro capitur; *Plin. Hift. Nat. lib. viii. cap.* 34.

————I have quoted thefe two paffages of Pliny, in which, under the denomination of *alce, machlis* and *tarandus*, he feems to point out three different animals. But I fhall after-wards fhow, that both *machlis* and *alce* apply folely to the elk; and that, though moft naturalifts believe the *tarandus* of Pliny to be the elk, it is much more probable that he means the rain-deer by this appellation. I acknowledge, however, that the indications of Pliny are fo confufed, and even falfe, that it is difficult to determine this point with precifion. The commentators upon Pliny, though they had much erudition,
were

obscure intimations of the elk and rain-deer under the appellations of *alce*, *machlis*, and *tarandus*. The name *alce*, therefore, cannot be properly confidered as either Greek or Latin; but it appears to have been derived from the Celtic language, in which the elk is called *elch* or *elk*. The Latin name of the rain-deer is ftill more uncertain. Several naturalifts have thought that it was the *machlis* of Pliny; becaufe this author, when fpeaking of the northern animals, mentions, at the fame time, the *alce* and the *machlis*; the laft of which, he remarks, is peculiar to Scandinavia, and was never feen either at Rome, or any part of the Roman empire. In Cæfar's Commentaries*, however, we find a paffage, which can

---

were but little verfed in natural hiftory; and this is one reafon why we find fo many obfcure and ill interpreted paffages in his writings. The fame work is applicable to the commentators and tranflators of Ariftotle. We fhall, therefore, endeavour to reftore fome words which have been changed, and to correct fome paffages of thofe two authors that have been corrupted.

* Eft bos in Hercinia filva, cervi figura, cujus a media fronte inter aures unum cornu exiftit excelfius, magifque directum his quæ nobis nota funt cornibus: Ab ejus fummo ficut palmæ ramique late diffunduntur. Eadem eft fœminæ marifque natura; eadem forma, magnitudoque cornuum; *Jul. Cæfar de Bello Gallico, lib.* vi. *Note,* This paffage is decifive. The rain-deer, in fact, has brow antlers which feem to form an intermediate horn. His horns are divided into feveral branches, terminated by large palms; and the female has horns as well as the male. But the females of the elk, the ftag, the fallow-deer, and the roe-deer, have no horns. Hence
it

can apply to no other animal than the rain-deer, and seems to prove that it then existed in the forests of Germany: and Gaston Phœbus, fifteen centuries after Julius Cæsar, seems to speak of the rain-deer, under the name of *rangier*, as an animal, which, in his time, existed in the forests of France. He has even given a good description * of this animal, and of the manner

of

---

it is apparent, that the animal here pointed out by Cæsar, is the rain-deer, and not the elk; especially as, in another place, he mentions the elk, under the name of *alce*, in the following terms: Sunt item in Hercinia silva quæ appellantur *alces*: Harum est confimilis capris (*capreis*) figura et varietas pellium: Sed magnitudine paulo antecedunt mutilæ quæ sunt cornibus et crura fine nodis, articulifque habent, neque quietis causa procumbunt.——His sunt arbores pro cubilibus: Ad eas se applicant: Atque ita paulum modo reclinatæ quietem capiunt: Quarum ex vestigiis cum est animadverfum a venatoribus quo se recipere consueverint, omnes eo loco aut a radicibus subruunt aut abscindunt arbores tantum ut summa species earum stantium relinquatur: Huc cum se consuetudine reclinaverint, infirmas arbores pondere affligunt atque una ipsæ concidunt; *de Bello Gallico, lib.* vi. I allow that this second passage contains nothing precise but the name *alce*; and, to make it apply to the elk, the word *capreis* must be substituted for *capris*; and we must suppose, at the same time, that Cæsar had only seen female elks, which have no horns. All the rest is intelligible; for the elk has very stiff limbs; that is, their articulations are very firm and close; and, as the ancients believed, that there were animals, such as the elephant, which could neither bend their limbs nor lie down, it is not surprising that they attribute to the elk this fabulous story of the elephant.

* The *rangier* or *ranglier* is an animal that resembles the stag; but his horns are larger and much more branched. When hunted, he flies, on account of the great weight on his head.

of hunting it. As his defcription cannot apply to the elk, and as he gives, at the fame time,
the mode of hunting the ftag, the fallow deer,
the roebuck, the wild goat, the chamois goat,
&c. it cannot be alledged, that, under the article
rangier, he meant any of thefe animals, or that
he had been deceived in the application of the
name. It is apparent, therefore, from thefe pofitive evidences, that the rain-deer formerly exifted
in France, efpecially in the mountainous parts,
fuch as the Pyrennees, in the neighbourhood of
which Gafton Phæbus refided, as Lord of the county
of Foix ; and that, fince this period, they have
been deftroyed, like the ftags which were formerly

head. But, after running long, and doubling, he places his
buttocks againft a tree, to prevent any attack from behind,
and bends his head toward the ground. In this fituation,
the dogs dare not approach him, becaufe his whole body is
defended by his horns. If they come behind him, he ftrikes
them with his heels. The grey-hounds and bull-dogs are terrified when they fee his horns. The rangier is not taller than
the fallow-deer; but he is much thicker. When he rears his
horns backward, they cover his whole body. He feeds like
the ftag or fallow-deer, and throws his dung in clufters. He
lives very long. The hunters fhoot him with arrows, or take
him with different kinds of fnares. He is fatter than a ftag.
Like the fallow-deer, he follows the ftag in the rutting feafon.

As to the manner of hunting the *rangier* or *ranglier*; when
the hunters go in queft of this animal, they fhould feparate
the dogs, to prevent his running into the thickeft parts of
the foreft, which are inhabited by the fallow-deer and roebucks. He fhould feparate his nets and fnares according to the
fituation of the foreft, and lead his hounds through the wood.
As the horns of the rangier are high and heavy, few hunters
attempt to feize him with hounds; *La Venerie de Jacques
Dufouilloux, p. 97.*

common in this country, and which now exift not in Bigore, Couferans, nor in the adjacent provinces. It is certain that the rain-deer is found only in more northern latitudes. But we likewife know, that the climate of France was formerly much moifter and colder, on account of the many forefts and marfhes which have fince been cut down and drained. From the Emperor Julian's letter, we learn what was the rigour of the froft at Paris in his time. The defcription he gives of the ice on the Seine is perfectly the fame with what the Canadians tell us of the ice on the rivers of Quebec. Gaul, under the fame latitude with Canada, was, two thoufand years ago, exactly what Canada is at prefent, namely, a climate fufficiently cold to nourifh animals which are now found only in the more northern regions.

From all thefe facts, therefore, it is evident, that the elk and the rain-deer formerly exifted in the forefts of Gaul and Germany; and that the paffages in the Commentaries of Cæfar can apply to no other animals. In proportion as the lands were cleared, and the waters dried up, the temperature of the climate would become more mild, thefe animals, who delight in cold, would firft abandon the flat countries, and retire to the fnowy mountains, where they ftill fub- fifted in the days of Gafton de Foix. The rea- fon why they are no longer found there is ob- vious: The heat of the climate has been gradually

dually augmented by the almoſt total deſtruction of the foreſts, by the ſucceſſive lowering of the mountains, by the diminution of the waters, by the multiplication of the human race, and by culture and improvement of every kind. It appears, likewiſe, that Pliny has borrowed from Cæſar almoſt every thing he has ſaid of theſe two animals, and that he was the firſt who introduced confuſion into their names. The *alce* and the *machlis* he mentions at the ſame time; from which we are led to conclude that theſe two names denote two different animals[*]. But, if we conſider, 1. That he mentions the *alce* only once, without giving any deſcription of it; 2. That he only employs the word *machlis*, which is neither Greek nor Latin, but ſeems to have been coined[†], and, according to his commentators, is changed into *alce* in ſeveral ancient manuſcripts; 3. That he attributes to the *machlis* all that Julius Cæſar has ſaid of the

---

[*] Several of our moſt learned naturaliſts, and particularly Mr. Ray, have thought that the *machlis*, being placed ſo near the *alce*, could be no other than the rain-deer. *Cervus rangifer, the rain-deer; Plinio machlis; Raii Synopſ. Quad. p. 88.* Becauſe I am by no means of the ſame opinion, I have here given a detail of my reaſons.

[†] On the margin of this paſſage of Pliny, we have *achlin*, inſtead of *machlin: Fortaſſis achlin, quod non cubet*, ſay the commentators. This name, therefore, appears to have been coined on the ſuppoſition that the animal cannot lie down. On the other hand, by tranſpoſing the *l* in *alce*, they have made *acle*, which differs little from *achlis*. Hence we may ſtill farther conclude, that this word has been corrupted by the tranſcribers, eſpecially as we find *alcem*, inſtead of *machlin*, in ſeveral ancient manuſcripts.

alce;

alce; the paffage of Pliny muft unqueftionably have been corrupted, and thefe two names muft denote the fame animal, namely the *elk.* The decifion of this queftion will refolve another. As the *machlis* is the *elk,* the *tarandus* muft be the *rain-deer.* The name *tarandus* is found in no other author before Pliny, and has given rife to various interpretations. Agricola and Elliot, however, have not hefitated to apply it to the rain-deer; and, for the reafon above affigned, we willingly fubfcribe to their opinion. Befides, we fhould not be furprifed at the filence of the Greeks, nor at the ambiguity with which the Latins have mentioned thefe animals; fince the northern regions were abfolutely unknown to the former, and the latter had all their information concerning thefe regions from the relations of others.

Now, in Europe and Afia, the elk is found only on this fide, and the rain-deer beyond, the Polar circle. In America, we meet with them in lower latitudes; becaufe there the cold is greater than in Europe. The rain-deer, being able to endure the moft exceffive cold, is found in Spitzbergen*; he is alfo very common in Greenland,

---

* In every part of Spitzbergen, the rain-deer are found, but particularly in *Reben-feld,* a place which received its name from the number of rain-deer it produces. They are alfo very numerous in Foreland, near Mufcle-Haven.———We arrived in this country in the fpring, and killed fome raindeer, which were very meager; from which circumftance we conclude, that, notwithftanding the unfertility and coldnefs of Spitzbergen,

land *, and in the moſt northern regions of Lapland † and of Aſia ‡. The elk approaches not ſo

Spitzbergen, theſe animals make a ſhift to paſs the winter
there, and to live upon the ſmall quantity of food they can
procure; *Recueil des Voyages au Nord, tom.* ii. *p.* 113.

* Captain Craycott, in the year 1738, brought a male and
a female rain-deer from Greenland to London; *Edwards's Hiſt.
of Birds, p.* 51. where we have a deſcription and figure of this
animal under the name of the *Greenland fallow-deer*, which, as
well as the *Greenland roebuck*, or *Caprea Groenlendica*, mentioned
by Grew, in his Deſcription of the Muſeum of the Royal Society,
can be nothing elſe but the rain-deer. Both theſe authors,
in their deſcriptions, mention, as a peculiar character, the
down with which the horns of theſe animals were covered.
This character, however, is common to the rain-deer, the
ſtag, the fallow-deer, and all the deer kind. This hair or down
continues on the horns during the ſummer ſeaſon, which is
the time when they are growing, and the only time that veſſels can ſail to Greenland. It is not, therefore, ſurpriſing
that, during this ſeaſon, the horns of the rain-deer ſhould be
covered with down. Hence this character is of no importance
in the deſcriptions given by theſe authors.

Upon the coaſts of Frobiſher's Straits, there are ſtags nearly
of the colour of aſſes, and whoſe horns are higher and much
larger than thoſe of our ſtags. Their feet are from ſeven
to eight inches in circumference, and reſemble thoſe of our
oxen; *Lade's Voy. tom.* ii. *p.* 297. *Note,* This paſſage ſeems
to have been copied from Captain Martin's Voyage, *p.* 17.
where he remarks, ‘ There are great numbers of ſtags on
‘ the lands of Warwick road, the ſkin of which reſembles
‘ that of our aſſes. Their head and horns, both in length and
‘ breadth, ſurpaſs thoſe of our ſtags. Their foot is as large
‘ as that of an ox, being eight inches broad.’

† The rain-deer are numerous in the country of the
Samoiedes, and over all the north; *Voyage d'Olearius, tom.* i.
p. 126. *L'Hiſt. de la Lapponie, par Scheffer, p.* 209.

‡ The Oſtiacks of Siberia, as well as the Samoiedes, em-
ploy rain-deer and dogs for drawing their carriages; *Nouv.
Mem. de la Grande Ruſſie, tom.* ii. *p.* 181.——— Among the
Tongueſe, there are great numbers of rain-deer, elks, bears, &c.;
Voyage de Gmelin, tom. ii. *p.* 206.

X 3   near

near the pole, but inhabits Norway *, Sweden †, Poland ‡, Lithuania ||, Ruffia §, and Siberia and Tartary **, as far as the north of China. In Canada, and in all the northern parts of America, we meet with the elk, under the name of

* See the chafe of the elk in Norway, by the Sieur de la Martiniere, in his Voyage to the North, p. 10.

† Alces habitat in filvis Sueciæ, rarius obvius hodie, quam olim; *Linn. Fauna Suecica, p.* 13.

‡ Tenent alces prægrandes Albæ Ruffiæ fylvæ, fovent 'Palatinatis varii, Novogrodenfis, Breftianenfis, Kiovienfis, Volhinenfis circa *Stepan,* Sandomirienfis circa *Nifko,* Livonienfis in Capitaneatibus quatuor ad Poloniæ regnum pertinentibus, Varmia iis non deftituitur; *Rzaczynfki auctuarium, p.* 305.

|| The *Loff* of the Lithuanians, the *Lozzi* of the Mufcovites, the *Oelg* of the Norwegians, the *Elend* of the Germans, and the *Alce* of the Latins, denote the fame animal: It is very different from the Norwegian *Rhen,* which is the raindeer. . . . . . No elks are produced in Lapland; but they are brought from other places, and particularly from Lithuania. . . . . . . They are found in South Finland, in Carelia, and in Ruffia; *Hift. de la Lapponie, par Scheffer, p.* 310.

§ In the neighbourhood of Irkutzk, there are elks, ftags, &c.; *Voyage de Gmelin, tom.* ii. *p.* 165.—The elks are common in the countries of the Manheous Tartars and of the Solons; *Id. ib.*

** The Tartarian animal called *Han-ta-han* by the Chinefe appears to be the fame with the elk. ‘The han-ta-han,’ fay the Miffionaries, ‘is an animal which refembles the elk. ‘The hunting of it is a common exercife in the country of ‘the Solons, and the Emperor Kamhi fometimes partakes ‘of this amufement. There are han-ta-hans as large as our ‘oxen. They are only found in particular cantons, efpeci- ‘ally toward the mountains of Sevelki, in marfhy grounds, ‘which they are fond of, and where they are eafily hunted. ‘becaufe their weight retards their flight;’ *Hift. Gen. des Voyages, tom.* xvi. *p.* 602.

the

the *orignal*, and the rain-deer under that of *caribou*. Those naturalists who suspect that the orignal * is not the elk, and the cari-

bou

---

* The *elks* or *orignals* are frequent in the province of Canada, and very rare in the country of the Hurons; because these animals generally retire to the coldest regions. . . . . The Hurons call the elks *sondareinta*, and the caribous *ausquoy*, of which the savages gave us a foot, which was hollow, and so light, that it is not difficult to believe what is said of this animal, that he walks on the snow without making a track. The elk is taller than a horse. . . . His hair is commonly gray, sometimes yellow, and as long as a man's finger. His head is very long, and he has double horns like the stag. They are as broad as those of the fallow deer, and three feet in length. His foot is cloven like that of the stag, but much larger. His flesh is tender and delicate. He pastures in the meadows, and likewise eats the tender twigs of trees. Next to fish, he is the principal food of the Canadians; *Voyage de Sagard Theodat. p.* 308,—There are elks in Virginia; *Hist. de la Virginie, p.* 213.—We find in New England great numbers of *orignals* or *elks*; *Descript. de l'Amerique Septent. par Denys, tom.* i. *p.* 27.—The island Cape Britain was famed for the chase of the orignal, where they were very numerous; but they have since been extirpated by the Savages; *Id. tom.* i. *p.* 163.—The orignal of New France is as strong as a mule; his head is nearly of the same shape. His neck is longer, and his whole body more meager. His limbs are long and nervous. His foot is cloven, and his tail is very short. Some of them are gray, others reddish or black, and, when old, their hair is hollow, as long as a man's finger, and makes excellent mattresses, or ornaments for saddles. The elk has large, flat, palmated horns. Some of them are a fathom long, and weigh from a hundred to a hundred and fifty pounds. They shed like those of the stag; *Id. tom.* ii. *p.* 321. —The orignal is a species of elk, very little different from those we see in Muscovy. He is as large as a mule, and of a similar figure, except in the muzzle, the tail, and the large flat horns, which, if we may credit the Savages, some-

X 4

times

bou * the rain-deer, have not compared nature with the relations of travellers. Though fmaller, like all the other American quadrupeds, than thofe of the Old Continent, they are unqueftionably the fame animals.

We will acquire jufter ideas of the elk and rain-deer by comparing both with the ftag : The elk

times weigh three hundred, and even four hundred pounds. This animal commonly frequents open countries. His hair is long, and of a brown colour. His fkin, though not thick, is very ftrong and hard. His flefh is good, but that of the female is moft delicate; *Voyage de la Hontan, tom.* i. *p.* 86.

* The caribou is an animal with a large muzzle and long ears.—As his foot is broad, he runs with eafe over the hardened fnow, which diftinguifhes him from the orignal, whofe feet always fink; *Voyage de la Hontan, tom.* i. *p.* 90.—The ifland of St. John is fituated in the great bay of Saint Lawrence. There are no orignals in this ifland; but there are caribous, which feem to be another fpecies of orignal. Their horns are not fo ftrong; their hair is thinner and longer, and almoft entirely white. Their flefh is whiter than that of the orignal, and makes excellent eating; *Defcript de l'Amerique feptent. par Denys, tom.* i. *p.* 202.—The caribou is a kind of ftag, which is very nimble and ftrong; *Voyage de Dierville, p.* 125.—The caribou is not fo tall as the orignal, and its figure partakes more of the afs than of the mule, and equals the ftag in fleetnefs. Some years ago, one of them was feen on Cape Diamond, above Quebec. . . . The tongue of this animal is much efteemed. His native country feems to be in the neighbourhood of Hudfon's Bay; *Hift. de la Nouv. France, par le P. Charlevoix, tom.* iii. *p.* 129.—The fineft hunting in North America is that of the caribou. It continues the whole year; and, particularly in fpring and autumn, we fee them in troops of above three or four hundred at a time. . . The horns of the caribou refemble thofe of the fallow deer. When firft feen by our failors, they were afraid, and ran from them; *Lettres Edifantes, recueil* x. *p.* 322.

is

is taller, thicker, and ſtands higher on his legs ; his neck is alſo ſhorter, his hair longer, and his horns much longer than thoſe of the ſtag. The rain-deer is not ſo tall ; his limbs * are ſhorter and thicker, and his feet much larger. His hair is very buſhy, and his horns are longer, and divided into a great number of branches †, each of which is terminated by a palm : But thoſe of the elk have the appearance of being cut off abruptly, and are furniſhed with broaches. Both have long hair under the neck, ſhort tails, and ears much longer than thoſe of the ſtag. Their

* The ſtag ſtands higher on his legs, but his body is ſmaller than that of the rain-deer; *Hiſt. de la Lapponie, par Scheffer*, *p.* 205.

† Many rain-deer have two horns, which bend backward, as thoſe of the ſtags generally do. From the middle of each a ſmall branch iſſues, which divides, like thoſe of the ſtag, into ſeveral antlers that ſtretch forward, and, by their figure and ſituation, might paſs for a third horn, though it frequently happens that the large horns puſh out ſimilar branches from their own trunks : Thus another ſmall branch advances toward the front, and then the animals ſeem to have four horns, two behind like the ſtag, and two before, which laſt is peculiar to the rain-deer. The horns of the rain-deer are alſo ſometimes diſpoſed in the following manner; two bend backward, two ſmaller ones mount upward, and two ſtill ſmaller bend forward, being all furniſhed with antlers, and having but one root. Thoſe which advance toward the front, as well as thoſe which mount upward, are, properly ſpeaking, only branches or ſhoots of the large horns which bend backward like thoſe of the ſtag. This appearance, however, is not very common; we more frequently ſee rain-deer with three horns, and the number of thoſe with four, as formerly deſcribed, is ſtill greater. All this applies only to the males; for the horns of the females are ſmaller, and have not ſo many branches; *Scheffer, p.* 306.

motion

motion confifts not of bounds or leaps, like the
ftag and roebuck: It is a kind of trot, but fo
quick and nimble, that they will pafs over nearly
the fame ground in an equal time, without
being fatigued ; for they will continue to trot in
this manner during a whole day, or even two
days *. The rain-deer keeps always on the
mountains † ; and the elk inhabits low grounds
and moift forefts. Both go in flocks like the
ftag ; and both may be tamed ; but the rain-
deer is more eafily tamed than the elk. The
latter, like the ftag, has never loft its liberty.
But the rain-deer has been rendered domeftic by
the moft ftupid of the human race. The Laplanders have no other cattle. In this frozen
climate, which receives only the moft oblique
rays of the fun, where the night and the day
conftitute two feafons, where the earth is covered
with fnow from the beginning of autumn to
the end of fpring, where the bramble, the juniper, and the mofs, conftitute the only verdure of
the fummer, man can never hope to nourifh
cattle. The horfe, the ox, the fheep, and all
our other ufeful animals, could never find fub-

* The orignal neither runs nor bounds ; but his trot equals
the courfe of the ftag. We are affured by the Savages, that
he may be trotted three days and three nights without refting ;
Voyage de la Hontan, tom. i. *p.* 85.

† Rangifer habitat in Alpibus Europæ et Afiæ, maximo
feptentrionalibus ; victitat lichene rangifero. . . . . Alces habitat in borealibus Europæ Afiaque populetis ; *Linn. Syft. Nat.*
p. 67.

fiftence

fiftence there, nor be able to refift the rigours of
the froft. It would have been neceffary to fe-
lect from the deepeft forefts thofe fpecies of animals which are leaft wild and moft profitable.
The Laplanders have actually done what we
would be obliged to do, if all our cattle were
deftroyed. To fupply their place, it would then
be neceffary to tame the ftags and roebucks of
our woods, and to render them domeftic. This
end, I am perfuaded, might be eafily accomplifhed; and we fhould foon derive as much benefit from thefe animals, as the Laplanders do
from their rain-deer. This example fhould lead
us to admire the unbounded liberality of Nature.
We ufe not one half of the treafures fhe prefents
to us; for her refources are inexhauftible. She
has given us the horfe, the ox, the fheep, and
other domeftic animals, to ferve, to nourifh, and
to clothe us ; and fhe has other fpecies ftill in
referve, which might fupply the want of the
former: Thefe we have only to fubdue, and to
render them fubfervient to our purpofes. Man
is equally ignorant of the powers of Nature, and
of his own capacity to modify and improve her
productions. Inftead of making new refearches,
he is continually abufing the little knowledge
he has acquired.

By eftimating the advantages the Laplanders
derive from the rain-deer, we fhall find that this
animal is worth two or three of our domeftic
animals. They ufe him as a horfe in drawing
fledges

fledges and carriages. He is fo nimble and expeditious, that in one day he performs with eafe
a journey of thirty leagues, and runs with equal
furenefs on the frozen fnows as upon the fineft
downs. The milk of the female affords a more
fubftantial nourifhment than that of the cow.
The flefh of this animal is exceedingly good.
His hair makes excellent furs; and his fkin is
convertible into a very ftrong and pliant leather.
Thus the rain-deer alone furnifhes every article
we derive from the horfe, the ox, and the fheep.

The manner in which the Laplanders rear
and manage the rain-deer, merits particular attention. Olaus *, Scheffer †, and Regnard ‡,
have given interefting details on this fubject, of
which the following is an abridgment. Thefe
authors tell us, that the horns of the rain-deer
are much larger, and divided into a greater number of branches, than thofe of the ftag. During
winter the food of this animal is a white mofs,
which he knows how to find under the deepeft
fnow, by digging with his horns, and turning it
afide with his feet. In fummer, he prefers the
buds and leaves of trees to herbs, which the pro-
jecting branches of his horns permit him not to
browfe with eafe. He runs on the fnow, into
which the breadth of his feet prevents him from

* Hift. de Gentibus feptent. Autore Olao Magno, p. 205.

† Hiftoire de la Lapponie, traduite du Latin de Jean Scheffer, p. 205.

‡ Oeuvres de Regnard, tom. i. p. 172.

finking.

finking. . . . . Thefe animals are extremely
gentle, and are kept in flocks, which bring great
profits to their owners. The milk, the fkin, the
finews, the bones, the hoofs, the horns, the hair,
the flefh, are all ufeful articles. The richeft
Laplanders have flocks of four or five hundred;
and the pooreft have ten or twelve. They are
led out to pafture, and, during the night, they
are fhut up in inclofures, to protect them from
the wolves. When carried to another climate,
they foon die. Steno Prince of Sweden fent
fome of them to Frederic Duke of Holftein;
and more recently, in the year 1533, Guftavus
King of Sweden tranfmitted to Pruffia ten male
and female rain-deer, which were let loofe in the
woods. They all perifhed without producing,
either in the domeftic or free ftate. ' I had a
' great defire,' fays M. Regnard, ' to carry fome
' live rain-deer to France. This experiment
' has been frequently tried in vain. Laft year,
' fome of them were brought to Dantzick,
' where, being unable to endure the heat of that
' climate, they perifhed.'

In Lapland there are both wild and domeftic
rain-deer. During the rutting feafon, the females are let loofe into the woods, where they
meet with wild males; and, as the latter are
ftronger and more hardy than the domeftic kind,
the breed from this commixture is better adapted
for drawing fledges. Thefe rain-deer are not
fo mild as the others; for they fometimes

not

not only refuse to obey their master, but turn against him, and strike him so furiously with their feet, that his only resource is to cover himself with his sledge, till the rage of the animal abates. This carriage is so light, that a Laplander can turn it with ease above himself. The bottom of it is covered with the skins of young rain-deer, the hair of which is turned backward, to make the sledge advance easily up the mountains, and prevent its recoiling. The rain-deer is yoked by means of a collar, made of a piece of skin with the hair on it, from which a trace is brought under the belly between the legs, and fixed to the fore part of the sledge. The only rein used by the Laplander is a cord tied to the root of the animal's horn, which he sometimes lays upon the one side of its back, and sometimes on the other, according as he wants it to turn to the right or the left. The rain-deer can travel, in this manner, at the rate of four or five leagues in an hour. But the quicker he goes, the motion becomes the more incommodious; and it requires much practice to be able to sit in the sledge, and to prevent it from overturning.

Externally, the rain-deer have many things in common with the stag; and the structure of their internal parts is nearly the same *. From this natural conformity, many analogous habits and similar effects result. Like the stag, the rain-deer annually casts his horns, and is loaded

* Vide Rangifer. anatom. Barth. Act. 1671. No. 135.

with

with fat. The rutting feafon of both is about
the end of September. The females of both fpecies go eight months with young, and produce
but one fawn. During the rutting feafon, the
males have an equal difagreeable odour; and
fome of the female rain-deer, as well as the
hinds, are barren *. The young rain-deer, like
the fawns of the ftag, are varioufly coloured,
being firft red mixed with yellow, and afterwards
become of a blackifh brown colour †. The
young follow their mothers two or three years;
and they acquire not their full growth till the
end of the fourth year. It is at this age alfo that
they are trained to labour. At the age of one
year, they are caftrated in order to make them
tractable. The Laplanders perform this operation with their teeth. The uncaftrated males
are fierce, and very difficult to manage; and,
therefore, are not ufed for labour. To draw
their fledges, the moft active and nimble geldings are felected, and the heavieft are employed
in carrying provifions and baggage. One unmutilated male is kept for every five or fix females. Like the ftags, they are tormented with
worms in the bad feafon. About the end of
winter, fuch vaft numbers are engendered under

---

* Out of a hundred females, not above ten are barren, and,
on account of their fterility, are called *raoner*. The flefh of
thefe is very fat and fucculent in autumn; *Scheffer, p.* 204.

† The colour of their hair is blacker than that of the ftag.
. . . . The wild rain-deer are always ftronger, larger, and
blacker than the domeftic kind; *Regnard, tom.* i. *p.* 108.

their

their skin, that it is as full of holes as a sieve. These holes made by the worms close in summer; and it is only in autumn that the raindeer are killed for their fur or their hide.

The flocks of rain-deer require much attention. They are apt to run off, and to assume their natural liberty. They must be followed, and narrowly watched, and never allowed to pasture but in open places. When the flock is numerous, the assistance of several persons is necessary to keep them together, and to pursue those which run off. In order to distinguish them, when they wander into the woods, or mingle with other flocks, they are all marked. In fine, the time of the Laplanders is totally consumed in the management of their rain-deer, which constitute their whole riches, and they know how to derive all the conveniencies, or rather the necessities, of life from these animals. They are covered from head to foot with their furs, which is impenetrable either by cold or water. This is their winter habit. In summer, they use the skins from which the hair is fallen off. They likewise spin the hair, and cover the sinews they extract from the animal's body with it. These sinews serve them for ropes and thread. They eat the flesh, and drink the milk, of which last they also make very fat cheese. The milk, when churned, instead of butter, produces a kind of suet. This singularity, as well as the great extent of the horns, and the fatness of

the animal at the commencement of the rutting
feafon, are ftrong indications of a redundance of
nourifhment.   But we have ftill farther proofs
that this redundance is exceffive, or at leaft
greater than in any other fpecies; for it is peculiar to the rain-deer alone, that the female has
horns as well as the male, and that, even when
the males are caftrated, they annually fhed and
renew their horns*.   In the ftag, the fallow-deer,
and the roebuck, who have undergone this operation, the horns remain always in the fame condition
they were at the time of caftration.   Thus, of all
other animals, the rain-deer affords the moft con-

---

* Uterque fexus cornibus eft. ———— Caftratus quotannis
cornua deponit ; *Linn. Syft. Nat. p.* 93.   It is upon the authority of Linnæus alone that I have advanced this fact, of
which I am unwilling to doubt; becaufe, being a native of
Sweden, and having travelled into Lapland, he had an opportunity of being well informed in every article regarding
the rain-deer.   I acknowledge, however, that the exception
is fingular, as; in all other animals of the deer-kind, caftration
prevents the renewal of the horns.   Befides, a pofitive teftimony may be oppofed to Linnæus. *Caftratis rangiferis Lap-
pones utuntur.   Cornua caftratorum non dicidunt, et cum hirfuta
funt, femper pilis luxuriant;* Hulden, Rangifer. Jenæ 1597.
But Hulden, perhaps, advances this fact from analogy only;
and the authority of fuch a fkilful naturalift as Linnæus
is of more weight than the teftimonies of many people who
are lefs informed.   The known fact, that the female has horns
like the male, is another exception which gives fupport to
the firft; and it is ftill farther fupported by the practice
among the Laplanders, of not cutting away the tefticles, but
only compreffing the feminal veffels with their teeth; for, in
this cafe, the action of the tefticles, which feems neceffary to
the production of horns, is not totally deftroyed, but only
weakened.

fpicuous example of redundant nutritive matter; and this effect is perhaps lefs owing to the nature of the animal than to the quality of his food *; for the fubftance of the *lichen*, or raindeer liverwort, which is its only nourifhment, efpecially during the winter, is fimilar to that of the mufhroom, very nourifhing, and contains a greater number of organic particles than the leaves or buds of trees†. This is the reafon why the rain-deer has larger horns and a greater quantity of fat than the ftag, and why the females and geldings are not deprived of horns: It is alfo the reafon why the horns of the rain-deer are more diverfified in fize, figure, and number of branches, than any other of the deer kind. Thofe males who have never been hunted or reftrained, and who feed plentifully, and at their eafe, upon this fubftantial nourifhment, have prodigious horns, which extend backward as far as their crupper, and forward beyond the muzzle. The horns of the caftrated males, though fmaller, often exceed thofe of the ftag; and thofe of the females are ftill fmaller. Thus the

---

* See article *Stag*, vol. iv.

† It is remarkable that, though the rain-deer eats nothing during winter, but great quantities of this mofs, he always fattens better, his fkin is cleaner, and his hair finer than when he feeds upon the beft herbage, at which time he makes a hideous appearance. Their being unable to endure heat is the reafon why they are better and fatter in autumn and winter, than in fummer, when they have nothing but finews, fkin, and bone; *Scheffer, Hift. de la Lapponie, p.* 206.

horns of the rain-deer are not only fubject to variation from age, like others of the deer-kind, but from fex and caftration. Thefe differences are fo great, in the horns of different individuals, that it is not furprifing to fee the defcriptions given of them by authors fo exceedingly different.

Another fingularity, which is common to the rain-deer and the elk, muft not be omitted. When thefe animals run, though not at full fpeed, their hoofs*, at each movement, make a crackling noife as if all their limbs were difjointed. The wolves, advertifed by this noife, or by the odour of the animal, throw themfelves in his way, and, if numerous, they feize and kill him; for a rain-deer defends himfelf againft the attacks of a fingle wolf. For this purpofe he employs not his horns, which are more hurtful than ufeful to him, but his fore-feet, which are very ftrong. With thefe he ftrikes the wolf

---

* Rangiferum culex pipiens, œftrus tarandi, tabanus tarandi ad Alpes cogunt, crepitantibus ungulis; *Linn. Syft. Nat. p.* 93.——The feet of the rain-deer are fhorter and much broader than thofe of the ftag, and refemble the feet of the buffalo. The hoofs are cloven and almoft round, like thofe of the ox. Whether he runs or goes flowly, the joints of his limbs make a great noife, like flints falling on each other, or like the breaking of nuts. This noife is heard as far as the animal can been feen; *Scheffer, p.* 202.——Fragor ac ftrepitus pedum ungularumque tantus eft in celeri progreffu, ac fi filices vel nuces collidantur; qualem ftrepitum articulorum etiam in alce obfervavi. ——It is remarkable in the rain-deer, that all his bones, and particularly thofe of his feet, make a crackling noife, which is fo loud as to be heard as far as the animal can be feen; *Regnard, tom.* i. *p.* 108.

fo

so violently as to stun him, or make him fly off; and afterwards runs with a rapidity that prevents all further attacks. The *rosomack or glutton*, though not so numerous, is a more dangerous enemy. This animal is still more voracious, but not so nimble as the wolf. He pursues not the rain-deer, but lies in wait for it concealed in a tree. As soon as the rain-deer comes within his reach, he darts down upon it, fixes upon its back with his claws; and, tearing its head or neck with his teeth, he never quits his station till he has cut the animal's throat. He employs the same artifices, and carries on the same war against the elk, which is still stronger than the rain-deer *. This *rosomack* or *glutton* of the North is the same animal with the *carca-*

* There is another animal, of a grayish brown colour, and about the size of a dog, which carries on a bloody war against the rain-deer. This animal, which the Swedes call *jaert*, and the Latins *gulo*, conceals itself in the highest trees, in order to surprise its prey. When he discovers a rain-deer, whether wild or domestic, passing under the tree where he is watching, he darts down upon its back, and, fixing his claws in the neck and tail, he tears and stretches with such violence as to break the animal's back, then sinks his muzzle into its body, and drinks its blood. The skin of the jaert is very fine and beautiful, and has even been compared to that of the sable; *Oeuvres de Regnard, tom. i. p. 154.*———The caribou runs upon the snow almost as nimbly as upon the ground; because the broadness of its feet prevents it from sinking. The caribou, like the orignal, travels through the forests in winter, and is attacked in the same manner by the carcajou; *Hist. de l'Acad. des Sciences, année 1713, p. 14. Note,* The carcajou is the same animal with the *jaert* or *glutton.*

jou or *quincajou* of North America. His combats with the orignal of Canada are famous; and, as formerly remarked, the orignal of Canada is the fame with the elk of Europe. It is remarkable, that this animal, which is not larger than a badger, fhould kill the elk, which exceeds the fize of a horfe, and is fo ftrong as to flay a wolf with a fingle ftroke of his foot *. But the fact is attefted by fuch a number of authorities as render it altogether unqueftionable †.

The

---

* Lupi et ungulis et cornibus vel interimuntur vel effugantur ab alce; tanta enim vis eft in ictu ungulæ, ut illico tractum lupum interimat aut fodiat, quod fæpius in canibus robuftiffimis venatores experiuntur; *Olai Magni Hift. de Gent. Septent.* *p.* 135.

† Quiefcentes humi et erecti ftantes onagri maximi a minima quandoque muftela guttur infiliente mordentur, ut fanguine decurrente illico deficiant morituri. Adeo infatiabilis eft hæc beftiola in cruore fugendo, ut vix fimilem fuæ quantitatis habeat in omnibus creaturis; *Olai Magni Hift. de Gent. Sept.* *p.* 134. *Note,* 1. That Olaus, by the word *onager,* often means the *elk;* 2. That, with much impropriety, he compares the glutton to a fmall weafel; for this animal is larger than a badger.——The quincajou climbs trees, and, concealing himfelf among the branches, waits the approach of the orignal. When any of thefe animals come under the tree, the quincajou darts down upon its back, fixes his claws in its throat and rump, and then tears the creature's neck, a little below the ears, till it falls down; *Defcript. de l'Amerique Septentrionale, par Denys, p.* 329.——The carcajou attacks and kills the orignal and caribou. In winter, the orignal frequents thofe diftricts where the *anagyris fætida,* or ftinking bean-trefoil, abounds; becaufe he feeds upon it; and, when the ground is covered with five or fix feet of fnow, he makes roads through thefe diftricts, which he never abandons, unlefs when purfued by the hunters. The carcajou, obferving the

route

'The elk and the rain-deer are both ruminating animals, as appears from their manner of feeding, and the structure of their intestines * ; yet Tornæus Scheffer †, Regnard ‡, Hulden §, and several other authors, have maintained that the rain-deer does not ruminate. Ray ‖, with much propriety, considers this opinion as incredible; and, in fact, the rain-deer ** chews the cud as well as all other animals which have many stomachs. The duration of life, in the domestic rain-deer, exceeds not fifteen or sixteen

route of the orignal, climbs a tree near a place where it must pass, darts upon it, and cuts its throat in a moment. In vain the orignal lies down on the ground, or rubs himself against the trees; for nothing can make the carcajou quit his hold. The hunters have found pieces of his skin, as large as a man's hand, sticking on the tree against which the orignal had dashed him; *Hist. de l'Acad. des Sciences, année* 1707, *p.* 13.

* The elk, in its internal parts, and particularly in its bowels, and four stomachs, has a considerable resemblance to the ox; *Mem. pour servir à l'Histoire des Animaux, part.* i. *p.* 184.

† It is remarkable, that, though the rain-deer is cloven-footed, he does not ruminate; *Scheffer, p.* 200.

‡ Regnard makes the same observation, tom. i. p. 109.

§ Sunt bisulci et cornigeri, attamen non ruminant Rangiferi; *Hulden, Rangiferi, &c.*

‖ Profecto (inquit Peyerus) mirum videtur animal illud tam insigniter cornutum, ac præterea bisculum, cervisque specie simillimum, ruminatione destitui, ut dignum censeam argumentum altiore indagine curioforum, quibus Renones fors subministrat aut principum favor. *Hactenus Peyerus; mihi certe non mirum tantum videtur, sed plane incredibile; Raii Synops. Quad. p.* 89.

** Rangifer ruminat æque ac aliæ species sui generis; *Linn. Faun. Suecica, p.* 14.

years.

years *. But it is probable, that, in a wild ſtate, he lives much longer; for, as he is four years in acquiring his full growth, he ought, when in his natural ſtate, to live twenty-eight or thirty years. The Laplanders employ different me-thods of hunting the wild rain-deer, corſeſpond-ing to the difference of ſeaſons. In the rutting time, they uſe domeſtic females to attract wild males †. They ſhoot theſe animals with muſ-kets or with bows, and they let fly their arrows with ſuch violence, that, notwithſtanding the great thickneſs and ſtrength of their ſkin, one is generally fatal.

We have collected the facts relating to the hiſtory of the rain-deer with the more care and

* Ætas ad tredecim vel ultra quindecim annos non excedit in domeſticis; *Huldeu*. Ætas ſexdecim annorum; *Linn. Syſt. Nat.* p. 67.———Thoſe rain-deer which eſcape all misfortunes and diſeaſes, ſeldom live above thirteen years; *Scheffer, p.* 209.

† The Laplanders hunt the rain-deer with nets, halberds, arrows, and muſkets. The hunting ſeaſons are autumn and ſpring. In autumn, when the rain-deer are in ſeaſon, the Laplanders go to thoſe places of the foreſts which they know the wild males frequent, and there tie domeſtic females to the trees. The female attracts the male, and, when he is at the point of covering her, the hunter ſhoots him with a bullet or an arrow.———In ſpring, when the ſnow begins to melt, and theſe animals are embarraſſed by ſinking in it, the Laplander, ſhod with his rackets, purſues and overtakes them.———At other times, they are chaſed into ſnares by dogs. In fine, a kind of nets are employed, which are compoſed of ſtakes wat-tled together in the form of two hedges, with an alley be-tween them of perhaps two leagues in length. When the rain-deer are puſhed into this alley, they run forward, and fall into a large ditch made with that view at the end of it; *Scheffer,* p. 209.

circum-

circumfpection, becaufe it was not poffible for us to procure the live animal. Having expreffed my regret on this fubject to fome of my friends, Mr. Collinfon, member of the Royal Society of London, a man as refpectable for his virtues as for his literary merit, was fo obliging as to fend me a drawing of the fkeleton of a rain-deer; and I received from Canada a fœtus of a caribou. By means of thefe two, and of feveral horns which were tranfmitted to us from different places, we have been enabled to mark the general refemblances and principal differences between the rain-deer and the ftag.

With regard to the elk, I faw one alive about fifteen years ago. But, as it continued only a few days in Paris, I had not fufficient time to have the drawing completed; and, therefore, I was obliged to content myfelf with examining the defcription formerly given of this animal by the gentlemen of the Academy, and to be fatisfied that it was exact, and perfectly conformable to nature.

' The elk,' fays the digefter of the Memoirs of the Academy *, ' is remarkable for the length ' of its hair, the largenefs of its ears, the fmall- ' nefs of its tail, and the form of its eye, the ' largeft angle of which is much fplit, as well ' as the mouth, which is much larger than that ' of the ox, the ftag, or other cloven-footed

* Mem. pour fervir à l'Hiftoire des Animaux, part. i. p. 178.

animals.

' animals. . . . The elk which we diffected
' was nearly of the fize of a ftag. The length
' of the body was five feet and a half from
' the end of the muzzle to the origin of the
' tail, which was only two inches long. Be-
' ing a female, it had no horns; and its neck
' was only nine inches in length, and as much
' in breadth. The ears were nine inches long
' by four broad. . . . The colour of the hair
' was not much different from that of the afs,
' the gray colour of which fometimes approaches
' to that of the camel. . . In other refpects,
' this hair differed greatly from that of the afs,
' which is fhorter, and from that of the camel,
' which is much finer. The length of the hair
' was three inches, and equalled in thickneſs
' the coarfeft hair of a horfe. This thickneſs
' diminifhed gradually toward the extremity,
' which was very fharp : It diminifhed like-
' wife toward the root, but fuddenly became
' like the handle of a lancet. This handle was
' of a different colour from the reft of the hair,
' being white and diaphanous, like the briftles
' of a hog. . . The hair was as long as that
' of a bear, but ftraighter, thicker, fmoother,
' and all of the fame kind. The upper lip was
' large and detached from the gums, but by no
' means fo large as Solinus defcribed it, nor as
' Pliny has reprefented the animal he calls
' *machlis.* Thefe authors tell us, that this crea-
' ture is obliged to go backward when he paf-
' tures, to prevent his lip from being entangled

4

' between

' between his teeth. We remarked, in the dif-
' section, that Nature had provided against this
' inconveniency by the largeness and strength
' of the muscles destined to raise the upper lip.
' We likewise found the articulations of the legs
' closely embraced by ligaments, the hardness
' and thickness of which might give rise to the
' opinion, that the *aloe*, after lying down, was
' unable to raise himself. . . . . . His feet were
' similar to those of the stag; only they were
' larger, and had no other peculiarity. . . . . . .
' We remarked, that the large angle of the eye
' was much more slit below than in the stag,
' the fallow-deer, and the roebuck: It is sin-
' gular, that this slit was not in the direction
' of the opening of the eye, but made an angle
' with the line which goes from the one corner
' of the eye to the other; the inferior lachrymal
' gland was an inch and a half long, by seven
' lines broad. . . . . In the brain we found
' a part whose magnitude seemed to point out
' some relation to the sense of smelling, which,
' according to Pausanias, is more exquisite in the
' elk than in any other animal; for the olfac-
' tory nerves, commonly called the *mammillary*
' *processes*, were incomparably larger than in
' any other animal we ever dissected, being
' more than four lines in diameter. . . . . With
' regard to the lump of flesh which some au-
' thors have placed on his back, and others un-
' der his chin, if they have not been deceived
' or '

' or too credulous, it muſt be peculiar to the elks
' they mention.' We can add our teſtimony to
that of the gentlemen of the Academy; for, in
the female elk we had alive, there was no bunch
either under the chin, or on the neck. Linnæus, however, as he lives in the country inhabited by elks, and ought to have a more complete knowlege of them than we can pretend to,
mentions this bunch on the neck, and even
makes it an eſſential character of the elk: *Alces,
cervus cornibus acaulibus palmatis, caruncula gutturali; Linn. Syſt. Nat. p. 92.* There is no
other method of reconciling the aſſertion of Linnæus with our negative evidence, but by ſup-
poſing this bunch, *guttural caruncle,* to be peculiar to the male, which wc have never ſeen.
But, though this were the caſe, Linnæus ought
not to have made it an eſſential character of the
ſpecies, ſince it exiſts not in the female. This
bunch may likewiſe be a diſeaſe, a kind of wen,
common among the elks; for, in Gefner's *
two figures of this animal, the firſt, which wants
horns, has a large fleſhy bunch on the throat;
and, in the ſecond, which repreſents a male with
his horns, there is no bunch.

In general, the elk is much larger and ſtronger
than the ſtag or rain-deer †. His hair is ſo
rough;

---

* Gefner, Hiſt. Quad. p. 1. & 3.

† The elk exceeds the rain-deer in magnitude, being equal
to the largeſt horſe. Beſides, the horns of the elk are much
ſhorter, about two palms broad, and have very few branches.
His

rough, and his fkin fo hard, that it is hardly penetrable by a mufket ball *. His limbs are extremely firm, and poffefs fuch agility and ftrength, that, with a fingle blow of his fore-feet, he can flay a man, or a wolf, and even break a tree. He is hunted, however, by men and dogs, in the fame manner as the ftag. We are affured, that, when purfued, he often falls down fuddenly †, without being either fhot or wounded.

His feet, efpecially thofe before, are not round, but long, and he ftrikes with them fo furioufly as to kill both men and dogs. Neither does he more refemble the rain-deer in the form of his head, which is longer, and his lips are larger and pendulous. His colour is not fo white as that of the rain-deer, but, over the whole body, it is an obfcure yellow, mixed with a cinereous gray. When he moves, he makes no noife with his joints, which is common to all rain-deer. In fine, whoever examines both animals, as I have often done, will remark fo many differences, that he will have reafon to be furprifed how any man fhould regard them as the fame fpecies; *Scheffer*, *p.* 310.

* Alces ungula ferit, quinquaginta milliaria de die percurrit, corium globum plumbeum fere cludit; *Linn. Syft. Nat.* *p. 93.*

† We had not advanced a piftol fhot into the wood, when we defcried an elk, which, when running before us, fuddenly dropped down, without being fo much as fired at. We afked our guide and interpreter how the animal came to fall in this manner. He replied, that it was the falling ficknefs, to which thefe animals are fubject, and affigned that as the reafon of their being called *ellends*, which fignifies *miferable*. . . . If this difeafe did not often bring them down, it would be difficult to feize them. The Norwegian gentleman killed this elk while it was under the influence of its difeafe. We purfued another two hours, and would never have taken him, if he had not, like the firft, fallen down, after having killed three ftrong dogs with his fore-feet. . . . This gentleman prefented

wounded. From this circumftance it has been prefumed that the animal is fubject to the epilepfy; and from this prefumption (which is not well founded, fince fear might produce the fame effect) the abfurd conclufion has been drawn, that his hoofs have the power of curing, and even preventing, the falling ficknefs. This grofs prejudice has been fo generally diffufed, that many people ftill carry pieces of the elk's hoof in the collets of their rings.

As the northern parts of America are very thinly inhabited, all the animals, and particularly the elks, are more numerous there than in the North of Europe. The favages are not ignorant of the art of hunting and feizing the elks *. They fometimes follow the tract of thefe animals for feveral days, and, by mere perfeverance and addrefs, accomplifh their purpofe. Their mode of hunting in winter is particularly fingular. ' They ufe,' fays Denys, ' rackets, by means of which they ' walk on the fnow without finking. . . The ' orignal does not make much way, becaufe he ' finks in the fnow, which fatigues him. He

---

ed me with the left hind feet of the elks he had killed, and told me they were a fovereign remedy againft the falling ficknefs. To which I anfwered, fmiling, that, fince this foot had fo much virtue, I was furprifed that the animal to which it belonged fhould ever be afflicted with the difeafe. The gentleman likewife laughed, and faid that I was right; that he had feen it adminiftered without effect to many people who were troubled with the epilepfy; and that he knew, as well as I did, that it was a vulgar error; *Voyage de la Martiniere, p.* 10.

* Defcript. de l'Amerique, par Denys, tom. ii. p. 425.

' eats

'eats only the annual fhoots of trees. Where
'the Savages find the wood eaten in this man-
'ner, they foon meet with the animals, which
'are never very diftant, and are eafily taken,
'becaufe they cannot run expeditioufly. They
'throw darts at them, which confift of large
'ftaves, pointed with a bone, which pierces like
'a fword. When there are many orignals in a
'flock, the Savages put them to flight. The
'orignals, in this cafe, march at one another's
'tails, and make a circle fometimes of more
'than two leagues, and, by their frequent turn-
'ing round, tread the fnow fo hard, that they
'no longer fink in it. The Savages lie in am-
'bufcade, and kill the animals with darts as they
'pafs.' From comparing this relation with thofe
already quoted, it is apparent, that the American
Savage and the orignal are exact copies of the
European Laplander and the elk.

SUPPLEMENT.

Addition to the article Elk and Rain-deer, by Profeffor Allamand.

M. De Buffon is of opinion, that the European
elk is likewife found in North America under
the appellation of *orignal.* If any difference
exifts, it confifts in magnitude only, which varies

ries in proportion to climate and food. It is not even afcertained which of them are largeft. M. de Buffon thinks that thofe of Europe are larger than thofe of America, becaufe all the animals of the New Continent are fmaller than thofe of the Old. Moft voyagers, however, reprefent the orignal as exceeding the elk in magnitude. Mr. Dudley, who fent an accurate defcription of an orignal to the Royal Society, fays, that the hunters killed one which was more than ten feet high[*]. This ftature would be neceffary to enable the animal to carry its enormous horns, which weigh one hundred and fifty, and, if we believe La Hontan, three or four hundred pounds.

The Duke of Richmond, who delights in collecting, for public utility, every thing that can contribute to improve the arts, or augment our knowledge of Nature, has a female orignal in one of his parks, which was conveyed to him by General Carlton, governour of Canada, in the year 1766. It was then only one year old, and it lived nine or ten months. Some time before it died, he caufed an exact drawing of it to be made, which he obligingly fent to me, and of which I have given an engraving as a fupplement to M. de Buffon's work. As this female was very young, it exceeded not five feet in height. The colour of the upper part of the body was a deep brown, and that of the under part was brighter.

* Phil. Tranf. ann. 1721. No. 368. p. 165.

I re-

I received from Canada the head of a female orignal which was more advanced in years. Its length, from the end of the muzzle to the ears, is two feet three inches. Its circumference at the ears is two feet eight inches, and, near the mouth, one foot ten inches. The ears are nine inches long. But, as this head is dried, these dimensions must be smaller than when the animal was alive.

M. de Buffon is likewise of opinion, that the caribou of America is the rain-deer of Lapland; and the reasons with which he supports this idea have much weight. I have given a figure of the rain-deer, which is wanting in the Paris edition. It is a copy of that which was published by Ridinger, a famous painter and engraver, who drew it from the life. I have likewise been obliged to the Duke of Richmond for a drawing of the American caribou. This animal was sent to him from Canada, and it lived a long time in his park. His horns were only beginning to shoot when the figure was drawn; and it is the only true representation we have of the animal. By comparing it with the rain-deer, there appears, at first sight, to be a very considerable difference between the two figures; but the want of horns in the caribou greatly changes its aspect.

Addition

Addition by the Count de Buffon.

I Here give an engraving of a rain-deer, drawn from a living female in the poffeffion of the Prince of Condé. It was fent to him by the King of Sweden, along with two males, one of which died on the road, and the other lived only a fhort time after its arrival in France. The female refifted the effects of the climate for a confiderable time. She was of the fize of a hind; but her legs were fhorter, and her body thicker. Her horns, like thofe of the male, were divided into antlers, fome of which pointed forward, and others backward. But they were fhorter than thofe of the males. The following defcription of this animal was communicated to me by M. de Sève:

' The length of the whole body, from the
' muzzle to the anus, in a fuperficial line, is five
' feet one inch. The height of the withers is
' two feet eleven inches, and that of the crup-
' per two feet eleven inches nine lines. The
' hair is thick and clofe, like that of the ftag,
' the fhorteft on the body being an inch and
' three lines in length. It is longer on the belly,
' very fhort on the limbs, and very long about
' the fetlock. The colour of the hair which
' covers the body is a reddifh brown, more or

' lefs deep in different parts, and fprinkled with
' a kind of yellowifh white. Upon part of the
' back, the thighs, the top of the head, and
' chanfrin, the hair is deeper coloured, efpeci-
' ally above the eye-pits, which the rain-deer
' has as well as the ftag. The circumference
' of the eye is black. The muzzle is a deep
' brown, and the circumference of the noftrils
' is black. The point of the muzzle, as far as
' the noftrils, as well as the end of the under
' jaw, are of a bright white colour. The ear is
' covered above with thick white hair, approach-
' ing to yellow, and mixed with brown. The
' infide of the ear is adorned with large white
' hairs. The neck and upper part of the body,
' as well as the large hairs which hang on the
' breaft below the neck, are of a yellowifh
' white colour. Upon the fides, above the
' belly, there is a large band, as in the gazelle.
' The limbs are flender in proportion to the
' body ; and they, as well as the thighs, are of
' a deep brown, and of a dirty white colour on
' the infide. The ends of the hairs which cover
' the hoofs are likewife of a dirty white.
' The feet are cloven, like thofe of the ftag.
' The two fore-toes are broad and thin : The
' fmall ones behind are long, pretty thin, and
' flat on the infide. They are all extremely
' black.'

By the figure I have given, no judgment muft
be formed of the length and thicknefs of the

rain-deer's horns, some of which extend backward from the head as far as the crupper, and project forward in antlers of more than a foot long. The large fossil horns found in different places, and particularly in Ireland, appear to have belonged to the rain-deer species. Mr. Colinson informed me that he had seen some of these fossil horns with an interval of ten feet between their extremities, and with brown antlers, like those of the rain-deer.

It is to this species, therefore, and not to that of the elk, that the fossil bones of the animal called *mouse-deer* by the British are to be referred. We must acknowledge, however, that no rain-deer now exist of such magnitude and strength as to carry horns so long and massy as those found in a fossil state in Ireland, as well as in several other parts of Europe, and even in North America *.

Besides, I knew only one species of rain-deer, to which I referred the caribou of America, and the Greenland fallow-deer, described and engraven by Mr. Edwards: And it is not long since I was informed, that there were two species, or rather two varieties, the one much larger than the other. The rain- deer of which I have given a figure, is the small kind, and probably the

* In North America, we find horns which must have belonged to an animal of a prodigious magnitude. Similar horns are found in Ireland. They are branched, &c.; *Voyage de P. Kalm,* tom. ii. *p.* 435.

fame.

fame with the Greenland fallow-deer of Mr.
Edwards.

Some travellers tell us, that the rain-deer is
the fallow-deer of the North ; that, in Greenland, it is wild ; and that the largeft of them exceed not the fize of a two year old heifer *.

Pontoppidan affures us, that the rain-deer perifh in every part of the world, except the northern regions, where they are even obliged to
inhabit the mountains. He is lefs to be credited
when he tells us, that their horns are moveable ; that the animal can turn them either forward or backward ; and that, above the eye-lids,
there is a fmall aperture in the fkin, through
which he fees, when the fnow prevents him
from opening his eyes. This laft fact appears
to be imaginary, and borrowed from a practice of the Laplanders, who cover their eyes
with a piece of fplit wood, to avoid the great
fplendour of the fnow, which renders them blind
in a few years, if this precaution is neglected †.

It is remarkable, that thefe animals, in all their
movements, make a crackling noife : Independent of running, even when furprifed or touched, this noife is heard. I have been affured that
the fame thing happens to the elk ; but I cannot afcertain the truth of this affertion.

* Hift. Gen. des Voyages, tom. xix. p. 37.
† Pontoppidan's Nat. Hift. of Norway.

Obfervations

Observations on the Rain-deer, by Professor Camper of Groningen.

THE rain-deer sent to me from Lapland by the way of Drontheim and Amsterdam, arrived at Groningen the 21st day of June 1771. It was very feeble, not only on account of the heat of the climate and the fatigue of the voyage, but chiefly from an ulcer between the second stomach and the diaphragm, of which it died the next day. While it lived, it eat, with appetite, grafs, bread, and other things presented to it, and likewise drank very copiously. It did not die for want of nourishment; for, upon diffection, I found all its stomachs full. Its death was slow, and accompanied with convulsions.

It was a male of four years old. In all the bones of the skeleton, there were epiphyses, which proves that it had not yet acquired its full growth, which happens not till five years of age. Hence this animal may live at least twenty years.

The colour of the body was brown, mixed with black, yellow, and white. The hairs on the belly, and particularly on the flanks, were white, and brown at the points, as in other deer. The hair on the limbs was a deep yellow; and that on the head inclined to black. The hair on the flanks, as well as on the neck and breast, was long and bushy.

z 3

The

The hair which covered the body was fo brittle, that, when flightly pulled, it broke tranf-verfely. It lay in an undulated form, and its subftance refembled the pith of rufhes. The brittle part of it was white. The hair on the head and the under part of the legs, as far as the hoofs, had not this fragility, but, on the contrary, was as ftrong as that of a cow.

The coronet of the hoofs was covered on all fides with very long hair. Between the toes of the hind-feet there was a broad pellicle, com-pofed of the fkin which covers the body, but interfperfed with fmall glands.

In the hind-feet, at the height of the coronets, a kind of canal, fufficient to admit a goofe quill, and filled with very long hairs, penetrated as far as the articulation of the canon with the fmall bones of the toes. I difcovered no fuch canal in the fore-feet; neither do I know the ufe of it.

The figure of this animal differed much from that defcribed by other authors, becaufe it was extremely emaciated. The length of the body, from the muzzle to the anus, was five feet, and its height before three feet.

The eyes differ not from thofe of the fallow-deer or ftag. The pupil is tranfverfe; and the iris is brown, inclining to black. The eye-pits refemble thofe of the ftag, and are filled with a whitifh, refinous, and fomewhat tranfparent matter. As in the fallow-deer, there are two lachrymal ducts and canals. The upper eye-

lid

lid has very long black *cilia*. It is not perforated, as fome authors have fancied, but entire.
The Bifhop of Pontoppidan, and, upon his authority, Mr. Haller, have attempted to account
for this fuppofed perforation : They thought it
neceffary, in a country perpetually covered with
fnow, to defend the animal's eyes againft the
exceffive glare of reflected light. Man, who is
deftined to live in all climates, prevents blind-
nefs as much as poffible by veils or fmall perforated machines, which weaken the fplendour
of the light. The rain-deer, who is made for
this climate alone, has no occafion for fuch me-
chanifm. But he is furnifhed with a nictitating
membrane, or an internal eye-lid, like the birds,
and fome other quadrupeds. Neither is this
membrane perforated: It is capable of covering the whole cornea.

The nofe of the rain-deer is very large, like
that of the cow; and the muzzle is more or lefs
flat, and covered with long grayifh hair, which
extends to the internal part of the noftril. The
lips are likewife covered with hair, except a
fmall border, which is blackifh, hard, and very
porous. The noftrils are very diftant from each
other. The under lip is narrow, and the mouth
deep cut, as in the fheep.

He has eight cutting teeth in the under jaw;
but they are very fmall, and loofely fixed. Like
the other ruminating animals, he has no cutting
teeth in the upper jaw. But I thought I per-

ceived

ceived tufks, though they had not yet pierced
the gums; and I obferved no fuch appearance
in the under jaw.   Horfes have tufks in both
jaws; but mares feldom have any. The fallow-
deer, both males and females, feldom or never
have tufks.   But I lately procured the head of
a hind recently brought forth, which had a large
tufk in the left fide of the upper jaw: Nature
is fo various in this article, that no conftant rule
can be eftablifhed.   There are fix grinders in
each fide of both jaws, or twenty-four in all.

I have nothing to remark concerning the
horns; for they were only beginning to fhoot:
One of them was an inch, and the other an
inch and a half high.   Their bafe was fituated
nearer the occiput than the orbit of the eye.
The hair which covered them was beautifully
turned, and of a gray colour, inclining to black.
In viewing the two fhoots at a diftance, they
had the appearance of two large mice fitting on
the animal's head.

The neck is fhort, and more arched than that
of the fheep, but lefs than that of the camel.
The body feemed to be naturally robuft.   The
back is a little elevated toward the fhoulders, and
pretty ftraight every where elfe, though the vertebræ are fomewhat arched.

The tail is very fmall, bent downward, and
garnifhed with long bufhy hair.

The tefticles are very fmall, and appear not
without the body. The penis is not large

.The

The prepuce is naked, like a navel, full of wrinkles in the inside, and covered with a calcareous cruft.

The hoofs are large, long, and convex on the outside. The fpurs are alfo very long, and fome of them touch the ground when the animal ftands. They were hollow, probably becaufe he makes no ufe of them.

The inteftines were exactly fimilar to thofe of the fallow-deer. There was no gall-bladder. The kidneys were fmooth, and undivided. The lungs and wind-pipe were very large.

The heart was of a middle fize, and, like that of the fallow-deer, contained one fmall bone only. This bone fupported the bafe of the femilunar valve of the aorta, which is oppofed to two others, from which the coronary arteries of the heart derive their origin. It likewife gives firmnefs to the membranous partition between the two cavities of the heart, and to the triglochine valve of the right ventricle.

In this animal there is a fingular pouch, very large, membranous, and fituated under the fkin of the neck. It begins by a conical canal between the os hyoides and the thyroide cartilage. This canal gradually enlarges, and is changed into a kind of membranous fac, fupported by two oblong mufcles, which derive their origin from the inferior part of the os hyoides, precifely where the bafe, the pifiform bone, and the cornua unite.

This

This pouch opens into the larynx, under the root of the epiglottis, by a large orifice, which eafily admitted my finger.

When the animal pufhed the air forcibly out of the lungs, as in lowing, the air paffed into this pouch, fwelled it, and neceffarily produced a confiderable tumour, which greatly changed the found. The two mufcles drive the air out of the pouch, when the animal ceafes its lowing.

About twenty years ago, I fhowed a fimilar pouch in feveral baboons and monkeys; and, the year following, I demonftrated to my pupils, that there was a double pouch in the Ourang-outang.

Plate CLXXXVIII.

A.Bell Sculp!

ELK.

Plate CLXXXIX.

FEMALE RAIN-DEER.

The WILD GOAT*, the CHAMOIS GOAT †, and other GOATS.

THE Greeks, it is probable, were acquainted with the wild and chamois goats. But they have neither pointed out these animals by particular denominations, nor by characters so precise,

---

* The wild goat has large knotted horns, reclining backward, and a very small head. On the chin of the male there is a dusky beard: the rest of the hair is tawny, mixed with ash colour. The females are less, and have smaller horns, more like those of the common she-goat, and have few knobs on the upper surface. They bring one young, seldom two, at a time; *Pennant's Synopſ. of Quad. p.* 13.

In French, *Bouquetin, Bouc eſtain, Boucſtein*; that is, *rock-goat. Stein* denoting *rock* in the Teutonic language; in Latin, *Ibex*; in German and Swiſs, *Steinbock.*

Ibex, *Pliny, lib.* viii. *cap.* 53. *Geſner. Quad. p.* 303. *Raii Synopſ. Quad. p.* 77. *Briſon, Quad. p.* 39.

Bouc eſtain; *Belon, Obſ. p.* 14.

Bouc Savage; *Gaſton de Foix, p.* 99.

Capricorne; *Munſter, Coſmog. p.* 381.

Steinbock; *Kram. Auſt. p.* 321.

Capra Ibex, cornibus ſupra nodoſis, in dorſum reclinatis, gula barbata; *Linn. Syſt. Nat. p.* 95. *Klein. Quad. p.* 16.

† The chamois goat has slender, black, upright horns, hooked at the end. Behind each ear there is a large orifice in the skin. The forehead is white, and along the cheeks there is a dusky bar. The rest of the body is of a deep brown colour. The tail is short; the hoofs are long and much divided; *Pennant's Synopſ. of Quad. p.* 17.

In Latin, *Rupicapra*; in Italian, *Camuza*; in German, *Gemſſ*; in old French, *Yſard, Yſarius, Sarris.*

Chamois,

precise, as to enable us to distinguish them. They have denominated them in general, *wild goats* *. They perhaps regarded these animals as of the same species with the domestic kind †, having never bestowed on them proper names, as they have done to every other species of quadruped. Our modern naturalists, on the contrary, have considered the wild and the chamois goats as two distinct species, and both different from the common goat. There are facts and arguments in favour of both opinions, of which we shall only give a detail, till we learn from experience whether these animals can intermix together, and produce fertile individuals; as this circumstance alone can determine the question.

Chamois, *Cemas, Tsard*; Obs. de Belon. p. 54. Belon pretends that the French name *Chamois* comes from the Greek *Cemas* of Ælian; but he is not certain that *Cemas*, or rather *Kemas*, denoted the Chamois; see *Mem. pour servir à l'Hist. des Animaux, part.* i. *p.* 205.

Rupicapra; *Plinii, lib.* viii. *c.* 15. Gesner, *Quad. p.* 290. *Raii Synopf. Quad. p.* 78. *Scheut. It. Alp. tom.* i. *p.* 155.

Ysarus on Sarris; *Gaston de Foix, p.* 99. *Brisson. Quad. p.* 41. Gemse; *Klein, Quad. p.* 18.

Antilope rupicapra; *Pallas Miscel. p.* 4.

Capra rupicapra, cornibus erectis uncinatis; *Linn. Syst. Nat. p.* 95.

* Rupicapras inter capras sylvestres adnumerare libet, quoniam hoc nomen apud solum Plinium legimus, et apud Græcos simpliciter *feræ capræ* dicuntur, ut conjicio: Nam et magnitudine et figura tum cornuum tum figura corporis ad villaticas proxime accedunt; *Gesner. Hist Quad. p.* 292.

† Capræ quas alimus a capris feris sunt ortæ a queis propter Italiam, Capraria insula est nominata. *Varro.*

The

6

The male wild goat differs from the chamois
in the length, thickness, and figure of his horns.
His body is also larger, and he is more vigorous
and strong. The horns of the female wild goat
are smaller than those of the male, and have a
great resemblance to those of the chamois *.
Besides, the manners and dispositions of these
two animals are the same, and they inhabit the
same climate; only the wild goat, being stronger and more agile, goes to the summits of the
highest mountains, while the chamois never rises
higher than the second stage †. But neither of
them are found in the plains. Both of them
clear roads in the snow, and leap from one precipice to another. Both are covered with a
firm solid skin, and clothed, in winter, with a
double fur, the external hair being coarse, and the
internal finer and more bushy ‡. Both of them
have a black band on the back, and tails of nearly

* Fœmina in hoc genere mare suo minor est, minusque
fusca, major Capra villatica, Rupicapræ non adeo dissimilis:
Cornua ei parva, et ea quoque Rupicapræ aut vulgaris capræ cornibus fere similia; Stumpfius, apud Gesner, p. 305.

† Rupes montium colunt Rupicapræ, non summas tamen ut
Ibex, neque tam alte et longe saliunt; descendunt alquando ad in-
feriora Alpium juga; Gesner, Hist. p. 292.

‡ The chamois goat has longer legs than the domestic
kind; but his hair is shorter. That which covers the belly and
thighs is the longest, and exceeds not four inches and a half.
On the back and flanks the hair is of two kinds; for, as in the
beaver, beside the long external hair, there is a very short fine
hair, concealed round the roots of the longer kind. The
head, the belly, and the legs, were covered with coarse hair
only; Mem. pour servir a l'Hist. des Animaux, part. i. p. 203.

an

an equal fize. The number of external refemblances is fo great, and the conformity of the internal parts is fo complete, that we fhould be induced to conclude, that thefe two animals are not only fimple, but permanent varieties of the fame fpecies. Befides, the wild, as well as the chamois goats *, when taken young, and reared along with the domeftic kind, are eafily tamed, affume the fame manners, go in flocks, return to the fame fold, and probably couple and produce together. I acknowledge, howcver, that this laft fact, which is the moft important of all, and would alone decide the queftion, is by no means eftablifhed. We have never been able, with certainty, to learn whether the wild and chamois goats produce with the common kind †. We only fufpect this to be the cafe. In this refpect, we agree with the ancients; and, befides, our conjecture

* The inhabitants of the ifland of Crete might take the young of the bouc-eftain (of which there are great numbers) wandering in the mountains, and feed and tame them along with the domeftic kind. . . . They are covered with yellow hair. When old, they become gray, and a black line runs along the fpine of the back. We have fome of them in the mountains of France, and chiefly in places full of precipices, and of difficult accefs. . . . The bouc-eftain leaps from one rock to another, at the diftance of fix fathoms. An exertion almoft incredible to thofe who have not feen it; *Obferv. de Belon, p.* 14.—Audio Rupicapras aliquando cicurari; *Gefnq, de Quad. p.* 292.—Vaflefii ibicem in prima ætate captam omnino cicurari, et cum villaticis capris ad pafcua ire et redire, aiunt; progreffu tamen ætatis ferum ingenium non prorfus exuere; *Stumpfius apud Gefner. Hift. Quad. p.* 305.

† In the compilation of natural hiftory made by Meff. Arnault de Nobleville and Salerne, it is faid (tom. iv. p. 264.), that

conjecture feems to be founded on ftrong ana-
logies, which are feldom contradicted by experience.

Let us, however, confider the oppofite arguments. The wild and chamois goats both fubfift in the ftate of nature, and yet they always
remain diftinct. The chamois fometimes mingles
fpontaneoufly with the flocks of the domeftic
kind *; but the wild goat never affociates with
them, unlefs when tamed. The male wild goat
and the common he-goat have very long beards,
and the chamois has none. The horns of the
male and female chamois are fmall: Thofe of
the wild he-goat are fo large and fo long †, that

we

that the chamois goats are in feafon during almoft the whole
month of September; that the female goes with young nine
months; and that they generally bring forth in June. If
thefe facts were true, they would demonftrate that the chamois is not the fame fpecies with the goat, which goes with
young about fix months only: But I think they are fufpicious, if not falfe. The hunters, as appears from the paffages
already quoted, affure us, on the contrary, that the chamois
and wild goats do not come in feafon till the month of November;
and that the females bring forth in May. Thus the time of
geftation, inftead of being extended to nine months, fhould be
reduced to near five, as in the domeftic goat. But this matter
muft be decided by experience alone.

* Rupicapræ aliquando accedunt ufque ad greges capràrum
cicurum quos non refugiunt, quod non faciunt ibices; *Gefner. Hift.
Quàd. p.* 292.

†'Ibex egregium ut et corpulentum animal, fpecies fere
cervina minus tamen, cruribus quidem gracilibus et capite
parvo cervum exprimit. Pulchros et fplendidos oculos habet.
Color pellis fufcus eft. Ungulæ bifulcæ et acutæ ut in rupicapris; cornua magni ponderis ei reclinantur ad dorfum,
afpera et nodofa, eoque magis quo grandior ætas procefferit;

augentur

we could hardly imagine they belonged to an animal of his fize. The chamois feems to differ from the wild goat, and the common he-goat, by the direction of his horns, which incline a little forward in their inferior part, and bend backward at the point like a hook. But, as we remarked in the hiftory of the ox and fheep, the horns of domeftic animals, as well as thofe of wild animals living in different climates, vary prodigioufly. The horns of our female goat are not entirely fimilar to thofe of the male. The horns of the male wild goat are not very different from thofe of our he-goat: And, as the female wild goat approaches the domeftic kind, and even the chamois, in fize, and in the fmallnefs of its horns, may we not conclude, that the males of the wild, chamois, and domeftic goats, are only one fpecies of animal, in which the nature of the females is conftant and fimilar among themfelves, but that the males are fubject to confiderable variations? In this point of view, which is not, perhaps, removed fo far from nature as may be imagined, the wild goat would be the original male ftock, and the chamois would be the female *. I fay, that this point

of

augentur enim quotannis donec jam vetulis tandem nodi circiter viginti increverint. Bina cornua ultimi incrementi ad pondus fedecim aut octodecim librarum accedunt. . . . Ibex faliendo rupicapram longe fuperat; hoc tantum valet ut nifi qui viderit vix credat; *Stumpfius apud Gefner, p.* 305.

* The want of a beard in the chamois is a female character, which ought to be added to the others. The male chamoi

of view is not imaginary, fince we can prove from experience, that there are animals in nature, in which the female can equally ferve males of different fpecies, and produce from them both. The fheep produces with the he-goat as well as with the ram, and always brings forth lambs which are individuals of its own fpecies. The ram, on the contrary, produces not with the fhe-goat. The fheep, therefore, may be regarded as a female common to two different males; and, confequently, fhe conftitutes a fpecies independent of the male. The fame thing will happen to the wild goat. The female alone reprefents the primitive fpecies, becaufe her nature is conftant. The males, on the contrary, vary; and it is extremely probable, that the domeftic fhe-goat, which may be confidered as the fame female as thofe of the wild and chamois kinds, would produce equally with thefe three different males, which alone admit of varieties in fpecies; and, confequently, though they feem to change the unity, alter not the identity of the fpecies.

Thefe, as well as all other poffible relations, muft neceffarily exift in nature. It even appears, that the females contribute more to the fupport of the fpecies than the males; for,

mois appears, as well as the female, to participate of the feminine qualities of the fhe-goat. Thus it may be prefumed, that the domeftic he-goat would engender with the female chamois; and that, on the contrary, the male chamois could not engender with the female domeftic goat. Time will verify or deftroy this conjecture.

though both comcur in the firft formation of the
fœtus, the female, who afterwards furnifhes
every thing neceffary to its growth and nutri-
tion, modifies and affimilates it more to her own
nature, and muft, therefore, greatly efface the
impreffion of the parts derived from the male.
Thus, if we want to form a diftinct judgment
of a fpecies, we ought to examine the females.
The male beftows one half of the animated fubftance : The female gives an equal portion, and
furnifhes, befides, all the matter neceffary for
the developement of the form. A beautiful woman feldom fails to produce beautiful children.
The offspring of a beautiful man with an ugly
woman are generally ftill more ugly.

Hence, even in the fame fpecies, there may
fometimes be two races, the one mafculine and
the other feminine, which, by both fubfifting
and perpetuating their diftinctive characters, appear to conftitute two different fpecies ; and this
feems to be the cafe, when it is almoft impoffible
to fix the limits between what naturalifts term
fpecies and *variety*. Let us fuppofe, for example, that fome fheep were always ferved with
he-goats, and others with rams; after a certain
number of generations, a race would be eftablifhed among the fpecies of fheep, which would
partake greatly of the nature of the goat, and
would afterwards perpetuate its own kind ; for,
though the firft produce of the he-goat would
be little removed from the mother's fpecies, and

would

would be a lamb, and not a kid; yet this lamb is already covered with hair, and poſſeſſes ſome other characters of the father. Let theſe ſeveral mongrels be afterwards ſerved with a he-goat; the produce in this ſecond generation will make a nearer approach to the ſpecies of the father, and ſtill nearer in the third, &c. In this manner, the foreign characters will ſoon overbalance the natural ones; and this fictitious race might ſupport itſelf, and form a variety in the ſpecies, the origin of which it would be difficult to trace. Now, what might ariſe from the influence of one ſpecies on another, may be produced with greater eaſe in the ſame ſpecies. If vigorous females be conſtantly ſerved with feeble males, in proceſs of time a feminine race will be eſtabliſhed; and, if very ſtrong males are appropriated to females of inferior ſtrength and vigour, a maſculine race will be the reſult, ſo different in appearance from the firſt, that we could not aſſign to them a common origin, and, of courſe, would regard them as two diſtinct ſpecies.

To theſe general reflections, we ſhall add ſome particular facts. We are aſſured by Linnæus *, that

* Capra cornibus depreſſis, incurvis, minimis, cranio incumbentibus, gula barbata. Magnitudo hædi hirci: Pili longi, penduli; cornua lunata, craſſa, vix digitum longa, cranio adpreſſa ut fere cutem perforent: Habitat in America. Linnæus, I ſuſpect, has not been properly informed with regard to the country of this animal, and I believe it to be a native of Africa. My reaſons are, 1. That no author mentions this

ſpecies

that he faw in Holland two animals of the goat-
kind, of which the one had very fhort, thick
horns, lying almoft flat on the fkull; the horns
of the other were erect, and bended backward
at the points, and its hair was fhort. Thefe
animals, though they feemed to be more remote
in fpecies than the chamois and common goat,
failed not to produce together; which demonftrates that thefe differences in the figure of the
horns, and length of the hair, are not effential
and fpecific characters; for, as the animals produced together, they muft be regarded as belonging to the fame fpecies. From this example,
it may be concluded, that the chamois and our
goat, whofe principal differences lie in the form
of the horns and the length of the hair, are probably the fame fpecies.

In the royal cabinet, there is the fkeleton of

---

fpecies of goat, nor even the common goat, as being ever
found in America; 2. That all travellers, on the contrary,
agree in affuring us, that there are three kinds of goats in
Africa, a large, a middle, and a fmall kind; 3. That we have
feen an animal, which we received under the name of the
African Buck, and of which we have given a figure, that refembled fo much Linnæus's defcription of the *capra cornibus
depreffis*, &c. that we confidered it to be the very fame animal.
For thefe reafons, we are entitled to affirm, that this fmall goat
is an original native of Africa, and not of America.

Capra cornibus erectis, apice recurvis. Magnitudo hædi
hirci unius anni. Pili breves, cervini. Cornua vix digitum
longa, antrorfum recurvata apice: Hæc cum præcedenti co-
bat, et pullum non diu fuperftitem in vivario Cliffortiano pro-
ducebat. Facies utriufque adeo aliena, ut vix fpeciem eandem
at diverfiffimam, argueret; *Linn. Syft. Nat. p.* 96.

an

an animal, which was sent under the name of *capricorne*. In the form of the body and proportions of the bones, it has a perfect resemblance to the domestic he-goat ; and the figure of the under jaw is the same with that of the wild goat. But it differs from both in the horns: Those of the wild goat have prominent tubercles or knobs, and two longitudinal ridges, between which there is a well marked anterior face : Those of the common he-goat have but one ridge, and no tubercles. The horns of the capricorne have but one ridge, and no anterior face : Though they want tubercles, they have rugofities which are larger than those of the he-goat. These differences seem to indicate an intermediate race between the wild and the domestic goat. Besides, the horns of the capricorne are short and crooked at the point, like those of the chamois ; and, at the same time, they are compressed and have rings : Hence they partake at once of the he-goat, the wild goat, and the chamois goat.

Mr. Brown *, in his History of Jamaica, informs

---

* Capra I. cornibus carinatis arcuatis ; *Linn. Syst. Nat.* The nanny goat.

Capra II. cornibus erectis uncinatis, pedibus longioribus.

Capra cornibus erectis uncinatis ; *Linn. Syst. Nat.* The rupi goat. . . . .

Neither of these are natives of Jamaica ; but the latter is often imported thither from the Main and Rubee island ; and the other from many parts of Europe. The milk of these animals is very pleasant in all those warm countries for it loses

that

forms us, that there are in that island, 1. the common domestic goat of Europe; 2. the chamois; 3. the wild goat. He assures us, that none of these animals are natives of America, but have been transported from Europe; that, like the sheep, they have degenerated and become smaller in this new country; that the wool of the sheep is changed into hair as coarse as that of the goat; that the wild goat seems to be a bastard race, &c. Hence we are led to believe, that the small goat, with erect horns, and crooked at the points, which Linnæus saw in Holland, and was said to have come from America, is the chamois of Jamaica, that is, the European chamois degenerated and diminished by the climate of America; and that the wild goat of Jamaica, called the *bastard wild goat*

that rancid taste which it naturally has in Europe. A kid is generally thought as good, if not better, than a lamb, and is frequently served up at the tables of all ranks.

Capra III. cornibus nodosis in dorsum reclinatis; *Linn. Syst. Nat.* . . . . The bastard ibex.

This species seems to be a bastard sort of the ibex goat; it is the most common kind in Jamaica, and esteemed the best by most people. It was first introduced there by the Spaniards, and seems now naturalized in these parts.

Ovis I. cornibus compressis lunatis; *Linn. Syst. Nat.* The sheep. These animals have doubtless been bred in Jamaica ever since the time of the Spaniards, and thrive well in every quarter of the island; but they are generally very small. A sheep carried from a cold climate to any of those sultry regions, soon alters its appearance; for, in an year or two, instead of wool, it acquires a coat of hair like a goat. *The Civil and Natural History of Jamaica, by Patrick Brown, M. D. chap.* v. *sect.* iv.

by

by Mr. Brown, is our capricorne, which feems to be nothing elfe than the wild goat degenerated by the influence of climate.

M. Daubenton, after fcrupuloufly examining the relations of the chamois to the he-goat and ram, fays, in general, that it has a greater refemblance to the he-goat than to the ram. Next to the horns, the chief differences are found in the figure and fize of the front, which is lefs elevated and fhorter, and the form of the nofe, which is more contracted in the chamois than in the he-goat; fo that, in thefe two articles, the chamois refembles the ram more than the he-goat. But, by fuppofing, what is extremely probable, that the chamois is a conftant variety of the fpecies of the he-goat, as the bull-dog and grey-hound are conftant varieties in the dog-kind, we will perceive that thefe differences in the fize of the front and the pofition of the nofe, are not nearly fo great in the chamois, when compared with the he-goat, as in the bull-dog and grey-hound, which, however, produce together, and certainly belong to the fame fpecies. Befides, as the chamois refembles the he-goat in a greater number of characters than the ram, if he conftituted a particular fpecies, it muft neceffarily be an intermediate one between the he-goat and the ram. Now, we have feen, that the he-goat and ewe produce together: The chamois, therefore, which is an intermediate fpecies between the two, and, at the fame time,

A A 4

has

has a greater number of resemblances to the he-goat than to the ram, ought to produce with the she-goat, and, consequently, should be regarded as only a constant variety of this species.

Hence, as the chamois was transported into America, where it has become smaller, and produces with the small she-goat of Africa, it is more than probable that he would also produce with our she-goats. The chamois, therefore, is only a constant variety in the goat-kind, like the bull-dog in the species of the dog. On the other hand, the wild goat is unquestionably the primitive goat in a state of nature, and is, with regard to the domestic goats, what the mouflon is to the sheep. The wild he-goat perfectly resembles the domestic he-goat in figure, structure, habits, and dispositions; and there are only two slight external differences between them. The horns of the wild he-goat are larger than those of the common he-goat. The former have two longitudinal ridges, and the latter but one. They have also large transverse protuberant rings, which mark the years of their growth; whilst those of the domestic he-goat have only a kind of transverse striæ or furrows. The figure of their bodies is precisely the same. Their internal structure is likewise perfectly similar, with the exception of the spleen, which is oval in the wild he-goat, and approaches nearer to the spleen of the roebuck

or

or ftag, than to that of the he-goat or ram.
This difference may proceed from the violent
exercife of the animal. The wild he-goat runs
as fwiftly as the ftag, and leaps more nimbly
than the roebuck. His fpleen, therefore, fhould
refemble that of the fwifteft running animals.
Hence this flight difference depends more upon
habit than nature ; and it is probable, that, if
our domeftic he-goat fhould become wild, and
were obliged to run and leap like the wild he-
goat, his fpleen would foon affume the figure
moft conformable to this exercife. With regard to the difference of his horns, though very
confpicuous, they fail not to refemble thofe of
the domeftic he-goat more than thofe of any
other animal. Thus the wild and common he-
goat approach nearer each other, even in the
form of their horns, than any other animal; and,
as their refemblance is complete in every other
article, we fhould conclude, that, notwithftanding this flight and folitary difference, they are
both animals of the fame fpecies.

The wild, the chamois, and the domeftic goat
muft, therefore, be confidered as the fame fpecies, the males of which have undergone greater
variations than the females : I find, at the fame
time, in the domeftic kind, fecondary varieties, which are the lefs equivocal, becaufe they
belong equally to the males and females. We
have feen that the goat of Angora *, though very

* See Vol. III. p. 493.

different

different from ours in the hairs and horns, is neverthelefs of the fame fpecies. The fame thing
may·be faid of the Juda goat, which Linnæus
has properly confidered as a variety of the domeftic fpecies. This goat, which is common in
Guiney*, Angola, and other parts of Africa, may
be faid to differ from ours only in being fmaller,
fatter, and more fquat. Its flefh is excellent;
and, in that country, it is preferred to mutton,
as we prefer mutton to goat's flefh. The Levant or Mambrina goat †, with long pendulous
ears, is only a variety of the goat of Angora,
which has alfo pendulous ears, though they are
not fo long. Thefe two goats were known to the
ancients ‡; but they did not feparate them from
the common fpecies. This variety of the Mambrina or the Syrian goat is more diffufed than
the goat of Angora; for we find goats with long

---

* In Guiney there are great numbers of goats fimilar to
thofe in Europe, except that, like all the other cattle, they
are very fmall. But they are fatter and plumper than wedders: It is for this reafon that fome people prefer the flefh of
thefe fmall he-goats; which the natives caftrate, to mutton;
Voyage de Bofman, p. 328.

† It is called the Mambrina goat, becaufe it is found on
Mount Mambrina in Syria. ——Capra Indica; *Gefner, Hift.
Quad. p.* 267. ——Hircus cornibus minimis, erectis, parumper
retrorfum incurvis, auriculis longiffimis pendulis.—Capra Syria-
ca; *La chevre de Syrie*; *Briffon, Regn. Anim. p.* 72.

‡ In Syria oves funt cauda lata ad cubiti menfuram: Capræ
auriculis menfura palmari et dodrantali, ac nonnullæ demiffis,
ita ut fpectent ad terram.—In Cilicia capræ tondentur ut alibi
ovis; *Ariftot. Hift. Anim. lib.* viii. *cap.* xxviii.

ears

ears in Egypt *, and in the Eaft Indies †, as well as in Syria. They yield a great deal of fine milk ‡, which the natives of the Eaft prefer to that of the cow or buffalo.

With regard to the fmall goat which Linnæus faw alive, and which produced with the American chamois, it muft, as formerly remarked, have been originally tranfported from Africa; for it fo ftrongly refembles the he-goat of Africa, that it is unqueftionably the fame fpecies; or, at leaft, it has fprung from the fame ftock. In Africa it is fmall; and it would become ftill lefs in America; and we learn, from the teftimony of travellers, that fheep, hogs, and goats, have frequently, and for feveral ages back, been tranfported from Africa, as well as Europe, into America, where they ftill fubfift, without any other change than a diminution of fize.

After examining the different varieties of goats, of which the nomenclators have made nine or ten different fpecies, I am convinced that they

* Ex capris complures funt (in Ægypto) quæ ita aures oblongas habent, ut extremitate terram ufque contingant; *Profper Alpin. Hift. Ægypt. lib.* iv. *p.* 229.

† At Pondicherry, there are kids which differ much from ours. They have large pendulous ears; and their afpect is mean and filly. Their flefh, though bad, is fometimes eaten; *Nouveau Voyage, par le Sieur Luiller, p.* 30.

‡ Goats are remarkable for the length of their ears.——— The fize of the animal is fomewhat larger than ours; but their ears are often a foot long, and broad in proportion; they are chiefly kept for their milk, of which they yield no inconfiderable quantity; and it is fweet, and well tafted; *Nat. Hift. of Aleppo, by Alexander Ruffel, M. D.*

ought

ought to be reduced to one: 1. The wild he-goat is the principal ſtock of the ſpecies. 2. The capricorne is the wild he-goat degenerated by the influence of climate. 3. The domeſtic he-goat derives his origin from the wild he-goat. 4. The chamois is only a variety in the ſpecies of the ſhe-goat, with whom, like the wild he-goat, he ſhould be able to mix and produce. 5. The ſmall goat, with erect horns, crooked at the points, mentioned by Linnæus, is the European chamois diminiſhed by the influence of the American climate. 6. The other ſmall goat, with horns lying flat on the ſkull, and which produced with the American chamois, is the ſame with the African he-goat; the fertility of theſe two animals is a proof that our chamois and domeſtic goat would alſo produce together, and, of courſe, that they belong to the ſame ſpecies. 7. The dwarf goat, which is probably the female of the African buck, is only, as well as the male, a variety of the common kind. 8. The ſame thing may be ſaid of the buck and ſhe-goat of Juda; for they are only varieties of our domeſtic goat. 9. The goat of Angora, as it produces with our goats*, belongs to the ſame ſpecies. 10. The Mambrina or Syrian goat, with very long pendulous ears, is a variety of the goat of Angora. Thus theſe ten animals are only different races of the ſame ſpecies, which have

* See Vol. III. article Goat.

been

been produced by the influence of climate. *Capra in multas similitudines transfigurantur*, says Pliny *. Indeed, from this enumeration, it is apparent, that the goats, though essentially similar among themselves, vary greatly in their external form; and, if we comprehend, like Pliny, under the generic name of *Goats*, not only those we have mentioned, but likewise the roebuck, the antilopes, &c. this species would be the most extensive in Nature, and contain more races and varieties than that of the dog. But Pliny, when he joined the roebuck, antilopes, &c. to the species of the goat, betrayed his ignorance of the real distinction of species. These animals, though they resemble the goat in many respects, constitute two different species; and we will perceive from the following articles, how greatly the antilopes vary both in species and in races; and after enumerating all the antilopes and all the goats, we will still find other animals which participate of both. In the whole history of quadrupeds, I have met with nothing so confused, so uncertain, and so obscure, as the accounts given us by naturalists and travellers concerning the goats, the antilopes, and the species which have a relation to them. I have exerted every effort to throw

---

* Capræ tamen in plurimas similitudines transfigurantur; sunt capreæ, sunt rupicapræ, sunt ibices.—Sunt et origes.—Sunt et Damæ et Pygargi et Strepsicerotes, multaque alia haud dissimilia; *lib*. viii. *cap*. liii.

light

light upon this fubject; and fhall not regret my labour, if what I now write fhould contribute to remove error, and to extend the views of thofe who incline to ftudy Nature. But to return to our fubject.

The goats are fubject to vertigos: This difeafe is likewife common to the wild and chamois goats*, as well as the inclination to climb upon rocks, and the habit of perpetually licking ftones †, efpecially thofe which are impregnated with nitre or falt. In the Alps, we find rocks hollowed with the tongues of the chamois. They are generally compofed of tender and calcinable ftones, in which there is always a certain quantity of nitre. Thefe conformities in natural difpofitions and manners appear to be

---

* In the mountains of Switzerland, the chamois or wild goats are very frequent.——The natives inform us, that thefe animals are fubject to vertigos; and that, when attacked with this difeafe, they fometimes come down to the meadows, and mix with the horfes and cows, when they are taken with eafe; *Extrait du Voyage de Jean-Jacques Scheuchzer*; *Nouvelles de la Republique des Lettres, p.* 182.

† Conveniunt fæpe circa petras quafdam arenofas, et arenam inde lingunt.——Qui Alpes incolunt Helvetii hos locos fua lingua *Fultzen* tanquam falarios appellant; *Gefner, Hift. Quad. p.* 292.——What is fingular, in the Alps there are feveral rocks which have been hollowed by the conftant licking of the chamois goats. This licking is not occafioned, as has been alledged, by falt contained in thefe ftones, which is very rarely the cafe; for the rocks are porous, and compofed of grains of fand, which are eafily detached; and they are fwallowed by the animals with great avidity; *Extrait de Scheuchzer, ibid. p.* 185.

infallible

infallible indications of identity of fpecies. The Greeks, as formerly remarked, did not divide thefe three animals into three diftinct kinds; and our hunters, who probably never confulted the Greeks, have alfo regarded them as the fame fpecies. Gafton Phœbus*, when treating of the wild goat, points him out under the name of the *wild buck;* and the chamois, which he calls *yfarus* and *farris,* in his eftimation, is only another wild buck. I acknowledge that all thefe authorities amount not to a complete proof: But, when joined to the facts and reafonings already employed, they form fo ftrong a prefumption, with regard to the unity of fpecies in thefe three animals, as leaves no room for hefitation.

The wild and chamois goats, which I confidered, the one as the male, and the other as the female ftock of the goat-kind, are only found, like the mouflon, which is the ftock of the fheep, in the deferts and in the higheft and moft rugged mountains. The Alps, the Pyrennees, the Grecian mountains, and thofe in the iflands of the Archipelago, are almoft the only places where the wild and chamois goats are to be found. Though both avoid heat, and inhabit the regions of fnow and froft; yet they equally avoid the exceffive rigours of cold. In fummer, they dwell on the northern fides of the mountains; in winter, they frequent the fouthern fides, and defcend

---

* La Venerie de Gafton Phœbus, p. 68.

from

from the fummits into the plains. Neither of them can fupport themfelves on fmooth fheets of ice; but, when the ice is rendered rough by the fnow, they run and bound with great firmnefs and agility. The chafe of thofe animals *, efpecially that of the wild he-goat, is

* There are two kinds of bucks; fome are called *wild bucks*, and others *yfarus* or *farris*. The wild bucks are as large as a ftag; but, though they have as much flefh, they are neither fo long, nor make fuch great bounds. The years of their age correfpond with the number of rings which encircle their horns. — When old, their horns, which have no branches, are as thick as a man's leg. They never caft their horns; but they continue to grow in length and thicknefs as long as the animal lives. They have a large beard, and their hair is brown like that of the wolf. A black bar runs along their back and down the buttocks. Their belly is yellow, and their legs black, and yellow behind. Their feet, like thofe of the domeftic goat, are cloven; and their tracks are large, and rounder than thofe of the ftag. The female, like that of the hind, or common fhe-goat, produces but one at a time.

The bucks feed upon herbage like other cattle.——Their dung refembles that of the domeftic goat. They come in feafon about All-Saints-day, and their rutting feafon continues a month. When that feafon is over, they are much emaciated; and they defcend from the rocks and mountains, where they had dwelt during the fummer, to the plains, in queft of food. They remain at the foot of the mountains, till toward Eafter, when they return to the moft elevated places they can find, and each takes poffeffion of his bufh, like the ftags. The females, at this period, feparate from the males, and retire near the brooks, in order to fawn, where they remain during the fummer. When the bucks are thus feparated from the females, efpecially at the approach of the rutting feafon, they attack both man and beaft. They alfo fight among themfelves, like the ftags, but in a different

manner;

is very laborious; for dogs are almoſt uſeleſs in this kind of hunting. It is alſo ſometimes dangerous: When the animal finds himſelf hard puſhed, he gives the hunter a violent blow with his head, and often throws him over a precipice *. Though not ſo ſtrong as the wild bucks, the chamois goats are equally active †. They are

manner; for their quarrels are more formidable. The buck ſtrikes ſo furiouſly with his head, that he often breaks the legs of thoſe whom he attacks; and, if he runs a man againſt a tree, or throws him down on the ground, death is infallibly the conſequence. Such is the nature of the buck, that, though a ſtrong man gives him a blow on the back with a bar of iron, the animal's ſpine does not break. In the ſeaſon of love, his neck ſwells prodigiouſly: And, though he falls from a height of ten fathoms, he receives no injury.

The buck called Yſarus is of the ſame figure with the preceding, and is not larger than the domeſtic he-goat. His nature is the ſame with that of the wild buck.——Like the ſtag, both come in ſeaſon about All-Saints-day, and they ſhould be hunted till that period arrives. ——When they can find no other food in winter, they eat the leaves of the pine-tree, which are always green. Their ſkin, when properly dreſſed, is an excellent defence againſt the cold; for, when the hair is outmoſt, neither cold nor rain can penetrate it. Their fleſh is not very wholeſome; for it produces fevers.——The hunting of the buck is not very pleaſant; for we can neither accompany the dogs on foot nor on horſeback; *Gaſton Phœbus; Venerie de Dufoilloux, p. 68.*

* Ibex venatorem expectat, et ſolicite obſervat an inter ipſum et rupem minimum interſit ſpatium; nam ſi viſu dumtaxat intertueri (ut ita loquar) poſſit, impetu facto ſe transfert et venatorem impulſum præcipitat; *Stumpfius apud Geſner, p. 305.*

† M. Perroud, undertaker of the chryſtal mines in the Alps, brought a live chamois to Verſailles, and gave us the follow-

more numerous, and go generally in flocks. In the Alps and Pyrennees, however, they are not

now

ing excellent remarks on the nature and manners of this animal: " The chamois, though a wild animal, is very docile. He inhabits only the mountains and rocks. He is of the size of a domestic goat, which he greatly resembles. His vivacity is delightful, and his agility truly admirable. His hair is as short as that of a hind: In spring, it is ash-coloured, in summer it is yellowish, in autumn yellowish brown mixed with black, and, in winter, brownish black. The chamois goats are numerous in the mountains of Upper Dauphiny, Piedmont, Savoy, Switzerland, and Germany. They are very social among themselves: We find them going in pairs, or in little flocks of from three to twenty; and sometimes we see from sixty to a hundred of them dispersed in different flocks along the declivity of the same mountain. The large males keep at a distance from the rest, except in the rutting season, when they join the females, and beat off all the young. At this period, their ardour is still stronger than that of the wild bucks. They bleat often, and run from one mountain to another. Their season of love is in the months of October and November, and they bring forth in March and April. A young female takes the male at the age of eighteen months. The females bring forth one, but rarely two, at a time. The young follow their mothers till October, if not dispersed by the hunters or the wolves. We are assured that they live between twenty and thirty years. Their flesh is very good. A fat chamois goat will yield from ten to twelve pounds of suet, which is harder and better than that of the goat. The blood of the chamois is extremely hot, and it is said to have qualities and virtues nearly equal to those of the wild goat, and may serve the same purposes; for the effects are the same, when taken in a double dose. It is good against pleurisies, and possesses the property of purifying the blood, and promoting perspiration. The hunters sometimes mix the blood of the wild and chamois goats: At other times, they sell the blood of the wild goat for that of the chamois. It is very difficult to distinguish them; which

shews

now fo frequent as formerly. The term *Cha-moifeurs*, which was applied to all tranfporters of fkins,

fhews that the blood of the wild goat differs very little from that of the chamois. The voice of the chamois is a very low and almoft imperceptible kind of bleating, refembling that of a hoarfe domeftic goat. It is by this bleating that they collect together, particularly the mothers and their young. But, when alarmed, or when they perceive an enemy, or any thing the nature of which they cannot diftinguifh, they advertife one another by a kind of whiftling noife, which I fhall afterwards defcribe. The fight of the chamois is very penetrating, and his fenfe of fmelling is acute. When he fees a man diftinctly, he ftops for fome time, and flies off, when he makes a nearer approach. His fenfe of hearing is equally acute as that of fmelling; for he hears the fmalleft noife. When the wind blows in the direction between him and a man, he will perceive the fcent at the diftance of more than half a league. Hence, when he fmells or hears any thing which he cannot fee, he whiftles or blows with fuch force, that the rocks and forefts re-echo the found. If there are many of them near, they all take the alarm. This whiftling is as long as the animal can blow, without taking breath. It is at firft fharp, and turns flat towards the end. The chamois then ftops for a moment; looks round on all fides, and begins whiftling afrefh, which he continues from time to time. His agitation is extreme. He ftrikes the earth with his feet. He leaps upon the higheft ftones he can find: He again looks round, leaps from one place to another, and, when he difcovers any thing, he flies off. The whiftling of the male is fharper than that of the female. This whiftling is performed through the noftrils, and confifts of a ftrong blowing, fimilar to the found which a man may make by fixing his tongue to the palate, with his teeth nearly fhut; his lips open, and fomewhat extended, and blowing long and with great force. The chamois feeds on the fineft herbs. He felects the moft delicate parts of plants, as the flowers and the tendereft buds. He is very fond of fome aromatic herbs, particularly of the carline thiftle and genipay, which are the hotteft plants that grow in the Alps. When he eats green herbs, he drinks very little. He is very

fond

ſkins, ſeems to indicate, that the chamois ſkins were at that time the chief article of their com-merce ;

fond of the leaves and tender buds of ſhrubs. He ruminates like the common goat. The food he uſes ſeems to announce the heat of his conſtitution. This animal is admired for his large round eyes, whoſe ſize correſponds with the vivacity of his diſpoſition. His head is adorned with two ſmall horns, from half a foot to nine inches in length. Their colour is a fine black, and they are placed on the front nearly between his eyes ; and, inſtead of being reflected backward, like thoſe of other animals, they advance forward above the eyes, and bend backward at the points, which are extremely ſharp. He adjuſts his ears moſt beautifully to the points of his horns. Two tufts of black hair deſcend from the horns to the ſides of his face. The reſt of the head is of a yellowiſh white colour, which never changes. The horns of the chamois are uſed for the heads of canes. Thoſe of the female are ſmaller and leſs crooked. The ſkin of the chamois, when dreſſed, is very ſtrong, nervous, and ſupple, and makes excellent riding breeches, gloves, and veſts. Gar-ments of this kind laſt long, and are of great uſe to manu-facturers. The chamois is a native of cold countries, and al-ways prefers rugged rocks and lofty places. They frequent the woods ; but it is only thoſe in the higher regions of the moun-tains. Theſe woods conſiſt of pines, larches, and beeches. The chamois goats are ſo impatient of heat, that, in ſummer, they are only to be found under the ſhades of caverns in the rocks, among maſſes of congealed ſnow and ice, or in elevated foreſts on the northern declivities of the moſt ſcabrous mountains, where the rays of the ſun ſeldom penetrate. They paſture in the mornings and evenings, and ſeldom during the day. They traverſe the rocks and precipices with great facility, where the dogs dare not follow them. There is nothing more worthy of admiration than to ſee theſe animals climbing or deſcending in-acceſſible rocks. They neither mount nor deſcend perpendicu-larly, but in an oblique line. When deſcending, particularly, they throw themſelves down acroſs a rock, which is nearly per-pendicular, and of twenty or thirty feet in height, without having a ſingle prop to ſupport their feet. In deſcending,

they

merce; but the skins of goats, sheep, stags, roe-bucks, and the fallow deer, are their principal objects.

With

they strike their feet three or four times against the rock, till they arrive at a proper resting-place below. The spring of their tendons is so great, that, when leaping about among the precipices, one would imagine they had wings instead of limbs. It has been alleged, that the chamois, in climbing and descending rocks, supports himself by his horns. I have seen and killed many of these animals; but I never saw them use their horns for this purpose; neither did I ever hear the fact supported by any hunter. It is by the strength and agility of his limbs that the chamois is enabled to climb and descend rocks. His legs are very free and tall; those behind are somewhat longer, and always crooked, which favours their springing to a great distance; and, when they throw themselves from a height, the hind-legs receive the shock, and perform the office of two springs in breaking the fall. It is said, that, when there are numbers of chamois goats together, one is deputed to stand sentinel, for the protection of the rest. I have seen many flocks of them, but never observed this part of their œconomy. It is true, that, when there are many of them, some always watch while others eat; but I remarked nothing more singular here than what happens in a flock of sheep: For the first who perceives any thing alarming, advertises the rest, and, in an instant, the same terror is communicated to the whole. In great snows, and during the rigour of winter, the chamois goats inhabit the lower forests, and live upon pine leaves, the buds of trees, bushes, and such green or dry herbs as they can find by scratching off the snow with their feet. The forests that delight them most, are those which are full of rocks and precipices. The hunting of the chamois is very difficult and laborious. The mode most in use is to kill them by surprise. The hunters conceal themselves behind rocks or large stones, taking care that the wind blows opposite to them, and, when a favourable opportunity occurs, shoot them with musket balls. They are like-

wise

With regard to the specific virtue attributed to the blood of the wild goat, against certain diseases, and particularly the pleurify, a virtue which is thought to be peculiar to this animal, and which, of courfe, would lead us to think it to be of a peculiar nature; it has been difcovered, that the blood of the chamois *, and likewife that of the domeftic he-goat †, have the fame properties, when the animals are nourifhed with the fame aromatic herbs; fo that even this property feems to unite thefe three animals in the fame fpecies.

SUPPLEMENT.

WE here give a figure of a Juda buck, which appears to be different from that publifhed in the original work. M. Bourgelat had it alive, and ftill keeps its fkin in his anatomical cabinet. It was confiderably larger than the one formerly

wife hunted in the fame manner as ftags and other animals, by polling fome of the hunters in narrow paffes, while others beat about to raife the game. Men are preferable for this purpofe to dogs; for dogs too quickly difperfe the animals, who fly off fuddenly to the diftance of four or five leagues." See alfo on this fubject, *La troifieme Defcript. du Voyage des Alpes de Scheuchzer, p.* 11.

* See above, *p.* 386.

† See l'Hift. des Animaux, par Meff. Arnault de Nobleville & Salerne, tom. iv. p. 243.

13 engraved.

engraved. It was two feet nine inches long, and one foot feven inches high, while the other was only twenty-four inches and a half long, and feventeen inches high. The head and whole body were covered with large white hairs. The points of the noftrils were black. The horns nearly touch each other at the bafe, and then recede. They are much longer than thofe of the former, which the prefent one refembles in the feet and hoofs. Thefe differences are too flight to conftitute two diftinct fpecies. They feem to be only varieties of the fame fpecies.

We formerly mentioned Syrian goats with pendulous ears, which were nearly of the fame fize with the domeftic kind, and produced with them even in our climate. In Madagafcar there is a goat confiderably larger, with pendulous ears fo long, that, when they fall down, they cover the eyes, which obliges the animal to move its head almoft continually in throwing them back. Hence, when purfued, it always endeavours to afcend. This notice was communicated to us by M. Comerfon; but it is too imperfect to enable us to determine whether this goat belongs to the Syrian race with pendulous ears, or to a different fpecies.

We had the following note from M. le Vicomte de Querhoënt:

' The goats which were left on Afcenfion

' ifland

‘ ifland have multiplied greatly; but they are,
‘ very meager, efpecially in the dry feafon.
‘ The whole ifland is beaten with their tracks.
‘ During the night, they retire into the excava-
‘ tions of the mountains. They are not fo large
‘ as the common goat. They are fo weak, that
‘ men fometimes feize them in the chace.
‘ Their hair is generally of a deep brown
‘ colour.’

Plate CXC.

A Bell sculp.

WILD-GOAT.

Plate CXCL

CHAMOIS GOAT.

Plate CXCIII.

A. Bell Sculpt.

DWARF GOAT.

Plate CXCV.

SHE-GOAT of JUDA.

Plate CXCVI.

BUCK of JUDA.

Plate CXCIV.

BUCK of JUDA.

Plate CXCII.

A Bell Sculp.

AFRICAN HE-GOAT.

The SAIGA, or SCYTHIAN ANTILOPE*.

IN Hungary, Poland, Tartary, and the southern parts of Siberia, there is a species of goat, called *Seigah* or *Saiga* by the Ruſſians, which, in the figure of the body and the hair, reſembles

---

* The Scythian antilope has horns a foot long, bending a little in the middle, the points inclining inward, and the ends ſmooth ; the other part is ſurrounded with very prominent annuli. They are of a pale yellow colour, and the greateſt part ſemipellucid. The length of the animal is four feet nine inches and a quarter ; the height before, two feet ſix inches and a half, and behind, two feet ſeven inches and a half. The tail is three inches long. The head is like that of a ſheep ; the noſe is very large, arched, and marked the whole length with a ſmall line, cauſed by the elevation of the *ſeptum narium.* The noſtrils are tubular and large. The upper lip hangs over the under. The noſe is formed of a muſcular ſubſtance mixed with fat. The cutting teeth are ſo looſe in their ſockets, as to move with the leaſt touch. The male is covered with rough hair, like the he-goat, and has a very ſtrong ſmell : The female is ſmoother. The hair on the bottom of the ſides and the throat is long, and reſembles wool ; that on the ſides of the head and neck is hoary. The back and ſides are of a dirty white colour. The breaſt, belly, and inſide of the thighs, are of a ſhining white. The females are hornleſs and timid : If attacked by wolves or dogs, the males place the females in the centre, and defend them ſtoutly. They bleat like ſheep. Their common pace is a trot ; when they go faſter, it is by leaps, and they are ſwifter than roe-bucks. When they feed, they lift up the upper mandible, and go backward ; *Pennant's Synopſ. of Quad. p.* 35.

Colus ;

refembles the domeftic goat. But the form of its horns and the want of a beard make it approach nearer to the antilopes; and, indeed, it feems to conftitute the fhade between thefe two kinds of animals; for the horns of the faigæ are perfectly fimilar in figure, tranfverfe rings, longitudinal furrows, &c. to thofe of the antilope, and they differ in colour only. The horns of all the antilopes are black and opaque; but thofe of the faiga are whitifh and tranfparent. This animal is mentioned by Gefner under the name of *colus* *, and Gmelin under that of *faiga*.

Colus; *Gefner, Quad. p.* 361.

Suhak; *Rzaczinfki, Hift. Polon. p.* 224.

Ibex imberbis; *Nov. Com. Petrop. tom.* v. *tab.* xix. *tom.* vii. *p.* 39.

Sayga; *Phil. Tranf.* 1767. *p.* 344. *Bell's Travels, vol.* i. *p.* 43.

Capra Tartarica, cornibus teretibus, rectiufculis, perfecte annulatis, apice diaphanis, gula imberbi; *Linn. Syft. Nat.* p. 97.

Antilope Scythica; *Pallas Spicil. p.* 9. *Faunul. Sinenf.*

* Apud Scytas et Sarmatas quadrupes fera eft quam *Colon* (Κολος) appellant, magnitudine inter cervum et arietem, albicante corpore; eximiæ fupra hos levitatis ad curfum; *Strabo,* lib. vii. . . . . Sulac (a quo litteris tranfpofitis nomen *Colus* factum videtur) apud Mofchovios vulgo nominatur animal fimile ovi fylveftri candidæ, fine lana: capitur ad pulfum tympanorum dum faltando delaffatur . . . Apud Tartaros (inquit Matthias a Michow) reperitur *Snack,* animal magnitudine ovis, duabus parvis cornibus præditum, curfu velociffimum, carnes ejus fuaviffimæ . . . In defertis campis circa Boryfthenem (iniquit Sigifmundus, Liber Baro in Herberftain in commentariis rerum Mofcoviticarum) Tanaim et Rha eft ovis fylveftris quam Poloni *Solbac,* Mofci *Scigak,* appellant, magnitudine capreoli, brevioribus tamen pedibus; cornibus

*saiga**. The horns in the Royal cabinet were sent under the denomination of *horns of the Hungarian*

nibus in altum porrectis, quibusdam circulis notatis, ex quibus Mosci manubria cultellorum transparentia faciunt, velocissimi cursus et altissimorum saltuum; *Gesner, Hist. Quad. p.* 361. et 362. ubi vide figuras.

* In the environs of Sempalat, there are a number of *Saigi* or *Saiga*. This animal has a great resemblance to the roebuck, except that its horns are straight. It is known in no other part of Siberia; for what is called *Saiga* in the province of Irkutzk is the musk. . . . The taste of its flesh, it is said, resembles that of the stag; *Voyage de Gmelin à Kamtschatka, tom.* i. *p.* 179.—*Note*, M. Gmelin has since published a more comprehensive description of the saiga, in the first volume of the New Memoirs of the Academy of Petersburg, under the name of *ibex imberbis*; but he has given no figure of it. M. Gmelin remarks, that this animal has the head of a ram, with a higher and more prominent nose, and the body of a stag, but smaller; for it never reaches the size of a roebuck. The horns are yellowish and transparent, a foot in length, have rings or circles toward the base, and are situated above the eyes. The ears are erect, pretty large, and terminate in a point. In the under jaw, there are four cutting, four canine, and five grinding teeth, each of the last having two roots. In the upper jaw there are an equal number of cutting and canine teeth, but only four grinders, each of which has three roots. The neck is pretty long. The hind are longer than the fore-legs. The foot is cloven. The female has four paps. The tail is thin, and about three inches long. The hair, like that of the stag, is of a yellowish brown colour on the body, and white under the belly. The female is smaller than the male, and has no horns. . . . Worms breed under their skin. . . . These animals copulate in autumn, and bring forth one or two young in the spring. They live upon herbage, and are very fat when the rutting season commences. In summer, they inhabit the plains along the banks of the Irtis. In winter, they go to the higher grounds; and they are found not only about the Irtis, but in all the countries watered by the Boristhenes, the Don, and the Wolga; *Vide Nov. Com. Acad. Petrop.*

tom.

Hungarian buck. They are fo tranfparent, that they are ufed for the fame purpofes as fhells. In natural difpofitions, the faiga has a greater refemblance to the antilopes than to the wild and chamois goats; for he does not frequent the mountains, but, like the antilopes, lives on the hills and plains. Like them, he is extremely fwift, and his motion confifts of bounds or leaps. His flefh is alfo better than that of either the wild or domeftic goat.

tom. v. *p.* 345.——The fecretary of the Peterfburg Academy adds, to what M. Gmelin has remarked, that the faiga goes backward when he feeds. . . . That their horns are purchafed by the Chinefe to make lanthorns. . . . That they are only found under the 54th degree of latitude; and that, in the Eaft, there are none beyond the river Oby; *Ibid. p.* 35.

The ANTILOPES, or GA-ZELLES*.

OF the animals called *antilopes*, we know thirteen ſpecies, or at leaſt thirteen diſtinct varieties. In this uncertainty with regard to ſpecies and variety, we thought it beſt to treat of the whole under one article, aſſigning to each, however, a proper name. The firſt of theſe animals is the common *gazelle*, or Barbary antilope †, which is found in Syria, Meſopotamia, and other provinces of the Levant, as well as in

* In Arabic, *Gazal*, a generic name applied to ſeveral ſpecies of animals.

† The horns of the Barbary antilope are twelve inches long, round, inclining firſt backward, bending in the middle, and then reverting forward at their ends, and annulated with about thirteen rings on their lower part. The upper ſide of the body is of a reddiſh brown colour; the lower part and buttocks are white. Along the ſides, the two colours are ſeparated from each other by a ſtrong duſky line. On each knee there is a tuft of hair; *Pennant's Synopſ. of Quad. p.* 33.

Gazella Africana, cornibus brevioribus, ab imo ad ſummum fere annulatis et circa medium inflexis; *Raii Synopſ. Quad. p.* 80.

Capra dorca, cornibus teretibus, perfecte annulatis, recurvatis, contortis; *Linn. Syſt. Nat. p.* 96.

Algazel ex Africa; *Hernand. Hiſt. Mexic. p.* 893.

Hircus cornibus teretibus, arcuatis, ab imo ad ſummum fere annulatis, apice tantummodo levi. . . Gazella Africana; La Gazelle d'Afrique; *Briſſon. Quad. p.* 15.

Dorcas, Dorcades Libycæ ventre ſunt albo, qui color eis ad laparas uſque adſcendit, ad ventrem vero utrinque latera nigris vittis diſtinguuntur; reliqui corporis color rufus aut flavus eſt, et pedes quidem eis longi ſunt, oculi nigri, cornibus caput ornatur, et longiſſimas aures habent; *Elian. de Nat. Anim. lib.* xiv. *cap.* xiv.

Barbary,

Barbary, and in all the northern parts of Africa.
The horns of this antilope are about a foot in
length. They have entire rings at their bafe, and
then half rings till within a fmall diftance from
the extremities, which are fmooth and pointed.
They are not only furrounded with rings, but
furrowed longitudinally. The rings mark the
years of growth, and they are commonly from
twelve to thirteen in number. The antilopes
in general, and this fpecies in particular, have a
great refemblance to the roebuck in figure, natural functions, nimblenefs of movement, vivacity, largenefs of the eyes, &c. And, as the
roebuck exifts not in the countries inhabited
by the antilope, we would at firft be led to conclude, that it is only a degenerated roebuck, or
that the roebuck is an antilope whofe nature
has been changed by the effects of climate and
food. But the antilopes differ from the roebuck
in the fubftance of their horns. Thofe of the
roebuck are a kind of folid *wood*, which falls off
and is renewed annually, like that of the ftag.
The horns of the antilopes, on the contrary, are
hollow and permanent, like thofe of the goat.
Befides, the roebuck has no gall-bladder. The
antilopes, as well as the roebucks, have hollows
before the eyes. They refemble each other ftill
more in the quality of the hair, in the white-
nefs of the buttocks, and in the tufts on their
legs; but, in the roebuck, thefe tufts are on the
hind-legs, and on the fore-legs of the antilopes.
Hence the antilopes feem to be intermediate

animals

animals between the roebuck and goat. But
when it is confidered that the roebuck exifts
equally in both Continents, and that the goats,
as well as the antilopes, are peculiar to the Old
World, we are led to think, that the goats and
antilopes, are more allied to each other than they
are to the roebuck. Befides, the only charachters
peculiar to the antilopes are the tranfverfe rings
and longitudinal furrows on the horns; the tufts
of hair on the fore-legs; a thick and well de-
fined band of black, brown, or reddifh hairs below the flanks; and, laftly, three ftripes of
whitifh hairs, which extend longitudinally upon the internal furface of the ears *.

. The

---

* Algazel ex Africa, animal exoticum . . . ex Africa Nea-
polim miffum; magnitudine Capreæ, *Capreoli* dichi, cui toto
habitu prima facie fimile, nifi quod cornibus nulli magis quam
hirco fimilioribus fit præditum. . . Pilo eft brevi, levi, flavi-
cante, at in ventre et lateribus candicante, ficut in internis fe-
morum et brachiorum, illoque capreolo molliori. Altitudo
illius in pofterioribus, quæ, fublimiora funt anterioribus tibiis,
tres fpithamas æquat. Corpus obefius, et collum craffius habet; cruribus et tibiis admodum gracile: Ungulis bifulcis admodum diffechis, illifque tenuibus, et hircinis oblongioribus,
et acutioribus fimilitudine alces, et nigricantibus. Caudam
habet dodrantem fere pilofam, hircinam, et a medio ufque ad
extremum nigrefcentem. . . . Hilaris afpechu facies; oculi
magni, nigri, lucidi, læti; aures longæ, magnæ, patulæ, in
profpechu elatæ, illæque intus canaliculatæ quinquefido ftri-
gium ordine nigricante, extumentibus circa illas ftriis pilofis
candicantibus, et linea tenui circumducha. . . Cornua pedem
Romanum longa, retrorfum inclinata, hircina, ex nigro cafta-
neo colore cochleatim ftriata, et interno fitu ad invicem finu-
ata, et poft dilatationem reflexa, atque deinde in extremo parum acie refupinata. . . Nafus colore magis rufo, ficuti ex
oculis

The second antilope is found in Senegal; where, according to Mr. Adanson, it is called *kevel* *. It is less than the common kind, and is nearly of the size of our small roebucks. Its eyes are also larger than those of the gazelle, and its horns, instead of being round, are flattened on the sides. This compression of the horns proceeds not from a difference of sex; for, in both males and females, the horns of the one species are round, and of the other flat. In every other article, the resemblance is complete. The kevel, like the gazelle, has short yellow hair, a white belly and thighs, a black tail, a brown band under the flanks, three white stripes on the ears, black horns surrounded with rings, longitudinal furrows between the rings, &c. The number of these rings, however, is greater in the kevel than in the gazelle; for the latter has generally twelve or thirteen, and the former at least fourteen, and often eighteen.

---

oculis parallelo ordine linea nigricans dependet ad os usque, reliquis candicantibus. Nares et labia, os et lingua nigrescunt, quod satis dum ruminabat observavimus; dentibus, ovium modo, exiguis et vix conspicuis; vocem edit non absimilem suillæ. *Fab. Columnæ*, Annot. et Addit. in rerum Med. Nov. Hisp. Nardi. Ant. Recchi. ... *Hernand. Hist., Mex.* p. 893 et 894.

* The horns of the kevel, or flat-horned antilope, are shaped like those of the last, but flatted on their sides. The rings are more numerous, being from fourteen to eighteen. It is of the size of the roebuck; and in colours and marks resembles the preceding species; *Pennant's Synops. of Quad.* p. 54.

Antilope kevella; *Pallas, Miscel.* vii. *spicil.* xii.

The

The third antilope we fhall denominate *corine**, from the name *korin*, which it bears, according to M. Adanfon, in Senegal. It has a great refemblance to the gazelle and kevel. But it is ftill fmaller than the kevel, and its horns are thinner, fhorter, and fmoother, the rings which encircle them being hardly perceptible. M. Adanfon, who communicated to me his defcription of this animal, fays, that it appeared to partake fomewhat of the chamois goat, but that it was much fmaller, being only two feet and a half long, and lefs than two feet high; that his ears are four inches and a half in length, the tail three inches, the horns fix inches long, and only half an inch thick; that they are two inches afunder at the bafe, and from five to fix at their extremities; that, inftead of rings, they have circular *rugæ*, very near each other in the inferior part, and more diftant in the fuperior; that thefe *rugæ*, which hold the place of rings, are about fixteen in number; that the hair of this animal, which is fhort, fhining, and clofe fet, is yellow on the back and flanks, white on the belly, and

---

* The corine, or fpotted antilope, has very flender horns, fix inches long, and furrounded with circular *rugæ*. It is lefs than a roebuck. On each fide of the face there is a white line. The neck, body, and flanks, are tawny; the belly and infide of the thighs white, which is feparated from the fides by a dark line. On the knees there is a tuft of hair. Some are irregularly fpotted with white. Perhaps thefe are the fpotted goats of Kolben, tom. ii. p. 115; *Pennant's Synopf. of Quad. p. 37.*

the infide of the thighs; that the tail is black; and that, in the fame fpecies, fome individuals have white fpots fcattered over their bodies without any order.

Thefe differences between the gazelle, the kevel, and the korine, though very confpicuous, feem to be neither effential, nor fufficient to make thefe animals three diftinct fpecies. In every other refpect, they refemble each other fo ftrongly, that they appear to be of the fame fpecies, varied a little by the influence of climate and food; for the kevel and gazelle differ lefs from one another than from the corine, whofe horns refemble not thofe of the other two. But all the three have the fame natural habits; they go in troops, affociate together, and feed in the fame manner; their difpofitions are gentle; they are eafily accuftomed to a domeftic ftate; and their flefh makes excellent eating. We may, therefore, conclude, that the gazelle and kevel certainly belong to the fame fpecies, and that it is doubtful whether the corine be a variety only of the fame, or really conftitutes a diftinct fpecies.

In the royal cabinet, there are fpoils, either entire or partial, of thefe three antilopes. We have likewife a horn, which greatly refembles thofe of the gazelle and kevel, but it is much larger. This horn is alfo engraven by Aldrovandus *. Its thicknefs and length feem to in-

* Lib. i. de bifulcis, cap. xxi.

dicate

dicate an animal of greater magnitude than the
common antilope ; and I imagine it belongs to
an antilope called *tzeiran* by the Turks, and *abu*
by the Perfians. This animal, fays Olearius *,
has fome refemblance to the fallow-deer, except that it is reddifh, inftead of yellow ; that
its horns have no antlers, and lie on the back,
&c. According to Gmelin †, who mentions
this

* We faw daily great numbers of a fpecies of ftag, called
tzeiran by the Turks, and *abu* by the Perfians. They had
fome refemblance to our fallow-deer ; but they were rather reddifh than yellow, and their horns want antlers, and lie on the
back. They are exceedingly fwift, and are only found, according to our information, in the province of Mokau, and in the
neighbourhood of Scamachia, Karraback, and Merragé ; *Relation d'Olearius, tom.* i. *p.* 413.

† I was fhewn a kind of deer, called *dsheren* in the language of the country. It refembles the roebuck, except that
it had the horns of a wild he-goat, which never fall off.
What is fingular in this animal is, that, in proportion as his horns
grow, the fize of the *larynx*, or *pomum Adami*, augments ; fo
that, when old, he has a confiderable fwelling on his throat. Dr.
Mefferfchmid afferts that this roebuck has an abfolute averfion
to water. But the inhabitants of Tongus affured me, that, when
hunted, he often takes to the water, in order to make his efcape ; and Brigadier Bucholz, at Selenginfck, told me, that he
had tamed one completely ; that it followed his fervant when
fwimming ; and that it often went to an ifland in the river
Selinga, which it never would have done, if it had a natural
averfion to water. Thefe roebucks are as fwift as the faigas
on the borders of the Irtis ; *Voyage de M. Gmelin en Siberie,
tom.* ii. *p.* 103.—M. Gmelin has fince given a more complete
defcription of this animal, in the New Peterfburg Memoirs,
under the appellation of *Caprea Campeftris gutturofa*, of which
the following is an abridgment :—This animal refembles the
roebuck in figure, fize, colour, and manner of going. . . It

has

this animal under the name of *dſkeren*, it reſembles the roebuck, except in its horns, which, like thoſe of the wild he-goat, are hollow, and never fall off. This author adds, that, in proportion as the horns grow, the cartillage of the larynx enlarges, and forms a conſiderable prominence when the animal is old. According to Koempfer *, the figure of the *abu* differs not from

has no cutting teeth in the upper jaw. The male differs from the female by having horns and a protuberance on the throat. The horns are ſomewhat compreſſed at the baſe. They have rings for a great part of their length; they are ſmooth at the points; and they are blackiſh, but perfectly black at the extremities. They are permanent, and ſhed not, like thoſe of the roebuck. . . . Upon the throat of the male, there is a large protuberance of five inches in length, and three in breadth : It is ſmaller when the animals are young, and it is not perceptible till they are near a year old. Its growth keeps pace with that of the horns. . . This protuberance is occaſioned by the ſtructure of the larynx and the orifice of the trachea, which are very large. . . The female is perfectly ſimilar to the female roe. . . . This animal differs from the *ibex imberbis*, or *ſaiga*. The noſe of the ſaiga is large and ſplit like that of the ram; but the noſe of this animal is entire and pointed, like that of the roebuck. . . . . The Monguls, and even the Ruſſians, call the male *dſeren*, and the female *ona*, &c.; *Nov. Comment. Acad. Petropol. tom.* v. *p.* 347.—The ſecretary to the Peterſburg Academy adds, that, in the manuſcripts of Meſſerſchmid, this animal is mentioned under the names of *obna*, *dſeren*, and *ſcharchoeſchi*; *Id. p.* 36.

* Ipſum animal (*abu*) a cervis nihil habet diſſimile præter barbam, et cornua non ramoſa quibus ſe caprino generi adſociat; cornua ſunt ſimplicia, atra, rotundis annulis, ultra mediam uſque longitudinem diſtincta, levia et quaſi ad modulum tornata; in mari quidem ſurrecta, pedalis longitudinis, in medio levi arcu disjuncta, faſtigiis rectis mutuo utcunque imminentibus;

from that of the ftag: But he approaches to the goats by his horns, which are fimple, black, and encircled with rings, for more than one half of their length, &c.

Some other travellers * have likewife mentioned this fpecies of antilope under the name of *geiran* or *jairan*, which, as well as *dfheren*, may be eafily referred to the original name *tzeiran*. This antilope is common in South Tartary, in Perfia, and feems alfo to be found in the Eaft Indies †.

To thefe four fpecies or races of antilopes, we may add other two, which have a great refemblance to them. The firft is called *koba* ‡ in Senegal,

---

tibus; in foemina vero præparva vel nulla; *Koempfer, Amœnitates, p. 404.—Note,* The defcriptions here given by Koempfer of the *pafen* and *abu,* correfpond not with the figures.

* Upon the rout from Tauris to Kom, we faw a kind of wild animals, whofe flefh was good, and the Perfians called them *geirans* or *garzelles*; *Voyage de Gemelli Careri, tom.* ii. *p.* 63. ——In the deferts of Mefopotamia, there are vaft numbers of antilopes, which the Turks call *jairain*; *Voyage de la Boullaye-le-Goux, p.* 247.

† In the forefts of Guzarat, every kind of game, or venifon, abounds, particularly fallow-deer, roebucks, *abus,* and wild affes; *Voyage de Mandelflo, tom.* ii. *p.* 195.

‡ The horns of the koba, or Senegal antilope, are almoft clofe at the bafe, and bend out greatly a little above; they approach again towards the ends, and recede from each other towards the points which bend backwards. The diftance in the middle is fix inches and a half, above that, four inches, at the points fix. The length of the horns is feventeen inches, and the circumference at the bottom eight. They are furrounded with fifteen prominent rings, and the ends are fmooth and fharp.

Senegal, where the French give it the denomination of the *great brown cow*. The second, which we shall call *kob* *, is also a native of Senegal, and called the *small brown cow* by the French. The horns of the kob have a great resemblance to those of the gazelle and kevel. But the form of the head is different; the muzzle is longer, and there are no pits under the eyes. The koba is much larger than the kob. The latter is about the size of a fallow-deer; and the former is as large as the stag. From the information of M. Adanson, it appears, that the koba is five feet long from the extremity of the muzzle to the origin of the tail; that the head is fifteen inches long, the ears nine, and the horns from nineteen to twenty; and that the horns are compressed on the sides, and surrounded with eleven or twelve rings; whilst those of the kob have only eight or nine rings, and exceed not a foot in length.

The head is large and clumsey, being eighteen inches in length; the ears are seven inches long. The head and body are of a light reddish brown. Down the hind part of the neck, there is a narrow black list. The rump is a dirty white. On each knee, and above the fetlock, there is a dusky mark. The hoofs are small. The tail is a foot long, covered with coarse black hairs, which hang far beyond the end. The length of the whole skin, which I bought at Amsterdam, was seven feet; *Pennant's Synopf. of Quad. p.* 38.

* The horns of the *kob*, or Gambian antilope, are thirteen inches long, five inches and a half round at the bottom, very distant in the middle, and pretty close at the base and points. They are surrounded with eight or nine rings, and are smooth at their upper part; *Pennant's Synopf. of Quad. p.* 39.

The

The seventh antilope is found in the Levant, and still more commonly in Egypt * and in Arabia. We shall call it by its Arabian name, *algazel* †. The figure of this animal is nearly the same with that of the other antilopes, and it is about the size of the fallow-deer. But its

---

* Gazella Indica cornibus rectis, longissimis, nigris, prope caput tantum annulatis; cornua tres propemodum pedes longa, recta, prope imum seu basin tantum circulis seu annulis eminentibus cincta, reliqua parte tota glabra et nigricantia. Animal ipsum ad cervi platycerotis, *Damæ* vulgo dicti, magnitudinem accedit, pilo cinereo, cauda pedem circiter longa, pilis longis innascentibus hirta. Hæc *D. Tancred Robinson*, e pelle animalis suffulta in regiæ societatis museo suspensa. Cæterum hujus animalis cornua pluries vidimus in museis curiosorum; *Raii Syn. Quad. p.* 79. *Note*, Naturalists have improperly applied the appellation of *Indian antilope* to this species. It will afterwards appear, from the evidence of travellers, that it is only found in Egypt, Arabia, and the Levant.

Gazellæ quibus Egyptus abundat; *Prosper Alp. Hist. Egypt. p.* 232.

† The bezoar antilope has very long, slender, upright horns, bending at the upper part inward towards each other; some of them are much annulated, others smoother. It is of the size of a goat, and is red, mixed with ash-colour. It inhabits the inhospitable and rough mountains of Laar in Persia, and is one of the animals which produce the bezoar; *Pennant's Synops. of Quad. p.* 26.

Pasen, capricerva; *Koempfer, Amœn. Exot. p.* 398.

Cornu ignotum; *Gesner. Quad. p.* 309.

La gazelle; *Belon. Observ. p.* 120.; *Alpin. Hist. Egypt. tom.* i. *p.* 232. *tab.* xiv.

Animal bezoarticum; *Raii Synops. Quad. p.* 80.

La gazelle du bezoar; *Brisson, Quad. p.* 54.

Capra bezoartica, cornibus teretibus, arcuatis, totis annularibus, gula barbata; *Linn. Syst. Nat. p.* 96.

horns

horns are very long, pretty thin, and they bend little till toward their extremities. They are black and almost smooth, the rings being very flight, except near the base, where they are better marked. They are near three feet in length, while those of the gazelle or common antilope exceed not one foot; those of the kevel are fourteen or fifteen inches; and those of the corine are only six or seven inches.

The eighth animal is commonly called the *bezoar antilope* *; and it is denominated *pasan* by the eastern nations, which last name we shall preserve. The horns of this antilope are very well reprefented in the German Ephemerides †,

and

* The Egyptian antilope has ftraight flender horns, near three feet long, and annulated. At their bafe, there is a triangular black fpot, bounded on each fide with white. A black line extends from the neck to the loins. The neck, back, and fides, are of a dark gray colour. The breaft and belly are white. The tail is about two feet long, terminated with black hairs. The length of the whole fkin is fix feet; *Pennant's Synopf. of Quad.* p. 25.

Gazella Indica cornibus rectis, longiffimis, nigris, prope caput tantum annulatis; *Raii Synopf. Quad.* p. 79.

Capra gazella, cornibus teretibus, rectiffimis, longiffimis, bafi annulatis; *Linn. Syft. Nat.* p. 96.

La gazelle des Indes; *Briffon. Quad.* p. 43.

† Miffum mihi Hamburgo his diebus fuit ab amico — Schellamero — cornu — capri Bezoardici. — Longitudino et facie qua hic depingitur, durum ac rigidum, fibris rectis per longitudinem cornu excurrentibus tanquam callis (nefcio an ætatis indicibus) ad medium circiter, ubi fenfum elanguefcunt quafi, aut planiores redduntur, exafperatum; intus cavum, pendens uncias octo cum duabus drachmis, —

Jacobus

and the figure of it is given by Kœmpfer *. But, in this figure, the horns are neither fufficiently long nor ftraight. Befides, his defcription is by no means exact; for he fays that this bezoar animal has a beard like the he-goat, though he has given it no beard in his figure; which is more confonant to truth, the want of a beard being the chief characteriftic by which the antilopes are diftinguifhed from the goats. This antilope is of the fize of our domeftic he-goat, and it refembles the ftag in figure, colour, and agility. Befide two feparate horns, we have feen a head of this animal to which the horns were attached. The horns engraven in Aldrovandus's work have a great refemblance to thofe of the pafan. In general, the algazel and pafan feem to be very near allied. They likewife belong to the fame climate, and are found in the Levant, Egypt, Perfia, Arabia, &c. But the algazel inhabits the plains, and the pafan the mountains. The flefh of both is excellent.

The ninth antilope is an animal, which, according to M. Adanfon, is called *nangueur* or *nan-*

Jacobus Bontius (lib. i. de med. Indorum, notis ad cap. 45.). Videtur figuræ Bezoardici cornu mei propius accedere dum ita fcribit: ' Capræ iftæ non abfimiles valde funt capris ' Europæis, nifi quod habeant erecta ac longiora cornua,' &c. De cornu capri Bezoardici; *Obf. Jo. Dan. Majoris Ephemer. ann. 8.*

* Koempfer, Amœnitates, p. 398.——In Perfia, this kind of antilope is very numerous, and is called *bazan*, and the ftone itfelf *bazar*; *Voyage de la Compagnie des Indes de Hollande, tom. ii. p. 121.*

guer

gwer in Senegal*. It is three feet and a half in length, and two feet and a half in height. It is of the figure and colour of a roebuck, being yellow on the upper part of the body, white on the belly and thighs, with a white spot under the neck. Its horns are permanent, like those of the other antilopes, and they exceed not six or seven inches in length. They are black and round; but, what is singular, they bend forward at the points nearly in the same manner as those of the chamois goat bend backward. The nanguer, or swift antilope, is a very handsome animal, and easily tamed. All these characters, and chiefly that of the horns bending forward, incline me to think that the nanguer may be the *dama* or fallow-deer of the ancients. ' Cornua ' rupicapris in dorsum adunca, damis in adver- ' sum,' says Pliny †. Now, the nanguers are the only animals whose horns are bended in this manner; we may therefore presume, that the nanguer of Africa is the dama of the ancients, especially as we learn from another passage of

* The *Swift* antilope has round horns, eight inches long, and reverted at their ends. The length of the animal is three feet ten inches, the height two feet eight inches. The general colour is tawny. The belly, lower part of the sides, rump, and thighs, are white. On the fore part of the neck, there is a white spot. But this species varies in colour.

Dama; *Plinii, lib. xi. c. 37.*

Cemas; *Elian, An. lib. xiv. c. 14.*

Antilope dama; *Pallas Miscell. v. spicil. 8.*

† Hist. Nat. lib. xi. cap. 37.

Pliny,

Pliny*, that the dama was found only in Africa.
In fine, from the teftimony of other ancient authors †, we fee that the dama was a timid, gentle
animal, and had no other refources but in the
fwiftnefs of its courfe. The animal defcribed
and engraven by Caius, under the name of *dama
Plinii*, being found, according to the teftimony
of the fame author, in the North of Great Britain and in Spain, could not be the dama of
Pliny, fince he tells us, that it was only to be
met with in Africa ‡. Befides, the animal drawn
by Caius has a beard like a goat ; but none of
the ancients mention the dama as having a beard.
Hence I am led to think, that the dama defcribed by Caius is only a goat, whofe horns being
a little bended at the points, like thofe of the
common antilope, made him imagine it to be
the dama of the ancients. Befides, the horns
bended forward, which is the diftinguifhing character of the dama of the ancients, are well marked in the nanguer of Africa only. We are likewife informed by M. Adanfon, that there are three

---

* Sunt et damæ, et pygargi, et ftrepficerotes.——Hæc tranf-
marini fitus mittunt ; *Hift. Nat. lib.* viii. *cap.* 53.

† Horace, Virgil, Martial, &c.

‡ Hæc icon damæ eft quam ex caprarum genere indicat
pilus, aruncus, figura corporis atque cornua, nifi quod his in
adverfum adunca, cum cæteris in averfum acta fint. Capræ
magnitudine eft dama et colore Dorcadis.——Eft amicus
quidam meus Anglus, qui mihi certa fide retulit in partibus
Britanniæ feptentrionalibus eam reperiri, fed adventitiam.
Vidit is apud nobilem quemdam cui dono dabatur ; accepi
a quibufdam eam in Hifpania nafci ; *Caius et Gefner, Hift. Quad.
p.* 306.

I   varieties

varieties of those nanguers, which differ only in colour; but all their horns are more or less bended forward.

The tenth gazelle is an animal very common in Barbary and Mauritania, and is called *the antilope** by the British, which name I shall preserve. It is of the size of our largest roebucks. Though it has a great resemblance to the gazelle and kevel, yet it differs in so many characters, that it ought to be regarded as a distinct species. The pits below the eyes are larger in the *antilope* than in the gazelle. Its horns are almost fourteen inches long; and, though they nearly touch at the base, yet their points are fifteen or sixteen inches asunder. They are surrounded with rings and half rings, which are

---

* The *common antilope* has upright horns, twisted spirally, and surrounded almost to the top with prominent rings: They are about sixteen inches long, and twelve inches distant between point and point. In size, it is rather less than the fallow-deer or buck. The colour is brown mixed with red, and dusky. The belly and inside of the thighs are white. The tail is short, black above, and white beneath. The females want horns; *Pennant's Synopf. of Quad. p. 32.*

Strepsiceros; *Plinii Hist. Nat. lib. viii. c. 53. & lib. xi. c. 37.*

Gazelle; *Mem. pour servir à l'Hist. des Animaux, part. i. p. 95. fig. 11.*

Gazella Africana, the antilope; *Rail Synopf. Quad. p. 79.*

Hircus cornibus teretibus, dimidiato annulatis, bis arcuatis; *Briffon. Quad. p. 44.*

Tragus strepsiceros; *Klein. Quad. p. 18.*

Capra cervicapra, cornibus teretibus, dimiato-annulatis, flexuosis, contortis; *Linn. Syst. Nat. p. 96.*

Antilope cervicapra; *Pallas Miscell. p. 9. Spicil. 18. tab. 1 & 2.*

less

lefs raifed than thofe of the gazelle and kevel; and, what is peculiar to the *antilope*, its horns have a remarkably beautiful double flexion, which gives them the appearance of the ancient lyre. The hair of the *antilope*, like that of the other gazelles, is yellow on the back, and white on the belly: But thefe two colours are not feparated below the flanks by a brown or black band, as in the gazelle, kevel, corine, &c. We have only a fkeleton of this animal in the royal cabinet.

In the *antilope*, as well as the other gazelles, there feem to be different races. 1. In the royal cabinet, there is a horn which can only be attributed to an antilope of a much larger fize than that we have been defcribing. We fhall adopt the name *lidmée**, which, according to Dr Shaw †, the Africans apply to the *antilopes*. 2. We have feen in the cabinet of the Marquis de Marigny, whofe tafte extends both to the fine arts and to the hiftory of Nature, a kind of

* The lidmée, or brown antilope, is lefs than a roebuck; its horns refemble thofe of the laft. Its face, back, and fides, are of a very deep brown, the laft bordered with tawny. The belly and infide of the legs are white. Above each hoof, there is a black fpot. The tail is black above, and white beneath; *Pennant's Synopf. of Quad. p.* 32.

† Befides the common gazelle or antilope, (which is well known in Europe,) this country likewife produceth another fpecies, of the fame fhape and colour, though of the bignefs of our roebuck, and with horns fometimes of two feet long. This the Africans call *lidmée*, and may, I prefume, be the *ftrepficeros* and *adace* of the ancients; *Shaw's Travels, p.* 243.

offenfive

offenfive weapon, compofed of two fharp horns, about a foot and a half long, which, from their double flexion, appear to belong to an *antilope* fmaller than the others *. It muft be very common in India; for the priefts † carry this kind of weapon as a mark of dignity. We fhall call it the *Indian antilope*, becaufe it appears to be only a fimple variety of the African fpecies.

Thus, among the gazelles or antilopes, we have difcovered twelve fpecies, or diftinct varieties. 1. The common gazelle; 2. The kevel; 3. The corine; 4. The tzeiran; 5. The koba, or great brown cow; 6. The kob, or fmall brown cow; 7. The algazel, or Egyptian antilope; 8. The pafan, or pretended bezoar animal; 9. The nanguer, or dama of the ancients; 10. The *antilope*; 11. The lidmée; 12. The Indian *antilope*. After a careful comparifon of thefe twelve animals among them-

* Mr. Pennant calls this the *fmooth-horned antilope*; *Synopf. of Quad. p. 33.*

† The Indian antilopes are not entirely like thofe of other countries. They have more fpirit; and are diftinguifhable by their horns. In the common antilopes, the horns are gray, and not half fo long as thofe of India, which are black, and more than a foot and a half in length. They are twifted as far as the points, like a fcrew. The Faquirs and Santons generally carry two of them joined together in a parallel direction, and ufe them as fmall batons; *Relat. du Voyage de Thevenot, tom.* iii. *p.* 111.—Thofe in the Marquis de Marigny's cabinet are neither twifted nor annulated: They feem to have been polifhed from one end to the other.

felves,

felves, we are led to conclude, 1. That the common gazelle, the kevel, and the corine, are only three varieties of the fame fpecies; 2. That the tzeiran, koba, and kob, the varieties of another fpecies; 3. That the algazel and pafan are probably two varieties of the fame fpecies; and that the name of *bezoar gazelle*, which has been given to the pafan, is not a diftinctive character; for I fhall afterwards prove, that the Oriental bezoar is not produced by the pafan alone, but by all the gazelles and goats which inhabit the mountains of Afia; 4. That the nanguers, whofe horns are bended forward, and of which there are two or three varieties, have been pointed out by the ancients under the name of *dama*; 5. That the *antilopes*, which are three or four in number, and differ from all the others by the double flexion of their horns, were likewife known to the ancients, and mentioned under the names of *ftrepficeros* * and *addax*. All thefe animals are found in Afia and Africa. To thefe five principal fpecies, which contain twelve diftinct varieties, I will not add two or three other fpecies of the New World, to which the vague name of *gazelle*, or *antilope*, has been given, though they differ from all thofe formerly taken notice of. This would be to augment a confufion which is already too great. In the fub-

---

* Erecta autem cornua, rugarumque ambitu contorta, et it leve faftigium exacuta (ut lyras diceres) ftrepficeroti, quem addacem Africa appellat; *Plin. Hift. Nat. lib.* xi. *cap.* 37.

fequent article, we fhall give the hiftory of thefe
American animals under their true names, ma-
zame, temamaçame, &c. and fhall here confine
ourfelves entirely to the animals of this genus
which are found in Africa and Afia: For the
fame reafon, we fhall refer to the following
article feveral other African and Afiatic animals,
which have been regarded as antilopes or goats,
though they appear to be intermediate fpecies,
fuch as the bubalus, or Barbary cow, the con-
doma, the guib, the grimm, &c. without including the chevrotains or mufks, which have a
great refemblance to the fmalleft goats or antilopes! Of thefe laft we fhall likewife make a
feparate article.

It is now eafy to perceive the difficulty of arranging and diftinguifhing all thefe animals,
which are thirty in number, ten goats, twelve or
thirteen antilopes, three or four bubali, and as
many mufks. Many of them were unknown
to the naturalifts, or exhibited in promifcuous
groups; and the whole have been confounded
with each other by travellers. This, indeed, is
the third time I have written the hiftory of
thefe animals; and, I acknowledge, that the
labour overbalanceth the produce. I have the
fatisfaction, however, of having made every
poffible ufe of the knowledge and materials I
could acquire.

With regard to the gazelles, from comparing
all that has been faid of them, both by the ancients

cients and moderns, with our own experience, we find, 1. That the δορκας of Ariſtotle is not the gazelle, but the roebuck; though the ſame word δορκας has been employed by Ælian, not only to denote the wild goats in general, but partricularly the Lybian gazelle or Barbary antilope; 2. That the *ſtrepſiceros* of Pliny, or *addax* of the Africans, is the *antilope*; 3. That the *dama* of Pliny is the *nauguer* of Africa, and not our fallow deer, or any other European animal; 4. That the προξ of Ariſtotle is the ſame with the Ζορκες of Ælian, and the πλατυκερος of the more modern Greeks; and that the Latins have uſed this word *platyceros* to denote the fallow deer: ' Animalium,' ſays Pliny, quorundam cornua ' in palmas finxit natura, digitoſque emiſit ex ' iis, unde *platycerotas* vocant;' 5. That the πυγαργος of the Greeks is probably the Egyptian or Perſian gazelle, that is, the *algazel* or *paſan*. The word *pygargus* is employed by Ariſtotle ſolely to denote the *white tailed eagle*; and Pliny has uſed the ſame word to denote a quadruped. Now, the etymology of *pygargus* indicates, 1. An animal with white thighs, ſuch as the roebucks, or gazelles; 2. A timid animal; the ancients, imagining that white thighs indicated timidity, aſcribed the intrepidity of Hercules to his having black thighs. But as almoſt all the authors who ſpeak of the *pygargus* as a quadruped, mention likewiſe the roebuck, it is obvious that the name *pygargus* can only apply to fome fpecies of gazelle different from the *dorcas Lybica*, or common gazelle, and from the *ftrepficeros* or *antilope*, which are alfo mentioned by the fame authors. We are therefore led to conclude, that the *pygargus* denotes the algazel or Egyptian gazelle, which muft have been known to the Greeks as well as the Hebrews; for we find the name *pygargus* applied, in the Septuagint verfion *, to a quadruped which is reckoned among the pure animals whofe flefh might be eaten. Hence the Jews eat the *pygargus*, or that fpecies of gazelle which is moft common in Egypt and the adjacent countries.

Dr Ruffel, in his Natural Hiftory of Aleppo, tells us, that in the neighbourhood of that city, there are two kinds of gazelles; the one, called the *mountain gazelle*, which is the moft beautiful, and whofe hair on the neck and back is of a deep brown colour; the other, called *the gazelle of the plains*, which is neither fo nimble, nor fo handfome as the firft, and whofe hair is of a pale colour. He adds, that thefe animals are fo fwift, and run fo long, that the beft hounds cannot take them, without the affiftance of a falcon; that, though the gazelles are meager in winter, their flefh is excellent; that, in fummer, it is loaded with fat like that of the fallow deer; that thofe fed in houfes are not fuch good eating as the wild ones, &c. From the teftimo-

* Deuteron. chap. xiv.

nies

nies of Mr. Ruffel and of Haffelquift*, we learn
that the gazelles of Aleppo are not the com-

* Capra cervicapra. *The rock goat.*

This is larger, fwifter, and wider, than the common rock
goat, and can fcarcely be taken without a falcon. It is met
with near Aleppo. I have feen a variety of this, which is
common in the Eaft, and the horns appear different; perhaps it is a diftinct fpecies. This animal loves the fmoke of
tobacco, and, when caught alive, will approach the pipe of
the huntfman, though otherwife more timid than any animal.
This is perhaps the only creature befide man, that delights
in the fmell of a poifonous and ftinking plant. The Arabians
hunt it with a falcon (Falco gentilis, Linn.). I had an excellent opportunity of feeing this fport in Nazareth, in Ga-
lilee. An Arab, mounting a fwift courfer, held the falcon on
his hand as huntfmen commonly do: When we efpied the
rock goat, on the top of a mountain, he let loofe the falcon,
which flew in a direct line, like an arrow, and attacked the animal, fixing the talons of one of his feet into the cheek of the
creature, and the talons of the other into its throat, extending his wings obliquely over the animal; fpreading one towards one of its ears, and the other to the oppofite hip. The
animal, thus attacked, made a leap twice the height of a man,
and freed himfelf from the falcon; but, being wounded, and
lofing its ftrength and fpeed, it was again attacked by the
falcon, which fixed the talons of both its feet into the throat
of the animal, and held it faft, till the huntfman coming
up took it alive, and cut its throat, the falcon drinking the
blood, as a reward for his labour; and a young falcon which
was learning, was likewife put to the throat of the goat: By
this means are young falcons taught to fix their talons in the
throat of the animal, as being the propereft part; for, fhould the
falcon fix them in the creature's hip, or fome other part of the
body, the huntfman would not only lofe his game, but his
falcon alfo: For the animal, roufed by the wound, which could
not prove mortal, would run to the deferts, and the tops of the
mountains, whither its enemy keeping its hold, would be obliged
to follow; and being feparated from its mafter, muft of courfe
perifh; *Haffelquift, p.* 190.

mon

mon kind, but the Egyptian gazelles, whofe horns are upright, long, and black, and whofe flefh is extremely good; and that they are half-do-meftic, having been often and very anciently tamed, which, of courfe, has given rife to a great number of varieties, or different races, as happens in all other domeftic animals. Thefe Aleppo gazelles, therefore, are the fame with thofe we have called *algazelles*. They are ftill more common in Thebaid and Upper Egypt, than in the environs of Aleppo. They feed upon aromatic herbs, and the buds of trees*. They ge-nerally go in flocks, or rather in families, confift-ing of five or fix †. Their cry is fimilar to that of the goat. They are not only hunted with hounds, who are affifted by falcons, but by the fmall ‡ pan-

ther,

---

* Relat. du Voyage fait ou Egypt, par Granger, p. 99.

† In Egypt there are a number of antilopes.——They com-monly traverfe the mountains in flocks. The hair and tail of thefe animals refemble thofe of the hind; and their fore-feet, which are fhort, refemble thofe of the fallow deer. Their horns are ftraight as far as the extremity, which is crooked. Their cry refembles that of the other goats; *Voyages de Paul Lucas, tom.* iii. *p.* 199,

‡ Venantur non minus et gazellas quibus Egyptus abun-dat, quarum carnes, bonitate et guftu, capreolorum carnibus fimiles exiftunt. Bifulcum animal eft, filveftre, fed quod facile manfuefit, capræ fimile, colore igneo ad pallidum inclinante, duplici cornu, longo, introverfo lunæ modo, et nigro; auribus arrectis, ut in-cervis, oculis magnis, oblongis, nigris, pulcher-rimis. Unde in adagio apud Egyptos dicitur de pulchris oculis *ain el gazel,* id eft, oculus gazellæ: Collo longo et

gracili,

ther, which we have called *ounce*. In some places, the gazelles are taken by means of tam-ed

gracili, cruribus gracilibus atque pedibus bisulcis conftat. Pantheræ in defertis locis gazellas venantur, quibus ali-quandiu cornibus duriffimus, acutifque refiftant ; fed victæ eorum præda fiunt. Pili quibus conteguntur, videntur fane fimiles iis qui in Mofchiferis animalibus fpectantur : Pul-cherrimum eft animal, quod facile hominibus redditur cicur manfuetumque ; *Profper. Alpin. Hift. Nat. Egypt. p.* 232. *tab.* 14. *Note,* From the figure given by Profper Alpinus, it is ob-vious, that it is the *algazel* of which he is treating ; and his defcription fhows that the algazel is often, as well as the com-mon gazelle and keval, marked with white fpots, like the civet.———In India there are numbers of gazelles, which refemble our fawns. They generally go in feparate flocks, each confifting of five or fix, and accompanied with a male, who is eafily diftinguifhed by his colour. When the hunters difcover one of thefe flocks, they endeavour to point them out to the leopard, which they keep chained in a fmall cart. This cunning animal does not run ftraight upon them, but winds about, creeping and concealing himfelf, in order to ap-proach and furprife them ; and, as he is capable of making five or fix bounds with inconceivable quicknefs, when he thinks himfelf near enough, he darts upon them, tears open the throat and breaft, and gluts himfelf with their blood, heart, and liver. But, if he miffes his aim, which often hap-pens, he remains fixed on the fpot. It would be in vain to at-tempt to feize them by running ; for they run much fwifter and continue much longer than he can do. His mafter then comes gently up to him, flatters him, and throws pieces of flefh to him. By amufing the animal in this manner, he is enabled to throw a cover over his eyes : After which, he chains him, and replaces him on the cart. In the courfe of our march, one of thefe leopards exhibited this fport to us, which alarmed feveral of our people. A flock of gazelles rofe in the midft of the army, and, as often happens, they accidentally paffed near the two leopards, which are commonly carried along on a fmall cart. One of them, which was not hood-winked,

made

ed ones, with fnares of ropes fixed to their horns *.

The antilopes, efpecially the larger kinds, are much more common in Africa than in India. They are ftronger and fiercer than the other gazelles ; and they are eafily diftinguifhed by the double flexion of their horns, and by the want of a black or brown band below the flanks. The middling antilopes are of the fize of a fallow deer. Their horns are very black †, their belly pure white, and their fore-legs are fhorter than the hind-legs. They are very nu-

made fuch a fpring, that he broke his chain, and darted after them, but without effect. However, as the gazelles were terrified, and chafed on all fides, one of them was again obliged to pafs near the leopard, who, notwithftanding the whole road was embarraffed with camels and horfes, and notwithftanding the common notion that this animal never attacks its prey after having once miffed it, he fprung upon and feized it ; *Relat. de Thevenot, tom.* iii. *p.* 112.

* Inftead of a leopard, a tamed gazelle is employed to catch the wild ones. Round his horns a rope is twifted in various directions, and the two ends of it are fixed under his belly. When the hunters difcover a flock of gazelles, he is allowed to go and join them. But the male of the little flock advances to prevent him : This oppofition he makes with his horns, which are foon entangled in the mefh of ropes. He is then feized and carried off by the hunters; *Id. ibid.*———— The fame art is employed in taking the females. A domeftic female with a netting of cords is let loofe among a flock. The wild females immediately begin to fport with her ; and the horns of one of them are foon entangled ; and fhe falls an eafy prey to the Indians ; *Voyage de la Boullaye-le-Gouze, p.* 247.

† L'Afrique de Marmol, tom. i. p. 53. and Shaw's Travels.

merous

merous in Tremecen, Duguela, Tell, and Zaara. They are cleanly animals, and never lie down but in dry places. They are alſo extremely nimble, vigilant, and timorous. In open places, they look round on all ſides; and, as ſoon as they perceive a man, a dog, or any other enemy, they fly off with full ſpeed. But, notwithſtanding this natural timidity, they have a kind of courage; for, when ſurpriſed, they ſtop ſhort, and face thoſe who attack them.

In general, the eyes of the gazelles are black, large, vivacious, and, at the ſame time, ſo beautiful, that in the Eaſtern nations, they are employed proverbially in praiſing the eyes of a fine woman *. Their limbs are finer and more delicate than thoſe of the roebuck. Their hair is ſhort, ſoft, and luſtrous. Their fore-legs are not ſo long as the hind ones, which enables them, like the hare, to run with greater facility up than down hill. Their ſwiftneſs is equal to that of the roebuck; but the latter rather leaps than runs, whereas all the gazelles run uniformly †. Moſt of them are yellow on the back, and

* In the neighbourhood of Alexandria, the antilopes are very numerous. This animal is a ſpecies of roebuck, whoſe eyes are ſo large, vivacious, and piercing, that they are uſed figuratively in praiſing the eyes of the ladies; Defcript. de l'Egypt. par Maillet, tom. ii. p. 125.

† The hair of the gierans or gazelles is like that of the fallow-deer, and they run, like the dog, without leaping. In the night, they come to feed in the plains, and, in the morning, return to the mountains; Voyage de Gemelli Careri, tom. ii. p. 64.

white

white on the belly, and have a brown band which feparates thefe two colours below the flanks. Their tails are of different lengths, but always garnifhed with pretty long black hair. Their ears are long, erect, pretty open in the middle, and terminate in a point. Their feet are cloven, and fhaped nearly like thofe of the fheep. Both males and females have permanent horns; but thofe of the females are thinner and fhorter.

Thefe are all the facts we have been able to collect concerning the different fpecies of gazelles, and their natural difpofitions and manners. We fhall now inquire with what propriety naturalifts have afcribed to one of thefe animals only, the production of the famous ftone, called the *Oriental bezoar*, and whether this animal be the *pafen* or *pazan*, which they have mentioned fpecifically under the name of the *bezoar gazelle*. In examining the figures and defcription * given by Koempfer, who has written

much

---

* Repertus in novenni hirco lapillus voti me fecit quodammodo compotem; dico quodammodo, nam in beftia quam comes meus findebat, inteftina, a me ipfo diligentiffime perquifita, nullum lapidem continebant. Pronior alteri apparebat fortuna qui a nobis longius remotus feram a fe transfoffam dum me non expectato diffecaret, lapillum reperit elegantiffimum, tametfi molis perexiguæ.———Adeptus lapidem, antequam adeffem.———*Kœmpfer, Amœnit. p.* 392.———Bezoard orientalis legitimus. Lapis bezoard orientalis verus et pretiofus, Perfice Pafahr, ex quo nobis vox bezoard enata eft.——Patria ejus præcipua eft Pefidis provincia Laar.——Ferax præterea Chorafmia effe dicitur.——Genitrix, eft fera quædam montana caprini

generis

much on this subject, it is doubtful whether he means that the pazan or the algazel is the only animal

generis quam incolæ *paʃen,* noſtrates capricervam, nominant. ——Animal pilis brevibus ex cinereo rufis veſtitur, magnitudine capræ domeſticæ, ejuſdemque *barbatum* caput obtinens. Cornua fœminæ *nulla* ſunt vel exigua, hircus longiora et liberalius extenſa gerit, annuliſque diſtinċta inſignioribus, quorum numeri annos ætatis referunt: Annum undecimum vel duodecimum raro exhibere dicuntur, adeoque illum ætatis annum haud excedere. Reliquum corpus a cervina forma, colore, et agilitate nil differt. Timidiſſimum et maxime fugitivum eſt, inhoſpita aſperrimorum montium teſqua incolens, et ex ſolitudine montana in campos rariſſime deſcendens, et quamvis pluris regni regiones inhabitet, lapides tamen bezoardicos non gignit. *Caʃbini* (emporium eſt regionis *Irak*) pro coquina nobis capricervam, vel, ut reċtius dicam, Hircocervum prægrandem venebat venator, qui a me quæſitus, non audiviſſe ſe reſpondebat beſtiam illic lapidem unquam foviſſe, quod et civium, quotquot percunċtatus ſum, teſtimonia confirmabant. ——Quæ vero partes, tametſi capricervas alant promiſcue, non omnes tamen herbas ferunt ex quibus depaſtis lapides generaṛi, atque ii quidem æque nobiles poſſint, ſed ſolus ex earum numero eſt mons Baarſi.——Nulla ibi ex prædiċtis beſtiis datur ætate proveċta quæ lapidem non contineat; cum in cæteris hujus jugi partibus (duċtorum verba refero) ex denis in montium diſtantioribus, ex quinquagenis in cæteris, extra Larenſem provinciam ex centenis vix una ſit quæ lapide dotetur, eoque ut plurimum exigui valoris. In hircis lapides majores et frequentius inveniuntur quam in fœminis. Lapidem ferre judicantur annoſi, valde macilenti, colla habentes longiora, qui gregem præire geſtiunt.——Beſtiæ ut primum perfoſſæ linguam inſpiciunt, quæ ſi ſolito deprehendatur aſperior, de præſente lapide nihil amplius dubitant. Locus natalis eſt pylorus ſive produċtior quarti quem vocant ventriculi fundus, cujus ad latus plica quædam ſive ſcrobiculus, mucoſo humore oblitus, lapillum ſuggerit: In alia ventriculi claſſe (prout ruminantibus diſtinguuntur) quam ultima hac inveniri negabant.——Credunṭ quos plicarum alveoli non ſatis ampleċtuntur elabi pyloro poſſe,

animal which produces the *Oriental bezoar* *.
If we confult the other naturalifts and travellers,
we fhall be tempted to believe that all the gazelles, wild and domeftic goats, and even the
fheep, indifcriminately produce this ftone, the
formation of which depends more, perhaps, on
the

---

poffe, et cum excrementis excerni : Quin formatos interdum
diffolvi rurfus, præfertim longiori animalis inedia. *Clar. Jagerus*
mihi teftatus eft fe, dum in regna Golkonda degeret, gazellas
vivas recenter captas manu fua perquifiviffe, et contracto abdo-
mine lapillos palpaffe, in una geminos, in altera quinos vel fe-
nos. Has ille beftias pro contemplatione fua alere decreverat,
camera hofpicii fui inclufas ; verum quod ab omni pabulo ab-
ftinerent, quafi perire quam faginari captivæ mallent, mactari
eas juffit, inedia aliquot dierum macentes. Tum vero lapillos
ubi exempturus erat eorum ne veftigium amplius invenit, ex
quo illos a jejuno vifcere, vel alio quocumque modo, diffolutos
credebat.——Diffolutionem nullo poffe negotio fieri perfua-
deor, fi quidem certum eft lapides in loco natali viventis bruti
dum latent nondum gaudere petrofa quam nobis exhibent
duritie, fed molliores effe et quodammodo friabiles, inftar fere
vitelli ovi fervente aqua ad duritiem longius excocti. Hoc
propter recenter exfectus ne improvide frangatur, vel attrectus
nitorem perdat, ab inventoribus confuevit ore recipi, et in eo
foveri aliquardiu dum induruerit, mox goffypio involvi et af-
fervari. Affervatio ni primis diebus caute fiant, periculum eft
ne adhuc cum infirmior, importuna contrectatione, rumpatur
aut labem recipiat. Generationem fieri conjiciunt cum refino-
fa quædam ex herbis depaftis concoctifque fubftantia ventricu-
lorum latera occupat, quæ, egeftis cibis, jejunoque vifcere in
pylorum confluens, circa arreptum calculum, lanam, paleamve
confiftat et coaguletur ; ex primo circa materiam contentam
flamine efformandi lapidis figura pendet, &c. ; *Idem, p.* 389.
et feq.

* At Golconda, the king has great ftore of excellent bezoars. The mountains where the goats feed which produce
thefe

the temperature of the climate, than on the nature or fpecies of the animal. If we may believe

thefe ftones are about feven or eight days journey from Bag-
nagaar. They commonly fell at forty crowns a pound; and
the longeft kind are the beft. They are likewife found in certain cows, which are much larger, though not fo valuable, as
thofe produced by the goats. The bezoars extracted from a rare
kind of apes, which are fmall and long, are in the higheft eftimation; *Voyage de Thevenot, tom.* iii. *p.* 293.—Perfia produces
finer bezoar ftones than any other country of the world. They
are extracted from the fides of certain wild he-goats, to the
livers of which they are attached; *Voyage de Feynes, p.* 44.——
The bezoar, that famous medicinal ftone, ought to be ranked
among the number of drugs. It is a tender ftone, confifting of
coats or pellicles, like an onion. It is found in the bodies of the
wild and domeftic goats along the gulf of Perfia, in the province
of Coraffon, which is the ancient Margiana, and is incomparably better than that brought from the kingdom of Golconda.
But, as the goats were brought from a diftance of three days
journey, we found bezoars in fome of them only, and even
that in fmall quantities. We preferved thefe goats alive fifteen
days. They were fed with common green herbage; but, upon
opening them, nothing was found. I kept them during this
time, in order to difcover whether, as is alleged, it be a particular herb which heats thefe animals, and produces this ftone
in their bodies. We are told by the natives of Perfia, that the
more this animal paftures in parched countries, and eats dry and
aromatic herbs, the bezoar is the more falutary. Coraffon and
the borders of the Perfian gulf are the drieft countries in the
world. In the heart of thefe ftones, there are always pieces of
brambles, or fome other vegetable, that ferve as a nucleus, round
which the humour that compofes this ftone coagulates. It is
worthy of remark, that, in India, the fhe-goats produce bezoar,
and that, in Perfia, it is produced by the wedders and he-
goats. The Perfians efteem their own bezoar, being hotter
and better concocted, as four times more valuable than the Indian kind. The former they fell at fifty-four livres the cou-

rage

lieve Rumphius, Seba, and some other authors, the true Oriental bezoar proceeds from apes,

rag, which is a weight of three drachms; *Voyage de Chardin, tom.* ii. *p.* 16.——The Oriental bezoar comes from a northern province of the kingdom of Golconda, and is found in the stomach of the she-goats.——The peasants, by feeling the belly of the goat, know how many bezoars she has, and sell her in proportion to their number. This number they discover, by rubbing the sides of the stomach with their hands in such a manner as to bring all the contents towards the middle of it, and then they feel the stones distinctly.——The bezoar, like the diamond, is valued according to its size; for, if five or six bezoars weigh an ounce, they bring from fifteen to eighteen francs. But, if one bezoar weighs an ounce, it sells at one hundred francs. I sold one of four ounces and a half at two thousand livres.——The merchants who traffic in bezoars, brought me six of these goats, which I examined. It must be acknowledged that these animals are beautiful, very tall, and have hair as fine as silk.——I was told that one of these goats had but one bezoar in its stomach, and that others had two, three, or four, which I soon perceived to be true, by rubbing their bellies in the manner above described. These six goats had seventeen bezoars and a half, one of which was about the size of half a hazel nut. The inside resembled the soft dung of a goat. These stones grow among the dung in the animal's belly. Some of the natives told me, that the bezoars were attached to the liver, and others, that they were fixed in the heart. From these vague assertions, I could not learn the truth.——With regard to the bezoar produced by the ape, it is so strong that two grains of it are reckoned equal to six of that produced by the goat; but it is very rare, and is found principally in the island of Macassar. This kind of bezoar is round; but the other is of different figures. These bezoars which are supposed to come from the apes, are much rarer than the other kind. They are also much dearer, and in greater request; and, when one is found of the size of a nut, it sometimes sells at more than a hundred crowns; *Voyage de Tavernier, tom.* iv. *p.* 78.

8 ~ . and

and not from gazelles, goats, or wedders *.
But this notion of Rumphius and Seba is by
no

---

* *De lapidibus bezoard. orientalis.* Nondum certo innotuit, quibufnam in animalibus hi calculi reperiantur; funt qui ftatuant, eos in ventriculo certæ caprarum fpeciei generari (Raius fcilicet, Gefnerus, Tavernier, &c.) . . . Rumphius, in *Mufeo Amboin.* refert Indos in rifum effundi audientes, quod Europæi fibi imaginentur, lapides bezoardicos in ventriculis caprarum fylveftrium generari; at contra ipfos affirmare, quod in *Simiis* crefcant, nefcios interim, quanam in fpecie fimiarum, an in Bavianis dictis, an vero in Cercopithecis. Attamen id certum effe, quod ex *Succadana* et *Tambas*, fitis in infula *Borneo*, adferantur, ibique a monticolis conquifiti vendantur iis qui littus accolunt; hos vero pofteriores afferere, quod in certa *Simiarum* vel *Cercopithecorum* fpecie hi lapides nafcantur; adderc interim Indos, quod vel ipfi illi monticolæ originem et loco natalia horumce lapidum nondum prope explorata habeant. Scifcitatus fum fæpiffime ab illis qui lapides iftos ex Indiis Orientalibus huc transferunt, quonam de animali, et quibus e locis, hi proveniant; fed nihil inde certi potui expifcari, neque iis ipfis conftabat quidpiam, nifi quod faltem ab aliis acceperant. . . . Novi effe; qui longiufculos inter et fphæricos feu oblongo-rotundos, atque reniformes, dari quid difcriminis ftatuunt. At imaginarium hoc eft. Neque enim ulla ratione intrinfecus differunt, quando confringuntur aut in pulverem teruntur, modo fuerint genuini, nec adulterati, five demum ex fimiis aut capris fylveftribus, aliifve proveniant animalibus. . . Gaudent hi lapides nominibus, pro varietate linguarum, variis, Lufitanis, *Pedra* feu *Caliga de Buzio*; Sinenfibus, *Gautsjo*; Maleitis, *Culiga-Kaka*; Perfis, *Pazar, Pazan*; feu *Belfabar*; Arabibus, *Albazar* et *Berzuaharth*; Lufitanis Indiæ incolis, *Pedra-Bugia* feu *Lapides-Simiarum*, juxta Koempferi teftimonium, vocantur. . . . . . Credibile eft nafci eofdem in ftomacho, quum plerumque in centro ftraminum lignorumve particulæ, nuclei, aut lapilli, et alia fimilia, inveniantur tanquam prima rudimenta circum quæ acris, vifcofa materies fefe lamellatim applicat, et deinceps, cruftæ

inftar,

no means well founded. We have feen feveral of thefe concretions, which are called *ape bezoars*. But they are totally different from the Oriental bezoar, which unqueftionably proceeds from a ruminating animal, and is eafily diftinguifhed, by its form and fubftance, from all the other bezoars. Its common colour is a greenifh olive, and brownifh within. The colour of what is called the *Occidental bezoar*, is a faint yellow, more or lefs dirty. The fubftance of the former is more tender and porous, and that of the latter, harder, drier, and more petrified. Befides, as prodigious quantities of the Oriental bezoar were confumed during the laft two or three centuries, being ufed both in Europe and Afia, in all cafes where our phyficians now employ cordials and antidotes againft

inftar, magis magifque aucta in lapidem durefcit. Pro varietate victus, quo utuntur animalia, ipfæ quoque lamellæ variant, fucceffive fibi mutuo adpofitæ, fenfimque grandefcentes. Fracto hæ facile feparantur, et per integrum fæpe ftatum ita a fe mutuo fuccedunt, ut decorticatum relinquant lapidem, lævi iterum et quafi expolita fuperficie confpicuum. Lapides bezoard, illis e locis Indiæ Orientalis venientes quibus cum Britannis commercium intercedit, pro parte minuti funt, et rotundi, filicumque quandam fpeciem in centro gerunt. Alii vero teneriores, et oblongi, intus continent ftraminula, nucleos dactylorum, femina peponum, et ejufmodi, quibus fimplex faltem, aut geminum veri lapidis ftratum, fatis tenue, circumpofitum eft. Unde in his ultra dimidiam partem rejiculi datur: Et nobis quidem hi videntur veri effe fimiarum lapides, utpote materies ab hifce animantibus per anum excreti, quam ut majorem in molem potuerint excrefcere; *Seba, vol. ii. p. 130.*

poifon,

poifon, may we not prefume, from this great confumption, which ftill continues in' fome degree, that the bezoar proceeds from a very common animal, or rather, that it proceeds notfrom one, but from feveral fpecies; and that it is equally extracted from gazelles, goats, and wedders; but that thefe animals can only produce it in the climates of India and the Levant?

From all that has been written on this fubject, we have not been able to find one diftinct obfervation, nor a fingle decifive argument. It only appears, from what has been faid by Monard, Garcias, Clufius, Aldrovandus, Hernandes, &c. that the Oriental bezoar animal is not the common domeftic goat, but a fpecies of wild goat, which they have not fufficiently characterifed. In the fame manner, all we can collect from Koempfer is, that the bezoar animal is a kind of wild goat, or rather gazelle, which is equally ill defcribed. But, from the teftimonies of Thevenot, Chardin, and Tavernier, we learn, that this ftone is not fo often extracted from the gazelles, as from the wedders, and the wild or domeftic goats. Thefe travellers merit the greater credit, becaufe they were eye-witneffes to the facts they mention, and becaufe, when treating of the bezoar, though they take no notice of the gazelles, yet, as they are well acquainted with thefe animals, and mention them in other parts of their works *, there is not the leaft appearance

* Voyage de Tavernier, tom. ii. p. 26.

of

of their having been deceived. We muft not, therefore, conclude, like our ancient naturalifts, that the oriental bezoar is produced folely by a particular fpecies of gazelle. I acknowledge, that, after having examined not only the evidence of travellers, but the facts themfelves which might decide this queftion, I am inclined to believe that the bezoar ftone proceeds equally from the moft part of ruminating animals, but more commonly from goats and gazelles. It is formed of concentric coats or ftrata, and frequently contains foreign fubftances in its centre. I endeavoured to inveftigate the nature of thefe fubftances, which ferve as a nucleus to the bezoar, in order to difcover the animal that fwallowed them. In the centre of thefe ftones, I found fmall flints, ftones of plums, and of tamarinds, feeds of caffia, and efpecially pieces of ftraw, and buds of trees. Hence I could no longer hefitate in attributing this production to animals which browfe herbage and leaves.

We are perfuaded, therefore, that the Oriental bezoar proceeds not from any one, but from a number of different animals. Neither is it difficult to reconcile this opinion with the teftimonies of travellers ; for, though each of them contradicts his neighbour, yet all of them make near approaches to the truth. The bezoar was unknown to the ancient Greeks and Latins. Galen is the firft who mentions its virtues againft poifon. The Arabians fpeak of the be-

zoar

zoar as poffeffing the fame virtues. But neither
the Greeks, Latins, nor Arabians, give any pre-
cife information concerning the animals by which
it is produced. Rabi Mofes, the Egyptian, only
remarks, that fome people pretend that this ftone
is formed in the angle of the eye, and others in
the gall-bladder of the eaftern wedders. Now,
bezoars, or concretions, are actually formed in
the angles of the eyes, and in the pits below
the eyes of ftags and fome other animals. But
thefe concretions are very different from the
oriental bezoar; and all the concretions in the
gall-bladder confift of a light, oily, and inflam-
mable matter, which has no refemblance to the
fubftance of the bezoar. Andreas Lacuna, a
Spanifh phyfician, in his commentaries on Dio-
fcorides, remarks, that the oriental bezoar is
extracted from a certain fpecies of wild goat, in
the mountains of Perfia. Amatus Lufitanus
repeats Lacuna's remark; and adds, that this
mountain-goat refembles the ftag. Monard,
who quotes all the three, affures us in a more
pofitive manner, that this ftone is derived from
the internal parts of a mountain-goat in India,
to which, fays he, I may give the appellation of
cervi-capra; becaufe it partakes both of the ftag
and the goat, is nearly of the fize and figure of
the ftag, and, like the goat, has fimple horns,
very much bended backward*, Garcias ab
Horto

* Lapis *bezaar* varias habet appellationes; nam Arabibus
bager dicitur, Perfis *bezaar,* Indis *bezar.* . . . Ifte lapis in internis

Horto tells us, that, in Coraffon and in Perfia, there is a fpecies of he-goats *, called *pa-fan;*

ternis partibus cujufdam animalis *capra montana* apellati generatur. . . . . In Indiæ fupra Gangem certis montibus. Sinarum regioni vicinis, animalia cervis valde fimilia reperiuntur, tum magnitudine, tum agilitate et aliis notis, exceptis quibufdam partibus quibus cum capris magis conveniunt, ut cornibus quæ veluti capræ in dorfum reflexa habent et corporis forma, unde nomen illis inditum cervicapræ, propter partes quas cum capris et cervis fimiles obtinent. . . . Eft autem animal (ex eorum relatu qui ex illa regione redeuntes animal confpexerunt) in quo reperiuntur ifti lapides, cervi magnitudine et ejus quafi formæ; binis dumtaxat cornibus præditum, latis et extremo mucronatis atque in dorfum valde recurvis, breves pilos habens cineracei coloris ceu admixta rufedo: In iifdem montibus aliorum etiam colorum reperiuntur. Indi vel laqueis vel decipulis illa venantur et maċtant. Adeo autem ferocia funt ut interdum Indos etiam occidant, agilia præterea et ad faltum prona: In antris vivunt gregatimque eunt; utriufque fexus mares fcilicet et fœminæ inveniuntur, vocemque gemebundam edunt. Lapides autem ex interioribus inteftinis aliifque cavis corporis partibus educuntur. . . . Dum hæc fcriberem quoddam animal confpeċtu ivi huic (ni fallor) fimile, quia omnes notas mihi habere videbatur quibus modo defcripta prædita funt; eft autem ex longinquis regionibus per Africam Generofo Archidiacono Nebienfi delatum: Magnitudine fervi, capite et ore cervino, agile inftar cervi, pili et color cervo fimiles; corporis forma capra refert, nam magno hirco fimile eft, hircinos pedes habens et bina cornua in dorfum inflexa, extrema parte contorta ut hircina videantur, reliquis autem partibus cervum æmulatur. Illud autem valde admirandum quod ex turre fe præcipitans in cornua cadat fine ulla noxa: Vefcitur herbis, pane, leguminibus, omnibufque cibis quæ illi præbentur: Robuftum eft et ferrea catena vinċtum, quia omnes funes quibus ligabatur rodebat et rumpebat; *Nic. Monardi de Lapide Bexoar. lib. interprete Carolo Clufio.*

* Eft in Corafone et Perfia Hirci quoddam genus, quod *paxan* lingua Perfica vocant, rufi aut alterius coloris (ego rufum

fan*; that the oriental bezoar is generated in their stomachs; that this stone is found, not only in Persia, but likewise in Malacca, and in the Island of Cows near Cape Comorin; and that, in great numbers of these goats, slain for the subsistence of the troops, these stones were very commonly found. On this subject, Christopher Acosta † repeats what had been said by Garcias and Monard, without offering any thing new. In fine,

sum et pragrandem Goæ vidi) mediocri altitudine, in cujus ventriculo fit hic lapis bezar. . . . Cæterum non solum generatur hic lapis in Persia, sed etiam nonnullis Malacæ locis, et in insula quæ a Vaccis nomen sumpsit, haud procul a promontorio Comorim. Nam cum *in exercitus annonam mactarentur istic multi prægrandes birci, in eorum ventriculis magna ex parte bi lapides reperti sunt.* Hinc factum est, ut quotquot ab eo tempore in hanc insulam appellant, hircos obtruncent, lapidesque ex iis tollant. Verum nulli Persicis bonitate comparari possunt. Dextri autem adeo sunt Mauritani, ut facile qua in regione nati sint singuli lapides, discernere et dijudicare possint. . . . Vocatur autem hic lapis *pazar* a *pazan,* id est, hircorum Arabibus, tum Persis et Corafone incolis: Nos corrupto nomine *bezar,* atque Indi magis corrupti *bazar* appellant, quasi dicas lapidem forensem : Nam *bazar* eorum lingua forum est ; *Garcias ab Horto, Aromat. Hist. interprete Carolo Clusio, p.* 216.

* Koempfer seems to have borrowed from Monard and Garcias, the names *cervi-capra, capri-cerva,* and *pasan,* which he has given to the oriental bezoar animal.

† Generatur iste lapis in ventriculis animalium hirco fere similium, arietis prægrandis magnitudine, colore rufo, uti cervi propemodum agili, et acutissimi auditus, a Persis *pazan* apellato, quod variis Indiæ provinciis, uti in promontorio Comorim, et nonnullis Malacæ locis, tum etiam in Persia et Corafone, insulisque quæ a Vacca cognomen adeptæ sunt, invenitur :— *Christophori Acosta, Aromat. liber, cap.* xxxvi. *interprete Carolo Clusio, p.* 279.

to

to omit nothing relative to the hiſtory of this
ſtone, Koempfer, an intelligent man, and an exact
obſerver, tells us, that, when in the province
of Laar in Perſia, he went with the natives of
the country to hunt the buck *paſan*, which produces the bezoar, and that he ſaw the ſtone
extracted; and he aſſures us, that the true oriental bezoar proceeds from this animal; that the
buck *abu*, of which he alſo gives a figure, likewiſe produces bezoar, but that it is of an inferior
quality. From the figures he has given of the
paſan and abu, we would be induced to think,
that the firſt repreſents the common gazelle rather than the true paſan; and, from his deſcription, we ſhould imagine his paſan to be a he-goat,
and not a gazelle, becauſe he has given it a beard
like the goats. Laſtly, from the name *abu*,
which he gives to his other buck, as well as from
his ſecond figure, we recogniſe the wild he-goat
rather than the genuine ahu, which is our tzeiran
or large gazelle. What is ſtill more ſingular,
Koempfer, who ſeems willing to determine the
ſpecies of the oriental bezoar animal, and who
aſſures us that it is the wild buck called *paſan*,
quotes, at the ſame time, a man who, he ſays,
is very worthy of credit, and who affirms, that
he felt the bezoars in the belly of the gazelle, at
Golconda. Thus all the poſitive evidence which
can be derived from Koempfer is reduced to this,
that there are two ſpecies of wild mountain-goats,

the

the pafan and ahu, which produce the bezoar in Perfia, and that in India this ftone is likewife found in the gazelles. Chardin remarks, that the oriental bezoar is found in the bucks and fhe-goats, both wild and domeftic, along the Perfic Gulf, and in feveral provinces of India; but that, in Perfia, it is alfo extracted from the wedders. The Dutch travellers alfo affert *, that it is produced in the ftomachs of fheep and goats. Tavernier, who is ftill more pofitive in favour of the domeftic goats, fays, that their hair is as fine as filk, and that, having purchafed fix of thefe goats alive, he extracted from them feventeen entire bezoars, and a piece of another as large as half a filberd nut. He then adds, that there are other bezoars fuppofed to proceed from apes, whofe virtues are ftill ftronger than thofe of the goat-bezoars; that they are alfo extracted from cows; but the virtues of thefe are inferior, &c. What can be inferred from this variety of evidence and opinions, unlefs it be allowed that the

* In the ifland of Bofner, we find the famous bezoar ftone, which is very precious and in great requeft, on account of its virtue againft poifon. It is formed, in the ftomachs of fheep or goats, round a fmall puftule or protuberance in the middle of the ftomach, and which is found in the ftone itfelf. . . . A conjecture has been formed, that the bezoar which proceeds from the ftomach of the fheep, and the gall-bladder ftone of the hog, are produced by the operation of fome particular herbs eaten by thefe animals. But they are found in all the countries of the Eaft Indies, though thefe animals feed promifcuoufly upon herbage of every kind. *See Voyage de la Compagn. des Indes de Hollande, tom.* ii. *p.* 121. and alfo *Le Voyage de Mandelflo, tom.* ii. *p.* 364.

oriental

oriental bezoar proceeds not from one fpecies, but from a number of different animals, and efpecially from the gazelles and goats?

With regard to the occidental bezoars, we hefitate not to pronounce, that they are produced neither by goats nor gazelles; for it will be fhown, in the fubfequent articles, that there are neither goats, gazelles, nor even any animal which approaches to this genus, throughout the whole extent of the New World. Inftead of gazelles, we find roebucks alone in the woods of America; inftead of wild goats and fheep, lamas and pacos*, animals totally different, are to be found in the mountains of Peru and Chili. The ancient Peruvians had no other cattle; and, at the fame time that thefe two fpecies were partly reduced to a domeftic ftate, they exifted, in ftill greater numbers, in their natural condition of liberty on the mountains. The wild lamas were called *buanacus*, and the pacos *vicunnas*, from which has been derived the name *vigogne*, that denotes the fame animal with the pacos. Both the lamas and the pacos produce bezoars; but the domeftic kind produce them more rarely than the wild.

M. Daubenton, who has inveftigated the nature of bezoar ftones more clofely than any other perfon, thinks that they are compofed of the fame matter as that fhining coloured tartar which

---

* See vol. v. art. *Of the animals peculiar to the New Continent.*

adheres

adheres to the teeth of ruminating animals; and it appears, from the numerous collection of bezoars in the royal cabinet, that there are essential differences between the oriental and occidental bezoars. Hence the goats of the East Indies, and the gazelles of Persia, are not the only animals which produce the concretions called *bezoars*. The chamois *, and perhaps the wild goat of the Alps, the he-goats of Guiney †, and several American animals ‡, likewise produce bezoars: And, under this name,

if

---

* In the country of the Grisons, balls as large, and sometimes larger, than a tennis-ball, are found in the stomach of the chamois goat. They are called *kemskougnel* by the Germans, who alledge that they are as useful as the bezoar, which likewise proceeds from the stomachs of certain Indian goats; *Travels to Italy, &c. by Jacob Spon and George Wheeler.* Near Munich, in a village called *Lagrem*, which is at the foot of the mountains, our host shewed us certain balls or brown masses, nearly of the size of a hen's egg, which were a kind of tender, imperfect bezoar, commonly found in the stomachs of the *roebucks*. He assured us, that these balls had great virtues, and that he often sold them to strangers at ten crowns a piece; *Voyage des Missionaires, tom.* i. *p.* 129.

† In Congo and Angola, when the wild goats begin to grow old, stones, resembling the bezoar, are found in their bellies. Those found in the males are supposed to be best; and the Negroes boast of them as specifics against many distempers, and particularly against the effects of poison; *Hist. Gen. des Voyages, par M. l'Abbé Prevost, tom.* v. *p.* 83.

‡ Accepimus a peritis venatoribus, reperiri lapides bezoard in ovibus illis Peruinis cornuum expertibus, quas *bicuinas* vocant; (sunt enim alia cornuta, *taruca* vocatæ, et alias quas dicunt *guanacas)* præterea in *teuhtlalmçame* quæ caprarum mediocrium paulove majori constant magnitudine. . . . Deinde

in

if we comprehend all fimilar concretions found
in the inteftines of animals, we may affirm, that
moft quadrupeds, except thofe of the carnivorous kinds, and even the crocodiles and large
ferpents, produce bezoars *.

In quodam damarum genere quas *macatlcbichiltic* aut *temamaçame* appellant. . . . Necnon in ibicibus quorum hic re-
dundat copia, ut Hifpanos et apud hanc regionem frequentes
cervos taceam, in quibus quoque eft lapidem, de quo præ-
fens eft inftitutus fermo, reperire: Capreas etiam cornuum
expertes, quas audio paffim reperiri apud Peruinos, et ut fum-
matim dicam, vix eft cervorum caprearumque genus ullum,
in cujus ventriculo, aliave interna parte, fua fponte, ex ipfis
alimoniæ excrementis, lapis hic, qui etiam in tauris vaccifque
folet offendi, non paulatim concrefcat et generetur, multis
fenfim additis et cohærefcentibus membranulis, quales funt
cæparum. Ideo non nifi vetuftiffimis et fenio pene confectis
lapides hi reperiuntur; neque ubique, fed certis ftatifque locis.
. . . . Variis hos lapides reperies formis et coloribus; alios
nempe candefcentes, fufcos alios, alios luteos, quofdam cine-
reos nigrofque, et vitri aut obfidiani lapidis modo micantes.
Hos ovi illos rotunda figura, et alios triangula, &c. *Nard. Ant.
Recchi. apud Hernand.* p. 325 *et* 326.—In the ftomach of a wild
goat, called *cornera de terra* by the Spaniards, Wafer found
thirteen bezoar ftones of different figures, fome of which refembled coral. Though perfectly green when firft expofed
to the air, they afterwards turned afh-coloured; *Hift. Gen.
des Voyages, par M. l'Abbé Prevoft, tom.* xii. p. 638.—*Nota,* This
cornera de terra is neither a goat nor gazelle, but the *lama* of
Peru.

* There is another ftone, called the *ftone of the hooded ferpent,*
a fpecies of ferpent which has a kind of hood hanging behind
its head . . . and, behind this hood, the ftone is found, the
fmalleft being as large as a hen's egg. . . . . Thefe ferpents
frequent the coafts of Melinda, and the ftones might be brought
by the Portuguefe failors or foldiers, when they return from
Mofambique; *Voyage de Tavernier, tom.* iv. p. 80.

To obtain a clear idea of thefe concretions, they muft be diftributed into feveral claffes, referring to the animals which produce them, and the climates and food that are favourable to their production.

1. The ftones formed in the bladder and kidneys of men and other animals, muft be feparated from the clafs of bezoars, and denominated by the appellation of *calculi*, their fubftance being totally different from that of the bezoars. They are eafily diftinguifhed by their weight, their urinous odour, and their ftructure, which is neither regular, nor compofed of thin concentric circles, like that of the bezoars.

2. The concretions fometimes found in the gall-bladder and liver of men and animals fhould not be regarded as bezoars. They may be diftinguifhed by their lightnefs, their colour, and their inflammability; befides, they are not formed of concentric circles round a nucleus.

3. The balls frequently found in the ftomachs of animals, and efpecially of the ruminating kinds, are not true bezoars. Thefe balls, which are called *ægagropili*, are compofed, internally, of hairs fwallowed by the animal, when licking itfelf, or of hard roots which it was unable to digeft; and, externally, moft of them are covered with a vifcid fubftance, which has fome refemblance to bezoar. Hence the *ægagropili* have nothing in common with the bezoars but this external

covering;

covering; and inspection alone is sufficient to distinguish the one from the other.

4. In temperate climates, we often find *ægagropili* in animals, but never bezoars. Our oxen and cows, the Alpine chamois [*], and the Italian porcupine [†], produce only *ægagropili*. The animals of hot countries, on the contrary, yield only bezoars. The elephant, the rhinoceros, the goats and gazelles of Afia and Africa, the lama of Peru, &c. instead of *ægagropili*, produce solid bezoars, whose size and consistence vary according to the animals and the climates under which they live.

5. The bezoars, to which so many virtues have been ascribed, are the oriental kind, and they are produced by the goats, gazelles, and sheep, that inhabit the high mountains of Afia. Bezoars of an inferior quality, which are called *occidental*, proceed from the lamas and pacas which are found in the mountains of South America. In fine, the goats and gazelles of Africa likewise yield bezoars; but they are not so good as those of Afia.

From all these facts we may conclude, in general, that the bezoars are only a residue of vegetable nourishment, which exists not in carnivorous animals, and is peculiar to those who

---

[*] See note, p. 439.

[†] We found an ægagropilus in a porcupine sent us from Rome in the year 1763.

live

live upon plants; that, in the southern mountains of Asia, the herbs being stronger, and more
exalted than in any other region of the world,
the bezoars, which are the residue of them, are
also superior in quality to all others; that, in
America, where the heat is less intense, and the
mountain herbs have not so much strength, the
bezoars which proceed from them are also greatly inferior; and, lastly, that, in Europe, where
the herbs are feeble, and in the plains of both
continents, where they are gross, no bezoars are
produced, but only *ægagropili*, which contain
nothing but hairs, roots, or filaments that are
too hard to be digested.

END OF THE SIXTH VOLUME.

Plate CXCVII.

A.Bell sculp.

GAZELLE.

Plate CXCVIII.

KÉVEL.

Plate CXCIX.

CORINE.

Plate CC.

A.Bell Sculp.

NANGUER

105